W9-BBF-336

The City in Modern Africa

The Praeger Library of African Affairs is intended to provide clear, authoritative, and objective information about the historical, political, cultural, and economic background of modern Africa. Individual countries and groupings of countries will be dealt with as will general themes affecting the whole continent and its relations with the rest of the world. The library appears under the general-editorship of Colin Legum, and each volume is written by an acknowledged expert on its subject.

Already Published

T. A. BEETHAM	*Christianity and the New Africa*
ALFRED GERTEINY	*Mauritania*
RICHARD GREENFIELD	*Ethiopia: A New Political History*
RICHARD HALL	*Zambia*
ALEX HEPPLE	*South Africa: A Political and Economic History*
JAMES R. HOOKER	*Black Revolutionary: George Padmore's Path from Communism to Pan-Africanism*
HORACE MINER	*The City in Modern Africa*
RICHARD P. STEVENS	*Lesotho, Botswana, and Swaziland: The Former High Commission Territories in Southern Africa*
CLAUDE WAUTHIER	*The Literature and Thought of Modern Africa: A Survey*

The City in Modern Africa

EDITED BY

HORACE MINER

FREDERICK A. PRAEGER, *Publishers*
New York · Washington · London

FREDERICK A. PRAEGER, Publishers
111 Fourth Avenue, New York, N.Y. 10003, U.S.A.
77-79 Charlotte Street, London, W.1, England

Published in the United States of America in 1967
by Frederick A. Praeger, Inc., Publishers

Library of Congress Catalog Card Number: 67-29714

Printed in Great Britain

To Donald Young

In recognition of his contributions to the development and utilisation of the social sciences

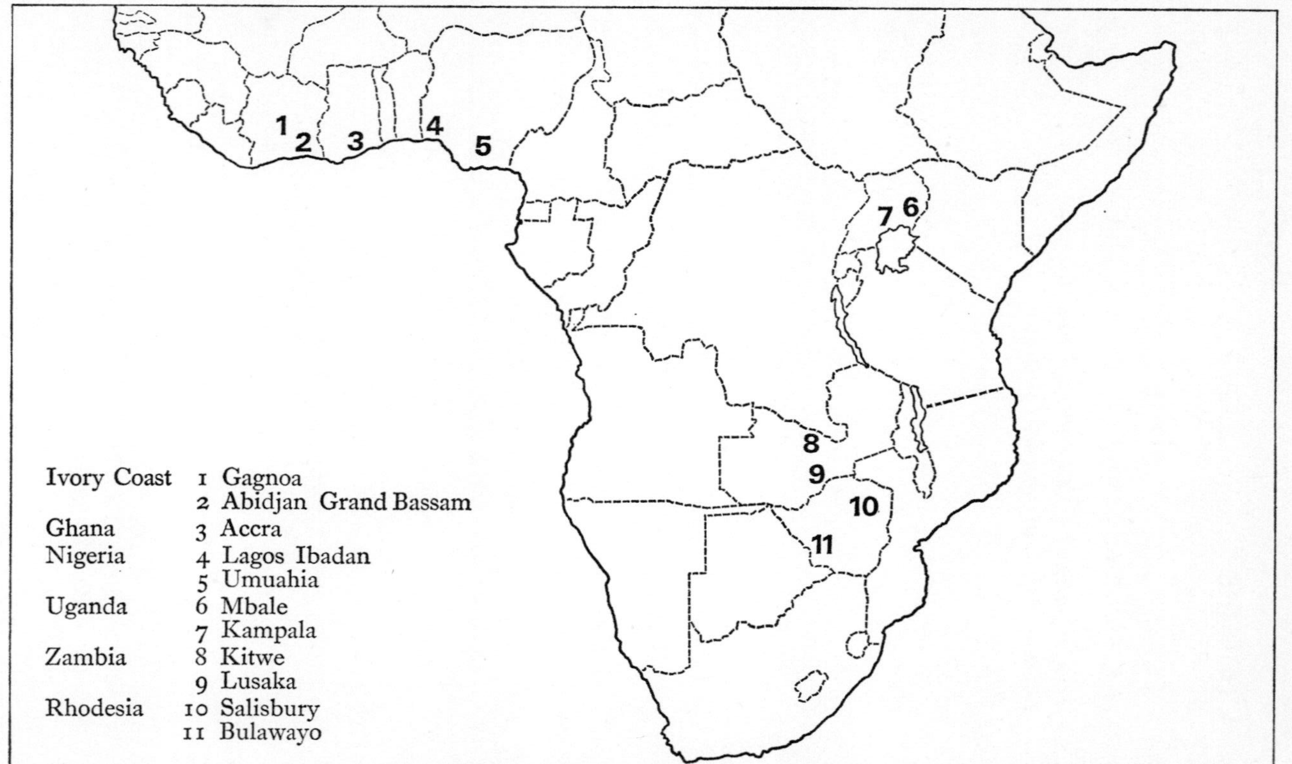

Sites of Urban Research Reported in this Volume

Contents

Preface

THE STUDY of modern African cities gathered initial impetus in 1954 from the UNESCO conference in Abidjan on the Social Impact of Industrialisation and Urbanisation in Africa South of the Sahara. The prime mover of those meetings, Professor Daryll Forde, subsequently wrote that the conference was 'remarkable for the fact that so many of its participants . . . were meeting one another for the first time and hitherto had little or no knowledge of each other's work'. In 1959 another international conference was held in Kampala to consider a variety of urban problems, and African urbanisation was more recently the focus of a conference at the University of Edinburgh. As Forde surmised, such interaction has contributed to the steady stimulation and development of urban African studies. The participation of Americans in these conferences was, however, notably limited, as also was their research on African cities.

The Joint Committee on African Studies of the American Council of Learned Societies and the Social Science Research Council took cognisance of this situation in 1963. American scholarly interest in Africa was high and it seemed appropriate to focus more of that concern on urban studies through a conference devoted to such research. There was apparent merit in bringing Americans already engaged in such work into contact with one another and with students of urban phenomena in developing areas other than Africa, as well as with foreign investigators of African cities. It also seemed desirable to embrace a variety of social sciences, a view which found support in the research recommendations of the Committee on Urbanization of the Social Science Research Council. The Committee on African Studies designated an *ad hoc* committee, consisting of Professors Lloyd Fallers, Robert LeVine and Leo Schnore, to give me assistance in the planning of such a conference. A strict limitation on conference size was stipulated in an effort to maximise the informality and intensity of interaction among the conferees. As a result, it was clearly impossible to include all relevant disciplines and all scholars who could have contributed to the sessions. In no instance was this more evident than in the category of foreign scholars, who were invited almost entirely from among professors then resident in North America.

The resultant Conference on Methods and Objectives of Urban Research in Africa was held under the sponsorship of the Joint Committee on African Studies at Airlie House, Warrenton, Virginia, April 1–3, 1965. The participants were:

William Barber	William O. Jones*	Rowland L. Mitchell, Jr.†
Remi Clignet	Leo Kuper	William Schwab
L. Gray Cowan*	Daniel Lerner	Roy Sieber*
Philip C. Curtin*	Robert LeVine	Aidan Southall
Norton Ginsburg	Peter Marris	Joseph Spengler
William Hanna	Dennis McElrath	Benjamin E. Thomas*
George Jenkins	Horace M. Miner*	Lionel Tiger

* Member of the Committee on African Studies. (Its Chairman, Alan P. Merriam, was unable to attend.)

† Social Science Research Council staff.

Revisions of papers prepared for the conference constitute the contents of this volume, apart from the introductory chapter which was written subsequently. American orthography and punctuation were Anglicised throughout during production of the book in England. I wish to express more than routine thanks to the *ad hoc* planning committee and to my fellow members of the Joint Committee for their support and assistance. The advice of my colleagues, Otis Dudley Duncan and Ronald Freedman, was very helpful. The co-operation of the collaborating authors has, of course, meant the most.

H.M.

I

The City and Modernisation: An Introduction

HORACE MINER

AFRICA is the least urbanised of continents, but this demographic fact belies the new importance of African cities. A decade ago the continent was a colonial patchwork and Africans a powerless people. Today the caucus of independent African nations has a third of the votes in the General Assembly of the United Nations. At home, African leaders are no longer traditional chiefs or renegade rousers of unrest, but are the holders of the economic, military and political power of the new nations. The habitat of this new elite is the city. Here is the centre of commerce, the seat of government, the source of news and innovation and the point of contact with the outside world. As in other modernising nations of diverse peoples, the emergence of national cultures in African countries is overwhelmingly an urban phenomenon. The bearers of these cultures are not to be found in yesterday's books with their wealth of material on tribal custom and rural life, on colonial organisation, and on history 'seen through blue eyes'. Even attempts to understand today's African as a mixture of primitive and modern runs the risk of overlooking him as a new kind of person dealing with new kinds of problems requiring new kinds of solutions.

Political imperatives demand that we understand the new Africa, and our lack of understanding challenges academic theories

NOTE: *The notes and references for Chapter 1 will be found on page 18.*

2—TCIMA

developed in too small a sphere too long ago. As part of the response of the social sciences to this challenge, the following studies shed some new light on African cities and, in so doing, highlight the possibilities of urban research on a variety of disciplinary fronts. The anthropologists, economists, political scientists, psychologists and sociologists whose discussions and writing led to this volume are not simply a multidisciplinary group. Individually, they reflect the interdisciplinary collaboration which occurs 'under the same hat'. Looking under some of these hats, we find Joseph Spengler writing as much as a demographer and ecologist as an economist, Robert LeVine being an anthropologist-cum-psychologist, Lionel Tiger acting as a sociologist of political life and Aidan Southall reflecting the British mix of anthropology and sociology as well as a concern with geography and history. We could go on, but let us, instead, wonder about the significance of such integrated scholarship.

First, be it noted that the collaborating authors were brought together because of their demonstrated interest in the study of urban phenomena in modernising states, not because of their disciplinary breadth. The fact that they possess such wide-gauge competence suggests that it serves their special research interest. It would seem that those who venture into other disciplines are inclined to pursue them into foreign lands. It is also interesting that their wanderlust leads them into overlapping bodies of literature. While the relative dearth of publication on African cities makes some common coverage of that literature probable, the shared theoretical literature is more extensive and more specialised. In this case, again, the nature of the city and of modernisation seems to encourage cross-disciplinary investigation. In their discussions, the collaborators explored some common ground and tested the limits of their *lingua franca*, but no attempt was made to map that ground or to look for a common morphology in their academic dialects. The following outline of some major features of the city and its role in modernisation is, therefore, offered as a frame of reference inherent to the ensuing studies and not as a synthesis or agreed-upon position of the collaborators.

The Essence of the City

Everyone knows what a city is, except the experts. For them, the city is many things, among which none is clearly dominant. As various definitions serve different purposes, it is important that there should be set forth a characterisation of the city which is meaningful to the spectrum of disciplines concerned with urban studies in modernising societies. But first a word about the Babel of definitions.

It is the sociologists who wonder most about the fundaments of the city, sometimes harried by irreverent anthropologists who find disconcertingly exceptional cases. Lack of agreement, however, lies mainly within the sociological fraternity itself. Summarising these views, Reiss states that the area of consensus is limited to the recognition of the city as a 'distinct form of human community'.[1] Beyond that, he finds no consistent frame of reference and concludes that no sociological theory exists for the study of urban communities among other communal forms. In its stead he finds three major approaches, used separately or in conjunction, to conceptualise the city: (i) ideal type constructs such as Toennies's *Gemeinschaft–Gesellschaft* contrast and Redfield's Folk-Urban typology; (ii) the 'trait complex' approach, which characterises the city in terms of clusters of empirical attributes such as size, density and occupation of the population; (iii) the rural-urban continuum of community types. With the possible exception of the occupational distinction, it is significant that all of these conceptualisations see 'cityness' as a matter of degree and not as qualitatively different from the essence of other sorts of communities. Even with regard to the farm/non-farm distinction, Weber recognised that 'the full urbanite of antiquity was a semi-peasant',[2] and Bascom has made us aware of the continuing agrarian character of Yoruba cities.[3]

The nebulous nature of city conceptualisation is indicated by the use of the crucial term urbanisation with at least two standard, but completely different, connotations. Thus Hauser writes:

The degree of urbanization of a nation for statistical purposes is

> generally defined as the proportion of the population resident in urban places. This demographic conception of urbanization, however, is transcended by many other uses of the term in which urbanization is recognized as a social process which has brought about great transformations in man's way of life.[4]

We observe that such transformations may even result from the urbanisation of rural areas, bringing increasing urbanism (city-like life) to the farmer while the density of the farm population declines! Of course the demographic definition also begs the question of what constitutes an 'urban place', except as some arbitrary standard is recognised. Such standards have varied among our own censuses and between them and commonly used international standards.

The fundamental difficulties are those of theory rather than of definition. The problem is that of discovering what is significant among the complexities of urban life. In this regard, a contributing factor to the conceptual smog over the city seems to be the prevalence of the view that urban phenomena must be explicable by some distinctive body of theory, if only we could discover it. An alternative position is recognised by Sjoberg in the most recent scholarly review of the field.[5] He favours regarding the city simply as a substantive area of study to be investigated through the use of all available theories and methods. In evaluating these alternative positions, we recall that the three traditional conceptualisations of the city dealt with it in contexts extending well beyond its limits. Modern ecologists also, despite the urban ambient of most of their research, understand the city only in a much broader frame of reference. One can hardly escape the conclusion that it is the nature of the city, rather than the dullness of its students, which has so long precluded the discovery of a distinctive body of urban theory. The search for a theory of stratification was comparably active and unsuccessful, and Parsons's observation regarding it seems applicable also to the analysis of urban phenomena. Such theory, he wrote, 'is not an independent body of concepts and generalizations which are only loosely connected with other parts of a general sociological theory; it *is* general sociological theory pulled together with reference to a certain fundamental aspect of society systems'.[6] Even if there is no independent urban theory, there remains the problem of distinguishing the fundamental aspect of society which underlies urban life.

Cities as Centres of Dominance

In his introduction to the translation of Weber's *Die Stadt*, Martindale tersely summarises his view of the theories to be found in modern books on the city: 'One may find anything or everything in the city texts except the informing principle that creates the city itself.'[7] Strangely enough, the basis for such a principle has long been at hand; we need only accept as definitive what is generally recognised as a universal feature of cities.

Going back with archaeologists to the very threshold of man's urban experience, we find temple-cities emerging from shrine-villages in Mesopotamia. A rising priestly class administered not only temple rites but also the wealth and labour contributed by the surrounding cultivators.[8] The power of the incipient cities lay in the power of religion, even as Fustel de Coulanges contended was the case in the cities of classical antiquity.[9] And so too, in West Africa, the ancient Yoruba city of Ife grew with the expanding sacred power of the Oni.[10] War ultimately came to Sumerian cities and from the war-lords arose an aristocracy whose armies exerted their might abroad, while, at home, complaining citizens were forced to wall their cities. Since then, the acropolis, the castle, and even the Anglo-Saxon 'burgh' have provided the foundation for cities.[11] In West Africa, we know that the walled city of Ibadan grew out of an armed camp near Ife. Extended trade and commerce were later additions to the generative power of the city-states of Sumer, where even public market-places were lacking in the sanctified and fortified centres of the earliest dynastic period. But subsequently, in Phoenicia, Tyre and Sidon put up their walls to protect the wealth of trade-built cities; later, in Venice, Genoa, Bruges and the Hanseatic cities, commerce so stamped their origins as to lead Pirenne[12] and Weber to see 'the market' as an urban requisite. In West Africa, trade alone built Timbuctoo—

never to be walled and only later ennobled with mosques and the 'university' of Sankore.

Finding history in the order of things, the archaeologist tells us: 'There is not one origin of cities, but as many as there are independent cultural traditions with an urban way of life.'[13] Finding system in the interdependence of things, the sociologist concludes: 'The key functions of preindustrial cities are political (both administrative and military), economic, religious, and educational. No city serves only one function to the exclusion of all others, but even so cities come to play special roles.'[14] Such agreement as to the diversity of urban origins and functions would seem to support Martindale's contention that no universally 'informing principle' exists. But through the diversity runs a unifying design—power and authority based on religious faith, physical force and wealth have combined or operated alone to create cities by making them centres of dominance over outlying areas.[15]

The 'agricultural revolution' did not produce cities, although it set the scene. The evidence leads Robert Adams to conclude: 'The rise of cities, the second great "revolution" in human culture, was pre-eminently a social process, an expression more of changes in man's interaction with his fellows than in his interaction with his environment.'[16] The most seminal aspect of that social change was the increase in social differentiation as a few men exerted more and more control over the lives of others. The local concentration of that control created the city by drawing in people and resources, initiating a spiral growth of division of labour and population and increasing the degree and extent of regional dominance exerted from the city.[17]

The view that the city is a power phenomenon does not rest on a foundation of archaeological ruins alone. Human ecologists have analysed community dominance in modern industrial society in terms so basic that they refer equally well to all biotic communities: 'Dominance attaches to the unit that controls the conditions necessary to the functioning of other units.'[18] As social units become differentiated in function, a hierarchy of power relations arises from the greater inherent influence of some functions, and particularly from the emergence of units to co-ordinate the differentiated parts. When the United States is regarded as such a system of interdependence, research results clearly support the contention that 'the units which mediate and control these dependency relationships tend to be localised in the large urban centers'.[19] On the whole, ecologists have stressed economic functions and the systematic nature of the dominance-dependence relationship between city and region rather than the operation of control within the system. In the final chapter of this book, Southall traces the development of Uganda's capital city, Kampala, as it spread over and beyond its 'seven hills'. With striking clarity, this crescive community illustrates the way in which one locus of power attracts other sorts of control. We see how the city grew in size and importance as hill after hill became the seat of control of one institution after another—the Kabaka's court, Lugard's fort, the Episcopal and Catholic cathedrals, and so on to the collegiate hill of Makerere. Between the hills spread the lines of commerce interconnecting the whole through the trade of the Asians—marginal to Ganda and English alike, and with no hill to call their own.

The city is not, however, to be understood solely as a microcosm, no matter how complex its structure. In the macrocosmic system of the nation, cities reflect the specialised functions which give them being. Thus Hance once pointed out the preponderant importance for Africa of coastal cities, particularly in West Africa where a port is the most important city in every country with access to the sea.[20] Even in the interior, the major position of inland ports and crossroad cities gives further evidence of the overwhelming importance of transport functions in the growth of African cities. The development of the littoral ports also reflects the economic power and aims of the Europeans. The fact that the ports became cities involved the establishment of the European powers on the mainland, from whence they controlled the development of the hinterland. Then too, as Hance says: 'It was logical that many of these cities were selected as colonial capitals.'

When we examine the logic which draws political and economic power together in the city, we find that, to a degree, they tend to have a single locus because they are different aspects of the same thing. But even when separate systems of control are discernible, one kind of power is used to secure another, and various sorts of control become concentrated in the same individual through his positions in the different systems. On the other hand, this very fact complicates the maintenance of the system boundaries. Thus, the universality of the problem of political corruption no more mirrors the venality of man than it does the difficulty of preserving the distinction between the legitimate distribution of spoils and the corrupt use of authority for personal advantage. The distinction is, to be sure, a useful precipitate of institutionalised government, but, by the same token, it is least clear and sometimes even dysfunctional during the formative period of the institutions themselves. This is evident in the pre-independence efforts of Africans to develop, within the framework of legitimacy imposed by Europeans, the national political parties required for self-government.

Even in Africa modern political activity depends upon mass media, the use of which is expensive. Beginning their political life without supporting private fortunes or broad public participation, African parties were forced to act as midwives at their own birth. In the well-documented case of Nigeria in the 1950s, we know 'that each major Southern party was supported by a bank, which in particular was responsible for keeping the party's main newspaper alive, and that each bank had in the past received a very substantial injection of public money from government agencies, the respective governments being controlled by the different parties'.[21] The continuous, reciprocal party charges of favouritism and corruption were neither surprising nor proven; nor was it always possible to distinguish legitimate from illegitimate activity. Politicians, who were already successful businessmen, encouraged —in their political capacity—state aid to African business, and—in their economic capacity—they gratefully accepted such help. For, businessmen or politicians, their habitat was the city, where opportunity existed and where the elite way of life was uniquely located.[22]

That Nigeria is typical in this regard is evident in Pye's characterisation of the political elite of most non-Western countries as consisting of 'those who have become urbanized, have received the appropriate forms of education, and have demonstrated skill in establishing the necessary personal relations'.[23] Political power is achieved, Pye believes, through manipulation of the prestige and influence which accrues to such personal attributes. While positions on policy issues are thus of secondary importance in achieving power, the elites of new nations of all political hues are committed to a policy of rapid industrial urbanisation. Not only does the revolution of rising expectations demand such development, but the very self-image of the elite requires it. If the new nations are to become respected in the world community, they must acquire the requisite economic base, and all that this implies, or face the alternative of some degree of elite-demeaning 'economic colonialism'.[24] The politics of economic development is part of the national search for self-respect.

Our probes into the nature of urban power bring us back to the observation that students of African cities tend to be disciplinary border-crossers. We have seen how this reflects the nature of the city itself, the improbability of there being a distinctive urban theory, and the necessity of following many paths of inquiry to arrive at an understanding of the whole. The suggestion that societal dominance is the city's raison d'être provides common focus for the spectrum of disciplines whose urban interests overlap. The new elites of Africa are not the new upper class or the new entrepreneurs or the new political leaders. Those who control the new nations are all of these—and urbanites as well.

What has been said is not uniquely true for Africa and what we learn of cities there can help us to understand them elsewhere. Yet Africa presents distinctive features which accentuate the dominance of its cities. It is only on the threshold of urban development; its nations are new; its cities are few. So also are its leaders new and few. In his essay on city size, Joseph Spengler discusses the demography of political leadership through which the very sparseness of cities makes possible such wide control by small elites. But even they have not secured economic dominance. Individual political influence is surely being converted into other coin, but sometimes a more dramatic conversion is sired by economists and mothered by international aid. The offspring—

planned national economy—places major economic controls in the hands of the government elite. So, by this and other means, small groups of powerful men in a few African cities work to create the sort of modern society which they require and which they have promised to the masses.

Modernisation

Modern Africa is our subject in two senses—we are concerned with the current scene in Africa and with the modernisation of life upon that scene. Daniel Lerner, who develops the theme in the following chapter, was influential in bringing the word 'modernisation' into formal scientific use.[25] In so doing, he moved away from terms like 'Europeanisation' and 'Westernisation' which disregard such non-Western models as Japan and the Soviet Union. Lerner sees modernisation as revolutionising all sectors of life—social, economic, cultural and political. He postulates that the evolution of this revolution follows a definite series of phases, recapitulating those evident in the history of Western modernisation. Beginning with urbanisation and the establishment of an industrial base, further development requires increasing literacy and involvement with mass media of communication and, finally, broad political participation. The fact that electronic media are not dependent upon literacy leads him, as well as Lionel Tiger, to ponder the rising level of frustration of African masses, whose abilities are bound by illiteracy but whose goals are set by the modern, urban images of elite life which are disseminated by radio, television and cinema. Lerner sees other 'people problems' resulting from such disjunctions in the modernisation process as growing urbanisation without industrialisation. Wilbert Moore recently characterised modernisation as the process of 'joining the modern world' economically, politically and socially.[26] His creative summary of the ways in which neophyte nations may achieve that membership recognised somewhat greater variability in the means of modernisation than does Lerner. The two agree, however, on the society-engulfing character of modernisation and on the central role of the city in that revolution.

The following studies range widely over the processes of modernisation,[27] particular facets of which find different treatment in separate contexts. The sequence of chapters follows a rough progression in emphasis: from general conceptual considerations to concern with demography and economics, then to studies of race relations and politics, and to analyses of the modernising family. The concluding sketch of the development of Kampala can be seen as illuminating the interdependence of the various approaches in arriving at some understanding of the urban whole. As no ordering of the contributions can portray the authors' mutual concern with the central phenomena of modernisation, the ensuing discussion provides an opportunity to follow a few of these processes from author to author.

It is usual to consider some of the inter-relationships among modernising forces in the context of the 'demographic transition' from high birth and death rates to low ones. As in the case of other theories of modernisation, a major problem is that of determining the degree to which the successive demographic changes which accompanied Western development are requisite for all modernisation. LeVine's comparison of traditional and modernised Yoruba families reveals many of the differences which would be expected in a transition from high to low mortality and from a preference for large families to small ones. It is possible, however, that the net impact is one of greater family size among the moderns, who are committed to family planning but who still want four or five children, almost all of whom will grow to maturity.[28]

In the Ivory Coast, Clignet finds that urban wives tend to have been married later in life than rural women. The former also differ sharply in their recourse to hospitals for the birth of their children. Despite such indications of modernising changes in the city, the birth rates appear roughly comparable for rural and urban married women of similar age. Although these data were not collected with demographic problems in mind, they are particularly valuable because they reflect dimensions of urbanisation. One of the striking findings is that progressive modernisation is not a unitary phenomenon, for it may lead to the partial resurgence of traditional ways. Thus, clerical workers are much more likely to be polygynous than are manual workers, who presumably would also like to have more wives if they could afford them. In a like vein, LeVine's data indicate that both traditional and elite Yoruba men have similar desires for living descendants, but they must pursue their goals by quite different means. Although the African situation is only sketchily known,[29] these studies contribute to the impression that the steps in the demographic transition may be quite varied.

Urbanisation is both a prerequisite and a product of industrialisation, yet we know that thousands of people can come together in communal life without benefit of industrialisation and without spawning it. So, in today's new nations, the urban accumulation of what Lerner calls the DPs from rural areas may lead only to the growth of unemployment and poverty. Such 'over-urbanisation' puts added demands on the economy of the city and even of the state. Because the leaders of such states are city-dwellers and because their power is disproportionately city-based, the needs of urbanites are proximate and pressing. In the city, the struggle is played out between the pressures to develop urban facilities and the pressures to facilitate economic development.[30]

Although the population of Africa is still overwhelmingly rural, even the prelude to independence increased the rate of urbanisation to levels above those then evident on any other continent. There is reason to believe that this was but the beginning—a crossing of the threshold to modernisation. Lerner concludes that Africa's very lack of development makes it the most favoured developing area in the world. This striking judgement rests on the argument that, because most new African states are still uncommitted to specific lines of development, they have more options open to them. They need not rush blindly ahead but can profit from the experience of others. The possible role of the social sciences in distilling such experience is more obvious than is the nature and utility of the distillate. Apparent options are not always real options, but our task is certainly to clarify the implications of the choices.

When urban growth is the question, Spengler shows the same sort of optimism as that expressed by Lerner. For most of Africa, the lack of cities in general, and of 'primate' cities in particular, means that there may be an opportunity to urbanise without creating the misery which stamps pre-industrial cities and which attended unplanned urban growth in the 'developed' nations. Spengler uses his encyclopedic knowledge of the functional implications of city size to spell out what the social sciences can say about the social and economic gains and losses associated with different sized cities and various systems of cityness.

'Mobility' has been called 'a one-word summary of the institutional requirements of economic development'.[31] With Lerner, we can differentiate between physical, social and psychic mobility, and see all three combining to liberate man from his traditional ties. Migration to the city is commonly the initial and perhaps the most dramatic step towards individual autonomy. In the form of labour migration, such mobility has been much studied in Africa by social anthropologists, who have stressed the effects of transient migrancy upon the social relations of urban workers. In contrast, when Barber considers the results of such migration to Rhodesian cities, he shifts the focus of inquiry from the impact of the urban economy on the roles of Africans to the impact of the Africans' urban roles on the economy.

Whatever else Talcott Parsons may have contributed to the social sciences, his delineation of the patterns of particularism-ascription and of universalism-achievement provided a context for the multidisciplinary examination of economic development.[32] In that context, it is held that urban industrialisation depends upon increasing specialisation of labour and upon labour recruitment on the basis of ability. It is therefore disconcerting to note, as Kuper does, that in South Africa—the continent's most industrialised country—the large urban African population is predominantly unskilled. So also in Rhodesia, Barber found that almost 90 per cent of the Africans employed in the largest cities were unskilled. Obviously, a society which is ascriptive in its racially-discriminatory patterns of education and labour recruitment can still have an industrial system based on the achievement orientation of its dominant group. Despite such lack of conformity of the total system to the ideal typical model, it is instructive to note that the urban African population tends to retain the traditional orientation of particularism-ascription, while the Europeans live more in terms of the modern pattern of universalism-achievement. Kuper skilfully dissects the unusually complicated social structure required to maintain such great cultural differences between interdependent and interactive groups.

Independence and Africanisation have eliminated such patterns of discrimination elsewhere on the continent, but the old patterns are frequently replaced by new ones based on African dominance, tribalism or some other form of ethnicity. As these seem likely to disturb modernisation efforts, it is particularly significant that the Hannas found structural similarities between the racial pluralism of South Africa and the polyethnic organisation of independent African countries, where the lines of urban politics can often be traced back to tribal areas. There is also evidence, notes Spengler, that the milieu of the large city is particularly conducive to the retention of such ethnic cleavages. Southall describes it thus for colonial Kampala, but residents of the new urban housing developments are mixed in origin. More importantly, the economic stratification inherent in the price structure of these housing estates is found to cross-cut the ethnic groups. Here, at least, occupation and class values over-ride tribal origins as the bases of social grouping. The picture which emerges is one in which the unskilled urban masses remain culturally fractionated and undigested by modernisation, while the new elite find common ground in their education, occupations and style of life. The elite are not a caste, however, but are committed to facilitating the upward mobility of their countrymen through the expansion of educational and occupational opportunities.

High expectations, however, are insufficient to maintain the impetus of new nations through the long struggle for modernisation. Many of the goals and motivations associated with the independence movement must be transformed and made self-sustaining if they are not to perish with white supremacy and with the charismatic fathers of the African dream. Two social mechanisms for institutionalising the dream are the 'routinisation of charisma' and the training of the new generation for greater autonomy than that decreed by tradition.

Weber's prediction that problems of politics become problems of administration is borne out by Tiger's evidence from Ghana, where he finds government by charisma giving way to a bureaucracy. Especially through its administrative role in the planning and execution of development programmes, the civil service has increasingly acquired control from the politicians, albeit with the support of Nkrumah, who was himself ordained to succumb to the trend. Progressive bureaucratisation is even evident in the dissociation of the civil service from the corruption of the politicians. This dichotomy Tiger finds at the top levels of government in Ghana and the Hannas note it at local government levels in Nigeria and Uganda. The subsequent overthrow of charismatic leaders in all three states reflects a culmination of the conflicts engendered in the taming of the revolution.

The lonely few who dreamed the dream of black power in Africa grew up, in large part, with white schoolmasters and professors as father surrogates. Before these young Africans left their homes for the world of boarding-schools, however, their feet were firmly planted in the traditional soil from which both their charisma and understanding grew. Today, we must ask, what sort of people does a modernising society require and what avenues exist for their emergence? There are suggested answers to the first question, answers which lead LeVine to define modernised child-rearing as that designed to produce highly-educated, self-directed, flexible and resourceful men and women. Such people seem best suited to the modern requirements of individual mobility in a continuously-changing system. No society has a completely modernised population in such terms, but the white-collar functions of fully industrialised societies do seem to be performed by people who are modern in this sense. Are parents from the African elite, asks LeVine, trying to produce such progeny? Yoruba members of the Nigerian elite answer him. Their origins are largely in traditional, illiterate, polygynous families, but families which made possible their children's education. These children, now grown to elitehood, show remarkable shifts towards familial values which foster the development of a yet more modern generation, but one still possessing a distinctly Yoruba flavour. Clignet's urban families of Abure and Bete are modernising too, but with their own distinctive variations. Modernisation does not appear to be the road to modernity but, instead, the general direction to be pursued.

To Know the City

Most of the social research conducted in Africa during the colonial period was done by anthropologists. The British variety in particular tended to consider themselves as much sociologists as anthropologists, or, as Radcliffe-Brown sometimes put it, they were comparative sociologists. As such, they not only studied the social organisation of African tribes, but they did not hesitate to follow the Africans into the cities. On the other hand, American anthropologists, reared in the traditional belief that urban-industrial civilisation was the province of sociologists, were apt to eschew the cities and the areas of their influence.

African independence and its anticipatory decade brought a surge of American anthropologists to Africa—even some to the cities—and a veritable tidal wave of political scientists. Disciplines such as economics and psychology, which had shown little prior interest in cross-cultural research, began to find the world of new nations a challenge to old notions; yet most American sociologists have continued to reflect their separation from anthropology by hesitating to venture afield. Because the research exploration of Africa must proceed as a collective and cumulative effort, it is fitting to conclude this overview by sketching, with broad strokes, the methodological paths the authors have followed.

The case study is, of course, the anthropologist's staple, but for other social scientists as well it is almost the *sine qua non* of African research. We are so familiar with the details of our own culture that we rarely examine the role of such understanding in research in American society. Peter Marris's discussion shows how the assumption of such common understanding is patently impossible in Africa. The case study of the African social milieu provides the necessary context for further social research in that setting. This is not to say that every social scientist must be an anthropologist or that anthropological analysis necessarily considers data of focal importance for every sort of social research. It is to say that such focal data can hardly be collected, much less understood, without reference to the cultural and social system of which it is a part.

Both the division of labour among the social sciences and their essential unity facilitate the process of developing such understanding. Thus Clignet depends heavily upon published ethnographies to grasp the traditional implications of the lineage systems whose contrast is built into his research. Each new study, in turn, contributes to the delineation of increasingly inclusive social configurations, such as that which emerges from Southall's synthesis based on the large accumulation of research on Kampala. Even in the case of Barber's dependence upon demographic and economic data from Rhodesian documentary sources, his protracted resident study of the area is evident in the social flesh he puts on the statistical bones; and Tiger's provocative essay on Ghanaian bureaucracy clearly reflects his long immersion in the life of Accra. Every case need not be enumerated to make the point that, if the collected studies beckon the researcher to African cities, it is not an invitation to a passing affair.

'Vive la différence' extends the sexual metaphor to comparative studies, for it is 'the difference' which invites discovery of the yet unknown or confirmation of the experienced past. Even a passion for dispassionate science leads to the pursuit of differences, as well as similarities, among societies. Such comparison may take the form of testing in one culture hypotheses derived from another, in the way Barber assays the applicability of Hoselitz's distinction between generative and parasitic cities, or as the Hannas use Riggs's model of 'prismatic society', or as LeVine tests social psychological conclusions from the works of Inkeles and Prothro.

But the use of comparison goes beyond that of subjecting hypotheses to culture shock. As a substitute for experimental research, controlled comparison[33] provides the best possible method of rising above the inherent limitation of conclusions drawn from a single case. It is true that the cross-cultural test of a hypothesis is a sort of comparison of cases, but one which demands much of the stipulation that other things be equal. By more narrowly limiting the differences between cases to those contrasts which are of crucial theoretical importance, the data can, of course, be made to speak less ambiguously. Among our collaborators, Marris reviews some of the theoretical and policy implications of his experience with the wide spectrum of comparisons in which his study of slum clearance in Lagos was conceived; the Hannas report on a unique comparison of the political system of a community in Uganda with another in Nigeria, the two being matched in fundamental respects. Clignet uses large population samples of matched occupational groups from two different tribes. The occupations range from cash-crop farming to manual and clerical work in the cities, providing a series with progressively greater urban-industrial involvement. Simultaneous comparison of all of these factors throws light on the process of urbanisation in a context of ethnic variation. LeVine pursues his concern with a narrower range of problems by comparing two very small Yoruba samples, carefully selected to represent the traditional and modernised extremes, both found in the modernising, pre-industrial city of Ibadan.

Finally, and beyond the scope of particular research designs, the broadest possible comparisons provide the basis for such summarising and innovating studies as those of Lerner, Spengler and Kuper. Here, as well, are thoughtful attempts to relate the fruits of scholarship to the practical problems of the modern world of African cities.

Notes and References

1 Albert J. Reiss, Jr, "The Nature of the City", in Paul K. Hatt and Albert J. Reiss, Jr, eds., *Cities and Society*, Glencoe, Ill., 1957, pp. 17–21.

2 Max Weber, *The City*, trans. and ed. Don Martindale and Gertrud Neuwirth, New York 1962, p. 78.

3 William Bascom, "Urbanization among the Yoruba", *American Journal of Sociology*, Vol. 60, 1955, pp. 446–54; and "Some Aspects of Yoruba Urbanism", *American Anthropologist*, Vol. 64, 1962, pp. 699–709.

4 Philip M. Hauser, "Urbanization: An Overview", in Philip M. Hauser and Leo F. Schnore, eds., *The Study of Urbanization*, New York 1965, pp. 8–9.

5 Gideon Sjoberg, "Theory and Research in Urban Sociology", in Hauser and Schnore, op. cit., pp. 157–89.

6 Talcott Parsons, "A Revised Analytical Approach to the Theory of Social Stratification", in Reinhard Bendix and Seymour Martin Lipset, eds., *Class, Status and Power*, Glencoe, Ill., 1953, p. 128.

7 Don Martindale, "Prefatory Remarks: The Theory of the City", in Weber, op. cit., p. 10.

8 Robert M. Adams, "The Origin of Cities", *Scientific American*, Vol. 203, No. 3, September 1960, pp. 153–68.

9 Numa Denis Fustel de Coulanges, *The Ancient City*, Garden City, NY, 1956. First published in 1864, this work is not sophisticated by modern standards, particularly in its over-emphasis on the role of religion in the formation of Athens and Rome.

10 N. C. Mitchell, "Yoruba Towns", in K. M. Barbour and R. M. Prothero, eds., *Essays on African Population*, London 1961, pp. 279–301.

11 Weber, op. cit., pp. 81–4.

12 Henri Pirenne, *Medieval Cities*, trans. Frank D. Halsey, Princeton, NJ, 1925.

13 Adams, loc. cit.

14 Gideon Sjoberg, *The Preindustrial City*, Glencoe, Ill., 1960, p. 87.

15 Concerning the concentration of political and economic power in cities, see Bert F. Hoselitz, "The Role of Cities in the Economic Growth of Underdeveloped Countries", in his *Sociological Aspects of Economic Growth*, Glencoe, Ill., 1960.

16 Adams, loc. cit.

17 For an excellent elaboration of these ideas, see Eric E. Lampard, "Historical Aspects of Urbanization", in Hauser and Schnore, op. cit., pp. 519–54.

18 Amos H. Hawley, *Human Ecology*, New York 1950, p. 221.

19 This idea, which entered the sociological literature through R. D. McKenzie, finds explicit empirical support in Otis Dudley Duncan and Albert J. Reiss, Jr, *Social Characteristics of Urban and Rural Communities*, New York 1956, and in Otis Dudley Duncan et al., *Metropolis and Region*, Baltimore 1960.

20 William Hance, "The Economic Location and Functions of Tropical African Cities", *Human Organization*, Vol. 19, 1960, pp. 135–6. See also Norton S. Ginsburg, "Urban Geography and 'Non-Western' Areas", in Hauser and Schnore, op. cit., pp. 311–46; and Benjamin E. Thomas, "Geography", in Robert A. Lystad, *The African World: A Survey of Social Research*, New York and London 1965, pp. 245–70, particularly pp. 261–2.

21 K. W. J. Post, "The Use of Power", in *The Nigerian Federal Election of 1959*, London 1963, pp. 55–66; reprinted in William John Hanna, ed., *Independent Black Africa*, Chicago 1964, pp. 444–53, specifically p. 450.

22 Hugh H. Smythe and Mabel M. Smythe, *The New Nigerian Elite*, Stanford 1960, p. 45.

23 Lucian W. Pye, "The Non-Western Political Process", *The Journal of Politics*, Vol. 20, 1958, p. 469.

24 Gideon Sjoberg develops this idea in his "Cities in Developing and Industrial Societies: A Cross-cultural Analysis", in Hauser and Schnore, op. cit., pp. 213–63, especially p. 220.

25 Daniel Lerner, *The Passing of Traditional Society: Modernizing the Middle East*, Glencoe, Ill., 1958.

26 Wilbert E. Moore, *The Impact of Industry*, Englewood Cliffs, NJ, 1965. This is a short, non-technical introduction to the modernisation of traditional societies. More specialised coverage is to be found in Bert F. Hoselitz and Wilbert E. Moore, eds., *Industrialization and Society*, Paris and The Hague 1963.

27 Major summarising and generalising studies of what is known about social structure and process in African cities include: A. L. Epstein, "Urbanization and Social Change in Africa", *Current Anthropology*, Vol. 8, 1967; Philip H. Gulliver, "Anthropology", in Lystad, op. cit., particularly pp. 96–106; Peter C. W. Gutkind, "African Urban Family Life", *Cahiers d'Etudes Africaines*, Vol. 3, 1962, pp. 149–217; and "The African Urban Milieu: A Force in Rapid Change", *Civilisations*, Vol. 12, 1962, pp. 167–91; Leo Kuper, "Sociology: Some Aspects of Urban Plural Societies in Africa", in Lystad, op. cit., pp. 107–30; Kenneth Little, *West African Urbanization, A Study of Voluntary Associations in Social Change*, Cambridge 1965; J. Clyde Mitchell, "Theoretical Orientations in African Urban Studies", in Michael Banton, ed., *The Social Anthropology of Complex Societies*, London 1966, pp. 37–68; Aidan Southall, ed., *Social Change in Modern Africa*, London and New York 1961, particularly the "Introductory Summary", pp. 1–66; UNESCO, *Social Implications of Industrialization and Urbanization in Africa South of the Sahara*, Paris 1956.

28 Wilbert E. Moore, "Industrialization and Social Change", in Hoselitz and Moore, op. cit., p. 328, draws a similar conclusion from Hassan El Saaty's evidence from the United Arab Republic.

29 Frank Lorimer, William Brass and Etienne van de Walle, "Demography", in Lystad, op. cit., pp. 271–316.

30 Gerald Breese, *Urbanization in Newly Developing Countries*, Englewood Cliffs, NJ, 1966, pp. 43–6.

31 Moore, *Impact of Industry*, op. cit., p. 31.

32 Horace Miner, "Community-Society Continua", *International Encyclopedia of the Social Sciences*, New York.

33 For a discussion of the method, see S. F. Nadel, *The Foundations of Social Anthropology*, Glencoe, Ill., 1951, pp. 222–46.

2

Comparative Analysis of Processes of Modernisation

DANIEL LERNER

MODERNISATION is, in my lexicon, the social process of which development is the economic component. If economic development produces 'rising output per head', then modernisation produces the societal environment in which rising productivity is effectively incorporated. As an acceptable first approximation of a definition, I would consider as modernised a society that is capable of 'self-sustaining growth' over the long run.[1]

This definition, while oriented towards the economic process, is not as restrictive as it may seem at first glance. To begin with, economic development is in fact a high-priority objective of every modernising society—the prime mover, when it is not indeed the only motivation, for modernisation. Moreover, and this is the crux of the matter, the attainment of 'self-sustaining growth' involves far more than the economic processes of production and consumption. It involves the institutional disposition of the full resources of a society—in particular, its human resources. For an economy to sustain its growth by its own autonomous operation, it must be effectively geared into the main components of the skill infrastructure and the value suprastructure of its societal framework—i.e., the skills and values of the people who make it work. On this view, a society capable of operating an economy of 'self-sustaining growth' is *ipso facto* a modernised society.

NOTE: *The notes and references for Chapter 2 will be found on page 38.*

I orient my definition in this sense in order to focus attention upon the proposition that is central to the analysis presented here: that there is a single process of modernisation which operates in all developing societies, regardless of their colour, creed or climate and regardless of their history, geography or culture. This is the process of economic development; and, since development cannot be sustained without modernisation, I consider it appropriate to stress this common mechanism underlying the various faces of modernisation. Having stated this proposition so baldly, let me promptly add the necessary disclaimers. The proposition does not assert that colour, creed, climate are of no consequence in modernisation; nor does it assert that history, geography, culture are irrelevant to development. These characteristics of a society clearly modify the development process, by varying its mode and adjusting its tempo. But they cannot change the basic mechanism underlying the particularities of mode and tempo. If a society is to develop, it must achieve 'rising output per head'. And if a society is to modernise, it must bring development to the level of 'self-sustaining growth'. A society that did not give high priority to these objectives would have little motivation to undergo the trials and tribulations, the pangs and pains, that accompany modernisation everywhere. For these objectives impose their price: people make themselves behave in the ways required to operate the only mechanism whereby these objectives can be attained.

Note that nothing normative in favour of modernisation has been said. In fact, I do not believe that modernisation, as here conceived, is either desirable or indeed feasible in every society of the contemporary world—a judgement based on the estimate that, a generation or two hence, some types of society will be able to modernise more effectively at lower human cost. What I have said is that most traditional societies—and all that are new states—appear in fact to have opted for modernisation (without my advice or consent). Having done so, they have committed themselves to a process they may not comprehend, a process that imposes upon them demands they may neither understand nor accept, but a process whose demands cannot be ignored, unless the objectives of modernisation are abandoned.

Consider one set of demands imposed by the objective of 'rising output per head'. Economists are agreed that to achieve this a new division of labour must be created that will shift working people from the primary agricultural sector (which will continue to feed the society as well or better) into the secondary and tertiary sectors. This sounds simple enough in doctrine, but an enormous transformation of human lifeways—skills and values—is required to bring it off in practice. Most developed societies feed their entire population, at the rate of 3,000 or more calories per head per day, with 20 per cent or less of their labour force employed in agriculture. Most underdeveloped societies employ 80 per cent or more of their labour force in agriculture and still do not supply their entire population with the minimum caloric requirements stipulated by the Food and Agriculture Organisation and World Health Organisation—often, indeed, supplying only half or less of the quantities produced by the advanced nations. To achieve modernisation, the developing societies would have to double or triple their output, using only one-third or one-fourth of their present agricultural workers. This requires 'rising output per head' in orders of magnitude ranging from 600 to 1,200 per cent, simply to bring their agricultural sector into an acceptable relationship with the rest of the economy. To this must be added the extra order of magnitude imposed by the 'population explosion' in these same developing countries.

What is to be done with the 60 per cent or more of the labour force displaced from agriculture? They are to be re-employed in the industrial and service sectors. Again, if one says this fast, it is possible to overlook the enormous transformation in people's lives that this process requires. Transport must be built to move them, homes to house them, schools to train them, factories and offices to employ them, and the array of urban facilities to service them. These are the processes of urbanisation-industrialisation (they must be hyphenated) that, in the Western world, evolved over the course of several centuries. Even so, they entailed suffering and misery for many millions of people—as is revealed in the nineteenth century studies of the urban poor by Frederic LePlay in Europe, by Charles Booth in England and by Jane Hull in America.

But the modernising lands today are societies-in-a-hurry. Emulating what the advanced Western societies have become today, they want to get there faster. Accordingly, they force the tempo of Western development. Even more serious, as a result of their hurried pace, they often disorder the sequence of Western development. The most conspicuous symptom of the contemporary disorder is what happened to urbanisation in the developing areas. Every student of development is aware of the global spread of urban slums—from the *ranchos* of Caracas and *favellas* of Rio, to the *geçeköndu* of Ankara, to the *bidonvilles* and 'tin can cities' that infest the metropolitan centres of every developing country from Cairo to Manila.

The point that must be stressed in referring to this suffering mass of humanity displaced from the rural areas to the filthy peripheries of the great cities, is that few of them experience the 'transition' from agricultural to urban-industrial labour called for by the mechanism of development and the model of modernisation. They are neither housed, nor trained, nor employed, nor serviced. They languish on the urban periphery without entering into any productive relationship with its industrial operations. These are the 'displaced persons', the DPs, of the developmental process as it now typically occurs in most of the world, a human flotsam and jetsam that has been displaced from traditional agricultural life without being incorporated into modern industrial life.

The hapless condition of the DP enters into the lives of their children as well, thus prolonging displacement into the next generation. Typically, their children do not go to school, do not find work (other than the most menial and unrewarding), do not become urbane in any significant sense (other than the urbanity of big-city delinquency and crime). If they do go to school, rarely is attendance sustained enough for them to acquire truly functional literacy. What they learn they forget; what they remember is insufficient to serve any useful purpose. Thus the DP status, once acquired, is prolonged and even perpetuated. The postwar generation of urban DPs around most of the world provides the nucleus of 'urban poor' that will multiply well into the next century. Their existence, dreadful in personal terms, is at the same time one of the major drags on the developmental process, wherever they are. They are not merely unemployed and impoverished. They are counter-productive in the sense that considerable resources must be allocated to maintain them in even this miserable condition of life, since the social conscience of a modernising society will not allow—and its self-protection cannot afford—the sorts of death bred by squalor. While I was in Caracas, during January 1962, an eleven-month-old infant in one of the *ranchos* was eaten alive by a rat. If this sort of thing were to 'go too far' in the *ranchos*, what guarantee would there be for the safety of babies in the better neighbourhoods farther down the road? Indeed, what protection is there for decent folk against those DPs who survive infancy in the *ranchos* (and their functional equivalent around the world) in order to grow into juvenile delinquents, hoodlums or criminals? Every such new urban agglomeration makes substantial demands upon the resources of its environment: more police and firemen, more hospitals and schools, more housing and related facilities. Much of this outlay is wasted, but there is no way in which it can be saved, so long as the environment cannot provide the one productive outlet from the DP condition: a job.

The foregoing is intended to dramatise the need for comparative analysis of the processes of modernisation by focusing on one such process that has gone seriously awry in most developing countries. This is the flooding of great urban centres by people who have no work there. What this augurs is the contemporary decoupling of the twin processes of urbanisation and industrialisation whereby most of the developed countries of the world attained their present condition. In this sense, the rat in Caracas is not a cautionary tale but a piece of evidence for functional analysis. It is a principal thesis of this essay that the modernisation of most of the world is going badly—is costing too much for too little benefit—owing largely to the lack of comparative analysis on which rational control of the modernisation processes could be based. In support of this thesis, some of the important processes and their interaction will be identified, and then suggestions will be made on some of the priorities for the comparative analysis that is yet to be done.

Major Processes and Their Interaction

Some of the major processes that animate modernisation have already been identified: urbanisation, industrialisation, education, sanitation, transportation. The first two are 'basic' variables, in that they have to be generated first before the rest can come into productive operation. The last two are 'sequential' variables, in that they invariably come into operation once the first two are operative. Whether the last two operate more or less efficiently in cost benefit terms is an important but technical question, subordinate to the great policy decisions activating the first two. Historically, where people displaced from agriculture went to the towns and found work, their industrialisation-urbanisation entrained in due course the sequence of urban services that are symbolised by sanitation and transportation. I say 'symbolised' because there are literally hundreds of technical and administrative sequences that must be worked out for sanitation and transportation to be effective in the modernising environment.

Education is rather different from the others. It is an 'intervening' variable. It cannot be fully independent of the urban-industrial processes, for it depends upon the human motivations and material facilities supplied by these, yet it cannot be left to come along as part of the 'sequential' aftermath. For, while the urban-industrial processes may be initiated independently of education, they cannot long be sustained without equivalent growth of education as the main supplier of those skilled human resources upon which urban-industrial growth utterly depends. This point is illustrated in a variety of ways throughout the eight-volume report on the United Nations conference on the Application of Science and Technology for the Benefit of the Less Developed Areas. Perhaps the most simple and vivid statement of the case was made by Professor E. V. Garcia of Argentina: 'The very basis of the problems of development, the core of everything related to it, is *Man*. Technology cannot canalize his potential with the same speed as it can canalize, for example, a river. Today we know how to deal with a desert, to turn it into an orchard in relatively few years; but far more time is necessary to train men who are capable of growing oranges in a desert.'[2]

To grow oranges in a desert requires man to do something other than what comes naturally. A man used to orange-growing will be strange to deserts; one used to deserts will be strange to the culture of oranges. Either way, something new must be learned in order to bring into efficient working relationship sets of lifeways—the desert and the orchard—never before integrated in the experience of a single person. The skills required for the planting, tending and harvesting of citrus crops are considerable, but far more than technical skills must be learned. Living in orchard oases means blending two disparate 'cultures' with different, often divergent, values. At a rudimentary level it requires a recasting of one's perception and evaluation of the natural elements—sun and wind, sand and water. At a somewhat higher level, it reshapes one's use and valuation of animals and people. In the orchard oasis, one is less likely to give absolute priority to camels, and rather more likely to find uses for women and children, than elsewhere in the desert. Yet the men and families living in an orchard oasis cannot wholly abandon the lore and law of the desert, for it remains their proximate environment.

The case of the oasis orchard has been taken as only a more vivid instance of the process that is activated whenever people move from a less to a more developed environment. Something new, which transforms old values while reshaping old skills, must be learned. This 'something new' is nothing less than how to live productively in a new and strange and ever-changing environment. When people move from the familiar routines of village life, where each person's role and status is known to all, to the unrelated sets of 'contacts' imposed by urban living, their style of life abruptly undergoes a deep transformation. To cope with the consequences of their physical mobility, they must acquire psychic mobility. For mobility is the primary process whereby modernisation is activated—the process of which urbanisation-industrialisation is the major mode. However, the world's educational facilities are vastly inadequate to provide the quantity of psychic mobility required by the amount of physical mobility that is now occurring over most of the world. This is why I pointed first to the millions of DPs who now populate the periphery of the world's great urban centres and who form the most numerous class of people victimised by mobility without education. But people of the same class can be found as well in smaller towns and even in orchard groves.

These millions of people form the hard core of the 'revolution of rising frustrations' that confronts the modernising world over the next two generations—i.e., the rest of our century. This is the heavy price the developing countries must pay for their failure to understand and adapt the urban-industrial sequences revealed by the Western model of modernisation. The West spent most of the nineteenth century dealing inadequately with its unprecedented problems of the urban poor. From the French revolution of 1789 to the British general strike of 1925, the most 'advanced' countries of Europe failed to find satisfactory solutions for urban-industrial poverty and the effects of their failure can be traced in the revolutionary civil wars throughout Europe and the international wars that spread beyond the European continent. The agonising civil wars imposed communism on Russia in 1918, fascism on Italy in 1924, nazism on Germany in 1933, falangism on Spain in 1937. Its wider effects can be seen in the 'popular front' that invaded all of the Western world during those critical 1930s. These conflicting movements of protest ignited the global war of the 1940s and shaped the global Cold War of the 1950s. During these decades, the failures of the Western model were put on display for all the world to see. The persistence of urban poverty was the main failure. Its projection into civil and global wars certified the incapacity of modern society to maintain external peace without resolving its internal conflict. It was Hitler who divided Europe into 'have' and 'have-not' nations and declared that he would move Germany by force into the 'have' category. His effort laid waste to Germany and much of Europe. Paradoxically, if Germany thirty years later has become a 'have' nation, it was by losing Hitler's war, abandoning Hitler's aim of European hegemony and entering into co-operative economic development with its European partners.

We are spanning great historical sequences in apparently cavalier fashion. To articulate the propositions underlying this summary sketch of Western history over the past two hundred years would go far beyond the scope of my immediate concerns. Accordingly, I am limiting myself to pointing out that in these two centuries of Western history there is a cautionary tale of major import for the modernising societies of the rest of the world. Those new nations that permit their attention and resources to be focused on external 'confrontations'—as between Egypt and Israel, India and Pakistan, China and India, Indonesia and Malaysia—are likely to re-enact the worst follies of Western history. To follow Hitler's schema of dealing with an international map of haves and have-nots by using military force is to follow a devious, and deviant, course that cannot bring other than grievous effects in the form of civil and international wars. This sort of strategy is the more senseless in that none of the parties to these 'confrontations' between developing countries is very 'have'.

The idea of enriching yourself by the plunder and booty of a defeated adversary is, in this context, a capital error. Getting a bigger slice of the other fellow's small pie will impoverish him without enriching you. Beggar thy neighbour, in the neighbourhoods of poverty, is a game without profit to the 'winner'. The present level of aggressiveness among poor developing countries enjoins us, if we are to deal realistically with their severe problems of internal growth, to take cautionary note of their tendency towards fruitless external adventure. For the great strategy of development is not to snip a piece from a neighbour's little pie, but to learn how to bake bigger pies for oneself. For this, one needs the constructive guidance of political economy—what has been called the 'policy sciences of democratic development'—rather than the destructive operation of military force. Since the policy sciences of democratic development require nothing less than a comprehensive understanding of the development process in operational terms, it is to this requirement that I now turn.

On the Agenda of Comparative Analysis

The policy science approach to a comprehensive understanding of societal processes begins with a formulation of goals: the value-objective that we want developing societies to achieve. Next, it describes the trends of recent and current events, in terms of movement towards (or away from) the postulated goals. It then undertakes to analyse the conditions under which these trends are occurring. This, given the instability of most operational indexes and the inadequacy of most statistical time-series, is the most difficult, but scientifically the most essential, step in deriving policy-science projections of the probable future from a comprehensive map of the past and present.

The definition of goals for modernising societies is reasonably clear from my earlier references to the 'policy sciences of democratic development'. The notorious ambiguity of all such key symbols as 'democracy' need not obscure the meaning in this context since the institutional procedures that best serve democratic goals may vary in different societies at different times. France was not cast out of the democratic world when irresponsible parliamentary supremacy under the Fourth Republic brought it to 'l'immobilisme'; nor will France be cast out because the Fifth Republic is governed by an autocratic president with a strong 'cult of personality' tendency. The French municipal elections in March 1965 are an acceptable indicator that France remains democratic, however its institutional procedures may change from one decade to another. This much could not have been said for the Indonesia of Sukarno or the Ghana of Nkrumah. It cannot be said today for the Egypt of Nasser who is trying harder than most 'charismatic' leaders to involve his people, but whose autocratic cult of personality still remains unchecked by public opinion and uncontrolled by popular vote. Without some institutional procedure to activate these popular controls, there is no democracy and no democratic development.

For the essential elements of a democracy are the mobility and participation of its individual citizens. Mobility is essential because it liberates the individual who was bound to his inherited place in traditional society. Liberated from his native soil, he gains physical mobility by changing his position in space; liberated from his native status, he gains social mobility by changing his position in society; liberated from his native self, he gains psychic mobility by changing his personality to suit his new place and status in the world. This powerful transformation frees the individual from the constraints that bound him, in the traditional society, to his place and kin. However, liberation from place and kin also implies isolation from the *communitas* whereby individuals were related to each other by traditional custom. As this passage from community to society has been sufficiently articulated in the sociological literature of the past century, it need only be alluded to here, but I must stress that as a man transforms himself—from being defined as his father's son to being defined as the citizen of a nation—he acquires a need for participation in public life that was not felt in the traditional society. As a citizen, each man must make and remake his own relations with the larger social environment in which he lives. This is why the participant citizen rapidly becomes the cash customer, the radio listener and the voter, for a citizen of a modern society can function only by participating actively in its market, its forum and its *vox populi*. These distinguishing marks of citizenship in ancient Athens and Rome are still the principal traits of the urban man today. In the modern urban-industrial context, however, these traits take on significantly new forms.

The modern forms are associated largely with the rapid tempo of modernisation in the contemporary world. In previous centuries, two full generations might elapse before the transition from rural to urban living would slowly enter the lifeways of a village or clan. Today, around much of the world, this transition is occurring within the lifetime of millions of individuals. Clearly, swifter means are needed to teach and train modernising individuals in the lifeways of urbanity. The chosen instruments for this process are the mass media, which have come to function, only in the past two decades, as a 'mobility multiplier'. The multiplier power of the mass media derives from their capacity to reach a vast number of individuals rapidly and repeatedly. The messages they transmit operate directly, continuously and simultaneously upon people of diverse place and status, in isolated rural hamlets as in crowded city slums. They are thus capable of diffusing an 'apperceptive mass' that transforms individual personalities while weaving threads of interaction among them. Because the mass media have this power of affecting millions of individuals severally and collectively, they are uniquely empowered to carry forward the two processes of 'interest articulation' and 'interest aggregation' which Gabriel Almond has identified as principal components of political development[3]—or, in our more comprehensive term of reference, of modernisation.

It is my conviction, based on a decade of data-collection and evaluation, that the wartime and postwar spread of the mass media around most of the world has been the most important single factor in producing the global 'revolution of rising expectations' that animated development activity in the 1950s. It is my further conviction that the activity of the 1950s produced a severe setback to rising expectations in many developing areas, owing to a faulty communication strategy for the mass media, or the absence of an informed communication strategy, on the part of the charismatic leaders of the emerging nations and their technical advisers from the advanced societies. Largely as a result of the strategic failure to use the mass media effectively for development purposes, much of the underdeveloped world in the 1960s faces a 'revolution of rising frustrations'.

The source of frustration is the large—and growing—disparity between the bright new world 'promised' by the mass media (at least by implication) and the miserable world in which the audience for these promises actually live. The mass media, for two decades or more, have led people to believe that with the achievement of independent nationhood would come the beginnings of paradise on earth. In the event, however, independence brought only the beginning of new and harder problems than the peoples of the emerging nations had ever faced while they were in a condition of dependence. As they rapidly learned, independence did not automatically bring prosperity. It brought only the opportunity to enter the long hard road of raising 'output per head' whereby prosperity may, in some distant future, be attained. Small wonder that peoples who thought income would rise along with the raising of their new national flag have found themselves frustrated by the facts of independent political life.

The fault lies with the communication strategy of the new

leaders because they, eager to mobilise popular support and maintain public morale, either promised good things they could not deliver, or—if they were more prudent (not necessarily more wise)—they permitted people to believe that these good things had been promised to them. In short, they allowed their peoples to learn to want more than they could hope to get. This created the unbalanced want:get ratio which is the psychosomatic malady affecting most of the underdeveloped world today. As I have described this malady elsewhere at considerable length, I need say here only that I consider this an essential starting point for comparative analysis of the process of modernisation in the years ahead.

Future research may well start from the recognition that, within the comprehensive process of modernisation, there is a relatively autonomous component, usually called 'economic development'. Economic development is autonomous in the sense that its basic rules are applicable to all developing peoples, regardless of colour, creed or culture. The rule of 'rising output per head' governs economic development regardless of the socio-political environment or the psycho-cultural context. The latter components may, in any given society, facilitate or hinder the achievement of 'rising output per head', but the rule remains that without it there is no economic development. The larger form of this proposition is that a truly modern society is capable of 'self-sustaining growth'. This means that an input-output level has been achieved which guarantees that overall economic growth will continue without requiring inputs external to the system. Future researchers will do well to start from the conception that only a modern society is capable of self-sustaining growth, and, *ipso facto*, that any society capable of self-sustaining growth is modern. The reason, as I have indicated, is my data-based conviction that no society can achieve self-sustaining growth in its economy without having attained a reasonably full measure of modernity in its polity and in the matrix of its social relations.

Africa and the World Environment

I am not qualified to illustrate in detail how this general conception, developed from the empirical observation of other regions striving for modernisation, may best be applied to Africa. My colleagues in this volume, with their superior knowledge of African places and peoples, are far better equipped for this task. It may be suggested, however, that Africa has some considerable advantages over many other developing regions of the world. Possibly the most promising of these is its favourable man: land ratio. In most of Africa, there is not yet the overpopulation that in many areas of Asia puts insatiable demands for food and fibre upon every acre of usable land. With foresight and planning, much of Africa can avoid the disastrous pseudo-urbanisation that merely transfers an unproductive rural jetsam to an equally unproductive, but more frustrated and counterproductive, urban flotsam.

The existence of a potential advantage does not automatically guarantee its rational utilisation. We have seen that Latin America, also blessed with a favourable man: land ratio, has failed to utilise it effectively for development purposes. Instead, over the past generation or so, Latin America has become the most abusively over-urbanised continent in the world: as a result, in several Latin American countries, half or more of the national population is now concentrated in the capital cities—as in the Uruguayan capital of Montevideo and, notably, in the Cuban capital of Havana. In Venezuela, where some 80 per cent of the population is living on 10 per cent of the national territory, the great regions of the *llanos* that were once so rich in cattle and grains now lie sere and barren. Meanwhile, Venezuela spends many millions of dollars annually to import food products—including, of all things, storage eggs—while its own vast acreage lies idle and nearly 20 per cent of its metropolitan population remains unemployed.

How is Africa to avoid such inhumane, inefficient and eventually disruptive waste of its lands and peoples? There is no single prescription that cures development ailments in all times and climes. There is, however, a general perspective on societal growth that significantly increases the probability of working out a particular formula suitable for any specific time-clime situation. This perspective, as has been discussed above, perceives that the main motive force for social change in our times is the desire for economic development. It perceives, further, that economic development is a process whose principal components are approximately the same in all climes. It perceives, finally, that economic development requires integral planning and simultaneous growth in all the dimensions of individual and institutional behaviour that condition the life of a society. Where these three elements of perception are coherently integrated in a general perspective, there emerges a new capability for dealing with the means of social change empirically rather than ideologically, for rational rather than theological ends.

It is my impression, gained largely from close study of the essays by my colleagues in this volume, that much of Africa is well-positioned to derive maximum practical benefits from a theoretical perspective that links its own lot with that of other regions in more advanced stages of the development process. One fundamental advantage is that Africa is the least developed continent in the world today. The paradox here is more apparent than real. That Africa can survey a variety of modernising efforts in different times and climes, and can evaluate them with reference to its own conditions of life, is an important resource no longer so readily usable in areas where the main lines of development have already been laid down in ways that engage the thinking and behaviour of transitional persons. The essential corollary is that, in much of Africa, the conceptual and behavioural lines of modernisation have not yet been activated by the indigenous elites. Accordingly, traditional patterns of behaviour persist—notably with respect to the factor of urbanisation that is central to the concerns of this volume. This gives African elites a degree of freedom, in their rational planning based on empirical observation, that has been severely compromised by the facts of social change in other regions—including Africa north of the Sahara. This is a considerable advantage. A third related advantage that belongs in the projection of African development is the growth-favourable conjuncture of physical and human resources. I have already referred to the favourable man: land ratio, an important resource for the rational expansion of agricultural life. Associated with this, as has been indicated, is the favourably low rate of urbanisation, an important resource for the rational expansion of industrial life.

These 'advantages' are negative rather than positive. They assert that Africa suffers from fewer disadvantages than most countries that initiated development planning twenty, or even ten, years ago. The absence of disadvantages can be as positive a factor for rational planning of development as the presence of advantages. Much depends on the particular case, at least in the short run. What happens in the long run must ultimately depend on the wisdom of the governing Africans who take charge of developmental policy, and on their skill in mobilising the governed Africans to behave in ways that promote the most development at the lowest cost.

To close with an instance of negative advantage that can be turned to very positive purposes, consider the state of the world environment. Most of the 'emerging nations' have emerged during the past twenty years. These years since 1945 have witnessed three major processes: (i) the weakening of Europe; (ii) the decolonisation of European empires in Africa and elsewhere; (iii) the bipolarisation of world politics between the United States and the Soviet Union.

Most of the political energy of new nations that have emerged since 1945 has been expended on decolonisation. It was the organisation of political resistance that counted so heavily in the personality-budgets of Chinese, Indians, Burmese, Indonesians, Malaysians, Syrians, Egyptians, Algerians and others. As a result of these colonial efforts, coupled with the imperial crise de conscience of postwar years, virtually all the European empires were liquidated—British, French, Dutch, Belgian, and even part of the Portuguese. There emerged during the crucial years 1944–54 (from Yalta to the defeat of the European Defence Community) a bipolarisation of world politics. Europe itself was the first region to be bipolarised—the Eastern part going to the Soviet bloc, the Western part to the American bloc. This way of structuring world politics virtually imposed upon the newly-emerging nations of the first postwar decade a politics of blackmail-and-bribery. The rule was: If we can't get what we want from the United States, on our terms, we'll get it from the Soviet Union. This phase, during which all of the Middle East and most of Asia gained their independence, produced certain boomerang effects. What was gained by blackmail-and-bribery techniques turned out not to be worth the candle. The certification of this historic fact occurred in 1956, when the United States failed to go beyond radio reassurance at Budapest and when the Soviet Union failed to go beyond nuclear bluffing at Suez. Clearly, the bipolar superpowers had put themselves outside the blackmail-and-bribery game for the years ahead.

Once this was clear, there developed opportunities for 'splitting' interests within each of the bipolar camps. The bipolar structure of the world had been undermined by previous events—the passage of Japan from East to West, the passage of China from West to East. The East-West division of world power, based mainly on the bipolar division of Europe, could no longer function effectively. Under these circumstances, each of the bipolar camps underwent a major splitting operation—China split from the Soviet bloc and France split from the American bloc. These splits provided the novelties of the second postwar decade. The bipolar world became, at least in appearance, pluripolar. The effects of this change were especially strong in Africa. Because of France's strong bargaining position in Europe, much of Central Africa sought association with the European Common Market—a phenomenon that is likely to be extended by current attempts to 'associate' ex-British territories across the African continent, from Nigeria to Kenya. The second postwar decade enabled France to use its partial strategic independence from the 'American guarantee' (vis-à-vis Russia) and its partial economic surplus (granted by the European Common Market) to make heavy inroads on the future design of African modernisation. Much of Middle Africa has delivered itself to short-term political control by de Gaulle in the hope that this will eventually produce long-term economic freedom via the European Common Market. Areas of peripheral Africa, such as Zanzibar, have permitted themselves the short-term luxury of a 'political revolution' under Chinese auspices. But neither of these pluripolar essays of the second postwar decade, as contrasted with the bipolar constraints of the first postwar decade, is likely to produce a durable model of African development.

The hope is that, in the third postwar decade, the enriched sense of alternatives derived from more developed foreign countries will help Africans to select and refine a more workable image of their own development. This was the key idea that Karl Marx tried to express when he wrote in his preface to *Capital*: 'The more developed society presents to the less developed society a picture of its own future.' What Africa has gained, by being the last of the world's continents to undertake its own development, is a greater variety of 'pictures' presented by developed societies elsewhere. Africa moves into the process of modernisation in a decade when 'pictures' coming from America and Russia, from China and France, from Japan and India are equally available for inspection, adaptation and transformation. It would be a pity if Africa neglected this most important of all capabilities bestowed by the modern system of international and intercontinental communication in order to seek short-term gains by the blackmail-or-bribery routine. The important thing for Africa is that it is not obliged to emulate the societies-in-a-hurry that undertook development planning in the first two postwar decades. Africa, in this third phase, can afford to wait and see, to plan and ponder, to try and test. In this perspective, which enables it to minimise the costs and maximise the benefits of all the trials that have gone before, Africa is today the most favoured development area in the world.

Notes and References

1 A portion of this paper was presented both to the Conference on the Methods and Objectives of Urban Research in Africa, upon which this volume is based, and to the Conference on Comparative Social Science Research, sponsored in April 1965 by the International Social Science Council and the Social Science Research Council.

2 United Nations, *Science and Technology for Development*, 1963, Vol. 6, p. 1.

3 Gabriel Almond and James Coleman, eds., *The Politics of Developing Areas*, Princeton, NJ, 1960.

3

Motives and Methods: Reflections on a Study in Lagos

PETER MARRIS

WHY DO WE CHOOSE to study urban African society? Heterogeneous, unstable, undocumented, it presents much greater difficulties—especially to an outsider—than more familiar fields of enquiry. We cannot, I think, answer only by appeal to the intriguing variety of human experience, to the value of comparative studies, or simply to the accidents of personal history which led us to an interest in Africa. We could surely have found topics nearer home with as sound an intellectual and moral justification. There is another, and I believe more general motive. The evolution of modern African civilisation dramatises our own ideological dilemmas.

I begin with this question of motive, because motive must determine the intellectual preoccupations which frame the enquiry. We can only start from questions which we already recognise to be important to us. At the same time, if the preoccupations we bring to the study of Africa derive from our own society, we may impose concepts which are not relevant in their new context. The development of urban African studies depends, I think, on whether we can discover a more relevant frame of reference without losing the thread of interest. There is the risk, on the one hand, of impertinent moralising; and, on the other, of elaborating a new terminology which we use to say nothing important. In this essay,

NOTE: *The notes and references for Chapter 3 will be found on page 54.*

I shall try to show how this translation of our interests into more African terms may come about. And, by way of illustration, I shall discuss a study I made in Lagos, in 1958 and 1959, of a slum clearance scheme.[1] It was not a very sophisticated study but, since it is the only one where I have intimate knowledge of the investigator's motives, I have no choice but to use it.

The Lagos study was conceived in an intellectual context that derived partly from housing policy in Britain, and partly from sociological theory. The theory argues that industrialisation has fragmented the cohesion of community life. The individual is no longer absorbed, as an integrated personality, into a group, but forms discrete relationships in each of which he fulfils a different role. His behaviour as worker or voter is regulated independently of his behaviour as husband and father. From this derives the economic potential of industrial society—the mobility of labour, the specialisation of skills, the ruthless isolation of market relationships from humane sympathies—and also the loneliness, the anomie of modern man. The studies in which I have been involved, in London, set out to question this theory.[2] Especially, they showed that the fragmentation of kinship relationships in a working class borough had been exaggerated. After one hundred and fifty years of an industrial economy, the people of Bethnal Green still seemed, characteristically, to belong to widespread, cohesive kin groups, and this seemingly amorphous district of monotonous row housing had a strong sense of community. The findings of these studies have been sporadically confirmed in other working-class districts of England and here and there in America. They suggest that an industrial economy does not, after all, impose so extreme a disruption of community life, at least for the majority who subordinate vocational ambition to their group loyalties. Within their family circle and the intimacy of the few streets where they are known and accepted for themselves, people find their greatest satisfaction. They also enjoy the mutual exchange of gifts and services which has protected them in a harsh world.

Here the argument became involved in questions of policy. The London County Council was committed, by its leftwing ideals, to a vigorous programme of slum clearance. This meant building to a much lower density in central London. Many of the people of Bethnal Green were, therefore, to be moved to the suburbs, where housing of a much higher standard could be built for them. From the standpoint of the studies I have described, the policy was questionable. It forced people to choose between a new home and their kin group, whose cohesiveness and pattern of mutual services could not survive this geographical dispersion. We argued instead for much denser building in the centre, with less regard for arbitrary standards of open space; rehabilitation rather than clearance; and, generally, for a more sensitive appreciation of the quality of life rather than of buildings. The argument was, of course, conservative, though its spokesmen saw themselves as radical reformers. At bottom, it questioned the conventional assumptions about the social concomitants of industrial growth. It questioned, too, whether the values which that growth encouraged —individualism, over-riding ambition for a higher standard of living, adaptability—were shared by most people in an industrial society. If not, such growth might be compatible with much more varied and even incompatible systems of values.

Given what we had learned from the Bethnal Green study, it seemed to me that an African city would provide an especially relevant setting in which to explore the argument further. Here was a society only just emerging from the paradigm of cohesive communal life where—as I assumed—the individual merged his identity with his kin group, and kin, polity and economy fused in a single system. At the same time, the society was under great pressure to modernise, and looked towards the industrial nations for a lead. It so happened, as I was exploring several African cities to choose one for the study, that I learned of the Lagos slum clearance scheme. Everything about the scheme suggested that both its conception and its execution followed British housing policy. The squalor of the slum area was condemned without regard to the quality of its community life, and the new housing estate assumed that husband, wife and children constituted the proper pattern of a household. Shops replaced markets and the new residential area was segregated from industry. Here, then, was an example of how a questionable theory of social change was promoting a policy I believed, from the London studies, to be misconceived. It seemed obvious to me that the policy would cause much hardship, and, in fact, I was told it had already done so. You can see that I went out to Lagos with strong preconceptions, although I knew scarcely anything about the city or its people. I would still defend this brashness. It provided a frame of reference about which to organise the enquiry. And my expectations were so specific that, if they were wrong, I could hardly ignore it. Whatever the outcome, the study would surely be relevant to one aspect of social change at least—the consequences of a housing policy.

I was able, then, to draw out a plan of investigation without delay. To see how transfer to the new housing estate had influenced peoples' lives, I needed a sample from the rehousing estate and from the clearance area. Since the rehousing estate was planned so much on European lines, with neat rows of bungalows each designed for a single household, a sample of households was easily drawn from the housing authority's record of its tenants. But, in central Lagos, the streets sprawled and wound through densely-built blocks of ramshackle dwellings, which might house a dozen or more households. I did draw a sample from the housing authority's census of the area, which supposedly listed, by household, every person entitled to rehousing. But the list was very inaccurate, and the team of interviewers I recruited were too inexperienced—and sometimes too casual—to produce findings of much reliability. I therefore concentrated on a block of houses which seemed typical and interviewed each household. The block was due to be cleared very shortly, and I hoped to follow up the families afterwards and see how they had got on. Thus the enquiry was designed to allow four comparisons:

1. Between the life of those interviewed in the central area before they were moved, and after.
2. Between the life of those interviewed on the rehousing estate, and what they told me of their life before they moved there.
3. Between these two samples.
4. Between this study, and our findings in London.

Actually, I was not able to make the first comparison, as the area was not pulled down on schedule. Most of it was still standing two years later. This weakened the reliability of my conclusions, since there is no certainty that those I interviewed on the rehousing estate and in central Lagos were comparable groups. I knew, in fact, that some of the people from the centre had refused to go to the rehousing estate in the first place.

I guess that most enquiries will run into snags of this kind. Records prove inadequate, government plans change, the administrative regulations which define a sample are not scrupulously observed. The more the enquiry depends only on statistical data, the more tiresome these lapses from logical rigour are likely to prove. A research report in which the sample adds to a different total in every table, and in which the tables themselves are studded with qualifying footnotes, is intellectually unsatisfying. And it may be hard to determine what influence the unobtained or unusable figures might have had on the results. An enquiry which depends more on the interpretation of the quality of life is less vulnerable. Though the interpretation may be questionable and its wider relevance speculative, an intimate description of the lives of even a few African city dwellers tells us much that we did not know before. The qualitative analysis enables us to guess, at least, at the way the statistical findings may have been influenced by weaknesses in the sample. Pragmatically, if we are willing to go beyond the strict logic of our method, a combination of sampling techniques and descriptive analysis will reinforce each other.

I do not want to claim too much for the Lagos enquiry. Some of its inferences were certainly questionable. But it showed conclusively enough, I think, that slum clearance brought more hardships than benefits to most of its victims. The Housing Authority itself—though it rejected my recommendations to stop the scheme —was bound to admit as much. More recently, a United Nations planning team came to similar conclusions, and I believe that the scheme, if it has not been abandoned altogether, is now in abeyance.

Though my expectations were confirmed, this did not in itself add very much to the understanding of urban African society.

Anyone who had studied, for instance, the social consequences of urban renewal in the United States could have predicted the outcome in Lagos. The findings repeated the obvious, if neglected, truth that any reconstruction of living space must take account of the social and economic factors which shaped the original structure. It was, I hope, useful to demonstrate this in an African setting. But the study also raised in my mind ideas which I had not foreseen. And these ideas, which were derived from African society rather than imposed upon it by my preconceptions, may be more relevant to African research.

Firstly, a minority of those transferred to the rehousing estate welcomed the disruption of their family ties. They were only too pleased to put a distance between themselves and the rapacity of aunts and cousins, whose demands for help ate into their salaries. They were characteristically young, salaried employees, Christian rather than Muslim, and Ibo rather than Yoruba (who predominated in central Lagos). I think, most probably, their occupation chiefly influenced their repudiation of traditional kinship obligations. A man with a secure, pensionable post in, say, government service, is less dependent on his kin to support him in old age, and less vulnerable to the hardships of sickness and unemployment. And, as he looks to his children's future, he will see that education rather than the support of their loyal kinsfolk is the most rewarding asset. Since education is expensive, he is led to concentrate his resources on his own children rather than distribute them amongst his kin, and he finds moral support for his individualism in the bourgeois English conception of marriage encouraged by Christian churches. He may, too, find it easier to take this stand if he belongs to a minority tribe in the town where he lives, already somewhat apart from the dominant social pressures.

However, this style of life is open only to the fortunate. For the rest, faced with the insecurity of urban life, traditional loyalties become more than ever important. Here there seems to be an important qualification. Young women are attracted by the emancipation and sophistication of urban life; through prostitution, casual liaisons and trade, they find they can earn an independent livelihood. In many African societies, it is still, I think, only by repudiating the ties of marriage altogether that a woman can assert her equality with men. So, besides the bourgeois and more or less traditional conceptions of life, there emerges an emancipated household of mother and children, in which the children's fathers play a casual and intermittent role. Such a household may be supported by the woman's own blood relations, especially her own mother, who may have herself adopted the same way of life. This kind of household does not seem to face serious social disapproval in Lagos.

Altogether, I was impressed with the way in which economic factors seemed to influence the evolution of family life. The pressures of urban society reinforced some kinship ties, weakened others, and people reacted differently according to their circumstances. But the trend was always consistent with the search for economic security. If their occupation seemed to protect them against hardship more surely than their marriage, women would give it precedence. If the reciprocal obligations of kinship no longer balanced, the prosperous would try to limit their involvement. But if the family association could be formalised as a resource for recruiting capital, exploiting family property or rationalising the distribution of welfare and educational support, the wealthier and more sophisticated members of the family might be active in its promotion. If fathers lost their influence when the family farm was no longer the economic basis of life, mothers might become powerful matriarchs, acquiring wealth and property in their own right from business enterprise. The vesting of property in individual titles rather than in families, which is characteristic of an urban economy where land must be freely marketable, redistributes control of resources, in Africa as in America, to the advantage of the elderly widow.

I doubt if this appraisal of kinship in economic terms is new or peculiarly urban. In everyday speech, the people of Lagos justified their family loyalties by mutual advantage. I remember the heart-rent letter a son wrote to his mother, to commiserate on the death of an only daughter. He had burst into tears, he said, when he learned the news, and he went on: 'I know how hard it must be for you, after the sacrifice of bringing Victoria up, to lose her just when she was old enough to help and support you.' The words jar a little, but in Lagos they seemed to be a natural and accepted way of expressing the meaning of kinship. I do not mean to suggest that affection there is less deeply felt, but rather that, where we often express affection, meaning advantage, the people of Lagos mention the advantage and take the affection for granted. Where we explore the emotional psychology of relationships, they explore the economics.

I suggest, then, that in predicting the evolution of family relationships in urban Africa, we should explore the influence of occupation, property holding, education as an economic investment and the institutions of social insurance—loan clubs, pension funds, funeral societies and more or less informal family associations. Conversely, the kinship structure itself will influence the expression of economic relationships. As the Lagos study progressed, the economic importance of a reliable system of mutual expectations became more and more apparent.

At the outset, I was preoccupied with the disruption of family ties by slum clearance: in London, this had been the main argument against the policy. But in Lagos the economic disruption turned out to be an even stronger objection. Craftsmen and traders who worked for themselves lost their contacts when they moved to the rehousing estate, and they seemed unable to establish new ones. A delicate informal network of personal relationships was pulled apart. In part, they lost their livelihood because they could not afford to commute between the suburbs and the centre, and their old customers could not afford the time or trouble to trace them to their new homes. But their misfortune also raises more fundamental questions about the demands of a system of exchange.

In Lagos, most customers expect credit. Few people hold reserves of capital; their retailer buys and sells on credit, recovering his money at the end of the month when salaries are paid, and then paying his own debts. The system depends on trust. This is true of economic relationships elsewhere in the world, but the means by which confidence is established differ. The bank manager looks you up and down, he takes hints from your clothes and your accent, he appraises your salary and your commitments and reflects on the prospects of your profession. He may demand securities whose value he can assess. The employer, hiring staff, believes he can judge reliability and performance from diplomas, testimonials and—as much—from the candidate's bearing. A conventional wisdom informs these estimates, which are backed by an elaborate, impersonal system of checks—credit ratings, black lists, formal qualifications, references. Most economic relationships in Africa lack these assurances. Even a man's name and address—as research interviewers discover to their frustration—identify him very uncertainly. Trust depends much more on face to face relationships and is confirmed by habit. Hence any disruption of established patterns of exchange is likely to damage a business severely, even when the disruption is apparently irrelevant to economic viability. In the circumstances, ties of kinship may produce a unique source of knowledge about people and of sanctions to enforce economic contracts. The family may be your only source of credit for a business venture, for they alone know what you are worth and how to bring pressure to bear if you fail to meet your obligations. You may choose to employ relatives for the same reasons, irrespective of the claims of kinship.

Membership of a family—and of a village or a tribe—does not in itself frustrate the growth of relationships appropriate to city life. On the contrary, it may provide the only point of departure from which to take your bearings in an unfamiliar and uncertain world. From it, the newcomer draws the confidence in conventional expectations which enables him to make his way. As he establishes himself in the city, he begins to discard the obligations of membership which no longer suit his economic needs and to adapt and reinforce others. I do not mean to suggest that kinship ties and economic advantage never conflict. But the conflict is between the conceptions of kinship which suit the advantage of different members of the family, not between kinship and profit in themselves. Nor of course do economic needs alone determine the evolution of family relationships; love rivals money as a source of security, and mingles with it. But however people are driven by the need to belong, to be approved and loved, they try hard to satisfy it without jeopardising their economic interests, as they see them.

If these inferences from Lagos society are valid, urban Africa is under pressure to evolve diverging patterns of life and, at the same time, to hold this divergence from destroying the foundation of meaningful interaction. Different occupations and levels of income will promote different conceptions of kinship, justified by different systems of values. But the confusing variety of expectations will create a pervasive anxiety. There will be, too, a countervailing pressure to sustain tribal, village and kinship loyalties in the city, so long as they remain the best understood and most widely accepted conventions of mutual exchange. The issue may be resolved by the hardening of these differences into exclusive social groups. The obligations of kinship would then extend only to those who saw them in the same light and shared similar economic interests. This would lead—since the disparities of income are so great, and the gap between bourgeois European and traditional African values so wide—to class divisions more obtrusive than in our own society. Alternatively, class solidarity may seem too unfamiliar a source of security, and the people of the city may evolve a conception of kinship loose enough to accommodate their different economic needs yet still universally reliable.

The alternative seems to promise a more egalitarian society, but it may discourage the growth of political democracy. If, as political scientists have suggested, democracy depends upon the institutionalisation of class interests in opposing parties, the survival of kinship ties, and therefore of ethnic loyalties, will militate against it. The evolution of political, economic and family relationships react upon each other. Hence to recommend policy from the examination of only one of these must, I think, be abortive.

I began by discussing the intellectual preoccupations which I brought to the Lagos study. Re-examined in the light of these reflections on Lagos society, they no longer seem adequate. Our view of working class London was, perhaps, a little sentimental. We noticed the warmth, the disparagement of individualistic self-seeking, the emotional ease, rather than the economic determinants which had matured their way of life. And the society was in many respects very unlike Lagos—homogeneous, stable and class bound.

I had thought of family relationships as the fulfilment of emotional needs, which conflicted with, and might for many people supersede, economic pressures. The Lagos study suggested, rather, that the two are inseparable. I wonder even whether the traditional pattern of African family relationships was especially emotionally satisfying or free of conflict. It may well have generated as much anxiety as our own self-pitying culture. Its strength lay more in the security of a reliable convention of behaviour, on which all manner of relationships could be based.

This line of thought leads towards a universal problem. Our actions assume a predictable response. We know how to behave towards others only in so far as we know how they will react. Our conception of ourselves depends on the response we evoke; we are defined by the love, hate, admiration, hostility, acceptance or rejection others bear towards us. Bereft of this knowledge, we are at first anxious, then paralysed and finally driven into fantasy. This we call the disintegration of personality, though it may be a more consistent performance to the inward eye than outreaching manipulation of the common world of experience. In search of sanity and reassurance, we cling to the familiar patterns of relationship. But in any radically changing environment, these patterns no longer hold. The characteristic cry of distress in an African city is 'I was deceived'. My girl deceived me; my business partners cheated me; my husband betrayed me; my enemies are plotting against me. The anxiety shows in a pervasive paranoia that mistrusts every relationship. How, then, is the predictability of human relationships to be maintained when they also need to be continually revised?

The dilemma arises alike in political, economic and family life, and bedevils every attempt at reform. It is illustrated by the uneasy courtship of an African city couple, by the frustrations of experimental community action in American cities, by the struggle of the British Labour government to introduce new financial strategies in the face of the conventional expectations of international bankers. The boldest reformer seeks to establish an entirely new convention of behaviour; the revolution extends, as it must, to every aspect of life. Communism, for instance, prescribes a code for marriage as much as for agriculture, industry, government, art and science. In frustration and anxiety, the solution is attractive. But the revolution cannot hold to its own creed: the new order is continually revised to meet the problems of the day, and the anxieties of uncertainty return. The alternative is a more gradual evolution, in which the familiar is exploited rather than rejected and the anxiety of innovation is held within tolerable limits. I do not know how this can be achieved, nor whether it is possible in every circumstance. Perhaps change is impossible without the ruthless destruction of some who defend themselves against its intolerable strain. But the dilemma seems to me especially relevant to urban Africa and to touch, at the same time, upon fundamental problems of our own societies. It concerns, ultimately, the nature of a social being and its survival in a world that continually threatens its integrity.

I have brought the argument back to its starting point in the motives which underlie the study of societies. I have tried to describe how the experience of a study can react upon the preconceptions of an investigator, to make his thinking more relevant to Africa without its being any less relevant to these underlying motives. Urban African studies must, I think, develop from this co-ordination of concepts derived from the analysis of what is happening with those derived from the definition of ultimate purpose.

The essays presented in this book converge from both starting points. Social anthropologists tend to take their departure from the impartial exploration of relationships. Wary of the prejudices of missionaries and colonial administrators, they have traditionally held aloof from questions of policy. Sensitive to the ethnocentric bias of their own social preoccupations, they have tried to interpret the rationality of other peoples' modes of living in *their* terms. In the confused society of an African town, this moral humility encourages the investigator to ask not whether behaviour is appropriate to need but why. He is led to accept whatever definition of their situation is acknowledged by those he studies. But while he challenges the preconceptions of alien reformers, he also runs the risk of repudiating altogether the relevance of other societies' experience. If this approach is to inform policy and clarify purpose, it has to work out the correspondences between one society and another, identifying the processes of adaptation which they share.

At the other extreme, we can begin, as Daniel Lerner does in this volume, by defining a universal motive: '. . . there is a single process of modernisation which operates in all developing societies, regardless of their colour, creed or climate and regardless of their history, geography or culture. This is the process of economic development. . . .'[3] This point of departure stresses the aims which are universally desired; the power of films, radio and television to stamp the aspirations of all mankind with the same symbols of achievement; and the relentless logic of the means to these ends. This view leads towards a conception of societies as more or less developing along a single line, and looks for the correlates which will indicate their progress most concisely. So long as we assume that self-sustaining economic growth is the over-riding aim, and that there is essentially only one way to it, this approach offers an immediate framework of comparison. However convincing these assumptions seem, only experience can test them. Nations sacrifice their economic interest to pride of independence, as their citizens weigh economic opportunity against other means to dignity and status. The strains of innovation provoke a reaction in favour of the security of custom. The gains of economic growth may be spent on the restoration of a disrupted tradition rather than the goods of modern manufacture. In Southern Africa, forced to choose between growth and a racial ideology, it seems that the white minority will forgo the economic advantage. As economic means conflict with other purposes, men and their governments continually reinterpret their aims. Unless research revises its concepts accordingly, it will be left with the prescriptive analysis of a process which, in practice, urban African societies neither desire nor pursue.

I believe, then, that the description of a particular society in its own terms remains intellectually barren, unless its social processes can be related to a more general discussion of means and ends. Equally, the definition of means and ends in abstraction drifts towards irrelevant moralising, unless it recognises the subtle inter-play of large ideals and pragmatic adjustment. Research in African cities will be most pointed when it is most concerned with the processes by which this interaction between general purposes and particular circumstances works itself out. The forms of social organisation which mediate between tradition and modernity seem to me especially pertinent—the Yoruba cultural societies, indigenous churches, loan clubs, the ambiguous neighbourhoods of Kampala which straddle the boundaries of a segregated pattern of settlement, the ethnic loyalties which sustain locally the structure of modern party politics, the family associations, the unions of villagers who migrate to the cities. We know very little about the social or psychological genesis of these attempts at synthesis. How do these adaptations arise, and at what stage? What happens when they outlive their use? Who creates and exploits them? Does a man whose own position in society is ambiguous—being of an ethnic or religious minority—come into his own when society at large becomes disorientated? And is ambiguity, itself the simultaneous assertion of incompatible values, an enabling characteristic of these mediating structures?

This line of enquiry starts from the analysis of what is happening, without prejudging the nature of the process, and leads towards an interpretation of its relevance as an expression of universal aspirations. Starting instead from these aspirations may be government policy. They are the most accessible point of departure, especially for a European or American sociologist in Africa; they bridge the familiar and the unknown. The policies of African governments derive largely from their European and American advisers or from the example of industrial nations; the political leaders have themselves been mostly trained in these countries. Thus, the thinking behind these policies is already familiar to us. We know something about their social and economic implications, their historical origins, their political and ideological connotations. We have some empirical evidence of their consequences in other countries. Whether we are concerned with government action or with the society to be manipulated, policy provides a framework by which to take our bearings. And since government action is an important influence on the societies we wish to study, it tends to react upon other pressures to realise latent change. It is a catalyst, crystallising the elements from which change is compounded, even where its own influence is secondary.

But if the enquiry is not to be imprisoned in the preconceptions of policy, it must also be designed to assimilate new ideas and redirect its search in the light of them. It needs to observe directly how people behave, how they interpret their actions, thoughts and feelings. Above all, I believe that the intensive study of the quality of life will lead most quickly to the heart of the matter. If, in an unstable environment, the search for a pattern of relationships at once predictable and economically viable is a crucial dilemma, research must be sensitive and detailed enough to catch the subtleties of the conflict. The economic, psychological and political inferences will be as speculative as the evidence is limited, but, at the outset, it seems more important to develop these inferences and to explore new concepts than to test the generality of findings. The snatches of conversation, for instance, recorded by Aidan Southall and Peter Gutkind's investigators in a Kampala bar; the organisation of life about illegal beer brewing, described in Ellen Hellman's study of a Johannesburg slum yard; the 'Red' and 'School' Xhosa values of East London (South Africa) and the conflict of generations analysed by Philip Mayer; Clyde Mitchell's interpretation of tribal identity from the symbolism of the Kalela dance; M. J. Field's speculative psychology of prophecy in Ghana —these insights,[4] like Oscar Lewis's guided autobiographies, seem to reveal something essential and new about the quality of relationships.

I do not mean to discount other approaches to research, to which I may have done less than justice. But no comparisons are meaningful unless we have the same questions to ask of the societies we compare. Whatever the method, we need to identify in the interplay of experience and ideals the processes by which a way of life takes shape and purpose. From this, the study of urban Africa will lead, not so much to concepts appropriate to the analysis of African societies in itself, as to concepts of more universal relevance which illuminate African, European and American society alike.

Notes and References

1 Peter Marris, *Family and Social Change in an African City*, London 1961.

2 See especially Michael Young and Peter Willmott, *Family and Kinship in East London*, London 1957, and Peter Townsend, *The Family Life of Old People*, London 1957.

3 See page 22.

4 Aidan Southall and Peter Gutkind, *Townsmen in the Making*, Kampala 1957; Ellen Hellman, *Rooiyard: A Sociological Study of an Urban Native Slum Yard*, Cape Town 1948; Philip Mayer, *Townsmen or Tribesmen*, Cape Town 1961; J. Clyde Mitchell, *The Kalela Dance*, The Rhodes-Livingstone Papers, No. 27, 1957; M. J. Field, *Search for Security*, London 1960

4

Africa and the Theory of Optimum City Size

JOSEPH J. SPENGLER

Not only can choice mimic chance, but chance can mimic choice.

M. G. Kendall[1]

If an economy is stable at all, the reason is that it is in motion. . . . Such evidence as exists . . . is not overwhelmingly in favour of the stability of the system under which we now live. . . . Our ideas about wants and utilities and the whole theory of acts of choice in an aggregate may have to be reshaped.

M. G. Kendall[1]

Through the discovery of inherent regularities . . . we may hope to bind Leviathan.

F. C. Mills[2]

THE IMMEDIATE concern of the following discussion is the applicability of optimum-size theory to the formation and distribution of cities in Africa, and mainly in Africa south of the Sahara. The ultimate concern, however, is the relation between the well-being of man and the distribution of population in space. The presentation is divided into four parts: Optimum City Size and Inter-City Population Distribution; The Relative Non-Urbanness

NOTE: *The notes and references for Chapter 4 will be found on page 78.*

of Africa and the Range of Choice Respecting Urban Patterns; Economic, Cultural and Political Advantages Varying with City Size; The Role of Deliberate Policy.

I. Optimum City Size and Inter-City Population Distribution

The subject of this section is but a component of a more inclusive subject—the optimum distribution of population in social and geographical space, which roughly encompasses two types of population distribution: that of the whole population between the urban sector and the non-urban sector, and that of the urban population among towns and cities of varying sizes. It is this urban distribution that is of main concern here, though the relative size of a given country's urban sector is conditioned mainly by how small a fraction of its total population is needed to supply its agricultural requirements. By focusing upon inter-city distribution, account may be taken of the fact that there is not *an* optimum city size, but a *set* of optimum sizes. Furthermore, although the distribution pattern of a country's cities may in the end assume a lognormal form, it will be argued later that this may not be a necessary outcome of what appears to be a stochastic process.[3]

Cities, though dominated by one or several sets of functions,[4] may be looked upon as collections of activities, some economic and some non-economic in nature; all of these activities in turn draw upon and absorb inputs of physical resources, space and time which, even when free (i.e., economically non-scarce) or non-committed (e.g., discretionary time), have alternative uses.[5] No such collection, not even one constituting a city of optimum size, can be self-sufficient; a portion of these activities will be used to satisfy domestic needs and the balance will be employed in providing what can be sold to visitors or 'abroad' in exchange for purchasing power wherewith to finance 'imports'. Furthermore, if it be granted that there are cities of optimum size, it must then also be granted that there is more than one such size. In each specific instance, size depends largely upon the kinds of activities in which a city specialises and upon what constitutes minimum-unit-cost size for the plant or producing unit in each of the various activities pursued. Accordingly, whatever tends to reduce optimum plant size tends to reduce optimum city size; this is true not only of manufacturing plants but also of such institutions as hospitals which, even though relatively small, can now communicate effectively with large medical centres and, when necessary, transfer difficult cases there.

Application of a variety of criteria suggests that, for most purposes, cities of 50,000 to 300,000 inhabitants suffice. The amount of time consumed per worker travelling to and from work tends to be at a minimum in relatively small cities, with the result that the worker's discretionary time is at a maximum. Space per inhabitant within cities, as well as access to space outside city perimeters, is greater within smaller cities, since population density rises with city size and access to parks tends to be greater in smaller cities.[6] While, in the past, health facilities have been better in larger than in smaller cities, the inferiority of the latter is diminishing with improvement in means of communication. Very large cities are inferior to, or at least not superior to, small cities in respect to public safety, exposure to atomic warheads, municipal efficiency and avoidance of traffic congestion, and they tend to be inferior in respect to some aspects of education and public recreation.[7] Colin Clark, postulating a 'desirable' population density of about fifteen persons per acre, concluded that, for Australia, 'the best pattern of population location . . . appears to consist of regions with some 250,000 population, comprising up to thirty or forty rural, and sixty or seventy urban neighbourhoods of 2,500'.[8]

In an earlier study, Clark reached the following conclusions:

1. That the principal function of the city is now the provision of service industries rather than manufactures and will be so to an increasing degree.
2. That a region can give its inhabitants an adequate range of commercial services when the population of its principal city is somewhere in the neighbourhood of 100,000 to 200,000.
3. That, in the case of the other service industries, a smaller population will generally suffice.

4. That manufactures tend to be concentrated in the older settled communities; in the more newly settled communities, where the manufacturing population is lower, a city somewhere between 200,000 and 500,000 population is necessary for full development of manufacture.

The range of size 100,000–200,000 also closely accords with the administrative optimum for municipal services as calculated from English experience by Mr K. S. Lomax. He showed, after making all qualifications, that the cost of such services per head rose when population rose above 150,000, and rose sharply when it exceeded 300,000. A size not greatly exceeding 200,000 also appears to be indicated from another aspect, namely, traffic and parking. On the assumption (as will be the case in many countries in the next generation, and as is already the case in the wealthier states of the USA) that nearly every family possesses a car and that a large proportion of the working population prefers to drive to work in its own car, it is hard to see how any larger city can prevent traffic congestion during the rush hours, or provide adequate parking space in the central business zone.

In future, with agriculture occupying only 10–15 per cent of the working population and the whole rural population (including rural traders, teachers, etc., and their families) therefore constituting at most 30 per cent of the whole, a city of 175,000–200,000 would correspond to a total regional population of 250,000. A population of this size is regarded by many writers as providing a satisfactory administrative unit for a number of public services including medical and hospital service and education. Such a population also might be expected to support a satisfactory University with 1,000–3,000 students.[9]

The argument underlying the notion of optimum size for cities is somewhat parallel to that underlying the notion of optimum size for industrial plants, though less so than at first appears.[10] However, a city is subject, in a measure that a firm is not, to economies and diseconomies associated with variation in size and agglomeration, many of which amount to externalities from the point of view of a plant or a firm. A city is also less exposed to the selective influence of the survivor principle which favours those firm and plant sizes that cope most profitably with the problems confronting entrepreneurs.[11] Indeed, whereas cities are fixed in space and not very prone to diminution in size, plants may be relocated and may shrink as well as increase in size as technological conditions and price structure change. It is much more difficult, furthermore, to assess the performance of cities than that of plants and firms. For example, a suitable indicator of the quality of performance of a plant or firm is much easier to contrive than is a corresponding indicator of the quality of a city's performance, subject as the latter index is to the difficulties that beset formulation of a community welfare function. Even so, we may conceive of increases in a city's size, under the equivalent of *ceteris paribus* conditions, as being accompanied by increases in the aggregate of private plus public costs and in the aggregate of private plus public returns or benefits. Then we may define the optimum size, under the existing activity-mix, as being that with which equivalance of marginal cost and marginal benefit is associated. The basic problem, of course, is that of identifying, measuring and appropriately aggregating all costs and all benefits and correlating changes therein with changes in city size, also appropriately defined. I shall not attempt this, though later I shall draw attention to some advantages and disadvantages associated with variation in city size. Relevant intra-urban conditions, of great concern to underdeveloped as well as developed countries, will also be touched upon inasmuch as they are functionally related to size of city.

II. The Relative Non-Urbanness of Africa and the Range of Choice Respecting Urban Patterns

Africa remains the least urban of continents, its degree of urbanisation resembling that of the world in 1900. In the mid-twentieth century, agriculture engaged a larger proportion of the population of Africa than of any other continent, though the population so occupied also performed for itself many non-agricultural services.[12] Little more than 7 per cent of the population of Tropical Africa lived in cities of 5,000 or more inhabitants, a fraction below the percentage found in North and Southern Africa and much below the 30 per cent reported for the world as a whole. Only about 5 per cent of Africa's population lived in cities of 100,000 plus, and only 9 per cent in cities of 20,000 plus. The corresponding percentages for Asia were 8 and 13; for Europe, 21 and 35; for Japan, 25·6 and 41·7; and for the United Kingdom, 38·2 and 66·8. In 1960, according to the Economic Commission for Africa, 'only some 6 per cent of the population of Africa south of the Sahara' and between 20 and 30 per cent of that of North Africa (excluding the Sudan) lived in cities of 20,000 or more inhabitants; the corresponding fraction for the world's population was about one-third.[13]

The uneven distribution of cities in Africa reflects its uneven past history, as does the fact that, in many African countries, most of the urban population is concentrated in one or two towns or cities. Lack of industrialisation in much of Africa is responsible for this relative absence of urban development, especially in Tropical Africa where the towns (outside West Africa) owe their origin mainly to non-African initiative and where the level of urbanisation is approximately what it was in the world as a whole about 1850. Though industrialisation is not the only source of cities, it does presuppose conditions which tend to produce agglomeration of population.[14] Smallness of many of the political units comprising Africa—only 8 out of 50 number over 10,000,000 inhabitants—together with the fact that few have adequate sea frontage, tends to prevent the growth of large urban centres, though less so now than in the past; a few decades ago Africa's economy resembled that of the world around 1700, when inland transport was quite inadequate and only the maritime fringe and large navigable river systems could accommodate heavy-duty transport.[15] The resulting uneven distribution of access to the sea contributed in an important way to the formation in Africa of what Hance calls an 'islandic pattern of economic activity', a collection 'of productive "islands" often set in vast seas of emptiness'.[16] It has also affected the pattern of city location in Africa; in 1950, only 32 of the world's 875 cities of 100,000 plus were situated there.[17] Close to one-third of Africa's cities of 30,000 and over are port cities, while many interior cities are inland ports or crossroad cities located at landroute nodes. Mining, climate and security requirements account for most of those not dominated by transport conditions.[18] In some African countries, as may happen when underdeveloped countries have been dependent upon foreign power, one particular city, often the capital, became primate and dominant over other towns and cities.[19] This tendency towards dominance by one or two cities (or urban hypertrophy) could, of course, be sustained in the future by excessive growth of capital and port cities, uncompensated by the adequate development of industrial cities; and it may be supported by the indisposition of most African states to enter a pan-African union within which population and mobile capital can freely circulate.

While the relative non-urbanness of Africa's population correctly implies that, in most African states, there exists a wide range of choice in respect to the distribution of population in geographical space, this range may yet prove quite narrow. Two forces may operate to restrict the number of options available: the anticipated high rate of population growth and the operation of what Kendall felicitously called 'a kind of the-higher-the-fewer rule'.[20]

It is expected that, over the next thirty-five years and probably for a longer period, Africa's population will be growing at a rate much above 2 per cent per year and perhaps around 3 per cent per year.[21] This rate is close to that (about 2·75 per cent) experienced in the United States during much of the nineteenth century, a century which saw the urban population of the country grow much faster than 3 per cent (about 4·75 per cent per year), even though America, unlike parts of Africa, was not yet overpopulated.[22] Whether, despite easing population pressure in rural areas, so high a rate of urban population growth is attainable in Africa is doubtful, for food to support this growing urban population, as well as capital to shelter and employ it, must become available in amounts not at present forthcoming. Though over 40 per cent of its income originates in agriculture, Africa has become a food-deficit area. Even with its population growing less than 1·5 per cent per year, it failed to keep its output of grain abreast of increasing demand originating in population growth and rising per capita income.[23] At the present time, productivity is certainly too low and improving too slowly to permit existing agricultural populations to feed the population in prospect. A portion of the annual increment of population will have to remain in agriculture and output per agriculturalist and per acre will have to be increased in a measure realisable only through the modernisation of African agriculture.[24] For example, suppose population grows 2·5 per cent per year, the aggregate demand for food increases 3 per cent per year, and output per agriculturalist rises 2 per cent per year. If, in 1965, 80 per cent of the population was rural and 20 per cent non-rural, by the year 2000 the total population will be 137 per cent greater than in 1965 and about 60 per cent of it will be rural and 40 per cent non-rural.[25] The non-rural population will have increased some 380 per cent, or about 4·5 per cent per year, and the rural some 76 per cent, or about $1\frac{3}{8}$ per cent per year. Given so high a rate of increase in the urban population, many would crowd into a few initially well-situated cities, unless the number of potential urban communities were increased. Excessive centralisation would result; the likelihood of eventually achieving an optimum distribution would be greatly diminished.

It has been observed that a country's cities sometimes tend to get distributed in an orderly manner among size categories.[26] Illustrative is the rank-size rule

$$r \cdot P^q = K$$

where q (which approximates unity) and K are constants for a given group of cities, r stands for the rank of a particular city in population, and P for its population.[27] According to this rule, which is, or at least can be made, comparable with a variety of explanatory hypotheses, the size of the nth city approximates one-nth of the size of the largest city. The distribution underlying this rule can be regarded as lognormal and obeying the law of proportionate effect; it also implies that 'cities of each order (but the lowest) have a fixed number of satellite cities of the next lower order' and this is compatible 'with ideas on hierarchies of market areas and their central cities'.[28] The rank-size and similar rules are outcomes of stochastic processes in that random mechanisms generate the end result and maintain it as a steady state condition.[29] Of especial concern for this discussion, if the rule were over-riding, the search for sets of cities of supposedly optimum size could prove a quest for a will-o'-the-wisp, at least in large countries where many factors operate.

It is possible, however, that the rule, though often useful as a summary descriptive formula,[30] does not necessarily operate so universally as to render unacceptable the usefulness of the concept of urban optima. For example, while Vining suggests that a 'chance process'—'a stochastic process possessing ergodic properties'—'determines the distribution of individuals over an area such as that of this nation' and finally gives it stable form, he points out that legislative policy can introduce constraints which modify the limiting form of the distribution.[31] Again, of 38 best-fitting city-size-distribution curves, only 13 fell into the rank-size lognormal category. The remaining 25 fell into one of three additional categories: 15, from both developed and underdeveloped countries, approximated primate distributions; 9 distributions fell in between the primate and the lognormal categories; one, that for England and Wales, consisted of primate cities grafted on a lognormal distribution. Since no type was especially associated with either relative economic development or degree of urbanisation of countries, Berry concluded that 'when a few strong forces obtain, primacy results; and when many forces act in many ways with none predominant, a lognormal city size distribution is found'.[32] His analysis does not offer much support for the ascendancy of a distribution resting upon cities of optimum size, at least in the absence of appropriate constraints. Yet these constraints must not be of the kind that are self-defeating, such as constraints which eliminate potential city sites and pull population and activities towards administrative centres.[33] For this danger exists, especially in small countries in which a rank-size distribution is less likely to emerge.

The relative non-urbanness of Africa's population not only permits the development of a relatively favourable inter-urban distribution of population, but it can also permit the achievement of a better intra-urban disposition of residential, manufacturing, commercial and servicing activities than has been attained in many

Western cities. For there, in the absence of careful planning or of considerable urban 'redevelopment', continual areal expansion occurs through the addition of zones (or sectors or nuclei) and a resulting periodic partial relocation of various activities. Urban form not yet having come markedly into being in Africa except in the large primate cities, it cannot yet limit growth as it eventually will when growth has generated relatively inflexible form.[34]

Disposition of men's activities can therefore still be made to reflect prospective traffic facilities and income levels, both of which have a bearing upon community structure and the distribution of population and activities therein. Let us, with Colin Clark, write:

$$y = Ae^{-bx}$$

Here A measures the peak level of density which citizens are 'prepared to tolerate at the centre of the city'; e is a constant; x is the distance in miles from the centre of the city; y is the density of the resident population in thousands per square mile; b measures the rate of decline in density, a high value signifying a compact city in which density falls off rapidly, and a low value indicating a spread-out city in which density declines gradually. Whatever increases the efficiency and speed of intra-urban transport, or the capacity of individuals to purchase such transport, tends to reduce the value of b, and conversely. Those who live near the centre exchange relative 'spaciousness' for time and money, while those who live out from the centre exchange time and money for relative 'spaciousness'; for the price of land and probably the associated price for a given amount of housing diminishes as one moves outward, with the result that the ratio of land inputs to other inputs rises as one proceeds from the centre. In Western countries, the values of b have diminished over time as transport has been improved and cheapened relative to incomes, whereas in non-Western countries these values have remained constant. In recent decades the values of A have also fallen in Western countries (after having risen), though they have increased in some non-Western countries, where compactness is much more common and where (unlike in the West) the least mobile groups occupy the periphery.[35]

There is a limit, of course, to what improvements in transport can do to diminish the time and other costs of access to 'spaciousness' and to reduce the overall density of intra-urban population. It is mainly through locating in relatively small cities that one can combine nearness to work with 'spaciousness' and life in a relatively uncongested community and with relatively easy access to less crowded space.[36]

The discussion in the preceding paragraph does not allow explicitly for other demands on urban space than that flowing from residential demands. These are not important, however, until one has moved out from the centre where non-residential demands predominate in far greater measure than in other parts of a city. In general, while activities entailing a high man-land ratio are of overwhelming significance near the centre, this ratio diminishes as one moves outwards.[37] The great post-1900 redistribution of economic activities within urban areas could get under way effectively, however, only with the development of rapid transit, trucking, etc. Changes in the character of industry also played a part, as did a decline in the extent to which industrialisation and urbanisation were correlated.[38]

III. Economic, Cultural and Political Advantages Varying with City Size

Within a city are situated sets of physical and organisational facilities that administer to the wants of the population. These may be divided into those serving economic, political or cultural needs. The units within each of these sets vary in degree of divisibility and hence are subject to variation in economies of scale or in capacity to perform allotted functions. Let us examine these under the three heads indicated.

(i) The paramount desideratum in the economic sphere is the maximisation of output per head, subject to constraints warrantable on political or cultural grounds and to the qualification that output per head is a weighted average of such outputs, which vary with type of activity. Some of these activities are oriented mainly to local demands and some to demands originating outside the urban area under analysis, with the relative importance of the latter turning mainly on the size of this area and the composition of its labour force. Thus, if e represents 'export' and d 'domestic' sales, with e plus d equal to unity, the ratio $e : (e + d)$ will decline with an increase in both city size and average income (and the associated relative increase in services); it will probably also fall with a decrease in the relative importance of manufacturing. (The export of governmental services is significant only in national or regional administrative centres.)[39] Within an activity, the level of output per head is dependent chiefly on conditions unconnected with city-size, such as capital-labour ratio, state of the arts, education and quality of the population. These affect the level of output principally through the medium of economies (diseconomies) associated with the agglomeration of complementary or other activities,[40] and through economies of scale which are pertinent mainly in respect to products that fall in the d category,[41] since external sales make economies attainable by e-category plants.[42] It has been possible, therefore, to achieve both considerable diversification of industry and full economies of plant scale in cities of quite small size.[43] This possibility has increased inasmuch as plant size has been tending to decrease and as improvements in communication and decision-affecting apparatus (e.g., computers) are facilitating the combination of greater plant scatter with a given input of administration.[44]

Insofar as real output per worker under *ceteris paribus* conditions is attainable in plants that can be located in relatively small cities, or (as is discussed below) in relatively small public administrative units, city growth beyond this size may entail increase in the waste of inputs, potential discretionary time and space. Emphasis needs to be placed not upon mere consumption, which often entails waste (i.e., unnecessary absorption of actual or potential inputs), but upon utilisation as a source of satisfactions (other than those associated with conspicuous consumption).[45] Mention has already been made of potential discretionary time which is consumed going to and from work,[46] and of access to space for day-to-day living and for recreation, both of which become less available as city-size increases and congestion grows. Waste of resources eventually becomes greater also with increase in the size of private and public administrative units. Prevention of waste becomes more difficult as the span of control is lengthened and as those adversely affected find it increasingly difficult to take corrective action; dearth of information blunts the force of homeostasis.

While the data here presented are based upon Western (mainly American) experience, they do suggest that in African states it should be possible to establish a sufficient number of smaller-sized cities to permit achievement of most economies associated with optimum dimensions of plant size, urban scale and agglomeration, and yet avoid the costs that emerge as urban size and concentration rise above certain levels. Current American experience might suggest otherwise, of course, since cities are being expanded and rearranged within spreading metropolitan areas that embrace multiple nuclei; we find not a multiplication of cities of 100,000–500,000, but often spread and sprawl under the aegis of improved transport, rising incomes and greater relative inputs of land in many sectors of the economy. Current American practice, however, is the product of response, not to a virtually new range of opportunities, but to a set of obsolete linkages and past decisions (many of them questionable even when made) which, when mixed with improved transport, changing land-price patterns and diverse subsidies and hidden costs,[47] makes for the spreading out of existing units.

(ii) While recreational and cultural opportunities increase with urban size up to a point, it is questionable if there is much net gain after a city attains several hundred thousand, for the availability of these opportunities depends largely upon income levels. There may be more opportunity for the spectator, but there will be less for the would-be participant. Given modern communication, access to most of what is transmitted probably does not vary greatly with city size. Within limits, access to live performances varies with size of city, but these are increasingly being squeezed out of existence in high-income countries such as the United States. Demand for the services of performers apparently is not shifting upwards fast enough to permit their payment in keeping with the alternative use-value of their labour. Thus greater reliance may have to be put upon amateur performances, which are not much more likely to flourish in large than in small communities. In general, given an income structure, access to recreational and cultural advantages probably does not vary enough with city size beyond some level (say 100,000) to affect the optimum range significantly.[48] In time, this could be true of African cities.

(iii) The political functions of a city are of three sorts: (*a*) provision of a milieu within which 'the good life' may be realised,[49] technical progress and freedom of inquiry may flourish and ethical norms may prove effective enough to insure adequate civic responsibility; (*b*) provision of adequate municipal services at minimal input cost per unit of output; and (*c*) transformation of the heterogeneous urban migrant elements into a sufficiently homogeneous population to permit accomplishment of the two preceding functions.[50] This last function is of primary importance in countries with very heterogeneous populations, or in cities with populations that, though homogeneous, are continually being augmented through the addition of culturally dissimilar elements; it is of particular importance in much of Africa.

Under (*a*) note may be taken of conditions, other than those to be discussed under (*c*), which can affect the quality of the milieu. Lampard concludes, on the basis of Western experience, that the domination of a country by a primate city of the sort that emerged in pre-industrial times, or in some African countries, 'may act as a curb rather than a stimulus to wider economic growth'. This it does by facilitating the relatively unproductive use of resources that might have been used in light manufacture or material processing, etc.[51] Such a large community also can make for political and hence economic instability by unduly centralising population and unemployment,[52] provided that job-seekers and others may freely migrate and settle in cities (which they could not or did not do under European rule).[53] Sufrin and Paul have concluded that in underdeveloped countries it is preferable to discourage further growth of centres which have become overcrowded and to encourage the formation of new industrial centres and the expansion of lesser industrial towns.[54]

It has been pointed out that, in developing countries, the form which cities have assumed or may assume tends to differ from the forms encountered in the West, where similar mechanisms are tending to produce similar morphological results. Given motor transport and ample land, there may be considerable urban spread in Africa, though physical limitations often give rise to congestion in coastal and inland port cities,[55] and in tropical lands the search for the advantages of micro-climate may prompt settlement in mountain valleys etc.[56] Cities in developing countries are likely, therefore, to become patchworks of areas, especially given the probable high rates of urban growth and the tendency of the poor to form slums on the periphery when there is not (as there was in the West) old, cheap housing near employment in the centre. With motor transport available, industry is likely to locate near the periphery, both because land is available there at lower price than towards the centre and because labour is near at hand. In time, of course, higher income groups may also move to the periphery and deterioration of the centre may set in.

(*b*) Economies of scale in the supply of urban public services do not seem to be very pronounced,[57] particularly when smaller units, though decentralised, are able to participate in organisational arrangements patterned somewhat after the market.[58] Only water and sewage services (which normally account for less than one-tenth of total urban expenditures) show continuous economies of scale. Full economic efficiency in the supply of other services (e.g., public education, fire protection, police protection, refuse collection, central administration) apparently can be attained in medium-sized communities of 50,000 to 100,000 residents.[59] Presumably the pattern of economies of scale in African cities will not differ materially from that found in the United States, particularly if uneconomic distribution of administrative responsibility among overlapping jurisdictions is avoided.

(*c*) Congregation of populations in cities is almost always a necessary though not a sufficient condition for generating that universalistic-achievement pattern so favourable to economic development.[60] In cities, role achievement supersedes ascription, and role allocation tends to be commensurate with performance and in keeping with generalised rules, universalistic values and a large amount of freedom from group pressures. 'Heterogenetic transformation' takes place within the city; 'local cultures are disintegrated and new integrations of mind and society are developed'.[61]

The conditions with which a universalistic-achievement pattern is associated, Max Weber's analysis suggests, gradually came into being in the Occidental city rather than in the Oriental city where 'magical animistic and sib constraints' tended to prevent the gradual emergence of social and legal equality.[62] Indeed, McKimm Marriott anticipates that, in Indian cities, life is likely to continue in keeping with a 'particularistic-achievement' value pattern.[63] Constraints analogous to those encountered in Asia, though less powerful, are found associated with tribal differences in Africa, with its hundreds of tribes (or culture-bearing units), many in each country, and its 730 distinct languages in use south of the Sahara.[64] Movement into cities does not, of course, produce 'agglomerations of "detribalized" and disorganized individuals', but rather organisations, deriving from tribal affiliations or emerging *de novo*, which relate individuals to other individuals and to the city and thus cushion the impact of city life on those newly settling there.[65]

Of concern here is the relation between city size and the transformation of the populations of African cities into relatively homogeneous cultural and political units. Even in cities in the United States, patterns of segregation developed and persisted in the wake of successive waves of ethnically distinct groups of immigrants,[66] though in time these patterns became less distinct in so far as they were not undergirded by ineradicable, genetically inherited differentiae.[67] Should tribal 'ghettoes' be more likely to develop in relatively large than in relatively small cities, congregation in the latter would be more favourable to the generation of values conducive to modernisation and economic development. Hoselitz's account suggests that in underdeveloped countries such as are found in Africa and Asia the circumstances which retard the development of new forms of social cohesion and solidarity and of 'universalistic, achievement-oriented social values', are more pronounced in relatively large than in relatively small cities.[68]

Concentration of a nation's population in several very large cities rather than in a number of smaller ones makes a higher degree of concentration of political power possible, even in the absence of a control-centring hierarchical structure. A large amount of control can be exercised by a small and resolute bloc or minority if the remainder of a population is indifferent. Let a population P consist of a resolute bloc B and an indifferent, random-voting majority M. Then given an M of size n, a B of size $\sqrt{n}$ can always carry 84 per cent of the decisions; and a B of size $^{x}\sqrt{n}$ can carry $\frac{1}{2}(1 + a)$ decisions where a is the area under the normal probability curve as given in the usual tables. This works out as in Table 4.1.[69] If a population were distributed among (say) five cities of one million

TABLE 4.1

M	Percentages of decisions controlled by B		
	84%	97·7%	99·9%
	Population of resolute bloc B		
10,000	100	200	300
1,000,000	1,000	2,000	3,000
100,000,000	10,000	20,000	30,000

each, instead of among 500 cities of 10,000 each, decision-making power could be concentrated in the hands of a much smaller fraction of the population, one perhaps only about one-tenth as large. While the *B*s in the various cities could enter into communication with one another, they would find it much harder to arrive at a concensus if there were 50 or 500 of them than if there were 5. Indeed, Coleman reports that even when there are two or more major cities, instead of just one that serves as the epicentre of political life, political leadership is dispersed and it proves much more difficult to 'organize a comprehensive nationalist party on a territorial basis'.[70]

In this section I have treated city size as a socio-economic and political variable and have indicated that the advantages associated with increases in city size are usually exhausted before a city becomes large (say, in excess of 100,000 in most instances).[71] Considering some of the difficulties which come in the wake of great population implosions, such as will be experienced in Africa, I have pointed to rising capital and service costs, to pollution of air and water, to impediments to urban beautification, to congestion, and to waste of time, space and capital and labour inputs.[72] It will be suggested below that a great deal of urban planning is required to hold adverse tendencies in check, for city growth is greatly stimulated by the illusion that it is easier and cheaper to expand a given urban centre than to establish a new one. In view of the lowness of incomes and the small measure in which African cultures have been modernised, however, regulatory undertakings will prove difficult.[73]

IV. The Role of Deliberate Policy

City size as well as the distribution of a nation's urban population among cities is in part the product of policy. Such policy is, however, subject to constraints flowing from the natural environment and the forms imposed by past growth, as well as from the limitations inherent in the policies themselves. They may range from those reflecting a very wide dispersal of autonomy in decision making (as in a hypothetical economy characterised by simple competition and unrestrained consumer sovereignty and freedom of choice) to policies reflecting great centralisation of decision making, together with relatively little response to the values and inclinations manifest in the general population. Limitations imposed by natural environment and the state of the arts have already been noted[74] and reference has been made to the restraining influence of existing forms. Attention will be devoted, therefore, to limitations which are inherent in urban growth or which may vary with the quality and the capacity of those whose decisions can affect such growth. Consideration of these limitations is useful, even when not empirically underpinned, for much the same reason that a tautological 'natural law' is useful; it helps us to shape our thinking about the scope of deliberate policy.[75]

At issue is whether a city, being a structure, is subject to the principles underlying structural growth. If so, the emergence of either a rank-size or a primate-dominated distribution of cities is subject to constraint. The growth of a structure is necessarily non-proportional, with the result that its size is 'limited by its ultimate inability to compensate for . . . non-proportional changes', among them the growing need for administration. Furthermore, since growth generates form which in turn limits or channels further growth, it becomes inimical to that minimal flexibility with which adaptability to change is necessarily associated in a dynamic world.[76] Because the elements composing a structure must be kept adequately adjusted to one another, it is preferable that adjustments and readjustments be continually made homeostatically as growth proceeds. A preconceived and rigid plan of growth is not likely to be able to restrict the variability of the individual parts sufficiently to continue a good fit. Given provision for continuing adjustment and readjustment, however, the growth of a city is more likely to proceed in keeping with comparative advantage and the most profitable use of the inputs absorbed by city growth.[77] In the absence of such provision, however, difficulties arise—difficulties analogous to those arising when organisms seek to exceed their appropriate dimensions.[78]

Let us return to the rank-size rule, $rP = K$, and assume the exponent of r as of P is unity. This rule, a product of 'the law of proportionate effect', implies that the growth of any city during any interval 'is a random proportion' of its size at the beginning of this interval. This law in turn may be interpreted as indicating the eventual and stable distribution of city sizes to be the result of 'a large number of causes operating simultaneously'.[79] If this law is fully operative, cities, large and small, will tend to grow, through natural increase and/or net immigration, at about the same rate. The number of cities will tend to grow at the same rate. As a result, the proportion of the urban population situated in relatively large cities (say, those 100,000 and over) will increase as the total urban population (say, in places 2,500 and over, or 20,000 and over) increases. This urban growth pattern has not yet manifested itself in Africa, however. There, the fraction of the population in urban centres of 20,000-plus which is found in cities of 100,000-plus is often abnormally large.[80] Even so, the larger cities found in most African states remain relatively small, because the states are too small to support even a large primate city. Presumably rank-size distributions will be slow to develop in Africa, where conditions for such growth are currently even less favourable than in other countries where such distributions have not emerged.[81]

Examination of individual cities often reveals their size to be subject to external or internal limitations. A city's growth in certain directions may be blocked by waterfronts or unfavourable terrain,[82] or by the presence of another city which limits expansion in the region of common interface.[83] Internal limits may also develop for, while urban growth manifests what Myrdal has called 'cumulative causation' (a process based in part upon statistical laws),[84] such growth cannot persist if expansion of the economic base of a city is restricted by municipal or business diseconomies associated with urban size. Awareness of some of these diseconomies may, of course, be slow to develop, if projected marginal private costs fall short of projected marginal social costs at a time when enterprises are deciding whether or not to locate in a given urban area.[85] Disparity between marginal social and marginal private costs can be averted, or at least minimised, however, much as stochastic processes tending to give rise to lognormal distributions can be subjected to constraints.[86]

Careful study of the urbanisation process will usually reveal it to be complicated and subject to cultural as well as economic and physical-environmental conditions. Such at least is the impression one has of the process in Nigeria, in whose 329 urban centres of 5,000-plus lived, in 1952, over 20 per cent of the country's thirty-two millions.[87] There, social attachments, institutions, geographical immobilities and accumulated investment militate against the relocation of cities and their populations. When to these sources of immobility is added a shortage of funds for the financing of infra-structure, the case becomes strong for investing initially in growing centres, even at the cost of neglecting, at least temporarily, relatively stagnant centres. Even so, the position of a country that has recently acquired political autonomy tends to be dynamic, for the socio-economic welfare function and the economic objectives of an independent state differ from those of a state under foreign rule. The result is that transport and trade undergo reorientation, together with occupational pursuits and population distribution.[88]

The amenability of the process of urbanisation to control through deliberate policy is governed by the skill of policy makers and the instruments at their disposal. Control through policy may involve the transfer to administrators of functions which the market system formerly performed effectively and almost gratuitously. Such transfer could prove impossible, however, should suitable administrators and requisite equipment and information be lacking, or should the sheer managerial difficulties be too great.[89] In most African states, moreover, other demands tend to be made on the state, albeit unwisely, and to absorb personnel that might otherwise have been available for urban administration.[90] Furthermore, excessive central direction may make for too much reliance upon high but ineffective motives instead of upon strong and tested material incentives. As a result, social cohesion is dissipated and a sense of frustration produced.[91]

Despite the difficulties which already beset efforts to regulate urban development in Africa, a large and perhaps increasing amount of such regulation will prove necessary for some decades, given current population growth. For regulation is indicated when, as in urban development, heavy expenditure upon infra-structure is involved and investment decisions, having been carried out, are not easily reversed.[92] Urban development thus differs markedly from processes involving decisions which, if found wanting, may be reversed at little cost; typical is a labour-management agreement which, upon being found unsatisfactory, is easily renegotiated. The heavy public and private investment required in urban development often entails a particularly high opportunity cost in capital-short underdeveloped countries. Furthermore, this investment, if uneconomically carried out, is not easily metamorphosed into quite useful economic investment. It is evident, therefore, that, as a rule, a large amount of regulation of urban development is required. Fortunately, while speedy urban construction or reconstruction may call for dynamic programming,[93] a great deal of urban planning can be accomplished through the establishment of constraints and guidelines within whose confines free play may be given to many market forces. Failure to plan urban growth in Africa will permit the appearance, in new and old forms, of the very problems which neglect of urban planning produced in Europe.

> Many underdeveloped countries can hardly afford not to plan. Public authorities should provide a master plan for every community and, where necessary, supplement the activities of private investors in such critical segments as housing and utilities. Furthermore, they must be furnished with ample enforcement power in order to make good their regulatory gestures. . . . The social costs of chaotic growth have been a burden on almost all the developed communities; they are responsible, in part, for some of the deeper antagonisms and tensions which still plague the social scene.[94]

In view of what was said in the preceding section, urban planning in Africa is likely to have at least four somewhat inter-related objectives, besides the avoidance of that formlessness of which Lewis Mumford complains.[95] First, the development of large primate cities had best, as a rule, be avoided, in view of the multiplicity of costs associated therewith. Second, development of the internal structure and form of African cities needs to be regulated in keeping with climatic, situational, and other relevant conditions. Third, in so far as important advantages are believed to be associated with cities of optimum size, it may prove necessary to impose constraints on the stochastic processes in effect, especially should they threaten to generate a distribution of city size in keeping with the rank-size rule and give rise to unduly large cities. Of course, given the smallness of most African states, the largest city in prospect in most states will remain quite small for some decades. Fourth, it may prove desirable to develop small urban islands around some of the scattered centres of development now found in African states, and to establish other such centres. This procedure is in keeping with the genesis of hierarchic systems, of which collections of cities are partial examples. Thus urban islands, exemplary of stable intermediate forms, may evolve into the more complex hierarchic systems of cities underlying modern economies, into systems of units which, though characterised by considerable autonomy, still adjust and readjust in a manner consistent with the maintenance of the system.[96] Objectives two to four can be most effectively achieved if adequate play is given to homeostatic processes.

Conclusion

Most of the material presented in this essay relates to non-African cities—to American cities in particular. This material is at present of but limited applicability to the interpretation of African urbanisation; material based entirely upon Asian and North African centres would not be of much greater applicability. Africa, however, is still little beyond the threshold of urbanisation, and its progress is bound to be conditioned, if not also handicapped, by the lowness of incomes and the limited modernisation so far attained. At the same time, study of experience in the West illuminates the natural history of urbanisation under alternative modes of transport and under the impact of local physical constraints and outmoded forms inherited from the past. It reveals something of the processes at work, whether they are stochastic in character or the product of great disparity between marginal social costs and marginal social benefits; and it suggests that both sets of processes can be brought under some control by careful urban planning. All of these considerations lend much support to the view that economic and social welfare in African states will be promoted more effectively if the urban population is kept distributed among smaller cities rather than concentrated in a few very large cities.

Notes and References

1 The first Kendall quotation is from "Natural Law in the Social Sciences", *Journal of the Royal Statistical Society*, Vol. 124, 1961, p. 12; the second from *New Prospects in Economic Analysis*, The Stamp Memorial Lecture, 1960, London 1960, pp. 16, 22.

2 "Statistics and Leviathan", *Journal of the American Statistical Association*, Vol. 30, March 1935, p. 11.

3 See Rutledge Vining, "A Description of Certain Spatial Aspects of an Economic System", *Economic Development and Cultural Change*, Vol. 3, January 1955, pp. 147–95; Martin J. Beckman, "City Hierarchies and the Distribution of City Size", ibid., Vol. 6, April 1958, pp. 243–8; Brian J. L. Berry, "City Size Distributions and Economic Development", ibid., Vol. 9, Pt. 1, July 1961, pp. 573–88; John Q. Stewart and William Warntz, "Physics of Population Distribution", *Journal of Regional Science*, Vol. 1, Summer 1958, pp. 99–123; also Yu V. Medvedkov, "Applications of Mathematics to Some Problems in Economic Geography", *Soviet Geography*, Vol. 5, June 1964, pp. 36–53.

4 E.g., Grace M. Kneedler, "Functional Types of Cities", in Paul K. Hatt and Albert J. Reiss, Jr, eds., *Reader in Urban Sociology*, Glencoe, Ill., 1951, pp. 49–57; Otis Dudley Duncan et al., *Metropolis and Region*, Baltimore 1960, chaps. 2–3.

5 On use of time, see Wilbert E. Moore, *Man, Time, and Society*, New York 1963, pp. 18, 27, 35–6, 74. If a city is defined as a collection of activities, it must also be indicated that this collection must not fall below specified quantitative and qualitative levels.

6 Marion Clawson et al., *Land for the Future*, Baltimore 1960, pp. 77–95; Otis Dudley Duncan, "Optimum Size of Cities", in J. J. Spengler and Duncan, eds., *Demographic Analysis*, Glencoe, Ill., 1956, pp. 374–5, 382.

7 Ibid., pp. 374–85; Robert M. Lillibridge, "Urban Size: An Abridgment", *Land Economics*, Vol. 28, November 1952, pp. 341–52. D. M. Heer's findings indicate relatively higher mortality for very large population concentrations. See *After Nuclear Attack*, New York 1965.

8 Clark, "The Distribution of Labour Between Industries and Between Locations", *Land Economics*, Vol. 26, May 1950, p. 144. Urban neighbourhoods would be two or three miles 'apart from each other, separated by ranges of hills or other natural features'; each would supply much of its own requirements, thus reducing the transport burden and the tendency to generate transport congestion in the centre of the city; ibid.

9 Clark, "The Economic Functions of a City in Relation to Its Size", *Econometrica*, Vol. 13, April 1945, pp. 112–13. See also G. M. Neutze, *Economic Policy and the Size of Cities*, Canberra 1965.

10 A firm comprising more than one plant may situate different plants in different cities, much as the 'visible' or the 'invisible' mechanisms governing an economy may situate different activities in different

cities. As is noted later, a stochastic process may pervade the universe of firms as well as that of cities.

11 On the survivor principle see George J. Stigler, "The Economies of Scale", *Journal of Law and Economics*, Vol. 1, October 1958, pp. 54–71.

12 Norton Ginsburg, *Atlas of Economic Development*, Chicago 1961, pp. 32–3. See also D. H. Reader, "A Survey of Categories of Economic Activities Among the Peoples of Africa", *Africa*, Vol. 34, January 1964, pp. 28–45; Economic Commission for Africa, *Population Distribution, Internal Migration and Urbanization in Africa*, New York, October 16, 1962, E/CN.14/ASPP/L.3 and E/CN.9/CONF.3/13.

13 See ibid., Pt. III and tables; Kingsley Davis and Hilda Hertz, "The World Distribution of Urbanization", reprinted in Spengler and Duncan, eds., *Demographic Analysis*, pp. 324, 326, 333; United Nations, "Demographic Factors Related to Social and Economic Development in Africa", *Economic Bulletin for Africa*, Vol. 2, June 1962, pp. 60–4, and United Nations, *Demographic Yearbook*; also Glenn T. Trewartha and Wilbur Zelinsky, "Population Patterns in Tropical Africa", *Annals of the Association of American Geographers*, No. 44, June 1954, pp. 144–6.

14 E.g., see Leo F. Schnore, "The Statistical Measurement of Urbanization and Economic Development", *Land Economics*, Vol. 37, August 1961, pp. 229–45; also Sanford Labovitz and Jack P. Gibbs, "Urbanization, Technology, and the Division of Labor: Further Evidence", *Pacific Sociological Review*, Vol. 7, Spring 1964, pp. 3–9, and Gibb's earlier studies mentioned in ibid. On population patterns and urban origins in sub-Saharan Africa, see K. M. Barbour and R. M. Prothero, *Essays on African Population*, London 1961, pp. 66–7, 92, 113, 117–18, 133, 253–67, 279–301, 318–22; Jacques Denis, SJ, *Le phénomène urbain en Afrique centrale*, in Académie royale des sciences coloniales (classe des sciences morales et politiques), *Mémoires*, Vol. 19, fasc. 1, 1958, pp. 19–59, 82–108; T. E. Smith and J. G. C. Blacker, *Population Characteristics of the Commonwealth Countries of Tropical Africa*, Commonwealth Papers No. 9, London 1963, pp. 20–7; Glenn T. Trewartha and Wilbur Zelinsky, "The Population Geography of Belgian Africa", *Annals of the Association of American Geographers*, Vol. 44, June 1954, pp. 165–6, 176–7; R. W. Steel, "African Urbanization: A Geographer's Viewpoint", in Kenneth Little, ed., *Urbanization in African Social Change*, Edinburgh 1963, pp. 7–13.

15 G. Hamdan, "The Political Map of the New Africa", *Geographical Review*, Vol. 53, 1963, pp. 418–39, especially pp. 424–36; Edward J. Taaffe et al., "Transport Expansion in Underdeveloped Countries: A Comparative Analysis", ibid., pp. 503–29, especially pp. 505–11; William A. Hance, *The Geography of Modern Africa*, New York 1964, pp. 29–41. On the importance of efficient transport in Africa and elsewhere, see Colin Clark and M. R. Haswell, *The Economics of Subsistence Agriculture*, London 1964, pp. 117–18 and chap. 9.

16 Hance, op. cit., pp. 46–8, 54–6. On the impact of foreign trade on African urbanisation, see S. D. Neumark, *Foreign Trade and Economic Development in Africa: A Historical Perspective*, Stanford 1964, pp. 19, 47, 67–78, 165–78. See also Gavan McDonell, "The Dynamics of Geographic Change: The Case of Kano", *Annals of the Association of American Geographers*, Vol. 54, September 1964, pp. 355–71.

17 Davis and Hertz, op. cit., p. 329. In 1950 Africa contained about 9 per cent of the world's population.

18 Hance, op. cit., pp. 52–6, and "The Economic Location and Functions of Tropical African Cities", *Human Organization*, Vol. 19, Fall 1960, pp. 135–7; also McDonell, op. cit.

19 Ginsburg, op. cit., pp. 36–7; Brian J. L. Berry, op. cit.; G. Hamdan, "Capitals of the New Africa", *Economic Geography*, Vol. 10, July 1964, pp. 239–53.

20 Kendall, "Natural Law in the Social Sciences", op. cit., p. 4.

21 United Nations, *Provisional Report on World Population Prospects*, New York 1964, chap. 12.

22 Hance estimates that 28 per cent of Africa is overpopulated. The overpopulated portion, wherein live about 38 per cent of the continent's population, includes 'most of Mediterranean Africa, discontinuous belts in the steppe and coastal regions of West Africa, many of the highland areas of eastern Africa, Rwanda and Burundi and adjacent parts of Congo, Nyasaland, Basutoland, Mauritius, and Reunion': *The Geography of Modern Africa*, p. 52. On growth in the United States, see Conrad Taeuber and Irene B. Taeuber, *The Changing Population of the United States*, New York 1958, chap. 6.

23 N. V. Sovani finds in the push of rural population pressure an important cause of urbanisation. See "The Analysis of Over-Urbanization", *Economic Development and Cultural Change*, Vol. 12, January 1964, pp. 117–19. The Economic Commission for Africa endorses this explanation. See *Population Distribution, Internal Migration, and Urbanization in Africa*, pp. 26–9; Lester R. Brown, *Man, Land & Food*, Washington, DC, 1963, pp. 77–8; US Department of Agriculture, *The World Food Budget*, FEA Report No. 19, Washington, DC, 1964, pp. iii, 38–44. While output per capita in Africa has increased 10–20 per cent over the last two decades and imports average close to $30 per head, it is preferable that these be used as capital instead of as food. See Economic Commission for Africa, *Industrial Growth in Africa*, New York 1963, pp. 3–4, 13.

24 On agricultural modernisation as such, see T. W. Schultz, *Transforming Traditional Agriculture*, New Haven 1964. On African agriculture, see Bruce F. Johnston, *The Staple Food Economies of Western Tropical Africa*, Stanford 1958; M. Yudelman, *Africans on the Land*, Cambridge, Mass., 1964; US Department of Agriculture, *Nigeria, Determinants of Projected Level of Demand, Supply, and Imports of Farm Products in 1965 and 1975*, ERS–Foreign 32, Washington, DC, August 1962, chaps. 5–6; United Nations, *FAO Africa Survey*,

Rome 1962, chaps. 1, 7–13, 20; Clark and Haswell, op. cit., pp. 17–18, 32 *ff.*, 37 *ff.*, 41 *ff.*, 46, 59, 63, 80 *ff.*, 117 *ff.*, 153 *ff.* Clark and Haswell report that in Japan, between 1900 and 1925, with the total population growing close to 1⅜ per cent per year and with agricultural production per head of rural population growing about 3·5 per cent per year, the agricultural population remained approximately stationary; ibid., pp. 186–9. These data imply that Africa's agricultural population will continue to increase. The Economic Commission for Africa believes that small investment, coupled with currently non-utilised land and labour, could greatly increase agricultural output in Africa. See *Economic Bulletin for Africa*, Vol. 3, January 1963, pp. 64–5.

25 These proportions correspond to those found in the United States in 1900: Taeuber, op. cit., p. 118. On recent African urbanisation see Kingsley Davis and Hilda Hertz Golden, "Urbanization and the Development of Pre-Industrial Areas", *Economic Development and Cultural Change*, Vol. 3, October 1954, pp. 16–23. The income elasticity of demand for farm-produced foods in the Near East and Africa (excluding South Africa) was around 0·7 in the late 1950s: see Schultz, op. cit., p. 13.

26 E.g., see the accounts of empirical regularities in the space-economy in Walter Isard, *Location and Space-Economy*, New York 1956, chap.3, and *Methods of Regional Analysis: An Introduction to Regional Science*, New York 1960, chap. 11; August Lösch, *The Economics of Location*, New Haven 1954, chaps. 10–11, 24; G. K. Zipf, *Human Behavior and the Principle of Least Effort*, Cambridge, Mass., 1949, chaps. 9–10; John Q. Stewart, "Empirical Mathematical Rules Concerning the Distribution and Equilibrium of Population", *Geographical Review*, Vol. 37, July 1947, pp. 461–85; Philip M. Hauser and Otis Dudley Duncan, eds., *The Study of Population*, Chicago 1959, chap. 28.

27 On this rule and its application, see Vining, op. cit., pp. 147–95. This rule in generalised form reverses the axes of the rule which roughly describes size of place distribution in many countries. See G. R. Allen, "The 'Courbe des Populations': A Further Analysis", *Bulletin of the Oxford University Institute of Statistics*, Vol. 16, May 1954, pp. 179–89.

28 Martin J. Beckmann, op. cit., pp. 243–8. On lognormal distributives and proportionate effects, see J. Aitchison and J. A. C. Brown, *The Lognormal Distribution*, Cambridge 1957, pp. 22–5, 101–2; R. Gibrat, *Les inégalités économiques*, Paris 1931, pp. 62–92, 250–6.

29 Beckmann, op. cit., pp. 246–8; H. A. Simon, *Models of Man*, New York 1957, chap. 9; Kendall, "Natural Law in the Social Sciences", op. cit., pp. 14–15; Leslie Curry, "The Random Spatial Economy: An Exploration in Settlement Theory", *Annals of the Association of the American Geographers*, Vol. 54, March 1964, pp. 138–46. N. T. J. Bailey describes the nature of stochastic processes in *The Elements of Stochastic Processes*, New York 1964.

30 Otis Dudley Duncan, "The Measurement of Population Distribution", *Population Studies*, Vol. 11, July 1957, pp. 39–44, and "Population Distribution and Community Structure", *Cold Spring Harbor on Quantitative Biology*, No. 22, 1957, pp. 364–7; also Duncan et al., *Metropolis and Region*, on qualifications to which a hierarchic tendency in city-distribution is subject, chap. 3 and pp. 86–7, 122, 153–4, 221–3, 270–1, 275.

31 Vining, op. cit., pp. 184, 187, 194–5; also E. M. Hoover's comment on Vining's findings, ibid., pp. 196–8. See also Curry, op. cit., pp. 144–5; B. J. L. Berry and W. L. Garrison, "Alternate Explanations of Urban Rank-Size Relationships", *Annals of the Association of American Geographers*, Vol. 48, March 1958, pp. 83–91. On stages of settlement, see also Yu V. Medvedkov, op. cit., pp. 47–53. E. E. Lampard reports little tendency on the part of industry to disperse: "The History of Cities in the Economically Advanced Areas", *Economic Development and Cultural Change*, Vol. 3, January 1955, pp. 123–9.

32 Berry, "City Size Distributions and Economic Development", op. cit., pp. 575–9, 582–4, 587; also Wolfgang Stolper's comments on Lampard's paper, op. cit., pp. 145–6.

33 Stolper, op. cit., pp. 143–4. However, see note 51 below.

34 See K. E. Boulding, "Toward a General Theory of Growth", in Joseph J. Spengler and Otis Dudley Duncan, eds., *Population Theory and Policy*, Glencoe, Ill., 1956, pp. 117–18; also Allan R. Pred, "The Intra-metropolitan Location of American Manufacturing", *Annals of the Association of American Geographers*, Vol. 54, June 1964, p. 180.

35 Colin Clark, "Urban Population Densities", *Journal of the Royal Statistical Society*, Vol. 114, 1951, pp. 490–6; Brian J. L. Berry et al., "Urban Population Densities: Structure and Change", *Geographical Review*, Vol. 53, July 1963, pp. 389–405; Duncan, "Population Distribution and Community Structure", op. cit., pp. 357–61; Stewart and Warntz, op. cit., pp. 99–123; Hal H. Winsborough, "City Growth and City Structure", *Journal of Regional Sciences*, Vol. 4, 1962, pp. 35–49; William Alonso, *Location and Land Use*, Cambridge, Mass., 1964. On the influence exercised upon intra-urban population distribution by occupational stratification, availability of residential facilities and general improvement in income levels, see e.g., Otis Dudley Duncan and Beverly Duncan, "Residential Distribution and Occupational Stratification", *American Journal of Sociology*, Vol. 60, March 1955, pp. 493–503; Beverly Duncan et al., "Patterns of City Growth", ibid., Vol. 67, January 1962, pp. 418–29; Reynolds Farley, "Suburban Persistence", *American Journal of Sociology*, Vol. 69, February 1964, pp. 38–47; Karl E. Taeuber and Alma F. Taeuber, "White Migration and Socio-Economic Differences Between Cities and Suburbs", ibid., October 1964, pp. 718–29.

36 Clawson et al., op. cit., pp. 64–107; Isard, *Location and Space Economy*, pp. 65–76. In the hinterland of cities one encounters a distance pattern which is similar to that found in cities, though

characterised by much lower levels and concomitants of density; ibid.

37 Ibid., pp. 200–6; Duncan, "Population Distribution and Community Structure", op. cit., pp. 358–61; also Beverly Duncan and Otis Dudley Duncan, "The Measurement of Intra-City Locational and Residential Patterns", *Journal of Regional Science*, Vol. 2, 1960, pp. 37–54; Clawson et al., op. cit., pp. 64–6, 78–81; J. H. Niedercorn and Edward F. R. Hearle, "Recent Land-Use Trends in Forty-Eight Large American Cities", *Land Economics*, Vol. 40, February 1964, pp. 106–110.

38 Pred, op. cit., pp. 168–9, 180; also pp. 170–9, on the role of conditions other than transport in the emergence of modern intra-metropolitan location. See also N. V. Sovani, "The Analysis of Over-Urbanization", loc. cit., pp. 113–21, especially pp. 113–17. He finds the correlation coefficient between urbanisation and industrialisation 0·85 in underdeveloped countries, but only 0·395 in advanced countries.

39 A now extensive literature deals with the definition and measurement of *e* and *d*, whether in income or employment terms, and with the impact of changes in *e* and *d* through multiplier channels upon aggregate income and employment within given urban centres. E.g., see Isard, *Methods of Regional Analysis*, especially pp. 189–204, 621–30; E. L. Ullman and M. F. Dacey, "The Minimum Requirements Approach to the Urban Economic Base", *Proceedings*, Regional Science Association, Vol. 6, 1960, pp. 175–194, and Ullman, "The Nature of Cities Reconsidered", ibid., Vol. 9, 1962, pp. 8–11; R. W. Pfouts and E. E. Curtis, "Limitations of the Economic Base Analysis", *Social Forces*, Vol. 36, May 1958, pp. 303–10; C. E. Ferguson, "Statics, Dynamics, and the Economic Base", in R. W. Pfouts, ed., *The Techniques of Urban Economic Analysis*, West Trenton, NJ, 1960, pp. 325–39. For an attempt to supply a causal interpretation of city growth—not supplied by rank-size and similar rules—see C. E. Ferguson, "A Statistical Study of Urbanization", *Social Forces*, Vol. 37, October 1958, pp. 19–26.

40 E.g., see Isard, *Location and Space Economy*, chap. 8 and pp. 265–74 and *Methods of Regional Analysis*, pp. 404–5, 678–80.

41 On scale economies in general, see ibid., pp. 400–2. Estimates of minimal required market size and of degree to which distribution of activities differs from that of population are given by Duncan et al., *Metropolis and Region*, pp. 70–81. On markets and costs, see also Colin Clark, "The Distribution of Labour Between Industries and Between Locations", op. cit., pp. 143–4, and *The Conditions of Economic Progress*, London 1957, pp. 342–50; USICA, *Manual of Industrial Development with Especial Application to Latin America*, Washington 1958; J. Jewkes, "The Size of the Factory", *Economic Journal*, Vol. 62, June 1952, pp. 237–52; United Nations, "Problems of Size of Plant in Industry in Under-Developed Countries", *Industrialization and Productivity*, Bulletin 2, March 1959, pp. 7–25.

42 The position of a city is somewhat parallel to that of a small country.

The latter can achieve economies of scale by having its firms concentrate on a limited number of products and export the surplus above domestic consumption, thereby attaining firm economies of scale. A city can achieve plant economies of scale by having plants sell outside the city output in excess of domestic consumption.

43 If one person in ten is engaged in manufacturing, a city of 50,000 can accommodate 50 plants averaging 100 wage earners each. In the United States in 1929, when medium-sized firms were frequently the most efficient and plant size was at a maximum in cities with 10,000 to 25,000 wage earners, the average number of wage earners per plant was approximately 42, with 62·3 per cent of the nation's plants employing fewer than 251 wage earners. See V. D. Kazakevich, "The End of Plant Expansion in American Manufacturing Industries", *Science and Society*, Vol. 2, 1938, pp. 195 *ff*.; but compare data given in next footnote. See also Temporary National Economic Committee, *Relative Efficiency of Large, Medium-Sized, and Small Business*, Monograph 13, Washington, DC, 1941; National Resources Planning Board, *The Long-Range Planning of the Location of New Productive Capacity*, Washington, DC, 1940, p. 11.

44 In the United States in 1957, employees per manufacturing establishment averaged 59 while production workers averaged 49; in 1958 the corresponding averages were 54 and 39, but 42·8 per cent of the employees were in plants employing 500 or more. Only one person in eleven was engaged in manufacturing in 1960. These figures are based upon the US Census of Manufacturers. In Britain, S. Moos has found that, if there is any trend, it suggests a decline in plant size; see "The Scope of Automation", *Economic Journal*, Vol. 67, March 1957, pp. 26–39; also John M. Blair, "Technology and Size", *American Economic Review*, Vol. 38, May 1948, pp. 121–52; Jewkes, op. cit.

45 E.g., see K. E. Boulding, "Income or Welfare", *Review of Economic Studies*, Vol. 17, 1949–50, pp. 70–80.

46 Among earlier studies of this problem is P. A. Sorokin and C. Q. Berger, *Time-Budgets of Human Behavior*, Cambridge, Mass., 1939, p. 42.

47 On the current course of urbanisation see Ullman, "The Nature of Cities", op. cit., pp. 7–23.

48 E. L. Thorndike gathered data on this relationship twenty-five years ago; see "American Cities and States: Variation and Correlation in Institutions, Activities, and the Personal Qualities of the Residents", *Annals of the New York Academy of Sciences*, Vol. 39, December 1939, pp. 213–98; also Thorndike, *144 Smaller Cities*, New York 1940, and *Your City*, New York 1940.

49 This is the over-riding objective, according to philosophical interpreters of the role of the city since the day of Aristotle; e.g., see Lewis Mumford, *The Culture of Cities*, New York 1938, p. 492.

50 The (*c*) category resembles Parson's 'integrative sub-system of the society' which 'relates the cultural value-patterns to the motivational

structures of individual actors in order that the larger social system can function without undue internal conflict and other failures of co-ordination'. See Talcott Parsons and Neil J. Smelser, *Economy and Society*, Glencoe, Ill., 1956, p. 48.

51 Lampard, op. cit., p. 131. In Asia, however, B. F. Hoselitz argues, the primate city has played a very dynamic role: "Urbanization and Economic Growth in Asia", *Economic Development and Cultural Change*, Vol. 6, October 1957, p. 43.

52 In Dar es Salaam about one male in five of those aged 16–45 was unemployed in 1963: see J. A. K. Leslie, *A Survey of Dar es Salaam*, London 1963. In Sudan's 'three towns', which may be treated as one metropolitan area, somewhat less than one in eight of the males answers to the description of 'unemployed'; see Peter F. M. McLoughlin, "The Sudan's Three Towns: A Demographic and Economic Profile of an African Urban Complex", *Economic Development and Cultural Change*, Vol. 12, July 1964, pp. 291–3. On the association of disguised unemployment with job shortages, see Michael Banton's study of Freetown in *West African City*, London 1957, pp. 60–7.

53 Potential migrants, though free to migrate and settle, may prefer not to settle permanently in cities if the pull of their nonliquifiable 'share' in tribal culture and land is sufficient to draw them back to tribal communities.

54 S. C. Sufrin and S. Paul, "Over-Urbanization and Economic Growth", in *Special Publication Series*, No. 16, The National Academy of Economics and Political Science, American University, Washington, DC, 1960, pp. 19, 21, 24. But see Sovani's critique in op. cit. Location of more industry in smaller towns is advocated for the Soviet Union by Ye N. Slastenko, "The Distribution of Productive Forces and the Effacing of Differences Between Town and Countryside", *Soviet Geography*, Vol. 5, February 1964, pp. 24–31.

55 E.g., see Steel, op. cit., pp. 9–12; Denis, op. cit., pp. 54–9.

56 This and several other points mentioned in the present paragraph have been discussed by William Alonso in "The Form of Cities in Developing Countries", *Regional Science Association Papers*, Vol. 13, 1964, pp. 165–73.

57 I am abstracting from the distribution of functions among a multiplicity of uncoördinated and overlapping jurisdictions, often a cause of a shortage of services as well as of excessive service costs; e.g., see A. J. Reiss, "The Community and the Corporate Area", *University of Pennsylvania Law Review*, Vol. 105, February 1957, pp. 443–63; also next note.

58 E.g., Robert Warren, "A Municipal Services Market Model of Metropolitan Organization", *Journal of the American Institute of Planners*, Vol. 30, August 1964, pp. 193–204.

59 Werner Z. Hirsch, "Expenditure Implications of Metropolitan Growth and Consolidation", *Review of Economics and Statistics*, Vol. 41, August 1959, pp. 237–41. Harvey E. Brazer's study similarly

reveals no marked economies of scale; *City Expenditures in the United States*, New York 1959. See also K. S. Lomax, "The Relationship between Expenditure Per Head and Size of Population of County Boroughs in England and Wales", *Journal of the Royal Statistical Society*, Vol. 106, 1943, pp. 51–9; Isard, *Methods of Regional Analysis*, op. cit., pp. 527–33.

60 Talcott Parsons, *The Social System*, Glencoe, Ill., 1951, pp. 60–7, 182–91; my essay, "Social Structure, the State, and Economic Growth", in Simon Kuznets, Wilbert E. Moore, and Joseph J. Spengler, eds., *Economic Growth: Brazil, India, Japan*, Durham, NC, 1955, pp. 380–4.

61 Robert Redfield and Milton B. Singer, "The Cultural Role of Cities", *Economic Development and Cultural Change*, Vol. 3, October 1954, pp. 53–73, especially 59–60, 70–3.

62 Max Weber, *The City*, trans. and ed. Don Martindale and Gertrud Neuwirth, Glencoe, Ill., 1958, chaps. 2, 4–5; Gideon Sjoberg, *The Pre-industrial City*, Glencoe, Ill., 1960, chap. 11; Bert F. Hoselitz, *Sociological Aspects of Economic Growth*, Glencoe, Ill., 1960, pp. 40–2, and "The City, The Factory, and Economic Growth", *American Economic Review*, Vol. 45, May 1955, pp. 166–84, especially 174–7.

63 See his comment on W. L. Kolb's "The Structure and Function of Cities", in *Economic Development and Cultural Change*, Vol. 3, October 1954, pp. 50–2.

64 J. Ornstein, "Africa Seeks a Common Language", *Review of Politics*, Vol. 26, April 1964, pp. 205–14; Joseph H. Greenberg, *The Languages of Africa*, Bloomington, 1963, pp. 161–71.

65 J. S. Coleman, "The Politics of Sub-Saharan Africa", in G. A. Almond and Coleman, eds., *The Politics of the Developing Areas*, Princeton, NJ, 1960, pp. 272–3, also 319–22 on mutual aid and related associations and 327 *ff*. on aggregate mechanisms. In several unpublished but forthcoming papers presented at Symposium No. 26, under the auspices of the Wenner-Gren Foundation for Anthropological Research, August 27–September 8, 1964, Michael Banton seems to attach relatively little weight to barriers of tribal origin, perhaps because their significance is conditioned by the urban social structure. The titles of his papers are "Role Theory and Urbanization" and "Social Alignment and Identity in a West African City" (i.e., Freetown). But see also Audrey Richards, "Multi-Tribalism in African Urban Areas", in Little, ed., *Urbanization in African Social Change*, pp. 43–51.

66 Duncan, "Population Distribution and Community Structure", op. cit., pp. 360–1.

67 Milton M. Gordon, *Assimilation in American Life: The Role of Race, Religion, and National Origins*, New York 1964.

68 "The City, the Factory and Economic Growth", op. cit., pp. 177–80, and *Sociological Aspects of Economic Growth*, pp. 200–5. Even in smaller cities, tribal groups may tend to live apart when housing

policy permits this. See Richards, "Multi-Tribalism in African Urban Areas", op. cit., pp. 46–50; UNESCO, *Social Implications of Industrialization and Urbanization in Africa South of the Sahara*, Paris 1956, pp. 557 *ff*., 693 *ff*. See also S. M. Lipset's essay in Erik Allardt and Y. Littunen, eds., *Cleavages, Ideologies and Party Systems: Contributions to Comparative Political Sociology—Transactions of the Westermarck Society*, Vol. 10, Helsinki 1964, pp. 21–55, especially pp. 39–41, where it is suggested that, if modernisation proceeds too rapidly to permit absorption of all political elements, social instability results and progress is retarded. He does not deal with possible relations between city size and absorption.

69 L. S. Penrose, "The Elementary Statistics of Majority Voting", *Journal of the Royal Statistical Society*, Vol. 109, 1946, pp. 53–7, especially p. 54.

70 Coleman, op. cit., p. 273.

71 The problem is posed by W. F. Ogburn and O. D. Duncan in "City Size as a Sociological Variable", in E. S. Burgess and D. J. Bogue, eds., *Contributions to Urban Sociology*, Chicago 1964, pp. 129–47.

72 E.g., see Coleman Woodbury, "Economic Implications of Urban Growth", *Science*, Vol. 129, June 12, 1959, pp. 1585–90; J. W. Dyckman, "Life in Supercity", ibid., Vol. 138, December 7, 1962, pp. 1089–91.

73 One gets an impression of some of the difficulties involved from Peter Marris, *Family and Social Change in an African City*, London 1961. Even so, the difficulties are not much greater than those faced in many Western countries; e.g., see John Dyckman, "The Changing Uses of the City", *Daedalus*, Vol. 90, Winter 1961, pp. 111–31.

74 Instances of the role of environments are given in Barbour and Prothero, op. cit., pp. 116–19, 134–6, 152–6, 189–92, 232, 253–7, 268–9, 308–9.

75 See Kendall, "Natural Law in the Social Sciences", op. cit., p. 11; also p. 12, where he indicates that even though 'the laws which control [man's] social actions and interactions may themselves be subject to rapid change', they may still be described as 'laws' and used to describe social phenomena (as does the rank-size rule) though the description lacks the permanence of a physical law.

76 Rigidification is associated, as Arnold J. Toynbee has suggested, with idolisation of ephemeral institutions or techniques, exemplified in Manchester's failure to keep in step with industrial and organisational change. *A Study of History*, Vol. IV, London 1939, pp. 303, 423, 428–30.

77 My discussion in this paragraph has been influenced by Boulding, op. cit., pp. 117–23; also by Gunnar Myrdal.

78 E.g., see D'Arcy Wentworth Thompson, *On Growth and Form*, ed. by John Tyler Bonner, Cambridge 1961, chap. 2 on "Magnitude"; J. B. S. Haldane, "On Being the Right Size", in J. R. Newman, ed., *The World of Mathematics*, Vol. II, New York 1956, pp. 952–7.

79 Aitchison and Brown, op. cit., pp. 22, 24–5, 101–2; Gibrat, op. cit.;

also N. Rashevsky, *Mathematical Theory of Human Relations*, Bloomington 1947, chap. 12.

80 See Table 5 in *Population Distribution, Internal Migration and Urbanization in Africa*, cited in n. 12 above. In 16 of 27 states, one city is dominant.

81 Homer Hoyt, "Is City Growth Controlled by Mathematics or Physical Laws?", *Land Economics*, Vol. 27, August 1951, pp. 259–62.

82 If a city's growth is blocked on one side, a given degree of growth requires a compensatory extension of a city's unblocked boundaries. See maps in Denis, op. cit., and Barbour and Prothero, op. cit.; also A. S. Smailes, *The Geography of Towns*, London 1953, chaps. 5–6 on morphology of towns.

83 Compare M. Avrami Melvin, "Geometry and Dynamics of Populations", *Philosophy of Science*, Vol. 8, January 1941, pp. 115–22, 125.

84 Gunnar Myrdal, *An American Dilemma* (1944), New York 1962, pp. 75–77 and Appendix 3; M. S. Bartlett, *Essays on Probability and Statistics*, New York 1962, pp. 26–7, 59.

85 For example, part of the costs of extending urban boundaries may be supported by the core city, whence movement of business firms may not be easy. In the absence of such support, enterprises might discover that it would be cheaper to locate in smaller or newly-emerging communities. Such effect can be produced, for example, by the structure of taxes and subsidies utilised in urban areas. E.g., see unsigned, "The Great Urban Tax Tangle", *Fortune*, Vol. 71, March 1965, pp. 106 *ff*.

86 Vining, op. cit.; Aitchison and Brown, op. cit., p. 109; Bartlett, op. cit., p. 27.

87 The course of urbanisation in Nigeria has been carefully described and analysed in a splendid paper by Professor Akin L. Mabogunje, of the Department of Geography, University of Ibadan, "Urbanization in Nigeria—A Constraint on Economic Development", *Economic Development and Culture Change*, Vol. 13, July 1965, pp. 413–38.

88 The points raised in this paragraph have been treated by Professor Mabogunje in ibid. See also Taaffe et al., op. cit.; Isard, *Location and Space-Economy*, pp. 182–8.

89 E.g., see M. Polanyi, *The Logic of Liberty*, London 1951, chaps. 8–10.

90 E.g., see Elliott J. Berg, "Socialism and Economic Development in Tropical Africa", *Quarterly Journal of Economics*, Vol. 78, November 1964, pp. 549–73.

91 Ibid., pp. 556–60; Theodore Morgan, "The Theory of Error in Centrally-Directed Economic Systems", *Quarterly Journal of Economics*, Vol. 78, August 1964, pp. 412–13. Disregard of the nature of demand for housing often characterises even urban renewal theory and practice in the United States; see William Alonso, "The Historic and the Structural Theories of Urban Form: Their Implications for Urban Renewal", *Land Economics*, Vol. 40, May 1964, pp. 227–31.

92 Isard, *Location and Space-Economy*, op. cit., p. 183.

93 E.g., see Leland S. Burns and Leo H. Klassen, "The Econometrics of

Building a New Town", *Review of Economics and Statistics*, Vol. 45, November 1963, pp. 368–73.

94 Lampard, op. cit., p. 134.

95 Lewis Mumford, *The City in History*, New York 1961, pp. 544, 546.

96 On the properties of systems see Herbert A. Simon, "The Architecture of Complexity", *Proceedings* of the American Philosophical Society, Vol. 106, December 1962, pp. 467–82. See also Albert Ando, Franklin M. Fisher, and Herbert A. Simon, *Essays on the Structure of Social Science Models*, Cambridge, Mass., 1963, pp. 2–4, 100–2, 107–12.

5

Urbanisation and Economic Growth: The Cases of Two White Settler Territories

WILLIAM J. BARBER

THIS ESSAY is concerned with economic aspects of the process of urban growth in the territories formerly designated as Southern and Northern Rhodesia (now renamed Rhodesia and Zambia respectively).[1] Though the experience of these territories is far from representative of the sub-Saharan continent, the economic characteristics of their urban patterns raise a number of issues of wider interest. Throughout most of the postwar period, economic expansion in these territories (at least as measured by such standard indices as growth in the gross domestic product) has proceeded at rates well above the average for the continent. For this reason, study of their situation is likely to shed light on the relationships between urbanisation and economic expansion in an African context. Moreover, these cases provide a useful framework within which to raise broader questions about the forces now reshaping the role of urban centres and about the types of inquiry deserving priority if these processes are to be adequately understood.

I. Urbanisation: General Orders of Magnitude

When judged by widely used international criteria, 'urbanisation' in the Rhodesias cannot be said to have progressed very far. Only

NOTE: *The notes and references for Chapter 5 will be found on page 123.*

four cities in the area can meet the standard used in many United Nations reports—that of concentrations of 100,000 persons or more. If the index of urbanisation were made more elastic and reduced to population concentrations of 20,000 or more, some fourteen places would be included by 1962–63, accounting for roughly 15 per cent of the Southern Rhodesian population and approximately 18 per cent of the population in Northern Rhodesia (see Table 5.1).[2] In American economic history, one would have to go back to 1880—when about 17 per cent of the United States population resided in places of 25,000 or more—before encountering a roughly similar 'urban' claim on the total population. Even then, the analogy would be far from exact. In the United States of 1880, another 11 per cent of the population inhabited places in the size range of 2,500 to 25,000.[3] In the Rhodesias, smaller towns carry much less weight in the aggregate.

Although the population of the Rhodesias is far more heavily rural than urban, nevertheless the process of urbanisation has proceeded further in these territories than in most of sub-Saharan Africa. Comparative data appear to indicate that the proportion of the population inhabiting urban areas of 20,000 or more is higher in the two Rhodesias than in any sub-Saharan country outside South Africa.[4] These international comparisons, however, must be interpreted with considerable caution. For most African countries, the reliability of demographic statistics is extremely shaky. In a number of respects, the statistical coverage of population in the Rhodesias is above the average in its adequacy. Even so, systematic enumeration of the African population and its geographical distribution dates from the very recent past. Before 1962, official estimates of the size of the African population were built on projections of the results of sample surveys undertaken in the early 1950s and on the Native Commissioner's calculations of males of poll tax-paying age. In census years, African employees in the main towns were counted, but no thorough measure of the African town population was attempted. Nor was a comprehensive census of Africans undertaken before April/May 1962 in Southern Rhodesia and before May/June 1963 in Northern Rhodesia. These enumerations indicated that prior estimates had understated the

TABLE 5.1

Official Estimates of the Size of Main Towns, Southern Rhodesia and Northern Rhodesia (in 1000s)

Southern Rhodesia (December 1962):	
Bulawayo	210·9
Gwelo	38·2
Salisbury	314·2
Umtali	42·8
Population of four main towns	606·1
Population of Southern Rhodesia	3,941·7
Per cent of population in four main towns	15·4%
Northern Rhodesia (June 1963):	
Bancroft	30·2
Broken Hill	46·4
Chingola-Nchanga	56·6
Kitwe-Nkana	114·8
Livingstone	34·1
Luanshya-Roan Antelope	72·4
Lusaka	119·1
Mufulira	76·4
Ndola	88·9
Population of nine main towns	638·9
Population of Northern Rhodesia	3,500·0
Per cent of population in nine main towns	18·2%

Sources: Southern Rhodesian data from the *Economic Report, Federation of Rhodesia and Nyasaland*, 1963; Northern Rhodesian data from the *Monthly Digest of Statistics, Northern Rhodesia*, May 1964, and the *Preliminary Report of the May/June 1963 Census of Africans in Northern Rhodesia.*

African population in Southern Rhodesia by some 20 per cent and in Northern Rhodesia by approximately 35 per cent.[5]

Judgements based solely on aggregative population data, however, obscure an important aspect of the urban reality in the Rhodesias. In both territories, the bulk of the European population is bunched in a handful of main towns. The claim of urbanisation on this minority is far heavier than on the African majority. By 1961, more than two-thirds of Southern Rhodesia's Europeans and more than four-fifths of Northern Rhodesia's Europeans were town-dwellers (see Table 5.2). The differential between the Rhodesias is largely accounted for by the heavier weight of farming

TABLE 5.2

Percentage of European Population Resident in Main Towns, Selected Census Years

	Total European Population (in 1000s)	Percentage in Main Towns
Southern Rhodesia: (four main towns)		
1946	84·0	52·0
1951	135·6	61·6
1956	177·1	65·5
1961	220·6	68·6
Northern Rhodesia: (nine main towns)*		
1946	21·9	72·0
1951	37·1	77·9
1956	65·3	81·0
1961	74·6	82·8

* Northern Rhodesian estimates for 1946 and 1951 cover eight towns, as Bancroft had not yet come into being.

Source: Census Reports, Southern and Northern Rhodesia.

and of small-scale mining in the occupational distribution of Southern Rhodesia's Europeans and by the fact that the important mineral workings in Northern Rhodesia have been conducted on a scale sufficient to justify the creation of sizeable communities near the site; of the nine main towns in Northern Rhodesia, six are located on the Copperbelt. Europeans, however, still form a minority in the urban population. In 1962–63, Africans outnumbered non-Africans by well over two-to-one in all Southern Rhodesia's main towns and by six-to-one or more in the urban centres of Northern Rhodesia (see Table 5.3).

Perhaps the most important single fact about urbanisation in the recent economic history of the Rhodesias is the impressive rate at which the main towns have expanded. In the absence of reliable data on the pre-1962 size of the African population in the main towns, the full extent of urban growth cannot be satisfactorily

TABLE 5.3

Estimates of the Racial Composition of Main Towns, Southern Rhodesia and Northern Rhodesia

	Non-African (in 1000s)	African (in 1000s)	Ratio of Africans to Non-Africans
Southern Rhodesia: (December, 1962)			
Bulawayo	55·9	155·0	2·78
Gwelo	9·2	29·0	3·15
Salisbury	97·2	217·0	2·23
Umtali	9·8	33·0	3·37
Northern Rhodesia: (June, 1963)			
Bancroft	2·5	27·7	11·11
Broken Hill	5·8	40·6	7·01
Chingola-Nchanga	5·9	50·7	8·09
Kitwe-Nkana	13·2	101·6	7·68
Livingstone	4·8	29·3	6·10
Luanshya-Roan Antelope	6·2	66·2	10·85
Lusaka	14·5	104·6	7·21
Mufulira	7·1	69·3	9·76
Ndola	12·1	76·8	6·35

Notes and sources: In addition to Europeans, the 'non-African' population includes a small number of Asians and persons of mixed race. Data are drawn from the sources indicated in Table 5.1.

measured. However, the census returns for the fifteen years 1946–61 record a four-fold expansion of the non-African population of the main towns in Northern Rhodesia and a figure of three and a half times for Southern Rhodesia.[6] Though the number of Africans employed in urban centres expanded at a somewhat slower pace, it is clear that a major growth in the size of urban concentrations occurred between the end of the war and the early 1960s.

II. Characteristics of the Urban Pattern

Quantitative measures of the claim of the main towns on population, illuminating though they are in establishing general orders of magnitude, nevertheless considerably understate the significance of urbanisation in the Rhodesian economic pattern. With but a few qualifications, the present urban areas may be regarded as the spearheads of the monetised exchange economy introduced and organised by Europeans. In the 'dual structure' of economic life in this part of the continent—in which a monetised and highly organised set of economic institutions co-exist with traditional indigenous forms of economic organisation—urban concentrations have always played a strategic role. They have provided the channel through which commercial contacts with the outside world have been maintained as well as the facilities required for the conduct of monetised exchange and of orderly administration at home.

An approximation of the position of main towns in the economic life of these territories can be obtained from an inspection of their share of the labour force engaged in highly organised and monetised types of economic activity (Tables 5.4 and 5.5). In the main towns of both Rhodesias is to be found the bulk of the work force—both European and African—engaged in services generally (and in commerce, finance, transport and communications particularly). Indeed, in 1965, four main towns in Southern Rhodesia claimed more than 70 per cent of the economically-active European population and more than 30 per cent of the territorial total of African wage employees.[7] The remainder of the population engaged in economic activities organised along Westernised lines were to be found in a scattering of smaller towns, in European agriculture (the largest single employer of African labour in the territory) and in mining. In Northern Rhodesia, the dominance of the main towns in the pattern of organised economic activity has been even more striking. Nearly 80 per cent of the territory's economically-active Europeans and more than half of its African wage earners inhabit the nine main towns. This result reflects the fact that nearly all of the significant mining activity in Northern Rhodesia is carried on by residents of main towns.

While urban centres in this part of the world have been expected to specialise in certain economic functions, they have not been organised with solely productive ends in view. Other objectives of colonial urban policy have been described as follows for another settler community in Africa, in words equally valid for the Rhodesias: '(a) to develop centres in which non-Africans could live in healthy surroundings, and (b) to limit the trading activities of non-Africans in order to protect the way of life, land and trade of the indigenous peoples'.[8] In short, urban areas were construed predominantly as European enclaves. As such, they represented the highest expression of the general settlement sought between the races during the colonial era—a settlement which called for the partitioning of land into racial zones. In the spheres assigned to them, Europeans and Africans enjoyed special privileges that were denied to outsiders.

The original character of urban communities as residential, commercial and administrative centres for Europeans has subsequently undergone some alteration. Nevertheless, much of the initial pattern has been retained. Thus, in Southern Rhodesia, despite the substantial growth in the four main towns recorded by the mid-1950s, Europeans engaged in tertiary activities outnumbered those in manufacturing and construction by more than two-to-one. This result is even more striking when it is recalled that the bulk of the manufacturing and construction activity of the territory was then conducted in these same four towns. At the same time, domestic services employed about the same number of Africans as did manufacturing in these urban concentrations. In Northern Rhodesia, on the other hand, the primary economic base of urban communities is considerably more conspicuous by virtue of the population complexes built up around the Copperbelt mines.

Much of the influence of the original non-economic constraints on the urban pattern has survived subsequent modifications in the economic base. The terms of these social and political arrangements, in turn, have had a number of economic consequences:

TABLE 5.4

Occupational Distribution of the Economically-Active European Population, Main Towns, 1956

	Numbers engaged (1000s)	Share of each occupational group of total European labour force in main towns (%)	Share of 'Urban' European labour force of territorial total for each occupational group (%)
Southern Rhodesia: (four main towns)			
Total economically active Europeans	55·2	—	70·2
Engaged in:			
(*a*) Commerce and finance	16·7	30·2	84·6
(*b*) Services (includes government, educational and health services, personal and recreational services)	13·6	24·7	75·9
(*c*) Electricity and sanitary services	0·9	1·7	76·2
(*d*) Transport and communication	6·3	11·4	80·3
(*e*) Manufacturing	9·7	17·5	83·8
(*f*) Construction	6·8	12·3	74·7
Northern Rhodesia: (nine main towns)			
Total economically active Europeans	23·0	—	78·2
Engaged in:			
(*a*) Commerce and finance	4·6	20·0	89·5
(*b*) Services (includes government, educational and health services, personal and recreational services)	4·8	20·8	72·0
(*c*) Electricity and sanitary services	0·2	0·8	87·2
(*d*) Transport and communication	2·0	8·8	77·0
(*e*) Manufacturing	2·2	9·7	81·4
(*f*) Construction	2·8	12·0	64·4
(*g*) Mining	5·9	25·8	88·6

Source: Calculated from *Reports on the Census, 1956.*

TABLE 5.5

Occupational Distribution of African Employees, Main Towns, 1956

	Numbers engaged (1000s)	Share of occupational group of total African employees in main towns (%)	Share of 'Urban' African employees in territorial total for each occupational group (%)
Southern Rhodesia: (four main towns)			
Total African wage employees	194·1	—	31·8
Engaged in:			
(*a*) Domestic services	52·3	26·9	73·0
(*b*) Other services (including government, health, educational and personal services)	19·7	10·1	42·0
(*c*) Electricity and sanitary services	3·1	1·6	57·4
(*d*) Transport and communication	10·6	5·5	77·2
(*e*) Commerce and finance	21·7	11·2	72·3
(*f*) Manufacturing	54·2	27·9	72·0
(*g*) Construction	26·7	13·7	45·9
Northern Rhodesia: (nine main towns)			
Total African wage employees	146·6	—	55·7
Engaged in:			
(*a*) Domestic services	25·4	17·3	79·3
(*b*) Other services (including government, health, educational, and personal services)	13·9	9·5	35·8
(*c*) Electricity and sanitary services	2·4	1·6	80·0
(*d*) Transport and communication	5·7	3·9	73·0
(*e*) Commerce and finance	8·3	5·7	57·2
(*f*) Manufacturing	17·1	11·7	69·4
(*g*) Construction	37·6	25·6	58·6
(*h*) Mining	33·5	22·9	89·1

Source: Calculated from *Reports on the Census, 1956*.

among them, they have restricted the geographical scope of the urban pattern. The development of towns has effectively been confined to zones apportioned for European ownership and occupancy, and, even more particularly, to those portions of the European land areas enjoying proximity to the main arteries of communication. At least in part, the stimulating effects on the economy that might otherwise have arisen from a more pervasive geographical spread of monetised activity have been precluded. With the exception of new communities sited near freshly-developed mineral workings (such as the Bancroft complex in Northern Rhodesia) and the relocation of the Northern Rhodesian capital from Livingstone to Lusaka in the 1930s, urban growth since 1930 has swollen the size of existing towns but has not led to the creation of new ones.

Of more far-reaching significance has been the effect of non-economic constraints on the manner in which economic life has been conducted within the urban complexes. As these enclaves grew, more and more Africans were brought into contact with them as wage earners. The institutional setting, however, denied a permanent stake in urban life to those Africans attracted to towns. Their natural base was held to be in the native areas from which they came and to which they were expected to return. The organisation of the economy on this basis committed Africans—whether or not they would have been disposed otherwise—to a migratory pattern of employment.

In the early days of European settlement, these migratory arrangements offered advantages to all parties. European employers were permitted to obtain labour at low wage rates—and certainly at rates below those they would have been obliged to pay had circumstances demanded that the money wage be high enough to cover the minimum requirements of both the African worker and his family. As it was, African labour could usually be obtained in the required volume with wages sufficient to provide a 'single' worker with his sustenance plus an incentive bonus. These terms still enabled many African families to enjoy higher real incomes than would otherwise have been available to them. So long as manpower could be spared for intermittent periods without loss in agricultural output (a situation which traditional techniques of cultivation often permitted), spells of wage employment on the part of adult males could augment the income of the family group. But there were also other reasons why the migratory pattern could provide a workable solution to the problems of the nascent money economy in the early phases of European intervention. A migratory pattern which relied on male workers whose dependants stayed behind to till the family plots minimised the claims on resources for housing an urban African work force.

The impact of these arrangements is clearly discernible in the most recent studies of the characteristics of the urban African population. In the light of the general structure of the system, it should come as no surprise to discover that the age and sex composition of the urban African population differs substantially from that of the population as a whole or that the urban group should be heavily weighted in favour of working-age males (see Table 5.6). In the main towns of Southern Rhodesia, for example, males over sixteen years of age comprised nearly half the urban African population. In most of these towns, the terms on which housing was available meant that normal family life was a live option to only a minor fraction of the African labour force. Debarred until the mid-1950s from acquiring title to urban building plots,[9] most urban African families have been obliged to rely on the accommodation provided in organised townships. These townships have been financed through a 'pooled rental' system, an arrangement whereby employers are billed a standard fee to cover the housing costs of African workers, without regard to the amount of space occupied. This procedure had originally been instituted in order to forestall biases against family men in hiring practices. But, inasmuch as the housing authorities set rentals with the expectation that profits from the housing of 'single' workers would subsidise losses on family accommodation, the books could be balanced only by providing space for four to five single workers for each family housed.[10] The consequences of this practice are reflected in the recent series of demographic surveys of Southern Rhodesia's urban African population. In Salisbury, for example,

TABLE 5.6

Characteristics of the African Population in Main Towns

	(1) Main towns (1000s)	(2) Per cent of Urban African Population	(3) Territorial Total (1000s)	(4) (1) as a per cent of (3)
Southern Rhodesia: (four main towns) (April/May, 1962)				
Total enumerated population	432·7	100	3,618·2	14·2
Males:				
Over 16 years of age	208·3	48·2	964·4	21·6
16 years and under	74·9	17·3	898·8	7·5
Total males	283·2	65·5	1,863·2	15·2
Females:				
Over 16 years of age	82·0	19·0	867·1	9·5
16 years and under	67·5	15·4	887·8	7·6
Total females	149·5	34·5	1,754·9	8·5
Ratio of males over 16 to females over 16	2·55	—	1·11	—
Northern Rhodesia: (nine main towns) (May/June, 1963)				
Total enumerated population	562·2	100	3,409·1	16·5
Males:				
Over 21 years of age	160·9	28·6	747·9	21·5
21 and under	154·8	27·5	942·5	16·4
Total males	315·7	56·1	1,690·4	18·6
Females:				
Over 21 years of age	94·2	16·8	769·9	12·3
21 and under	152·3	27·1	948·8	16·1
Total females	246·5	43·9	1,718·7	14·4
Ratio of males over 21 to females over 21	1·71	—	0·97	—

Sources: Preliminary Report of the April/May 1962 Census of Africans in Southern Rhodesia, and *Preliminary Report of the May/June 1963 Census in Northern Rhodesia.*

fewer than 20 per cent of the African wage earners were heads of families accompanied by dependants.[11]

In Northern Rhodesia, the pattern of urban settlement has been a species of the same genus. As in Southern Rhodesia, adult males form the largest single component of the urban African population, though the urban age/sex balance is less heavily distorted from that of the territory as a whole. The initiatives of the large mining companies in seeking to stabilise their African work force (and the effect of this example on other urban employers) has resulted in the settlement of a relatively higher proportion of family groups than prevails in Southern Rhodesia.

The terms on which towns have been organised have also had an important influence on the distribution of income generated within them. As far as personal incomes are concerned, these communities have been structured on the premise of a sharp discontinuity in the distribution of income between the races. In the initial stages, this outcome could not easily have been avoided. African labour was unskilled, unreliable and not very productive, whereas Europeans—who expected higher real incomes than would be available to them elsewhere if they were to remain in these pioneering outposts—had to be rewarded at higher rates than their skills could command in other environments. Over the course of time, this pattern has tended to be self-perpetuating. Employers lacked incentive to invest in 'skilling' an African labour force which they could expect to be only migrant and transient. Nor did African employees, given prevailing wages and the terms of urban living generally, have either incentive or opportunity to commit themselves to urban occupations. The interlocking of these factors, in turn, imposed a low ceiling on the positions in the urban economy to which Africans could aspire—a ceiling made more rigid by restrictions in the labour market, backed by custom if not by statute. Though the colour bar in employment has been dented in the recent past, it remains the case that most African employees in the urban economy have yet to rise above the lowest rungs on the skill ladder, where they continue to receive low wages.

The persistence of this pattern is strikingly brought out in the findings of the 1958–59 round of demographic surveys of the urban

TABLE 5.7

Economically Active African Population in the Four Main Towns of Southern Rhodesia by Skill Category and Wage Rates, 1958-59

	Numbers (1000s)	Per cent of Urban African Labour Force	Median monthly wage (without rations) (£. *s.d.*)	Median monthly wage (with rations) (£. *s.d.*)
Skilled:				
Teachers	1·0		15. 2.0	
Carpenters	1·0		12. 3.0	
Painters	0·6		13.14.0	
Bricklayers, plasterers, etc.	1·0		15.12.0	
Other*	1·0			
Total skilled	4·6	2·6		
Semi-skilled:				
Clerks and clerk typists	2·1		12.13.0	
Shop assistants and shopkeepers	0·8		10. 2.0	
Drivers of motor vehicles	6·0		12.17.0	
Sewers, tailors and dressmakers	3·8		7.13.0	
Police, detectives, guards, firemen	3·7		10. 3.0	
Total semi-skilled	16·4	9·1		
Unskilled:				
Assistants to shop sales workers	4·3		7. 0.0	4. 0.0
Petrol pump attendants	0·8		7.17.0	
Gardeners, groundsmen	3·2		6.10.0	4. 3.0
Quarry workers	1·1		6.18.0	
Office messengers	5·5		7.17.0	
Cycle delivery workers	2·6		6.16.0	
Textile factory workers	3·0		6.17.0	
Shoe repairers and leather workers	1·5		6.14.0	
Brickfield workers	2·5		6.12.0	
Food process workers	3·8		6.14.0	4. 9.0

TABLE 5.7—*continued*

	Numbers (1000s)	Per cent of Urban African Labour Force	Median monthly wage (without rations) (£. *s.d.*)	Median monthly wage (with rations) (£. *s.d.*)
Tobacco floor and factory workers	6·1		6.13.0	4. 7.0
Packers and related workers	1·1		7. 1.0	
Storemen, warehouse-men and porters	1·0		7.12.0	
Truck and lorry loaders	5·0		6.13.0	
Labourers on railways	5·2		9. 1.0	
Labourers in building and construction	12·8		6.13.0	
Labourers in municipalities	2·8		6.17.0	
Other labourers	15·9			
Cooks	1·4		6.12.0	
Waiters and waitresses	2·3		7. 1.0	
Watchmen and caretakers	1·3		7. 9.0	
Cleaners	3·5		6.12.0	
Workers in laundries and dry cleaners	1·3		6.13.0	
Domestic servants:	58·1			
male				3. 4.0
female				3.17.0
Total unskilled	146·1	81·2		
Other: predominantly unskilled; plus occupation inadequately described	12·9	7·2		
Total economically active:	180·0			

* Predominantly nurses, for whom wage rates were unspecified.

Source: Calculated from "Occupations and Wage Rates of Africans in the Urban Areas of Southern Rhodesia 1958/1959", *Monthly Digest of Statistics, Federation of Rhodesia and Nyasaland*, July 1960, pp. iii-ix.

African work force in Southern Rhodesia's four main towns. When the occupational distribution is arrayed by skill groupings, it appears that less than 3 per cent of urban African wage earners can be classified as 'skilled'. Even when interpreted with latitude, the 'semi-skilled' category can account for less than another 10 per cent. The overwhelming mass of the urban labour force has acquired little or no skill and is engaged in ordinary labour or in domestic service. For most of these employees, money wages were less than £7 per month, with lodging, but not rations, provided by the employer (see Table 5.7).

The significance of these findings emerges more sharply when they are compared with the incomes of European urban families. If the results of the October 1960 sample survey of European family budgets are representative, the average monthly income of European families was then nearly £163 in Salisbury and more than £148 in Bulawayo. Not all of these receipts were attributable to the employment of the main bread-winner. The earnings of the wife and 'other income' (including property rentals, interest and dividends) accounted for about £30 of the family's total receipts in Salisbury and for £24 in Bulawayo.[12] These findings indicate that cash earnings of the average European head of family in these towns would be in the order of eight times greater than those of the 'skilled' upper 3 per cent of the African labour force and sixteen times greater than the cash wage of the average African urban employee.

Broadly speaking, the special character of the urban pattern in these territories stems from a blend of two contrasting properties: rigidity and fluidity. Rigidities are apparent in the terms on which Africans and Europeans are brought together and organise their relationships with one another. But these very rigidities have demanded from Africans a high degree of flexibility. The system has required most urban Africans to keep a 'foot in two camps'—one in his native district, the other in a wage earner's role outside it. For that matter, a high proportion of the European residents do not have both feet planted on Rhodesian soil. A substantial percentage are recent immigrants whose ties with the mother country have not been completely severed. It would appear that the character of cities in this part of Africa is some distance removed from that of the cities about which a distinguished economic historian of a generation back once wrote:

> The city is primarily an organ of civilization. As such, it has two main functions. On the one hand, it is an organ for the fusion of different races, tribes and castes; on the other, it is an organ for the differentiation of classes. By race, tribe and caste I mean social distinctions that resist and prevent social fluidity. By class I mean a social distinction that does not resist social fluidity, but promotes and gives a higher value to it.[13]

III. Urbanisation in the Context of Economic Growth

At this point, it may be appropriate to reflect on the wider significance of urbanisation in the Rhodesias and its relationship to economic growth. Until recently, many economists regarded the emergence and expansion of cities as a sound indicator of favourable change in the economy at large. After all, the argument went, the emergence of cities was possible only after productivity in agriculture had advanced sufficiently to feed the non-agricultural population. Further, in the build-up of transactions between urban and rural areas, cities would be cast in the role of suppliers of manufactured goods and services. Thus the natural course of evolution for a developing economy was held to be one in which the distribution of the labour force would shift progressively in favour of secondary (manufacturing and processing) and tertiary (services) activities and away from primary (agricultural and extractive) activities.

Urbanisation was expected to play an important part in the expansionary process. For technical reasons, most modern types of manufacturing could be conducted most efficiently in agglomerations in which the heavy overhead costs of the necessary supporting facilities could be spread. When thus clustered, production costs of individual firms were also expected to fall as a consequence of 'external economics'—such as the education of the labour force—

associated with an urban environment. Meanwhile, urban growth would itself generate secondary rounds of stimuli favourable to progress in the rural economy. New demands would be created, both for foodstuffs and for raw materials, which would propel the entire economic system forward. In the discussion of this process in the underdeveloped economies, another consideration has often been emphasised: the transforming power of urban modernism on traditional attitudes. An urban atmosphere, it has been maintained, stimulates productivity in the indigenous economy by exposing some of its members to regular rhythms of work and to new types of discipline. It is thus expected to instil new, and more productive, habit patterns as well as to condition tastes in a manner likely to unleash fresh incentives for sustained work.

More recently, it has been realised that this portrait of the economic role of cities in underdeveloped economies may be more accurate as a statement of desirable effects than as a description of reality. Indeed, cities in the underdeveloped world may not possess the 'generative' properties sketched above. They may, on the contrary, be 'parasitic', i.e., with effects that retard growth in the economy as a whole.[14] The classic case of the 'parasitic' city has usually been thought of as the tightly organised and self-contained colonial enclave which skims the cream of the indigenous system's able-bodied manpower and orients the bulk of its commercial activity abroad. Demand stimuli, whose effects might otherwise have spread throughout the local economy, thus largely leak away through expenditures on imports and through the repatriation of earnings. Meanwhile, the energies of a low-paid indigenous wage labour force are diverted from the tasks of raising production in the traditional system. In the extreme case of 'parasitic' urbanisation, the growth of cities might even provide a better index of economic deterioration than of economic progress. Circumstances are at least conceivable in which cities were swollen by refugees from rural distress—refugees who might have fled from a breakdown of law and order or who have been pushed out of agriculture by failure to gain access to land. A substantial part of the postwar urban growth in some South Asian cities can best be understood in these terms.

Which of these cases—the generative or the parasitic—best fits the relationship between urbanisation and economic growth in the Rhodesias? At first glance, it might appear that urbanisation in these territories has been of the generative variety. Without doubt, an impressive growth in aggregate real output has occurred during the period of rapid urban expansion. But the coincidence of these phenomena in time is insufficient to demonstrate a causal connection between them. Further exploration of the mechanisms linking urban growth to the economy at large is needed.

An inquiry along these lines can usefully begin with an inspection of the demand stimuli radiated from the expanding urban centres to the rest of the economy. The mere growth in urban numbers has swollen the demand for consumer goods and, most particularly, for food. The character of this demand, however, has obviously been influenced by the distribution of personal incomes. Among the Africans covered in the Southern Rhodesian urban budget surveys of 1958–59, food purchases accounted for more than 46 per cent of cash outlays.[15] European households, by contrast, allocated, in Salisbury, 20 per cent of family expenditures to food and, in Bulawayo, roughly 21 per cent.[16] The qualitative content of the food budgets of African and European households is, of course, totally different. African purchases are dominated by the cheapest foodstuffs; mealie meal (ground maize), low quality meat, dried and fresh fish, bread and sugar account for roughly 80 per cent of outlays for foods. Virtually all of these requirements can be met within the productive capabilities of the home economy. European food consumption patterns, on the other hand, include a much higher percentage of imported goods.

Despite some leakages into international trade arising from urban food purchases, urbanisation has still had favourable effects on Rhodesian agriculture. In one important respect, however, the generative impact of urban food demand has not been widely diffused. The greater part of the growth in marketable food supplies has been contributed by the European farming community. Participation of African farmers in this enlargement of markets has been much slighter. A number of factors have combined to yield this outcome; among them, the proximity of the European farming areas to the urban markets (as opposed to the remoteness of most African reserves), the low productivity of techniques in traditional agricultural practice, and the slow pace of adaptation of the African productive pattern to the requirements of the urban market. The expansion of food output by the European farming community augmented the demand for African labour. A substantial proportion of the African employees engaged by European farmers were drawn, however, from neighbouring territories. Extra-territorial workers, in the view of employers, could be hired at lower wages and, by virtue of their distance from home, were alleged to be more amenable to discipline.

The growth in home demand for manufactured consumer goods—and its consequent spread effects on the remainder of the economy—has perhaps been more directly influenced by the distribution of money incomes. The preference patterns of most Europeans (in whose hands effective consumer demand has been concentrated) have been heavily skewed towards imported manufactures. This is not to suggest that products of local manufacture were excluded altogether. European consumers have brought home-processed foodstuffs, beverages and tobacco in considerable quantity. The major soft-goods industries (particularly the manufacture of low-quality textiles), on the other hand, have been designed primarily to serve African buyers. The build-up of secondary industry on this base has been subject to limitations set by the money income at the disposal of the African population. Nearly half the disposable income of most urban African families has usually been earmarked for food purchases and, even then, food outlays have often been insufficient to maintain socially desirable standards of nutrition.[17] The local African market has been insufficient to absorb substantial outputs of locally-produced manufactures. Nevertheless, a modest amount of the demand stimulus for certain items—clothing and footwear, for example—has emanated from this source.

At another point, however, the consumption patterns of the European population have generated expansionary stimuli: in the demand for services that could be supplied by Africans. The ranking of 'domestic services' in the occupational distribution of the urban African labour force is impressive in both Rhodesias. As of 1956, this category accounted for more than a quarter of the urban African workers in Southern Rhodesia and for more than 17 per cent in Northern Rhodesia. These employments, to be sure, have augmented local demand. It may be pertinent to recall, however, that the analyses of economic growth worked out by the economists of the classical era described them—and for good reason—as 'unproductive' employments.

A more substantial 'generative' impact of urbanisation on the demand side can be traced through the effects of urbanisation on investment. The rapid expansion of urban areas during the post-war boom years quite naturally placed heavy requirements on the building and construction industry. Though the proportion of gross capital formation exclusively attributable to rapid urbanisation cannot be established with precision, a rough indication of its magnitude can be gleaned from the capital accounts of the Federation in the mid-1950s. (Unfortunately, the contribution of Nyasaland—the present Malawi—to these totals cannot be extracted, though it is safe to proceed on the assumption that its weight in gross investment for the Federation was then small.) These calculations indicate that, in the years from 1954 to 1958, capital expenditures unambiguously identifiable as 'urban' accounted for roughly one-third of the fixed capital formation recorded (see Table 5.8). These calculations probably understate the urban share, as they do not include capital expenditure of the central governments, a substantial part of which was undoubtedly associated with urbanisation. The inference that the urban share was in fact greater than the identifiable one-third is reinforced by the findings of the 1956 census on the geographical distribution of persons engaged in building and construction. The urban claim on European construction workers then amounted to nearly three-quarters of the Southern Rhodesia total and to nearly two-thirds of the Northern Rhodesian total; of the African wage earners in building and construction, roughly 46 per cent were urban-based in Southern Rhodesia and about 59 per cent in Northern Rhodesia (see Tables 5.4 and 5.5).

Imperfect though the data may be, one feature of the findings on

TABLE 5.8

Urban Gross Investment in Relation to Gross Capital Formation, Federation of Rhodesia and Nyasaland, 1954–1958 (in £1,000,000s)

	1954	1955	1956	1957	1958
I. Urban:					
a. Local authorities	10·5	10·9	12·6	13·6	12·1
b. Urban residential building	7·0	8·4	11·7	12·6	10·4
c. Urban industrial building	2·3	2·6	2·6	3·8	2·9
d. Urban commercial and other building	6·0	8·6	11·2	12·4	12·0
Identifiable Urban Total	25·8	30·5	38·1	42·4	37·4
Urban per cent of gross fixed capital formation	32·8%	33·7%	33·7%	33·8%	31·9%
II. Other Investment:					
a. Mining	17·5	21·9	25·4	19·9	15·5
b. Railways and statutory bodies (including electricity boards)	13·1	10·6	17·9	24·6	30·8
c. Agricultural machinery and equipment imported	3·3	4·5	4·8	5·5	4·1
d. Other machinery and equipment imported	5·2	6·3	9·3	10·9	10·3
e. Central government	13·9	16·6	17·6	21·9	19·5
III. Total recorded gross fixed capital formation	78·8	90·4	113·1	125·2	117·6

Note and source: Recorded gross fixed capital formation excludes changes in inventories as well as unrecorded items. Data are drawn from the *Monthly Digest of Statistics, Federation of Rhodesia and Nyasaland*, Supplement, Vol. VI, No. 3, p. 9.

the urban share of gross investment is especially striking. If the three components of investment most directly linked to mounting urban numbers (urban residential building, capital expenditures of local authorities and 'urban commercial and other buildings') are compared with the capital formation recorded in the productive sectors responsible for the bulk of foreign exchange earnings—mining and agriculture—it appears that in each year of this period capital expenditures on the first group of items exceeded those on the latter. If the urban component of central government capital expenditure could be established, it would probably turn out that the capital expenditures attributable to urban growth exceeded capital spending on directly productive enterprises, including the plant and equipment expenditure of industrial establishments as well as those of mining and agriculture. It may at least be questioned whether such an allocation of capital was compatible with the build-up of productive capacity at rates desirable in an underdeveloped economy.

Quite apart from the implications of this mix of capital formation for the growth rate of the economy, it is nevertheless clear that the investment demands generated by urbanisation did radiate further stimuli throughout the economy. In the first place, urban building augmented the demand for labour. During the boom years of the 1950s, employment in building and construction claimed a sizeable share of the urban labour force.[18] At the same time, the rising activity of the building and construction industry, much of it associated with urban expansion, had important linkages to the small but growing manufacturing sector. Local suppliers of building materials—notably of cement, bricks, tiles and (to a lesser extent) of iron and steel—emerged to fill much of this expanding market space.

A comprehensive analysis of the relationship between urbanisation and economic growth on the demand side should, of course, take account of the current expenditures of governments. Unfortunately, the impact of urbanisation on these expenditure items cannot be satisfactorily established. That urban growth has enlarged expenditure on current account is, however, self-evident. The mere growth in numbers has called upon governments to supply educational, health and sanitation services in increasing volume. In the context of the Rhodesias, a substantially heavier share of these outlays were allocated for the benefit of the European than for that of the African population. Nevertheless, the growth of expenditure on these services has swollen the income stream.

From the demand side, it would appear that the mechanisms associated with urban growth in the Rhodesias have had a stimulating effect on the economy. What then have been the consequences of urbanisation for the stimulation of production on the supply side? Two distinct issues are pertinent to the consideration of this aspect. The first concerns the manner in which agglomeration has itself induced economies and efficiencies in production that would not otherwise have been within reach in modern lines of production. The second concerns the extent to which urban development has—or has not—had negative effects on the productive capabilities of the traditional economy.

The economic structure of the urban communities, which (particularly in Southern Rhodesia) has been heavily oriented towards service activities, has not lent itself ideally to the cost-reducing effects expected from geographical concentration. The case for dynamic efficiencies from urbanisation is usually related to manufacturing, an activity which still accounts for only a small fraction of the urban labour force. The services available in urban areas—particularly those of transport, communication and power—may well offer cost advantages to manufacturers in such settings. Though some cost reductions have undoubtedly been achieved, it cannot be said that they have stimulated a dramatic increase in urban manufacturing activity.

In the theoretical literature on economic location, considerable emphasis is also given to the efficiency-stimulating effects flowing from the development of a pool of skills through urbanisation. Moreover, it is maintained that an urban climate is conducive to a re-shaping of work attitudes, thus fostering improvements in labour productivity. At least as far as the African work force is concerned, this case for the economic benefits of urbanisation in the Rhodesias is weak. The migratory pattern of employment, and the high rates of turnover associated with it, have frustrated the development of a substantial pool of African skills.[19] It is no doubt true that conditions of urban employment have demanded a considerable change from rhythms of work to which most

Africans were accustomed. But this effect is less a function of urban life *per se* than of the disciplines of wage employment in any location.

The larger and more interesting question about the impact of urbanisation on production concerns its effects on the wider economy, and particularly on the performance of the indigenous economic structure. One aspect of this is abundantly clear: the claim of urbanisation on the African labour force has been highly selective. Urban labour demand has concentrated heavily on the traditional economy's resources of able-bodied adult males. At one stage in the evolution of the migratory labour pattern, techniques in traditional agriculture were such that its prime manpower could be spared temporarily without sacrifice in the output of traditional agriculture. At the same time, the absence of a high proportion of its most vigorous members clearly stripped the African community of manpower which might otherwise have been allocated to expanding its agricultural productivity. Whether or not the energies of African workers would have been so applied if their presence in the traditional community had been uninterrupted is open to doubt. In all probability, some forceful external stimuli for innovation would have been required to accomplish a transformation in agricultural productivity. At least it can be said that Africans in those districts with access to farm produce markets have been less disposed to accept wage employment and more inclined to intensify agricultural production than have those from more isolated districts.[20]

Conceivably, negative effects on the production of the indigenous economy arising from the claim of towns on its ablest manpower might be more than compensated for should contact with urban life alter the skills, incomes or attitudes of African workers in ways that led to improvements in agricultural productivity. Much that is pertinent to complete assessment of these possible relationships remains unknown. On the surface, there would appear to be little to support the conclusion that urban contacts have transmitted many useful skills to the indigenous economy. After all, few Africans in the urban wage-labour force have received a significant degree of training. Moreover, the few productive skills that may have been acquired in an urban environment are not directly applicable to the tasks of agricultural uplift.

The possibility that earnings of urban wage earners may later flow back into indigenous agriculture (and with favourable consequences) deserves fuller consideration. On this point, the results of the urban African budget surveys supply several clues. In particular, they are instructive in indicating the general orders of magnitude of money transfers to the rural areas from the current income of urban employees. The gross flow was reported to have amounted to about £502,000 from the four main towns of Southern Rhodesia in 1958–59 and to roughly £246,000 from the eight towns surveyed in Northern Rhodesia in 1960. Even so, this accounted for only a petty proportion of the current outlays of urban African wage earners; the Southern Rhodesian studies suggest that only about 3·2 per cent of the aggregate outlays by urban Africans were allocated in this manner and in Northern Rhodesia the percentage was even lower—1·6 per cent.[21] These calculations fail to take into account the flows in the reverse direction in the form of goods transferred from the rural areas to augment the income of urban Africans. Though the aggregative significance of these transfers cannot be established, it is nevertheless clear that some groups of urban African workers receive more support from rural relatives than they transfer to them (see Table 5.9). Single men form the only group from which the flow in favour of rural areas is consistently positive. Among urban African families, some with much above-average income levels are in a net deficit position with respect to urban-rural transfers.

No budget surveys of a type that would assist in identifying the disposition of current flows from urban relatives have been taken among rural African families. Presumably, the bulk of these cash receipts were used to augment rural consumption. Conversion of urban earnings into capital improvements in agriculture, to the extent that it occurs, is more likely to be financed from savings accumulated over a substantial period of wage employment than from the current income flows recorded in the urban budget studies. In Southern Rhodesia's main towns, it would appear that the recorded money income of Africans exceeded recorded

TABLE 5.9

Monthly Flows of Money and Goods between Urban Africans and Rural Areas, Southern Rhodesia

Flows are measured in shillings and pence; (+) indicates flow favours rural areas; (−) indicates flow favours urban areas.

	Salisbury (1957–58)	Bulawayo (1958–59)	Umtali and Gwelo (1959)
Unrationed rent-free families by quintile income groups			
Highest	−9·4	+18·9	+16·10
Second	+1·7	+ 2·11	+ 1·8
Third	+0·2	+ 2·0	+ 0·2
Fourth	−0·6	+ 3·1	− 1·0
Lowest	−0·8	+ 0·6	− 3·3
Unrationed families in own houses by quintile income groups			
Highest	+6·9	0·0	
Second	+2·10	− 2·0	
Third	−1·2	+ 2·0	
Fourth	+0·1	+ 5·2	
Lowest	−1·4	− 1·10	
Single men	+6·2	+10·4	+10·1

Sources: Second Report on the Urban African Budget Survey in Salisbury, 1957/58, Salisbury 1959; *Second Report on the Urban African Budget Survey in Bulawayo, 1958/59*, Salisbury 1960; *Second Report on the Urban African Budget Surveys Held in Umtali and Gwelo in July, 1959*, Salisbury 1960.

expenditures (including current transfers to rural relatives) by about 6 per cent in 1958–59; a similar percentage was reported for Northern Rhodesian main towns in 1960.[22] Part of this 'unaccounted for' category was probably allocated to the purchase of large items—such as bicycles or motorcycles—that would not appear in monthly budget calculations. The residual portion available for transfer to the rural areas cannot be precisely established, but the aggregate sums would not appear to have been large. Nor does it follow that such accumulations would ultimately flow into agricultural improvement. If the parenthetical comments found in the reports of various district commissioners portray the situation accurately, more Africans return to their home districts determined to establish themselves as petty retailers than the market can sustain.

Since the conversion of traditional tenures to private ownership under the Native Land Husbandry Act in Southern Rhodesia, some urban employees have accumulated funds to purchase land in the African areas. It is not clear, however, whether the new landowners have bought intending to become progressive farmers or whether they have simply sought to regain a sense of security in traditional society. But even if funds flowing into productive improvements in agriculture are insignificant in magnitude, there still may be a sense in which contact with the money economy reinforces productivity improvements in agriculture. Fragmentary evidence indicates that, once exposed to the money economy as wage earners, Africans are more likely to produce for market upon their return to agricultural pursuits.[23] This effect, however, is not necessarily related to urbanisation. It might equally well have occurred through wage employment in a non-urban setting; in fact, the carry-over to African farming may be more forceful among those who have worked on European farms.

The various effects of urbanisation on the growth of output throughout the economy cannot be precisely quantified. It would appear, however, that the conditions of urbanisation in the Rhodesias have contained parasitic elements. They have not taken the extreme form found in some other parts of the world. Expansion of monetised economic activity in urban centres has not, for example, had a destructive backwash on traditional crafts similar to the one experienced by certain Asian countries; that this has not occurred is primarily a reflection of the low degree of development of indigenous 'manufacturing' in this part of Africa. Nor has contact with urban life had seriously harmful consequences for production through the creation of a sizeable class of 'educated unemployed' or, more properly, of a group partially assimilated to Western ways who disqualify themselves from work that soils the hands. Even though no acute symptoms of parasitism have been visible in this part of the continent, the suspicion remains that urban growth has suppressed productive improvements that might otherwise have been achieved within the indigenous economy. Meanwhile, the generation of external economies in urban-based production has not been highly conspicuous.

It would thus appear that the relationship between urbanisation and economic growth in this part of the continent is ambiguous. Some generative properties, to be sure, have been associated with the growth of cities. Their force, however, has been weakened by the conditions governing the distribution of income. Moreover, the expansionary stimuli themselves have been channelled largely towards productive activities organised by Europeans. In food production particularly, the potential impact of the growth in urban demand on African producers has been blunted. Meanwhile, Africans, by no means all of whom are residents of the territory in which urban growth has taken place, have shared in this process largely as wage earners. In this capacity, their energies have not been available for the tasks of improvement in indigenous agriculture. But if the generative impact of cities has not been notably strong, neither have been their parasitic effects. The latter must be thought of in terms of the productive uses to which the resources claimed by the urban economy might otherwise have been put, and of the different pattern of economic growth and income distribution that might then have emerged.

IV. Questions about the future Economic Role of Urban Centres

The experience of urbanisation and its relationship to economic growth examined in the preceding section has been concerned with an era in which economic life has been conducted within a framework established by a unique type of political and social system. That system has been and is being challenged. What forces are likely to shape the urban pattern in the future? A brief consideration must now be made of the more important economic factors which affect the urban pattern and with which economic policy must deal.

Perhaps the most immediate implication of change in the political balance is that one of the sources of generative impulse from urban centres—the influx of European immigrants—is likely to diminish sharply, if not to evaporate altogether. The effects of this stimulus for the improvement in the real income and productivity of the African population have not been conspicuously favourable. Nor has the allocation of resources to the build-up of towns at standards acceptable to Europeans constituted the most desirable allocation of capital resources, even though part of the finance so allocated was specific and would not readily have been available to augment the productive capacity of the economy. Whatever the long-term wisdom of this expenditure, it has at least spawned and sustained local industries supplying building materials and has generated employment in urban construction. Deceleration in the growth of the European population (if not an absolute decline in European numbers) is also likely to affect another important source of employment for urban Africans: i.e., domestic services.

Other established lines of employment in the urban pattern may be less vulnerable to change in the political environment. Urban employments associated with importing and exporting activities are regulated primarily by the state of foreign demand, rather than by local political arrangements.[24] Nor is the overall output of manufactured consumer goods likely to be severely affected by a decline in European demand. The geographical distribution of manufacturing activity between Zambia and Rhodesia, however, may be altered by political events (especially by a rupture of the common market arrangements of the federal period). Nevertheless, the short-term prospect is one in which the demand for urban labour in familiar forms is likely to be dampened. Concurrently, several changes on the supply side of the urban labour market are likely to occur—and quite independently of a further influx of workers from rural areas. Three aspects of this problem are particularly noteworthy: (1) the growth in labour supply arising from the natural increment in that part of the population which has been reasonably 'stabilised' in an urban environment; (2) the growth in labour supply associated with labour-displacing innovations; and (3) the availability of a pool of unemployed urban Africans.

On all three of these counts, the short-term problem of adjustment will probably be more formidable in Zambia than in Rhodesia. In the former, the proportion of the urban African population established in urban life—at least as measured by the ratios of heads of families to 'single' men in the working population and by the percentage of dependants in the total urban population —is substantially higher than in the latter. Even in the absence of any other factors tending to augment the urban labour supply, a substantial expansion of job opportunities in Zambia's urban centres will be required during the next decade simply to absorb the natural increment in the urban population of working age. This problem will also be present in Rhodesia, but the lower degree of stabilisation of African families in urban life reduces its dimensions there. The labour market in Zambian towns is also likely to be vulnerable to labour-displacing innovations. For some years, the number of Africans employed by the Copperbelt mining companies has tended to decline as newer techniques have been introduced. This trend may well continue to release more African labour than can be absorbed in the upgrading to positions formerly occupied by Europeans. The nature of the employment pattern in Rhodesia's main towns is less subject to labour-displacement through technical innovation. Additional complications in labour absorption are also presented by the growth of urban unemployment in the recent past. The magnitude of this problem is especially difficult to establish, as is the case in any society lacking a system of unemployment compensation. The results of the mid-1963 census throw some light on the matter, indicating that nearly 24,000 males (or about 14 per cent of the urban male labour force) were then unemployed but 'seeking paid work' in the nine main towns.[25] In Southern Rhodesia's four main towns, the unemployment rate among urban males was approximately 7 per cent at the time of the 1962 census.[26] The policy of adjusting the issuance of urban residence and work permits to fluctuations in urban labour requirements has had the effect of suppressing the emergence of open unemployment.

Absorbing the additions to the labour supply generated from within the present urban areas will itself be a considerable task in the years ahead. But, of course, the main towns will probably also continue to be fed by transfers from rural areas. In all likelihood, the glamour of urban life will attract newcomers for reasons other than the economic opportunities it can provide. This flow may indeed exceed the rates recorded in the recent past. After all, the restrictions imposed on the access of Africans to urban life in the days when towns were run primarily as European enclaves cannot be expected to be permanent. Meanwhile, should productivity in African agriculture fail to improve substantially, population growth in the rural areas may produce distresses that push people towards the towns. This possibility is by no means unthinkable. In Rhodesia, the partial implementation of the Native Land Husbandry Act has created a class of landless Africans but has failed to provide the technical supports required to raise agricultural productivity. In Zambia, the 1963 census revealed that overcrowding in African farming areas was far more serious than had previously been realised. Substantial urban growth on these terms would be a svmptom of economic deterioration, not of economic progress.

If this fate is to be averted, governments must address themselves more vigorously than their predecessors to the task of transforming traditional agriculture. The objectives of the job at hand can be stated simply: to create conditions in African agriculture which both raise its productivity and permit it to absorb productively the greater part of the natural increment in the rural population. The implementation of the required reforms, however, will not be easy; yet massive rural improvement is a necessary condition for healthy urban growth in the future.

Meanwhile, economic policy towards the present urban centres might usefully be framed with a dual objective: (1) to reinforce measures for agrarian reform by generating a growing demand for foodstuffs and industrial raw materials; and (2) to create urban conditions in which the potentially attainable external economies can be more fully realised than has been the case in the past. It would be consistent with both of these objectives to stabilise the present urban labour force by encouraging the urban settlement of families. At first, support from public funds would undoubtedly be needed to finance the additional housing required. This move would also augment employment opportunities in building and construction, generate increased requirements for marketable foodstuffs and for consumption goods of home manufacture, and create a climate more conducive to cumulative gains in efficiency. Restructuring the present urban centres, however, is both less essential and less demanding than an effective programme of agrarian uplift.

In short, the new governments in these territories now confront a choice between unambiguously generative cities (an outcome in which accelerated improvements in productivity, based on a stabilised urban work force, are achieved) and unambiguously parasitic cities (a possible outcome should agrarian transformation be neglected and should cities expand at rates faster than warranted by growth in demand for non-agricultural labour). When students of a generation hence seek to understand the phenomena of urbanisation in this part of Africa, they will be well-advised to begin their studies with an analysis of the course of events in the agrarian sector.

Notes and References

1 For convenience, pre-1964 names of territories will be used in contexts referring to pre-1964 events.

2 Only one community other than those listed as 'main towns' in Table 5.1 crosses the 20,000 threshold; Wankie, Southern Rhodesia, was reported to have a population of 20,200 in 1962.

3 *Historical Statistics of the United States, 1789–1945*, Washington 1949.

4 For estimates on the scope of urbanisation in African countries, see the *Economic Bulletin for Africa*, Vol. 2, June 1962, p. 63.

5 *Preliminary Report of the April/May 1962 Census of Africans in Southern Rhodesia*, Salisbury 1963, and *Preliminary Report of the May/June 1963 Census of Africans in Northern Rhodesia*, Lusaka 1964.

6 *Census Reports, Southern Rhodesia and Northern Rhodesia, 1946*, and *Preliminary 1961 Census Returns* as reported in the *Monthly Digest of Statistics, Federation of Rhodesia and Nyasaland*, November 1961.

7 One qualification should be added to the interpretation of the census returns on the number of African wage earners. Africans employed by other Africans in the rural areas were not covered by the census enumeration; their numbers, however, were believed to be slight.

8 Cmd. 9475, *East Africa Royal Commission Report*, London 1955, p. 201. The members of this commission, it may be noted, were highly critical of the racial and tribal restrictionism implied by this policy.

9 Though earlier legal disabilities have been relaxed, few Africans have had sufficient income to qualify as urban home owners. In the largest Southern Rhodesian city (Salisbury), 2,620 African families (in an African wage labour force of 102,000) were listed as 'owner-occupiers' in 1958. *Report on the Salisbury Demographic Survey, August/September, 1958*, Salisbury 1959, p. 12.

10 It deserves to be mentioned in passing that the 'pooled rental' system has been sharply criticised by the administrators of various urban townships; see the *Annual Report of the Director of African Administration, 1963*, City of Salisbury.

11 *Report on the Salisbury Demographic Survey, August/September, 1958*, p. 12.

12 *Preliminary Report on the Federal European Family Expenditure Survey, October, 1960*, Salisbury 1961, p. i.

13 George Unwin, "The Mediaeval City", in R. H. Tawney, ed., *Studies in Economic History*, London 1958, pp. 49–50.

14 This distinction has been drawn by Bert Hoselitz; see "Generative and Parasitic Cities", *Economic Development and Cultural Change*, Vol. 3, April 1955, pp. 278–94.

15 "The African Market in Salisbury, Bulawayo, Umtali and Gwelo", *Monthly Digest of Statistics, Federation of Rhodesia and Nyasaland*, Vol. 5, January 1959, p. iv.

16 *Preliminary Report on the Federal European Family Expenditure Survey, October, 1960*, p. 12.

17 Further light was shed on this point by an analysis accompanying the 1958 Report of the Urban African Affairs Commission in Southern Rhodesia. A 'minimum needs budget' for African families of varying size was constructed and designated as the Poverty Datum Line (PDL). When the actual circumstances of a sample of Salisbury's African families were measured against this criterion, it emerged that the 'sample of households had 57·1 per cent with incomes in the category "extremely impoverished", i.e., with incomes more than 35 per cent below the PDL level. Only 23·5 per cent had incomes within or above the limits of "PDL latitude".' The report concluded that 'the overall picture is one of poverty in all but a few households composed of childless couples or with one or two children. The majority of children in the sample are being brought up under conditions of extreme poverty and in want of the essentials of life.' D. G. Bettison, Appendix N, *Report of the Urban African Affairs Commission, Southern Rhodesia*, 1958, p. 193.

18 Not surprisingly, this share has dropped sharply in the recent past when the momentum of urbanisation slackened.

19 This is not to suggest that high labour mobility is necessarily incompatible with substantial economic advance. In nineteenth century American economic history, where conditions were quite different from those commented on above, high labour mobility probably made a substantial positive contribution to economic growth. See Stanley Lebergott, *Manpower in Economic Growth*, New York 1964, pp. 120–1.

20 For details on this point, see W. J. Barber, "Economic Rationality and Behaviour Patterns in an Underdeveloped Area: A Case Study of African Economic Behavior in the Rhodesias", *Economic Development and Cultural Change*, Vol. 8, April 1960, pp. 237–51.

21 *Monthly Digest of Statistics, Federation of Rhodesia and Nyasaland*, Vol. 6, January 1960, p. iv, and *Second Report on the Urban African Budget Survey Held in Northern Rhodesia, May to August, 1960*, Salisbury 1961, p. 15.

22 *Monthly Digest of Statistics, Federation of Rhodesia and Nyasaland*, Vol. 5, January 1959, p. iv, and *Second Report on the Urban African Budget Survey Held in Northern Rhodesia, May to August, 1960*, p. 7.

23 In this connection, M. Yudelman has argued that migrant labour is 'exposed to many of the "virtues" of scientific method and timing. Those who retain a residue of the techniques and values of the modern sector of the economy carry this form of "know-how" back to the African areas . . . the most progressive producers are frequently those who have been in the wage economy for some time': *Africans on the Land*, Cambridge, Mass., 1964, p. 133.

24 Barring, of course, the effects on Rhodesia's exports of her unilateral declaration of independence and the loss of export advantages in the British market.

25 *Preliminary Report of the May/June 1963 Census of Africans in Northern Rhodesia*, p. xiv.

26 *Final Report of the April/May 1962 Census of Africans in Southern Rhodesia*, Salisbury 1964, p. 71.

6

Structural Discontinuities in African Towns: Some Aspects of Racial Pluralism

LEO KUPER

THIS IS an analysis of the discontinuities in the social structure of African towns which have their basis in racial pluralism.[1] It describes some of the characteristics of the structural discontinuities, and some of the processes of change in their racial character and extent. Discussion is confined mainly to new towns in White settler societies, and to two situations of change: transfer of power to the African majority, and—quite hypothetically since there are few indications of it anywhere—a sharing of power between Africans and non-Africans.

I

By way of an extended introduction, I want to argue the case that African towns should be studied as structures in their own right. In particular, I suggest that it may be misleading to emphasise the qualities of the two parent societies, African and European, before contact, and to seek the key to the interaction of their members in some compounding or combustion of these qualities. It is likely to be even more misleading when the parent societies are identified

NOTE: *The notes and references for Chapter 6 will be found on page 149.*

with the developmental or morphological models of classical sociological theory.

By this I do not mean to imply that the culture and structure of the societies in contact or prior to contact do not have great relevance for the nature and results of their interaction. I argue only that preoccupation with the genetic approach may divert attention from regularities inherent in the context of racial pluralism. For example, a relatively low value placed on education by White townsmen, and a high value by their fellow African townsmen, as seems to be the case, can be explained by reference to the structure of White settler society and the different opportunities for dominant and subordinate groups, and not by reference to the values of the parent societies.

Regularities in interaction may occur, within certain limits, regardless of a wide range of variation both in the racially dominant and the racially subordinate groups. Thus racial segregation was ubiquitous in the new towns of Africa, both under colonial and settler regimes, notwithstanding the immense variety of the parent societies from which African and White townsmen derived. It seems to have made little difference to the pattern of racial segregation whether the colonising power was committed to a policy of assimilation or of separation, or whether the parent African societies were centralised kingdoms with established procedures for the segregation of strangers or acephalous societies segmented into kinship groups, nomadic or sedentary, agricultural or pastoral, warlike or peaceful.

The genetic approach may also mislead, by encouraging the analyst to perceive the townsmen as creatures of antecedent custom, and thus to underestimate the flexibility of the relationship to custom, the capacity of persons to use different cultural idioms in different social contexts and the role of human creativity.[2] However deeply an individual may have accepted the traditional authority of custom, there is certain to be some independence from particular customs and some measure of an instrumental or manipulative approach. Cultural pluralism is likely to foster these tendencies. Since the new towns of Africa present a great diversity of culture, they offer opportunity for comparison, they encourage experiment, improvisation and detachment from particular customs, and they invite selection between different customs, either generally or in specific situations.[3] Hence, accepting the significance of antecedent custom, it becomes important to analyse the structures and processes of urban society as they influence choice between different patterns of behaviour, and definitions of situational relevance.

This is, more or less, the argument advanced by Gluckman in a paper on "Anthropological Problems Arising from the African Industrial Revolution".[4] He attacks the 'tribalistic' tradition of anthropological urban African research which takes tribal society as its starting point of analysis. He emphasises instead a theoretical orientation, which views Africans in urban areas as acting primarily within a field structured by the urban industrial setting, and he demonstrates how, in certain urban situations, common urban interests and industrial forms of organisation may prevail over tribal interests and tribal forms of organisation.[5] Similar arguments apply to White townsmen, who also act within an urban context, responding to its cultural and structural pluralism, and to varied influences and imperatives of different situations. For Whites too the principle of situational selection operates, as may be seen for example in the different manifestations of tradition in church, state and industry.

The significance of antecedent custom may also be weakened by selective migration to the cities. Neither urban Africans nor Whites are fully representative of their societies of origin. The new towns may be expected to draw disproportionately from the adventurous, the rebellious, the discontented, the lowly placed, the young and those with modest expectations in their traditional societies. The very qualities which carry them to the towns may also predispose them to reject tradition and to deviate from established custom. Hence the influence of antecedent custom may often be expressed in the breach rather than the observance; or the leeway in custom may be so manipulated that what is exceptionally permitted in the old society becomes normative in the new.

Moreover, antecedent custom may have little or no relevance for many of the situations and relationships in the new towns. This is specially true for migrants from African societies which have no urban tradition. Initially, they are obliged to find many of the norms for appropriate behaviour within the towns themselves; later these norms become part of the traditional culture, not necessarily as guiding behaviour within the confines of the traditional societies themselves, but as knowledge of urban ways. So too, the norms of European urban society are often inappropriate, or transported with difficulty, in part because they are not compatible with urban African pluralism. Europeans are also obliged to find many of the norms for appropriate behaviour within the new towns, or they are obliged to invent new forms. This process may be charted, for example, in laws regulating race relations, or movement into the towns and residence within it, or curfew laws and labour regulation. Among Africans, the process may be observed in the improvisation and vitality of African urban settlements or in the varied experiments in formal association.

The emphasis on antecedent culture and structure is often accompanied by the use of the developmental models in sociological theory. The extreme points of the evolutionary process, or social polarities, are identified with the societies in contact. The parent societies of Whites are perceived as secular, or as characterised by *Gesellschaft* or organic solidarity, while the parent African societies are perceived as sacred, or in terms of *Gemeinschaft* or mechanical solidarity. If polarities of social traits are used, then the qualities of universalism, evaluation by achievement and specificity of obligations may be imputed to the parent European societies, and particularism, the ascription of status and diffuseness of obligations to the parent African societies. The effect, in equating ideal types with empirical description, is again to divert attention from the actual qualities of the urban groups and the actual nature of their interaction.

Clearly, the appropriateness of a characterisation of the parent societies in terms of the developmental models or polar concepts is a matter for empirical research, rather than complacent assumption—complacent because of the implication of the superiority of more 'evolved' societies. The societies in contact may have greater similarities than is suggested by stereotypes based on evolutionary models. Afrikaner and Xhosa societies, at the time of their first contacts in South Africa, could hardly be regarded as examples of very different forms of social organisation and development. There may be much affinity in values and organisation between a British bureaucracy and an African one, as Dr Audrey Richards shows in her analysis of Baganda "Traditional Values and Current Political Behaviour".[6] Even in cases where the parent societies are of sharply contrasted type, and the colonising society emphasises norms of universalism and achievement, there may nevertheless be available in the culture of the colonising society a very different model for behaviour towards, or administration of, 'backward' peoples or peoples of other race—a model which rests on the ascription of a subordinate status and discrimination in a wide range of roles. The significance of a heritage of *Gesellschaft* in the dominant society is thus much diminished in contact with Africans.

In some ways plural societies seem to be *sui generis*; they do not readily fit the developmental sequences or models. In theory, we might expect a complex division of labour and industrialisation to be associated with an emphasis on universal criteria of relationship rather than on bonds of race or blood, on achievement rather than ascription, and on specific contractual obligations rather than diffuse obligations attached to status. And yet, among urban African societies, it is precisely where the division of labour and the development of industry are most advanced—in South Africa—that the principle of ascription on the basis of race is extended to the widest range of situations and relationships.

No societies correspond precisely to the ideal types of sociological theory. The models exemplify tendencies or relative emphases. Empirically, elements of sharply contrasted ideal types and social polarities, in terms of structure and culture, are found within the same society.[7] It is the extreme nature of the contrasts, the extensive range of behaviour and the many segments of population affected by these contrasts, and the complexities of their juxtaposition and intermingling, which render African urban pluralism highly distinctive.

The African sector of the urban society cannot be described as

Gemeinschaft, the White as *Gesellschaft*. Rank is not defined for Africans by ascription, and for Whites by achievement: one cannot say that occupation determines rank for Whites and that rank determines occupation for Africans. There is a complex interplay of ascription and achievement in both sectors. The ascriptive criterion of race defines the respective life chances of the groups, affording Whites extended opportunities for achievement while restricting the scope for African achievement. Within this overall ascriptive framework, there is evaluation by achievement, but of a different character in the two sectors. Because of the narrow range of opportunity for Africans, high occupational achievement is relatively rare, and it may be accorded much greater prestige by both groups than the comparable achievement of a White. At the same time, this achievement does not qualify an African for those rights of citizenship which are enjoyed by Whites of the meanest occupational achievement. Indeed, one of the most characteristic expressions of this intermingling of societal types is status incongruity at the highest and lowest status levels of the racial groups. The high occupational achievement but low racial status of Africans confronts the low occupational achievement but aristocratic racial status of Whites; and tension is acute precisely between these strata of incongruous statuses.

The manner in which polar qualities or developmental models are intermingled may vary from one institution to another and even within the same institution. Thus, in the religious ethic, such universal standards as the quality of faith may guide the pursuit of salvation, while, in the religious organisation, the ascriptive criterion of race serves to segregate worshippers and to discriminate between them in houses of worship and in stipends to pastors. This discontinuity between ethic and structure is not invariable: the ethic may be modified to accord with the discrimination in structure, or the discrimination modified in greater congruence with the ethic.

The developmental theories and morphological forms of classical sociological theory may be adequate for the analysis of African plural societies, as long as they are not identified with empirical description of the different units. But perhaps new models for the analysis of plural societies may yield greater insight, or perhaps different questions should be asked in using the present models. The same problem arises as in the use of separate models of conflict (or cleavage) and of integration. Each yields relevant information as to the separate action of these social forces, but the really crucial questions concern the relations between them. Similarly, in using the developmental (or morphological) models in the analysis of plural societies, the important questions may concern the manner in which elements from the different models are combined in new patterns, and the distribution of these patterns in different structures and institutions. It may be valuable to enquire whether plural societies are characterised by distinctive patterns, transcending the accepted types, and, if so, the manner of their relationship to each other and to the structures in which they appear.

II

The distinctive characteristics of the structural discontinuities in the new towns are: first, the extreme social distance between the racial groups; next, the presence of special mechanisms, parallel and intercalary,[8] for both maintaining and bridging the discontinuities; and third, a dissonance or nonalignment between structure and culture, in the sense that cultural differences and structural divisions do not coincide.[9]

Extreme social distance arises from the convergence of many sources of power in the dominant group—political control, the wealth of industrial and commercial enterprise and cultural resources in technology, science and techniques of organisation. It is expressed particularly in stratification and segregation, and less markedly in social etiquette. Indeed, etiquette may be more expressive of extreme social distance in traditional African societies. Presumably elaborate forms of deference are not readily compatible with industrial and commercial development.

Race is the primary basis for stratification in the society as a whole. It pervades the general structure of the society, and it pervades all special or differentiated structures. The interaction between the general and special systems of stratification is a further source of extreme social distance. The interaction may be analysed, for example, in the hierarchical structure of employment, which is affected by social stratification in the wider society, recruitment to different levels of employment being from different racial strata. The following consequences seem to result.[10] There is a wider discrepancy between White and African wages, a greater discontinuity in the wage structure, than would be found between comparable levels of the wage structure in homogeneous societies of similar industrial development. The range of employment opportunities is restricted for Africans and expansive for Whites. Corresponding to this difference is a characteristic structure, with simplification at the lower or African levels and diversification at the White levels. This diversification is likely to include 'parasitic' posts, such as the 'non-working' supervisors of small African road gangs, and protected posts of unskilled work, with semi-skilled White status. The general structure of the society vests every White with a measure of authority, regardless of his position, so that authority rests partly on status outside the commercial or industrial enterprise, though exercised within it. Mechanisation is retarded and efficiency sacrificed in an attempt to maintain an occupational structure in harmony with the broad structure of racial stratification.

Comparable processes may be observed in the religious sphere, where differences in stipends reflect the general racial inequality and reproduce the wage structure of secular enterprise, and where the contrast between palatial and modest (or even daub and wattle) churches expresses the contrast in racial status, not differences in the concept or status of the deity. There is greater social distance between fellow worshippers of different race in consequence of the general stratification. Similar processes may be observed in politics and education. Moreover, the general stratification inhibits contrary processes which might transcend the racial discontinuities, such as class formation across racial barriers. Classes do form, but within each group and under the influence of the general racial stratification, which affects White and African class structure in different ways. Among Whites, the aristocracy of racial birth introduces some equalising tendencies. Among Africans, restricted opportunity enhances the significance of small differences and sharpens the awareness of social class.

Segregation is extensive, and interacts with stratification so that each is rendered more extreme. Africans and Whites live virtually in different urban worlds, and the African settlement is often a dormitory or satellite to the White. There is a wide disparity in housing standards, corresponding to the general racial discrimination. Since discrimination extends through the specialised structures, the disparity is expressed also in community facilities. Churches, administrative buildings, schools, clinics and shops all testify to the widely different statuses of the two races. In some respects the racial segregation resembles class segregation, but there are sharper contrasts in the standards of African and White areas; segregation is also more pervasive, and tends above all to exclude equal status contact; and it brings about greater social discontinuity. In the class structured society, there are often many levels of socio-economic residential status which shade off into each other. In the racially segregated White settler society, the transition is abrupt, there being little scope for residential differentiation among Africans.

Structural discontinuities between the dominant and subordinate groups are a potential threat to the political unity of the plural society. Indeed, a group which challenges this unity or seeks domination is likely to make deliberate use of structural discontinuities; thus, in South Africa, Afrikaners systematically created these separate ethnic structures in commerce, industry, culture, welfare, education and politics as weapons in their struggle for national domination. The dominant group, if it is to maintain its position, must therefore control the potentially disruptive consequences of structural discontinuities. The means of control are government regulation or force in a context of interdependence and stratification, and also such specific and typical mechanisms of control in plural societies as parallel and intercalary structures.

By *parallel structures*, I refer to a basic structural separation of the racial groups within the same organisation, combined with inter-racial contact and co-operation at various supervisory levels and effective control by the politically dominant racial group. The Christian churches in White settler societies are especially rich in parallel structures. For example, there may be segregated congregations, pastors of different race meeting together as a supervisory district missionary council, and together with lay representatives in an annual national conference to elect the office bearers of the church. Parallel structures vary in the nature of the activities which are separate or reserved for the dominant group or integrated, as well as in the structural and cultural patterns by which avoidance and contact are regulated. The variations in these experiments in integration by separation seem almost infinite and chart subtle differences in the pattern of race relations. But there are also regularities, as in the tendency for the racially dominant group to monopolise most executive functions and particularly financial policy and administration.

Parallel racial structures seem to arise mainly under the following conditions. There are shared interests, as in sport or religious conversion, which bring the members of different racial groups together, realisation of the interests being dependent on interracial co-operation. In the pursuit of these interests, the participants would meet as equals, as sportsmen or Christians, were it not for the parallel structures. The general racial inequality which pervades the society raises, for such specialised organisations as Christian churches, the problem of reconciling racial superiority and competition for ministerial stipends with racial equality and the non-competitive pursuit of transcendental or abstract goals. Cultural and class differences are often present, impeding ease of association. There is usually paternalism in the attitudes of the dominant group, and dependence in the subordinate group, but not invariably, since the parallel structure may be an interim response to the subordinate group's rejection of racial domination.

The functions of parallel racial structures are to avoid equal status contact; to assert racial inequality by the very fact of separation; and to reconcile inequality in competitive, and especially material, spheres with equality in noncompetitive ideal spheres, or the particularist criterion of race with such universal standards of qualification as religious virtuosity or grace. Parallel structures may have the same consequence as I suggested in the case of racial stratification in employment, namely that of restraining the diversification of positions for the subordinate group. Certainly, where Africans establish separate and independent structures, they may greatly extend the range of positions which are open to them, as for example in the Zionist churches with their many prophets and bishops.

Intercalary racial structures refer to structures inserted or forming between the racial groups, which serve both to separate and co-ordinate their activities; they may be formal or informal, institutionalised or in process of institutionalisation. Location advisory boards in South African towns will serve as an example. They consist of Africans representing the residents of segregated living areas and acting in an advisory capacity to the exclusively White city council, which exercises executive powers. They are linked to the council by a White councillor, who acts as chairman of the advisory boards, and a White administrator, who acts as director of African affairs. From the point of view of the Whites, this structural device facilitates government of Africans while excluding them from direct representation on the council and it provides a channel for transmitting instructions and for receiving views and reactions. For Africans, it facilitates being governed by providing the appearance of participation, a channel of communication, and a buffer between African residents and the city council.

Intercalary structures involve dualism in function, representation and identification. They are distinguished from segregated or parallel structures, such as sports associations or religious congregations, which serve many of the same functions for each of the racial groups. Intercalary structures serve different, though often complementary, functions for the two groups. Such structures are not identical with intermediate or marginal structures. For example, the conception of middle-class Africans as having a moderating role in White settler societies implies a dualism in their functions, and that they represent and identify with both racial groups, constituting, that is to say, an intercalary group by the definition I have used. But where identification is with fellow

Africans in a revolutionary struggle against White domination, the intermediate or marginal position of middle-class Africans in the class or economic system is not an intercalary position. Or again, by way of further example, the recruitment of Negro policemen for service in Negro districts during the period of civil rights demonstrations in the USA is based on a conception of an intercalary position with a moderating function. On the other hand, Africans have long been recruited to the police force in South Africa, where they act with much brutality towards fellow Africans, seemingly identifying with White policemen and acting as the representatives of White authority. Here again the intermediate position is not intercalary.

It seems to be in the nature of racial intercalary positions that they should be held by members of the subordinate racial group—an African 'boss-boy', for example, rather than a White foreman over African workers. In a racially homogeneous society, the position of a White foreman of working class background in a factory of White workers is generally conceived as intercalary, since it has varied functions for management and workers, is representative of both sectors, and evokes conflicting loyalties. But if the workers are African, then elements of dualism tend to disappear from the role of the White foreman who cannot identify with, or has difficulty in representing, Africans and therefore functions as an agent of management. Incumbency of intermediate positions by members of the subordinate group seems, in general, to be a necessary condition for the formation of intercalary structures, though not sufficient in itself.

Intercalary and parallel structures help to maintain the sharp racial discontinuities. There seem to be no comparable devices for maintaining cultural discontinuities, though segregated, parallel and intercalary structures, by the divisions they impose between the racial groups, encourage cultural distinctiveness. Even shared items of culture may acquire different significance for the racial groups as a result of the differences in structural context consequent upon structural discontinuity. This is most obvious in the case of common political institutions seen from the different perspectives of rulers and ruled, of subjects or active agents of government, and of objects or recipients of government. It may also be observed, for example, in membership of a Christian church, which is a mark of Westernisation and of distinctive status for persons of one racial group but of minor relevance for the status of other persons. It is an aspect of the exaggerated prestige accorded a member of a subordinate group for an achievement which is commonplace in the dominant group, thereby emphasising inferiority in the very moment of achievement.

Probably the meaning of most shared items of culture is affected by structural relativity. For this reason, participation in the same social values may be quite differently motivated in the racial groups. Moreover, the same values may serve different and, indeed, dialectical functions. Thus the attempt to realise democratic values by the subordinate group forces the dominant group to redefine these values. For the White radical, Marxism is an ideological basis for inter-racial co-operation; for the African radical it may justify racism by a racial identification of bourgeoisie with White and proletariat with African. Sometimes, the races appear to share the same cultural items, whereas in fact there has been a reinterpretation, as for example a change in the mood of worship from the sober gentility of White churchmen to the evangelical ardour of African churchmen, while the prayers, ritual and affiliation remain unchanged.

These different functions, meanings and interpretations of the same institution or values diminish the area of shared culture. But even so, there is greater continuity of culture, which diffuses and moves easily between groups, than there is of structure. Persons of different race may be effectively excluded from membership of many social structures; they cannot be so effectively insulated against acculturative influence and opportunity.

Finally, certain characteristic tensions result from the *non-alignment between structure and culture*. There is sharp tension between Africans and Whites at the point of maximum dissonance between cultural similarity and structural cleavage, namely in the relations between Africans of high achievement, who have acquired the culture of the Whites, and lowly Whites of poor achievement, to which I have already referred. From a different point of view this is a tension between the principles of evaluating status by achievement and of ascribing status by race. It is not surprising that acculturated Africans, after an initial accommodative phase in which they seek to be judged by the same standards of achievement as Whites, should be attracted by a reverse racism and a compensatory desire for a prescriptive right to high racial status.

The dissonance between culture and structure also affects relations among Africans themselves. Their cultural diversity receives small recognition, in terms of structure, from the dominant group; there is little or no exemption or emancipation from the common subordination. Within the African group, however, cultural differences function, as a basis for social differentiation, in much the same way as the means of production in Marxist theory. These differences are strongly emphasised, often as a basis of antagonistic division, and stand in contrast to common membership in a subordinate race. This is another form of the tension between ascription and achievement, but internal to the African group.

In terms of race relations, the consequences of cultural diversity among Africans are not entirely negative. The different distribution of cultural patterns and racial structures may serve to reduce racial tension by encouraging inter-racial association on the basis of interests which cut across the racial divisions.

The patterning of structural discontinuity and of cultural diversity varies in the different institutional spheres. There seem to be characteristic emphases on different structural forms. Thus, in the economic sphere, there is an emphasis on racial stratification in employment (and on segregation where there is equality of status, as for example, between traders). In religion, the characteristic structures are parallelism and voluntary separation; in education, parallelism and segregation; in government, stratification, segregation and intercalary structures. Similarly, the extent of cultural diversity varies, being at its maximum in the political sphere, and at its minimum probably in the educational sphere, at any rate at the higher levels. There may be regularities in the relationship between the forms of structural discontinuity and the nature and extent of cultural diversity and similarity. Thus parallel structures may be found where there is a shared culture within the framework of the institution and equality with reference to ultimate goals, intercalary structures where there is cultural diversity and explicit domination.

The different patterning of structural discontinuity and cultural diversity is often a source of tension between institutional spheres. This tension may be reduced or resolved by rationalisation, such as in the theory that spiritual equality has no relevance for temporal affairs; or there may be special devices to reconcile the different spheres, like the parallel structures in the Christian churches; or objectives and organisation may be changed in consonance with the dominant political or economic spheres. Alternatively, the tensions may be made explicit and indeed sharpened as an organisation seeks to express the logic of its own objectives and directly challenges the dominant values.

III

I have discussed the structural discontinuities as if only two racial groups were involved. This is largely the position in sub-Saharan Africa, outside South Africa with its large Coloured and Indian populations, and Kenya with its appreciable numbers of Indians. It is probably mainly in South Africa, and to a lesser extent in Kenya, that other settled racial groups are likely to be a significant factor in the process of change. These racial groups are often stereotyped as intermediate, with the implication that the transfer of their positions to Africans would give greater continuity in structure. This image is in some ways misleading, since a distinction must be drawn between stranger groups (corresponding to Weber's concept of 'pariah' groups), such as Indians in South Africa, and intermediate groups such as the Coloureds.

Indians hold some intermediate positions in the occupational structure: though South African commerce and industry are mainly monopolised by Whites, and most Indians are employed in manual work, there are appreciable numbers of Indian petty traders, some wealthy merchants and industrialists and a growing professional class. In educational level, Indians fall between Africans and Whites. In culture, they share with Whites traditions of urbanism and of commerce and they move more freely than Africans in the urban industrial environment. To this limited extent, Indians occupy a racially intermediate position. For the rest, the situation of Indians is marked by sharp cultural and structural discontinuity. The hesitation or reluctance of many Christian missionaries in South Africa to establish missions among the Indians greatly contributed to this situation. Islam and Hinduism, with their domestic rituals, remain the basis of a distinctive family life. Separate religious and cultural associations formed by Indians, together with segregation imposed by Whites, add to the insulation of Indians. There are few intercalary and parallel structures to link them with other groups, a further expression of their status as strangers.[11] Far from rejoicing as a third party in the conflict between Africans and Whites, Indians are a scapegoat for both the main racial groups. They are rejected by many Whites, who resent their commercial and competitive role, and they are rejected by many Africans, including strata for whom the removal or expropriation of Indian traders represents economic opportunity. At the same time, they hold so few intermediate positions that the movement of Africans into these positions would not materially bridge the structural discontinuities.

The Coloureds, by contrast, are an intermediate group. Though there are many divisions among them, including Islamic, their culture is largely a sub-culture of the dominant White groups rather than a distinctive culture. They are employed within the European sectors of the economy, at a higher level of skill than Africans, and do not compete as entrepreneurs. They are less segregated from other groups and less relegated to parallel structures than Africans. While they seek to maintain social distance from Africans, they in fact merge, physically and socially, with them and also with Whites. Both groups seem to feel some responsibility for Coloureds, and no political party has agitated for their removal, in contrast to the proposed expatriation of Indians. Coloureds bridge the racial discontinuities to a small extent and the South African government has responded to this threat by assimilating the administration of Coloureds under apartheid to the pattern of African administration and intercalary control.

IV

The process of change in structural discontinuities will depend on such antecedent conditions as type of economic development, extent of urbanisation, level and distribution of education and the racial and tribal composition of the population. And it will be decisively influenced by the manner of political change, whether evolutionary or revolutionary, and by the policies of the new government, whether directed towards centralised planning and state ownership of the means of production or continued encouragement of private enterprise. In this discussion, I am assuming evolutionary change, with a large measure of continuity in economic forms of development, and either a transfer of power to the African majority or a sharing of power between Africans and Whites; and I am drawing on recent experience to suggest some of the processes of change which might affect the extreme social distance between the races, the parallel and intercalary structures regulating their relations and the dissonance between structure and culture.

A transfer of power seems likely to have the following consequences. Since extreme social distance between Africans and Whites rests on the convergence of power, wealth and prestige, its basis is undermined by the transfer of power to the African majority. Possessing political power and the prestige of office, and responding to the desire or pressure to achieve an equilibrium in status, members of the African political elite either directly convert political power to wealth or seek alliance with the possessors of wealth. A new ruling class begins to form round the African and White elites of wealth and power. At this level, the boundaries of culture and structure come into closer alignment, many of the African elite being Western-educated. Segregation, at any rate in the form of White exclusion of Africans, can hardly persist in the face of political regulation, nor will it appear desirable when it no longer conserves privilege and prestige moves to the African political elite. In the process of desegregation, the parallel and intercalary racial structures immediately dissolve. The reaction of Whites may be expected to vary, some leaving the country in a spirit of disaffection, others seeking to retain a measure of exclusiveness in the domestic sphere or in such small associations as White separatist churches. Many will no doubt identify with Africans, and indeed overconform to African expectations,[12] experiencing a sense of frustration as they are denied full acceptance—the situation of the African évolué in reverse. The net effect will be to reduce the cultural diversity between the races.

I am assuming that, on independence, positions in government and economy are defined in much the same way as in the past, with extreme differences between the higher and lower positions. Initially it is not the structure which changes but the principle of recruitment; in the first instance, in government. The African elite moves into the highly rewarded positions previously occupied by Whites. The structural discontinuities remain, but they are transformed in part into structural discontinuities between Africans themselves. Inevitably they become a focus of political struggle. New opportunities must therefore be found for Africans, above all in the rapid economic expansion to which the African governments are committed, whether in state or private enterprise. Levels of skill may be raised by intensive training programmes and by apprenticeship under 'expatriates' serving for short terms, and organisation may be revised in closer relationship with available skills. There is some recruitment of Africans to senior positions in White commercial and industrial enterprises. But all these measures fall short of the high expectations raised by the struggle for, and the achievement of, independence. And the frustrated expectations find expression in political action directed against the present inequalities and towards a redistribution of opportunity and wealth.

Non-Africans are a first target of this political action, either in the form of an openly racist attack or a radical movement guided by Marxist thought. For members of the political elite, the sacrifice of non-Africans is one line of defence; but they are also committed to a policy of African advancement and may be expected to share much of the antagonism, or to feel ambivalance, towards non-Africans. There is thus convergence of sentiment between political leaders and protesting groups in support of opportunities for Africans by displacement of non-Africans.

Moreover this policy of Africanisation, extending beyond government to commerce, industry, education and religion, is conceived almost as a crusade, in terms of assumptions widely accepted not only by Africans but throughout the world. These assumptions are that Africa belongs to Africans; that non-Africans are exploiters of Africans; that justice therefore demands the redistribution of the desirable positions they hold; and that past racial discrimination against Africans justifies present racial discrimination against non-Africans. Those most immediately vulnerable to expropriation are 'stranger' groups, but the White elite will not be long exempt from the pressure to redistribute positions and resources in favour of Africans. And even this redistribution will not blunt the demand for a more radical restructuring of the society.

Transfer of power to Africans, in terms of this argument, stimulates two partly conflicting, partly converging, movements, affecting the structural discontinuity in the society. The conservative movement attacks the racial basis but maintains the structural discontinuity in the system in a coexistence, or indeed alliance, of African and White elites: in effect, the major change is in the system of recruitment. The second movement expresses its radicalism racially in a more thorough-going policy of Africanisation and, economically, in demands for a radical restructuring of the society. In either event, the ascriptive criterion of race retains, at the least, the significance it held in colonial society, and perhaps gains enhanced significance.

South Africa is the only territory in which there might conceivably be a *sharing of power* between Africans and other racial groups. The present situation follows a recent transfer of power to Afrikaners, in which the processes are much as I suggested for the transfer of power to Africans but with the following differences. The elite formation is within a single racial group and bridges not the racial discontinuities but only the ethnic discontinuity between

English and Afrikaners. The Afrikaner elite of power and the English elite of wealth draw closer together as Afrikaners convert political power to wealth and prestige. Racial antagonism is directed particularly against Indians and expressed in a policy which aims at the redistribution of their resources, a policy only partly executed however, presumably because Afrikanerisation, in contrast to Africanisation, is widely condemned. Since Afrikaners are in the minority, many of the expectations raised in them by the acquisition of power can be satisfied by further economic development in an already industrialised society and by exploitation of the racial majority. There is consequently no political movement of economic radicalism among Afrikaners, the challenge to the established elite continuously taking the form of a more extreme racism.

Current policy seeks to maximise racial discontinuity. The maintenance of Afrikaner rule is conditional on the maintenance of both ethnic and racial separation. But since Afrikaners lack the resources for exclusive dominion, there has been some relaxation of their separation from other White groups, though this relaxation is a political issue between different factions. On the principle of racial separation, however, there is apparently little disagreement, and racial discontinuity is being systematically extended and rigorously enforced throughout the country. At the same time, economic development increases the interdependence of the racial groups, imposing the need for more intercalary structures to contain the racial discontinuities.

Against this background, it is difficult to see how a sharing of power can come about by evolutionary means, and what its political form might be—a multiracial balancing of representation, or universal franchise and racially based political parties, or inter-racial parties divided by interests other than race. And the manner and forms of political change would be closely related to change in the structural discontinuities. Presumably a series of structural changes would precede the sharing of power, such as the conversion of intercalary structures to parallel structures and experiments in junior partnership and controlled desegregation.

Perhaps the processes of restratification and the associated political movements may not be very different in character from those processes which I suggested might follow a transfer of power. There is first a conversion of racial discontinuities into class discontinuities, with little basic change in the structure of the society. It may be possible to observe this type of process in some of the English churches in South Africa, if they carry out their declared intention to abolish racial discrimination in stipends, to eliminate parallel structures and to encourage desegregated worship. The effect will be to liberate a process in the churches comparable to class formation, enabling educated Africans to associate more freely with educated Christians of other race in prayer and in church government, while maintaining a *de facto* segregation of the mass of African members, who are widely separated from their fellow Christians in education, culture, occupation, economic and residential status. Similarly, the abolition of such intercalary structures as advisory boards might liberate Africans for civic leadership with representatives of other races, without affecting the basic segregation of Africans, rooted in the poverty of poorly-rewarded manual occupations. The opening of senior positions in commerce and industry to highly qualified Africans would similarly detach a privileged minority from the general body of Africans. The combined consequences of such changes in the specialised structures (political, economic and religious) could be the creation of an African elite, moving with greater freedom across racial boundaries.

Structural discontinuities, though they would be less explicitly racial, would nevertheless persist, with the African masses remaining in much their former situation. Stratification might not be so extreme, since Africans would share political power. New opportunities might be found for them in partial Africanisation of the civil service, in new state enterprises and other economic development, and by discrimination against intermediate stranger groups. But most of the land would still be held by Whites, unless there was a deliberate policy of redistribution; African traders could hardly compete with established traders of other race, but would require a measure of protection; and Africans would still be recruited to the lowest positions, in the absence of special opportunities for favoured employment or quota systems to effect a more equitable distribution.

As in the case of a transfer of power, political radicalism would find its social base in extreme inequality and its ideology in common class interests and the frustration of expectations raised in the struggle. But the racism is likely to be more extreme, since the sharing of power could arise only in a situation where there is a substantial and powerful White minority; and the economic demands are likely to be more revolutionary, since Whites may be expected to resist strongly any attempt to expropriate or redistribute the resources they acquired in the economic development and industrialisation of the country.

V

I have suggested that plural societies may be somewhat *sui generis* I do not know to what extent this would be true of the structural discontinuities in White settler societies as I have described them. Extreme social distance is certainly not unique to African pluralism, but may be found in other systems of hereditary stratification. Dissonance between culture and structure is to be observed in class societies, though it is not so marked nor so extensive as in White settler societies, since there is greater continuity in structure, and cultural diversity is more restricted to subcultural variation. Probably the extensive use of both parallel and intercalary structures is a somewhat distinctive characteristic The process of change by which talented subordinates are absorbed into the dominant group, and the conflict between this conservative evolutionary process and revolutionary demands for radical restructuring of the society, are again not unique; nor is the fusion of the universalism of Marxist revolutionary thought with various ascriptive particularisms unique, though their combination in Marxist racism is distinctive of colonial pluralism.

If the structure of African towns in White settler societies is *sui generis*, then this derives not so much from the presence of an particular characteristic as from the combination of element which contribute to the structural discontinuities, and the extent and pervasiveness of the cultural contrasts and social cleavages. Whether unique or not, it is difficult to place this type of structure within the developmental sequences of classical sociological theory.

Notes and References

1 By racial pluralism I mean racial differences in association with cultural diversity and social cleavage. North American scholars often use pluralism as an antithesis to totalitarianism. In England, students of colonial societies use the term particularly to describe racial and ethnic cleavages within a politically-constituted unit. For discussions of the concept in the second sense, see M. G. Smith, "Social and Cultural Pluralism", *Annals of the New York Academy of Sciences*, Vol. 83, 1959–60, pp. 763–77; J. Rex, "The Plural Society in Sociological Theory", *The British Journal of Sociology*, Vol. 10, 1959, pp. 114–24; J. C. Mitchell, *Tribalism and the Plural Society*, London 1960; P. L. van den Berghe, "Toward a Sociology of Africa", *Social Forces*, Vol. 43, 1964, pp. 11–18; and L. Kuper, "Sociology: Some Aspects of Urban Plural Societies in Africa", in R. A. Lystad, ed., *The African World: A Survey of Social Research*, New York and London 1965.

2 It is usually Africans who are thought to be ruled by custom, while Whites are perceived as innovators. This invidious contrast seems to be present also in discussions of modernisation. There may be a projection of sentiments of racial superiority in a conception of Africans as creatures, and Whites as creators, of custom.

3 Some African migrants to the towns may respond by incapsulating themselves against the new influences, as Philip Mayer describes in his analysis of the 'Red' Xhosa: *Townsmen or Tribesmen*, Cape Town 1961.

4 In A. Southall, ed., *Social Change in Modern Africa*, New York 1961, pp. 67–82.

5 For a fuller discussion of this point, see A. L. Epstein, *Politics in an Urban African Community*, Manchester 1958.

6 L. A. Fallers, ed., *The King's Men*, London 1964, pp. 308–16.

7 Almond demonstrates this quality of 'cultural dualism' in political systems. See Gabriel A. Almond and James S. Coleman, eds., *The Politics of the Developing Areas*, Princeton 1960, pp. 20–5.

8 Max Gluckman, J. C. Mitchell and J. A. Barnes analyse the intercalary position of the village headman in three articles contributed to *Africa*, Vol. 19, 1949, pp. 89–106. ("The Village Headman in British Central Africa", "The Yao of Southern Nyasaland", "The Fort Jameson Ngoni".) See also Max Gluckman, *Order and Rebellion in Tribal Africa*, London 1963, p. 41 *ff*., and especially the reference on page 66 to Fortes's discussion of intercalary lineages.

9 See discussion by M. G. Smith, op. cit., p. 768, of correspondence, or divergence, between the boundaries of cultural and social sections, and comments on the discontinuous status order of plural societies.

10 I phrase this hypothetically, since the consequences I suggest probably need to be examined further.

11 The South African government is now creating special intercalary structures for Indians. This change in policy was announced as government recognition that Indians are an integral part of South Africa.

12 This process can be seen in South Africa where many of the English elite of wealth have moved from disdain for the Afrikaner political leaders to deference. There is no reason to suppose that racial differences will inhibit this process.

7

The Political Structure of Urban-Centred African Communities

WILLIAM JOHN HANNA and

JUDITH LYNNE HANNA

URBAN-CENTRED communities have been the cauldrons of African nationalism and they continue to be the radiants of modernity. One observer has remarked that 'urban centres have been the principal arenas of acculturation, and African politics are primarily urban politics'.[1] The histories of most nationalist movements begin in what are now world cities: Accra, Dakar, Dar es Salaam, Kinshasa, and their counterparts. Today, many of these cities are the predominant arenas of intense state politics, while the hinterlands shade into objects of state policy and conflict.

The provincial towns and their peri-urban areas are also arenas of acculturation and modern politics, although perhaps somewhat less intensely so. Often forgotten because of the glamour of the capitals, these 'other' urban-centred communities may have a cumulative impact upon a country's population—and may determine the future direction of its politics—to an extent far exceeding that of the capital. It is often through the political structures of these communities that the new territorial political system becomes visible to the urban masses and village peasants, and it is through the same agency that primordial ties profoundly affect political modernity.

NOTE: *The notes and references for Chapter 7 will be found on page 180.*

Urban-centred communities are therefore crucial arenas for the processes of integration. Our object in this paper is to describe the principal political structures of two urban-centred African communities[2] and suggest how these structures relate to the integrative process—the interweaving of modern politics and primordial ties into the fabric that is contemporary Black Africa.

Data were collected during our 1963 comparative study of Umuahia in Eastern Nigeria and Mbale in Eastern Uganda.[3] A few comments are in order on our choice of the research settings, each of which includes a relatively small town.[4] Two localities were studied, using the same research procedures, in order to facilitate the search for general patterns and deviant cases. Selection of urban-centred communities was based upon our interest in politics within a framework of urbanisation and the conviction that urban politics in Africa cannot be properly comprehended without including the peri-urban area within the scope of research. This decision stemmed from the wide variety of research suggesting a close rural-urban link. (The strength of this link is probably inversely related to the size of the urban centre, since the small town dweller is likely to have travelled a shorter distance and his rural ties are more likely to be regularly reinforced.) Relevant research syntheses include Daryll Forde's that 'urban migrants tended initially to maintain close ties with their communities of origin'[5] and David Apter's that 'characteristically the towns in new nations have not experienced a sharp break between rural and urban life, but rather a blending of one into the other'.[6] Our choice of communities centred on small towns was based upon the likelihood that there we would be able to learn more about the grassroots foundations of modern politics and government in Black Africa while at the same time obtaining a community-wide view.

To minimise community variation, we chose research settings which were similar in traditional African culture, size, function, location and level of industrialisation. The Ibo people of Umuahia share a number of characteristics with the Bagisu and some Bakedi tribes of Mbale, including decentralised authority and an emphasis upon achievement.[7] Both urban-centred communities have urban populations of between 15,000 and 20,000 and total populations of about 100,000 (including peri-urban areas which appear to have regular political, social and economic interaction with their urban centres). Both are administrative, agricultural and transportation centres about three hours' driving time from the capital city, and they have undergone moderate industrial development: a brewery and a ceramics factory are located in Umuahia, and there are coffee and cotton processing plants in Mbale.

Before turning to the results of our research, brief historical descriptions of the communities in question are in order. Near the turn of the century, when the first European arrived in the vicinity of what is now Umuahia-Ibeku, he asked the name of the area and he understood the Ibo reply to be 'umuahia'. This could be one of two Ibo words: one which means 'market place' (there was a village market nearby), and the other, 'children of the river bed' (which the people in the proximate village were called). Whatever meaning was intended, the name stuck. (See p. 161, below, on how Umuahia became Umuahia-Ibeku.) Missionaries soon came to the area and it was not long before an administrative post of the colonial government was established. The railway reached Umuahia in 1913 and significantly changed the character of the previously all-rural area. By 1916, European businesses such as the United Africa Company had agents in the area buying produce, primarily palm oil and palm kernels, but at no time were there more than a few dozen European residents. 'Stranger' Africans began to settle in a central area, which soon took on the character of a town. The new transportation network continued to favour Umuahia and, by 1945, as the centrepoint of main roads going in all four directions, it became the largest cattle-trading and distribution area in Eastern Nigeria.

The municipality of Mbale (the origin of the name is uncertain)[8] is the third largest urban centre in Uganda. A staging post for traders was established in the vicinity in the 1880s, but it was not until 1904 that a government station was installed. Telegraphic communication was set up in 1909 and the railway reached Mbale in 1931. For almost thirty years, Mbale was the railhead to the north and, as such, it was favourably located for trade and trans-shipment. In 1963, the urban centre of Mbale was dominated by Asians, both as general influentials and economic dominants. They arrived shortly after the turn of the century, reaching their zenith of power during the recent interim period between European rule and full Africanisation.

In this paper we shall examine the political structures of Umuahia and Mbale from two perspectives: the trans-cultural and the particular. Although it is quite true that 'Western' models are sometimes not appropriate for 'non-Western' data, we believe that generalisations can be made across the confines of these categories. Our examination includes three principal structures: (i) poly-ethnic divisions, (ii) intercalary influentials, and (iii) bifurcated influence and authority.

I. Poly-Ethnic Divisions

Urban-centred communities in Africa tend to be poly-ethnic,[9] and this structure probably provides the predominant channels for political solidarities and conflicts. Personal identities are largely based upon ethnic group membership and individuals usually participate in politics through a screen of ethnicity. By 'ethnic group' we mean a collection of individuals who mutually identify on the basis of origin and/or culture. The term 'group' itself implies 'a collection of individuals who stand in regular and relatively permanent relationships, that is, who act towards and in respect of each other, or towards and in respect of individuals outside the group, regularly in a specific, predictable, and expected fashion'.[10] We believe this characterises the political behaviour of ethnic groups in the research communities, but there is no intention of proving the point by definition. A number of observers have, however, noted that political groups in the emergent nations tend to be formed on the basis of non-political attachments, such as ethnic ties. Thus Lucian Pye writes: 'In non-Western societies the political sphere is not sharply differentiated from the spheres of social and personal relations.'[11] And Richard Sklar conceptualises the phenomenon as 'communal participation', which means that a political party is perceived as an extension of the member's social order.[12]

Some of the residents of urban-centred communities have been inducted into the new territorial politics and deeply touched by world culture, but the majority are objects of the new politics and outside the mainstream of world culture. For the latter, especially, the boundaries of identity between ethnic groups are clearly drawn and reinforced by unflattering inter-ethnic stereotypes. During our interviews, we often heard remarks like this: 'Clannishness is shown in all phases of the life of the people. Clannish interest is very much projected. . . . There is rivalry among all the clans.'

Poly-ethnic structures are obviously not new, but some of the inter-ethnic hostility is undoubtedly due to urbanisation, increased contacts and changing concepts of identity. Reporting on urban research in what is now Zambia, Clyde Mitchell has written: 'People in rural areas are apt to take their tribe for granted, but when they come to the town their tribal membership assumes new importance.'[13] And the results of Jean Rouch's research in Ghanaian towns indicate that ethnic ties are greatly strengthened by separation from one's rural home, residence in an urban area, and job competition in a free market situation.[14] Indeed, it may have been that, in the rural area, self-identity was in terms of a compound or village, but when in a more heterogeneous situation there is an enlarged self-identity to encompass the entire ethnic group. On this point, Immanuel Wallerstein notes that 'membership in an ethnic group is a matter of social definition, an interplay of the self-definition of members and the definition of other groups. The ethnic group seems to need a minimum size to function effectively, and hence to achieve social definition.'[15]

The intensified need to define oneself ethnically provides the basis for emotional conflicts over symbols of prestige. As a result, it becomes very important whether, for example, the representative of one group or of another speaks first at a community-wide event, and just such a situation increased tension between two ethnic groups in Mbale. The use of one ethnic group's name to identify a poly-ethnically inhabited town is an issue obviously charged with emotion, and so it was when the Ibeku people petitioned to have the town's official name, Umuahia, changed to Umuahia-Ibeku. Much of the political life of our two research communities involves prestige, and that is one of the reasons why some major decisions are made far from the public eye.

Our research settings appear to be characteristically polyethnic. The town of Umuahia-Ibeku is surrounded by the territories of five clans; one of the clans (Ibeku) nominally owns the town's land, but all contribute to the population of the town and are involved in the community's politics. Only one of the clans has any apparent historic unity; the rest are composed of semi-autonomous villages or groups of villages in which only recent external contacts have stimulated the sense of identification that is coterminous with the entire clan. The town itself is divided into nine main groups. There are the members of the five local Ibo clans, the stranger Owerri Ibo (culturally linked to the indigenes), the stranger Onitsha Ibo (with whom cultural differences are marked), Yoruba from Western Nigeria and Hausa from Northern Nigeria.

Mbale is located virtually on the boundary between Bugisu and Bukedi Districts. The former includes three Bagisu clans; the latter, six distinct tribes. The Baganda, under the leadership of General Semei Kakunguru, were sent by the British in the late nineteenth century to pacify and rule the people near what is now Mbale. The British gave the general twenty square miles of land for his efforts and many of the invaders remained. Their holdings and presence are a continuing source of irritation to some indigenous Africans. Within Mbale municipality all the above groups are represented, and there are two additional stranger peoples (excluding the rapidly departing Europeans, who numbered about 200): Kenyan Africans and Asians from India, Pakistan and Goa. Most of the Kenyans are labourers who, many employers report, are harder working than the indigenous Africans, who can easily return to their *shambas* (farms) for subsistence and cash crop income. The Asians, who constitute about one-third of the municipality's population, are divided into Hindu groups (Patels, Lohanas, Sikhs, Jains and others), Muslims (including Sunni, Shia, and Ismaili sects) and Catholic Goans. Thus one can say that in the Mbale community there are approximately nineteen main ethnic groups, most of which consider themselves distinct from all others.

The organisational expression of ethnic group solidarity and shared interest is the welfare association. Usually membership is based on ethnicity, and the organisation is dominated by an active minority which pursues the interests of the ethnic group (or the interests of the ethnic group's active minority) in politics, welfare and other spheres. These organisations are similar to what Riggs has called 'clects'. He describes them as follows: 'Each clect draws its membership from a particular community [in the present usage: ethnic group]; it applies its norms [without discrimination] to members of that community; and its poly-functional goals always include a communal-orientation as well as whatever economic, religious, political, educational, or social objectives constitute its manifest functions.'[16]

In one form or another almost every ethnic group in our two research communities has such an organisation. Those in Umuahia are usually clan unions or youth associations; the Asians of Mbale have their welfare associations, socio-religious groups and clubs; the Africans of Mbale use welfare associations and co-operative unions. Whatever their form, these organisations tend to have similar activities: development projects, welfare assistance for individual members, resocialisation of members (in Mbale, governmental community developmental organisations are also active in these areas) and, most important for our present purposes, a significant political role. Their political activities are seemingly internal, including the settling of disputes and the selection of local candidates. But both these activities have an external impact and, in addition, the organisations act as interest groups in the larger political arena. Illustrative of these points is the following comment: 'The greatest organisations for solving problems', said one of our Nigerian respondents, 'are the town and clan unions—the cultural organisations. They were the greatest weapons against the British. Once a decision is made, it is carried out. No power can force them to go back.'

Some welfare associations are equivalent to ward-level machines, the territorial party leaders (not the urban leaders) being the 'big bosses'.[17] Necessary for the development of machines are clientele groups which are willing to exchange their independent voting decisions for the rewards a boss can offer, which in the African case might include affection, well-being and the distribution of scholarships and jobs. These rewards are not the same as the American boss's food, shelter and clothing—usually not needed by the African who lives in, or can easily return to, his rural home—but they are the approximate equivalents because rising aspirations have created new necessities of life for which the African is willing to exchange his vote. Of course, it is important to remember that many of the rank-and-file do not have psychically possible alternatives, since a vote against the wishes of the boss is also an implicit rejection of the group and, because of the singularity of the individual's identity, a rejection of himself.

There are relatively few horizontal links in the poly-ethnic communities of Africa, with the result that identity-modifying cross-pressures are slight. 'The vast multiplicity of criss-crossing groups existing in more advanced societies', writes Eckstein, 'does not exist . . . in the less advanced. Group politics in such societies . . . become almost by definition social politics.'[18]

Several important horizontal links do exist in our research communities. The major religions of Umuahia include Protestantism and Roman Catholicism; in Mbale, Hinduism and Mohammedanism are added to the list. (The religious horizontal link is not relevant in examining the behaviour of Asians because religion is related to the formation of their ethnic groups. Traditional African religions are excluded from this discussion because of the village or compound locus characteristic in our research communities.) We found that about half the African ethnic groups are internally divided by religion, due to the establishment of competing missions within the group's territory. However, the unexpected result is intra-ethnic conflict rather than intra-denominational solidarity. The remaining African ethnic groups tend to be internally united religiously, with a consequent reinforcement of ethnic ties.

A second horizontal link is occupation—one's relationship to the means of production and distribution. But in the communities studied, there tends to be a correspondence between ethnic group and occupation (especially in Mbale, where the Asians are economically dominant) and most attempts to organise permanently on the sole basis of occupation have failed. A contractor's guild in Umuahia has been ineffective because of strong government counterpressure; rivalry caused *de facto* disbanding of a chamber of commerce in Mbale; and as yet there are only slight signs of labour union activity in either community.

A third horizontal link is politics, the result of multi-party competition and trans-ethnic political alliance. Party activity tends to be cyclical, however, so that, during periods of low activity, only a thin horizontal link remains. Most ethnic groups predominantly support one party or another (especially in Umuahia); party patronage tends to be based upon ethnic ties; and party branches outside the urban centre are based upon ethnic groups or sub-groups, depending upon the intensity of intra-group factionalism. Illustrative evidence includes the importance of the ticket-balancing issue in both communities[19] and the high priority given to ethnic-group-oriented welfare projects by the central government.[20] From another point of view, ethnic identities in our communities provided a fairly reliable organisational base for political parties.[21] Thus we can say that ethnic groups are being co-opted into political organisations and also that political organisations are being co-opted into the ethnic group structure.[22]

Each of the ethnic groups with which we became acquainted in Umuahia and Mbale is politically divided into at least two factions, usually because of traditional rivalries, the rewards of modern politics, or a combination of the two. Modern politics intrudes because ethnic backing is almost a necessary condition of influence and because, with the transfer of sovereignty, power is available. As David Apter has so colourfully put it: 'Power is left to the nationalists like gold dumped in the streets, and many are bruised in the hectic scramble to gather it up. . . .'[23] An additional contributing factor is the stress of change generally. Previous research suggests that change, with its correlates of competing belief systems and community stress, proliferates leadership claimants.[24]

Although the horizontal links of religion, occupation and political party do not appear to provide strong cross-pressures to identity based upon the ethnic group, this does not imply that their impact upon ethnicity (or vice versa) is likely to be uniform. Each institution forms a sub-system having a particular interaction with each ethnic group. As A. L. Epstein has written, 'the tempo and character of change [and persistent ethnic penetration] are not evenly distributed over the whole field'.[25]

There are numerous ethnic conflicts and coalitions in Umuahia and Mbale, but two major patterns emerge. These are (i) rural poly-ethnic politics projected into the urban centres, and (ii) strangers as buffers or balancers in the communities' politics.

(i) The urban centre of an African community is often a legally distinct entity, but it may become the focus of conflicts which originate in the surrounding rural area. This is due to the prestige of owning or controlling the town, the material welfare which can accrue to the group which is dominant in the town, and the various ties which link the rural and urban sectors. The process of rapid urbanisation which began after European intervention is largely responsible for conflict's being focused on the urban centre. New towns were established throughout Black Africa to facilitate administration and the new economy. Soon, Africans began to come to the towns and urban population explosions occurred. Each of our research towns, for example, had grown ten-fold during the thirty years prior to our arrival. But the combination of European administrators and immigrant Africans often meant that there was an indigenous power vacuum and a poly-ethnic urban society. The transfer of state sovereignty led to symbolic and/or substantive battles for control of the urban centre. These have been only slightly moderated by national mobilisation and the urban melting pot.[26]

The most intense conflict in the Umuahia community is between the Ohuhu clan and the Ibeku clan (both with allies and the latter with defections). The Ohuhu people had poor land and a strong achievement orientation, leading them to become the first well-educated people in the community. A rival put it this way: 'Ohuhu area was not fertile, so they had to struggle. They got into politics before we did; they read politics in school.' Some Ohuhu young men joined the nationalist movement early, and they rose to prominence when representative government was introduced. The first three representatives from the Umuahia community were Ohuhu. When the former leader of the NCNC (National Council of Nigerian Citizens) and Premier of Eastern Nigeria, Nnamdi Azikiwe, resigned to become the first President of Nigeria, Dr M. I. Okpara, a son of Ohuhu, succeeded him in both positions. Thus, in 1963, the Ohuhu were powerful. The Ibeku people, on the other hand, had sufficient fertile land and were slow to take advantage of the new education. One member of the clan stated: 'Ibeku feed copiously. My people became lazy and did not go to school.' As a result, they fell behind politically and educationally, encouraging such out-group comments as this: 'As far as we know, the Ibeku have low mentality. They didn't go to school; they work for the Hausa selling cattle.' Although the Ibeku did have one significant advantage in the Umuahia community—they were the traditional owners of the town land and still retain at least nominal ownership of approximately one-half of the town—the quest for local parity with the Ohuhu has coloured their recent political activities.

Illustrative conflicts between the Ohuhu and the Ibeku are those over the name of the town and the control of the town council. (The constituency's election of a regional representative, the most bitter incident, will be described in the following sub-section.) In 1949, the railway station was moved from a non-Ibeku area just outside the town into the town proper. The station's sign, 'Umuahia', was also moved. This evoked a sharp reaction from the Ibeku people, who petitioned the government to have their clan name added to the town name and the sign changed to 'Umuahia-Ibeku'. (The station's sign was one of the first visible displays of the town's name.) This met with Ohuhu protests, but an agreement was nevertheless made to have the change take effect—but not until 1959. The delay and the Ohuhu persistence in officially and unofficially calling the town 'Umuahia' (their persistence is especially meaningful since they controlled relevant regional and county governments) have been catalysts of ill-will. The other conflict, over the control of the town council, has for the past few years been quite heated. In 1962 an Ohuhu influential won an easy contest for chairman, but in 1963 he was overthrown by an Ibeku-stranger coalition. The former vice-chairman, an Ibeku man, was elected chairman when the opposition came into the open on the day the council met to vote. In another bitterly-fought contest, the Ibeku man retained his post in the 1964 election. The Ohuhu Premier apparently chose not to intervene because he was engaged in a delicate attempt to woo the Ibeku people away from their support of a party rebel.

In the Mbale community, the conflict between Bagisu and Bakedi is projected into the town. Available historical evidence indicates that the area which is now Mbale municipality was unoccupied seventy-five years ago. Nevertheless, it has been claimed by both peoples in recent decades. The colonial administration complicated the matter by putting Mbale within one jurisdiction and then another until it became such a sensitive issue that an independent Mbale municipality with federal territorial status was established in the first independence constitution of a sovereign Uganda. But the constitution also called for a jurisdictional decision to be made by October 1963, a decision which has been postponed indefinitely because it is so explosive. The Bagisu-Bakedi conflict affects the town in a number of ways, including 'an undercurrent of friction' as one university-educated African put it. The District Offices of Bugisu and Bukedi are both located in the town as symbolic beachheads on the prized land—each occupying half of the same building! At celebrations, representatives of the two peoples compete for prestigious seating positions and speaking order. Service at the municipality's hospital, whose employees are predominantly Bagisu, is said to favour Bagisu, with Bakedi often standing in line for hours, or even days, to be treated. A band of Bagisu came into the town a few years ago, trying to circumcise non-Bagisu townsmen in the tradition of the tribe. But perhaps the greatest impact the conflict has had upon the town is to make its future insecure. If the Bakedi rule the town, the Bagisu will suffer; if the Bagisu rule, the Bakedi will suffer; and if either is in firm control, the Asians' situation will probably deteriorate further. 'One thing is certain', an Asian professional man told us, 'wherever the land goes, Mbale will face difficulty. The non-owner will riot.

The Asians will be the first to suffer; the shops will be broken in.' This insecurity, added to those caused by a new central government dominated by Africans resulted in the virtual cessation of private initiative in the economic sphere on the part of local Asian businessmen.

(ii) Strangers tend to be buffers or balancers in the community's politics. The stranger, as Georg Simmel has noted, is not 'radically committed to unique ingredients and peculiar tendencies of the [hosts], and therefore approaches them with the specific attitude of "objectivity" '.[27] This makes it possible for strangers to participate in the politics of the community in a variety of ways (not all mutually exclusive), depending of course upon the constraints established by the hosts.

The first possibility for stranger participation is as the balancer in a balance-of-power system, and this tends to be the behaviour of strangers in Umuahia. Second, they can absorb the aggressions of the indigenous groups and thus buffer their poly-ethnic conflicts; this is the pattern which is crystallising for the Asians of Mbale. Third, the strangers can occupy a neutral position among indigenous antagonists, striving to befriend all and offend none. This is what many Asians of Mbale are trying to achieve. Fourth, it is possible for strangers to throw their support to the indigenous faction thought likely to obtain, or hold, predominant power. Several leading Asians have tried to follow this strategy. Its success, however, depends upon acceptance by the powerful, a condition which existed in 1963 but, with Africanisation, is soon likely to attenuate. Fifth, strangers can withdraw from manifest politics, as most Europeans living in Umuahia and Mbale have done. Other possibilities (not found in the two communities studied) include taking the identity of an indigenous group, as has been common in Kinshasa, Congo, and bipolar conflict between strangers and indigenes, an example of this being Onitsha, Nigeria.[28]

Whatever pattern predominates, strangers are usually in a precarious position because their residence is, at least to some extent, at the pleasure of the indigenes. The feelings of strangers are illustrated by informant comments. 'The natives are selfish', said one non-Umuahia Ibo. 'They don't love strangers.' And an Mbale Asian observed: 'Anything said by anyone here, in this small place, goes around very fast. People who used to take active part in public life are afraid to talk.' One explanation for this relates to the past sponsors of immigration. 'The new [i.e., after imperial occupation] strangers entered these foreign areas under the aegis of the Europeans, even when they were not directly brought by them. The result was that, unlike the earlier strangers, they have only secondary relationships with the local African political authorities.[29]

The role of strangers in Umuahia illustrates the balance-of-power system. The largest single stranger group in Umuahia town is the Onitsha Ibo, and it has dramatically influenced the conflict between the Ohuhu and Ibeku clans. The most important relevant event was the election of a representative from a new constituency comprised of the town and the lands of three clans, including the Ibeku but excluding the Ohuhu. In 1961 constituency lines had been redrawn and single-member districts established for the first time. As a result there was only one home seat for two Ohuhu incumbents, and one of them was the Premier. The influential members of the Ohuhu clan resolved the issue by sending the other incumbent to contest in the constituency which included Ibeku clan land and the town, where he had a second residence. With the help of the NCNC executive committee, which was controlled by Ohuhu people, the nomination for the constituency which included the town was given to the Ohuhu man and prospective Ibeku candidates were denied. An Ibeku candidate had actually won the local NCNC committee's nomination, but the executive committee's action over-ruled the previous decision. The locally chosen Ibeku candidate was persuaded by his people to contest as an independent, and the battle was joined. Here is the Ohuhu explanation of that candidacy: 'Politics is the headache we have in the township. We have stranger elements. When the election came out, the stranger elements corrupted the Ibeku, saying that the Ohuhu were lording it over them and they should have someone.' With the two communities pitted against each other, the strangers' votes were a significant factor in the election. For a number of reasons, one of which was probably implicit adherence to the balance-of-power necessity 'to oppose any coalition or single actor which tends to assume a position of predominance with respect to the rest of the system',[30] the strangers sided with the Ibeku and the latter's candidate won a sweeping victory. But the role of balancer may carry with it dangers. As Elliott Skinner has observed, stranger groups which support one indigenous faction against another often cause a great deal of antagonism to be directed against themselves.[31]

The Mbale strangers include both Asians and Africans, each with a significant buffer role. When Europeans relinquished sovereignty in October 1962, the Asians' economic and administrative positions were strong, and there were few Africans capable of manning key posts in the administration or economy who were willing to remain in a provincial town. As a result, the European/Asian/African stratification became Asian/African, with the remaining Europeans largely out of the mainstream of politics and economics. In a sense, the town is really an Asian town, even though Africans outnumber them two to one. 'After the Second World War', writes A. Bharati, 'the Asian minority [in East Africa] experienced a tremendous boom. What had been potentially the most affluent group in East Africa, now definitely turned into the richest. In urban East Africa, more than 75 per cent of all buildings and real estate, and about an equal proportion of investments belonged to the Asians. [Many cities] . . . have the appearance of an Indian bazaar rather than anything else.'[32] The situation in Mbale is well-represented in this comment by an informant: 'Africans are not influential in Mbale. None of them commands respect among the Africans or Asians. The entire life of the town is in the hands of the Asians. The African politicians are from the outside—they come into the town by serving on the Bugisu or Bukedi District Councils.'

As noted above, some Asians have supported an indigenous faction while others have tried to remain neutral in conflicts among African groups. It appears likely, however, that the Asians will increasingly be relegated to the role of buffers. Their importance is due to the dearth of skilled and educated Africans at the local level, and to the central government's shrewd tolerance of the situation as an interim measure. But soon there will be Africans who can more-or-less replace the Asians and, in addition, targets will be needed for aggressions arising from the Africans' frustrated aspirations. Total dedication to the African cause, as is manifested when the personality defends itself through identification with a rival, may be a solution for some. Others give 'protection money', as this Asian informant reveals: 'I get sympathy with the Africans. I spend much time. . . . We give to these people; we like it here and we want to stay, so we have to give some sacrifices to these people. Anyone comes to me for financial aid, I give to them.' Unfortunately, the evidence from elsewhere in East Africa suggests that dedication or support will not obviate later rejection or scapegoating. 'What the Africans cannot forget', A. Bharati argues, 'is the disdain in which the average Asian had been holding Africans since Asians came and settled.'[33]

Most Asians do not (and dare not) openly favour particular African ethnic groups or political parties, and it is they who have tried to make Mbale into a neutral zone. One African reports: 'Asians are not participating in party affairs. It might ruin their business. It is difficult to know who is DP [Democratic Party] and UPC [Uganda People's Congress].' But it is unlikely that many Asians will be able to insulate themselves from the processes of change. The attitudinal precondition already exists. The Asians' religions and languages and their sense of cultural superiority led some of our African informants to make remarks such as this: 'They are a tight group, so it is hard to understand them.' Even more resented is the predominant role Asians play in the community's economy. 'They are great cheats in every business they perform. They are very unkind. Once an Asian finds you on the way, he cannot give you a lift at all.' And again: 'The Asians are not interested in the problems of the town; they are only interested in their businesses.' Already, some African politicians make a practice of letting Asians pay their bills. A few of the more aggressive African customers threaten severe reprisal if service is not to their satisfaction. An Asian comments: 'Anything said against an African is considered against the country. For example, a clerk wanted a loan for a car. He earned very little. When refused a loan from an Asian, the African clerk complained to the UPC that he was mistreated and all Africans were insulted.' Although such incidents are still infrequent in Mbale, the likely developmental pattern is emerging.

The most important African strangers are Baganda and Kenyans. Since their 'pacification of the natives', the former have, in ever-lessening degree, had a self-image of superiority to the indigenes. As warrant chiefs for the British, the Baganda were placed in key administrative posts throughout the locality; some of them were the first African teachers and religious leaders. One of the last holdovers of this regime is the son of Kakunguru, who served as 'Native Administrator' within the town. Although in recent years the Baganda have become less important, they still play the roles of neutral and buffer. The Kenyans, numbering about five hundred, are employed as manual labourers. Although they have pre-empted some jobs, the indigenes have not been seriously hurt economically because they can easily return to farming. 'There is much labour in Mbale, particularly Kenyan labour', commented one African civil servant. 'The people here don't want to do the dirty work. Government wants to limit the number of Kenyans, but they are hard-working. The people here don't have to work; they go dig.' The Kenyans are not active in politics, both because they are not eligible to vote and because they want to minimise provocation of local Africans.

II. Intercalary Influentials

Recent attempts to apply the concepts of political theory to the emergent nations have directed attention to the need for middle positions between polar ideal types. Fred Riggs has constructed the entire model of a 'prismatic society' on the premise that there is a theoretically important type located between modern industria and traditional agraria.[34] There is obviously a tremendous gap between the relatively modern sphere of the political and social leaders at the centre of new African states, and the ethnic-group-oriented sphere of the rank-and-file in rural, peri-urban and crowded urban areas. But the gap is far from complete, both because there are no 'pure' modern men or traditional men, and because there are people who occupy the middle positions, those who 'make up the social bridges between otherwise distinct and separated political subcommunities'.[35] Such thinking has resulted in Dankwart Rustow's conceptualisation of the 'amalgamate' as one whose behavioural patterns 'are neither traditional nor Western but that are the result of this interaction',[36] and Lucian Pye's conceptualisation of 'transmitters' as those who 'communicate the ideas and values of one system to the other'.[37] In this section we have a similar concern; the mediation function of community influentials.[38] This mediation generally takes place between the influential's rank-and-file co-ethnics, on the one hand, and those who participate in his local, regional and national orbits, on the other.

People whose behavioural patterns are the result of traditional and Western interaction can be viewed in several ways. One is that they are marginal men burdened by the weight of role conflicts. Thus Lloyd Fallers, writing about the Basoga people of Uganda, suggests that 'chiefs and most other Basoga hold both value systems and both systems of belief at the same time. This results in frequent conflict, both between persons and within persons. . . . Whichever way he jumps, he will be punished, both by his own remorse at having contravened values which are part of his personality, and by sanctions applied by others.'[39] This view of inevitable negative psychic and social sanctions fails to take into account that: (i) it is possible to buffer role conflict, (ii) multiple role playing is a basis of social integration, and (iii) there is a tendency to integrate or redefine apparently diverse systems in order to avoid cognitive dissonance.

The role-buffering concept directs attention to the possibility that not all apparently conflicting demands impose themselves with equal force upon the locus actor. One or more of the demands may be partly absorbed by those who stand between the source of the demand and the man in the middle.[40] For the community influential, the demands of a central government minister may be buffered by members of the minister's staff; the demands of a village elder may similarly be buffered by local political party functionaries. In a sense, this arrangement tends to convert conflicts between the roles of one individual into conflicts between several individuals within a social system.

Concerning role conflict Aidan Southall writes: 'Multiple role playing and multiple status incumbency confront the most mobile and influential individuals with the necessity of mediating, in their own persons, between the very diverse clients, relatives, cliques, networks, institutions and publics among whom they must move. . . . Thus, fortunately, the strivings of the individual contribute to the maintenance of society. . . .'[41] One of the concerns of our research in Umuahia and Mbale was the ways by which the apparently diverse systems of modernity and tradition are bound together. The community influentials who have multiple roles help to form this bond by functioning as elements of an intercalary structure.[42]

Focusing upon the cognitive dissonance of cultural duality, we assumed that 'the existence of dissonance in a person leads to a process of social communication by which he attempts to reduce the dissonance'.[43] The community influential's cultural duality is constantly reinforced by regular contacts with modern industria and traditional agraria. Perhaps in order to create consonance in the face of this cultural duality, most influentials seek to modify each cultural sphere so that it is more compatible with the other. This obviously has an important integrating effect upon the larger society. A reconceptualisation of the situation is also possible. Thus the locus actor may not perceive one of the conflicting demands, or if he does, he may not believe that the demands are conflicting and therefore will not be disturbed by them.[44]

As moderator or transmitter, the influential in an urban-centred African community is in an important respect equivalent to the opinion leader which Paul Lazarsfeld and his associates identified in Erie County. They report that 'ideas often flow *from* radio and print *to* opinion leaders and *from* them to the less active sections of the population'.[45] From this finding the concept of the two-step flow of communications developed. Similarly, the influential member of an urban-centred African community is the mediating middleman in a communications network. The research most relevant for translating this finding to Black Africa has been carried out by S. N. Eisenstadt who, writing about the leaders of immigrant groups in Israel, concludes that 'the elites perform a very important function as "mediators" between the primary groups of the immigrants and the wider social structure. . . . The identification of the immigrants with the new society is to a large extent effected through their identification with the elites, and the elites seem to influence the formation of the values and activities of the primary groups.'[46] Kenneth Post sees this clearly in the African setting:

> The new men performed for their people an 'interpretative function', which was of vital importance politically. They acted as intermediaries between the new modern world in which they were busily making their way and the old traditional society from which they had sprung. The new world, through its chief agent the Government, made heavy demands upon the old. . . . In such a situation the ordinary citizen in contemporary Nigeria was bewildered and often afraid. Usually illiterate and unable to speak English, he would have been quite lost without someone to explain the Government's demands and to help him to meet them.[47]

Some scholars have argued that the mediating, interpretive role is so difficult that an almost complete communications gap has developed.[48] There are, they say, no equivalents in the two spheres whereby a concept could be communicated from one to the other. We have found this to be true only if the would-be mediator is not closely integrated with the prospective receivers of the communication. During our field research, several advanced secondary school students were tried out as research assistants for interviewing heterogeneous subsamples of respondents. We found that they could neither communicate with most selected respondents nor even tolerate them. When we interviewed these interviewers, they complained of the stupidity, the filth and the primitive state of the respondents. It seems that most students—and bureaucrats and party leaders—do not have the necessary link with ethnic groups other than their own—and sometimes not even with their own.[49] But the influentials in our communities, despite their higher standard of living, education and so forth, were well integrated with their home ethnic groups and able to perform the mediating role quite effectively.

Let us examine some of the links between the community influentials and the central leadership, as well as between the influentials and the rank-and-file. The link between the influentials and the leaders at the centre is direct and communication is constant. In Umuahia, most of the men whom we identified as community influentials actually went to the capital when any issue of importance arose, and the Premier would visit Umuahia periodically, calling many influentials in for meetings to make sure that his political organisation was running smoothly. The same pattern was found in Mbale, where several key men communicated frequently with the government ministers, either in person or by telephone. The communications amount to more than taking orders from the government, as the following remark suggests: 'If the Patels [Mbale's most influential ethnic group] want something, the Prime Minister will listen.'

Many national leaders appear to be acutely concerned with integrating community influentials—most of whom are leaders of their respective ethnic groups—into the larger structure. Justification for their concern can be found in the successes of indirect rule and the results of several research projects. For example, Alexander Leighton concludes, on the basis of research at a Japanese relocation camp, that 'one of the major tasks of a new administration is that of integrating itself with the patterns of leadership and authority which exist in the community. . . . The matter is doubly difficult and doubly important in a community that is under stress.'[50] Without this integration between administration and community leadership, it is extremely difficult to bridge the gap to the rank-and-file.

The link between the influential and the rank-and-file can best be understood by conceiving of the African masses as ethnic-group-oriented immigrants (from far *or* near) to a new society, and of towns as dormitories as well as settlements.[51] Normally, we think of the geographical immigrant, but trans-cultural immigration is also important, and the combination is an especially profound experience for the individual. Initially, African immigrants were partly oriented to the new society by European contact or direction and by the efforts of the nationalist movement and the political messiah.[52] However, the movement in many countries is torn by factionalism resulting from the scramble for power, and the messiah's charisma is wearing thin now that heaven has not come to earth. This kind of disillusionment was recently shown to us by a former true believer who said about his idol: 'He is better dead.' The passing of initial nationalist fervour has put an especially heavy burden upon local influentials.

Almost all the influential members of our research communities were prominent and active in their own ethnic groups. Since they participate successfully in a disproportionate number of the groups' decisions, they are political elites. But they are also probably influential beyond the political arena. Ronald Lippitt and his associates conclude, on the basis of research in American boys' camps, that 'perception of power, rather than sheer activity output, is a major determinant of contagion pick-up' and that 'the higher a member's attributed power, the more likely it is that each of his influence attempts will be successful'.[53] Although in our research communities Europeans tend to remain the social elites, using S. F. Nadel's strict specification of the term,[54] our evidence suggests that the influentials of Umuahia and Mbale are imitated by the rank-and-file to a significant extent.

The rank-and-file appear to be relatively willing to follow the lead of influential co-ethnics. This is not to suggest that the mass will accept direct dictation, but only that the power and prestige of the leading members have considerable weight and, with skilful use, can often carry the day. Who promotes the alternative is often more important than what the alternative is, whether in a political party or a community development scheme. Of course, this situation prevails partly because the immigrants confront new situations, are faced with new decisions, and yet may be without all the controls and securities which home and tradition provide.

Probably another reason why the rank-and-file are willing to follow is that the ethnic group's influentials are also material benefactors. In explaining the attribution of influence, this is the kind of answer we often heard: 'He helps to find jobs for people when vacancies exist and helps in giving scholarships. He is one of those who helped us maintain our clan.' The situation in the American army that Edward Shils calls to our attention appears to be similar: 'More than any other single characteristic, veteran enlisted men mentioned helpfulness towards their men, and the display of personal interest in them and their problems, in describing the characteristics of the best officer they had known in combat.' There is a need, Shils continues, for 'personal relationships with a protective exemplary authority whose qualities permit identification.'[55]

A local influential need not have the interests of his ethnic group in mind in order to contribute to the group's integration into the larger society. Integration can be the spill-over effect of self-interest. Writing about American immigrants at the turn of the century, E. Cornwell argues that 'the selfish quest by the politician for electoral support and power was transmuted by the "invisible hand" into the major force integrating the immigrant into the community'.[56] Although many influentials in Umuahia and Mbale had not recently run for public office, they campaigned for others and sought support for themselves in intra-ethnic and inter-ethnic conflicts, probably with a similar result. They also involved themselves in community projects, possibly to validate their leadership. Charles Adrian has written: 'It appears to be necessary for community leaders always to have some project underway lest they implicitly vacate their claims to leadership. By striving thus to lead, they often push above the public threshold of attention matters that might otherwise be ignored by the bulk of the citizenry and even by the formal leadership.'[57]

III. Bifurcated Influence and Authority

The third main political structure of the urban-centred communities studied came dramatically to our attention with the discovery of a low correlation between influence and authority. In Umuahia, we found that only two members of the town council (the chairman and the leader of the opposition) were among the nineteen men identified as community influentials. Seven members of the council representing the county surrounding the town were also classed as influentials, but six of these were honorary appointees who rarely attended meetings. Although six of the fourteen Mbale influentials were on the municipality's council and another two were on councils of the surrounding districts, the trend there is towards a diminishing number of influentials in the councils. (In the years since our departure, several influentials have ceased to be active in a council.) One Mbale influential explained his inactivity this way: 'It was formerly a pleasure to serve on the council. Problems were solved by friendly debate. Now it becomes personal. Even the aldermen say, "Why should we bother? What do we gain?" ' The pattern of influence in Mbale appears to be evolving towards the one which prevails in Umuahia. An influential in the latter community put it this way: 'Important people don't want to soil their hands.' Thus there has been a partial separation —a bifurcation—between the influentials of the communities and the incumbents of local authority positions. Three factors appear to have contributed to the bifurcation: the European legacy, a cosmopolitan interest leading to a local division of political labour, and the ethnic base of power. Each factor will be examined.

'The most significant legacy of colonialism', writes Donald Kingsley, 'is the existence of institutions in the newly emerged states which reflect levels of political development [or styles of political behaviour] not yet reached by those states.'[58] The institutional legacy of imperial local government has in part been retained because of its symbolic contribution. During the half-century of imperial rule, European clothes, languages and governing institutions became synonymous with 'civilisation', whereas their African counterparts were manifestations of the 'primitive'.

The Europeans were social elites, and therefore models of behaviour. Many Africans have imitated the models, consciously or unconsciously attempting to partake of the envisioned power and wisdom.[59] This behaviour prevails among many Africans today, but it is ambivalently combined with the belief that Africans should have and practice independence (rather than let the model Europeans continue to control). When our African interviewers asked respondents about Europeans, the two predominant themes that emerged from their answers were: (*a*) the Europeans were good, but (*b*) we should try to run our own affairs now.

How well are the local authorities considered to be running community affairs? The overall image of local government is very negative with local councillors the objects of severe denigration. Twenty-eight per cent of our respondents evaluated these councillors negatively and another 31 per cent offered mixed evaluations. However, two qualifications should be stated. In the first place, the local government activities of Asians and Europeans have been relatively free from such criticism, the former perhaps because they were originally drafted by imperial administrators on the basis of possessing such proper British qualities as honesty and amenability. Second, local civil servants tend to be exempt from criticism. This may be because they represent greater continuity with the European regime and because they are very careful to stay out of the limelight.

Local councillors were commonly criticised for being inherently bad people and for not properly representing the rank-and-file. In the first instance, they were seen as self-interested, of questionable character, corrupt, weak and so forth. Improper representation included not consulting the rank-and-file—except perhaps at election time—and not adequately representing constituents' interests in the local councils. The widespread negative comments about councillors are encapsulated by a departing European's evaluation: 'The most important problem here is the completely unrepresentative quality and the incompetence and the lack of maturity of the elected council. It applies mostly to the African, who doesn't know what he is doing and is vicious.' These criticisms suggest that a fissure has developed between the perceptions of local government as it ought to be conducted according to the proper models established and articulated by the Europeans, and local government as it is in fact conducted by councils composed largely of petty politicians. The fissure has been driving community influentials out of the local councils (or at least out of active participation in them), inhibiting leaders of the central government from expanding the limited authority of the formal institutions of local government, and stimulating the development of informal networks of influence which can perform the increasing requirements of local governance.

The second factor which appears to have contributed to the bifurcation of influence and authority in Umuahia and Mbale is the development of a cosmopolitan orientation among some of the prominent residents of the areas. Most of the influentials in the communities we studied were cosmopolitan in that they had important orientational links to the world beyond their home community. They contrasted with most local authorities (e.g., councillors), for whom Umuahia or Mbale appears to constitute a large proportion of their orientational world.[60]

Most influentials in both communities have economic, social and political interests which transcend the local scene. Umuahia is linked to the outside by its two major industries and by the fact that the premiership passed to a member of the Ohuhu clan. In addition, one influential owns a catering company that does business throughout half the country, another has a transportation company that is regional, others have their main business interests in other towns, and so forth. In the case of Mbale, the Asians own large cotton ginneries and other industries which have important economic links beyond the community. They retain strong ties with India or Pakistan. This stranger group is being replaced in minor economic activities, however, by the Africanisation of petty trade and petty politics. Yet, in both Umuahia and Mbale, major rewards, such as the siting of development projects, the appointment of government board members and the distribution of licences for big business, come from the central government and national political party headquarters. Thus the influentials' external interests are maintained.

Although our field research did not focus directly upon the orientations of local authorities, it was obvious that most councillors and local government administrators had a relatively restricted scope of political, social and economic interest. This was especially true in Umuahia, where no big businessman held a position of local authority which was not honorary and relatively inactive. Thus the typical councillor in this community lived within the confines of his home village and/or the urban centre; the modal administrator would, in addition, respond passively to the stream of decisions which came from the central government.

The tendency for influentials to be cosmopolitan in orientation and for local authorities to be more exclusively oriented to the community has resulted in a local division of political labour. The influentials dominate in matters that involve extramural relations and decisions on matters of high value, such as the supervision of local political party units and the distribution of major contracts to favoured residents. The local authorities tend to specialise in intramural matters that are not of high value, such as the allocation of market stalls and the naming of streets. This contrast is greater in Umuahia than Mbale. (Areal specialisation is greater in Mbale, where some influentials concern themselves almost exclusively with the town and others only with rural areas. In Umuahia, by contrast, most influentials are interested in the town and their home rural area.)

Umuahia and Mbale are not unique in having such a division of political labour. An important study of this phenomenon was made in Ypsilanti, Michigan, by Robert Schulze;[61] his developmental explanation probably applies with equal force to our African communities. He observes that the relatively small and self-contained town tends to be characterised by a fused power structure. With urbanisation and industrialisation, local economic interests are directed outwards and external economic interests and personnel are linked to the town. The result is that the economic elite withdraws from local politics, which becomes the province of middle-class business and professional men. The African equivalent of the latter groups would, at the present stage of development, be the small businessmen, and indeed small businessmen do predominate in the councils of Umuahia and Mbale.

The third factor which appears to have contributed to the bifurcation of influence and authority in Umuahia and Mbale is the ethnic base of influence. Most influentials in the two research communities have such a base, often formalised and enhanced by being an officer in the group's welfare association or by holding a chieftaincy recognised by the central government. Perhaps the ideal types are the formal (not traditional) clan or tribal leaders, called 'second class chiefs' in Umuahia and 'constitutional heads' in Mbale. There are six such leaders in Umuahia and two in Mbale, all appointed by the government with (except for one) the advice and consent of their clan or tribal constituents. The reason for their influence has been well stated, in another context, by Peter Rossi. Listing 'control over solidary groups' as one of the bases of power, he reasons: 'Persons who are at head of cohesive organised groups or who are reputed to have influence over large segments of the public can wield power by threatening to withhold support.'[62] Thus the authority of local government is not the basis of influence—a supportive cohesive ethnic group is.

Bifurcation is also a reflection of the preferences of most rank-and-file co-ethnics. Although often easily manipulated, they are also able to exert some control over their group representatives, who derive a large part of their influence from the group. Members of the formal government structure, on the other hand, can rely upon their offices between elections and upon the proper arrangement of nominations at election time to retain their positions without relating to the ethnic structure. 'They don't consult us!' 'They don't represent us!' our respondents say. On the other hand, the mediating influentials remain, in an important sense, part of both the traditional and modern structures.

The picture that emerges is a local government denigrated because it does not meet imported standards, shunned by the cosmopolitans because it does not readily serve their interests, and somewhat isolated because the poly-ethnic structure of power is not satisfactorily incorporated. As a result, in Umuahia and Mbale as elsewhere, to the extent that the formal institutions of government do not perform the required community functions, informal structures arise to meet the need. In the case at hand, the informal structures reflect the informalisation of influence, thus the bifurcation of influence and authority. The situation is strikingly similar to that of the boss politician in urban America. Robert Merton's observation could easily be translated to the African setting: 'In this struggle between alternative structures for fulfilling the nominally same function of providing aid and support to those who need it, it is clearly the machine politician who is better integrated with the groups which he serves than the impersonal, professionalised, socially distant and legally constrained welfare worker.'[63] The boss is powerful because he fulfils needs more effectively than the welfare worker, and the influential ethnic group leader is more powerful than the local government councillor or administrator partly for the same reason.

Bifurcation of authority and influence is not an uncommon social systemic phenomenon. More than two decades ago, J. L. Moreno wrote: 'The discovery that human society has an actual, dynamic, central structure underlying and determining all its peripheral and formal groupings may one day be considered as the cornerstone of all social science.'[64] Informal structures undoubtedly exist in every political system, and one might speculate that they are encouraged by the needs of the national leadership for reliable control systems and by the influence vacuum resulting from weak local governments. Thus C. I. Barnard sees informal structures as channels of executive control[65] and Herbert Simon suggests that weak formal systems of communication probably encourage clique development.[66]

Conclusion

The structures which have been described direct attention to the integration of the community and the larger society. The evidence suggests that in Umuahia and Mbale there is no sharp conflict between *Gemeinschaft* and *Gesellschaft*, but a subtle 'prismatic' blending of the two. In his discussion of the traditional norms, Bert Hoselitz seems to have described a situation which applies to our communities. They may, he says, 'provide stability in a situation of constant and rapid change. They may tend to carve out areas of social action in which known and well-understood behaviour patterns prevail, and they may in this way provide a feeling of security in a situation in which there are strong forces pulling into the direction of disorganization, fear and anxiety.'[67] In the political arena, poly-ethnicity, intercalary influentials and bifurcated influence and authority emerge from the interaction of rapid change and traditional ways to make possible the larger integration which is probably necessary for the continuity of the new states of independent Black Africa.

Notes and References

1 James S. Coleman, "The Politics of Sub-Saharan Africa", in Gabriel A. Almond and James S. Coleman, eds., *The Politics of the Developing Areas*, Princeton 1960, p. 270.

2 Leo Kuper argues, in this volume, that 'African towns should be studied as structures in their own right'. We should note here that there are several structural similarities between the racially plural communities analysed by Kuper and the poly-ethnic communities in independent Black Africa with which we are concerned.

3 This report is based upon 1963 field research supported by a Ford Foundation/Michigan State University Office of Internal Programs grant, administered through the African Studies Center. The authors wish to thank Horace Miner, Joseph Spengler, Howard Wolpe and Alvin Magid for their helpful comments.

4 "Umuahia" is both the name of the urban-centered community's encompassing province and the town's former name; "Mbale" is the name of the urban centre. We use these names to refer to communities composed of urban and peri-urban areas, but in neither research setting is this always the practice of local residents. We have chosen to employ the territorial name "Eastern Nigeria" because in 1963 it was the name of the relevant regional entity. At press time, the fate of the Republic of Biafra was uncertain. Changes in the research communities which have taken place since 1963 have not, for the most part, been incorporated into this report.

5 Daryll Forde, "Social Aspects of Urbanization and Industrialization in Africa: A General Review", in *Social Implications of Industrialization and Urbanization in Africa South of the Sahara*, Paris 1956, p. 38.

6 David Apter, "Non-Western Government and Politics: Introduction", in Harry Eckstein and David E. Apter, eds., *Comparative Politics: A Reader*, New York 1963, p. 652.

7 See Simon Ottenberg, "Ibo Receptivity to Change", in William R.

Bascom and Melville J. Herskovits, eds., *Continuity and Change in African Cultures*, Chicago 1959, pp. 130–43; J. S. La Fontaine, *The Gisu of Uganda*, London 1959; Fred G. Burke, "Bukedi: From Tribes to Counties", *Local Government and Politics in Uganda*, Syracuse, NY, 1964, pp. 178–222; Victor C. Uchendu, *The Igbo of Southeast Nigeria*, New York 1965.

8 One Kigisu historian writes: 'But where does "Mbale" get its name from? First because the area was sandy and stony, secondly there was at the time of the coming of Kakungulu an important man called Wambale. It is very important to note that some of the place names in Bugisu get their names from important men of particular clans. Thirdly, Kakungulu remembered the name "Mbale"—Mpigi in Buganda. After all, there is a village and a river in the neighbourhood of Mbale called Nambale, four miles on Mbale–Tororo Road called so practically for the same reasons.' George Wamimbi, "Historical Analysis of Bugisu", *Mulembe*, March 1963, p. 19. The activities of the Baganda in the Mbale area are noted later in this chapter.

9 The term 'poly-ethnic' is suggested by Fred W. Riggs's 'poly-communal' in his model of the prismatic society (an ideal-type society located between, and having characteristics of, traditional-fused agraria and modern-diffracted industria) and is used to designate a population partially mobilised but only slightly assimilated. See Riggs, *Administration in Developing Countries: The Theory of Prismatic Society*, Boston 1964, pp. 158–60 et passim.

10 S. F. Nadel, *The Foundations of Social Anthropology*, Glencoe, Ill., 1951, p. 146. We do not argue an explanatory group theory, but think it necessary for analysts to consider the importance of a collection of men who mutually identify and act in the political arena in terms of their group membership. 'What group theory accomplishes', Harry Eckstein has argued, 'is nothing more or less than to call our attention to the "real forces" in political processes.' ("Group Theory and the Comparative Study of Pressure Groups: Introduction", in Eckstein and Apter, op. cit., p. 393). We hope to demonstrate that, at least in our two research settings, ethnic groups were 'real' political forces.

11 Lucien Pye, "The Non-Western Political Process", *The Journal of Politics*, Vol. 20, 1958, p. 469.

12 Richard Sklar, *Nigerian Political Parties: Power in an Emergent African Nation*, Princeton 1963, pp. 474–80.

13 Clyde Mitchell, "Africans in Industrial Towns in Northern Rhodesia", in *H.R.H. The Duke of Edinburgh's Study Conference*, No. 1, p. 5, cited in Immanuel Wallerstein, "Ethnicity and National Integration in West Africa", *Cahiers d'Etudes Africaines*, No. 1, October 1960, pp. 130–1.

14 Jean Rouch, "Migrations au Ghana (Gold Coast)", *Journal de la Société des Africanistes*, Vol. 26, 1956, pp. 33–196.

15 Wallerstein, op. cit.

16 Riggs, op. cit., p. 171.

17 See Fred I. Greenstein, "The Changing Pattern of Urban Party Politics", *The Annals of the American Academy of Political and Social Science*, Vol. 353, 1964, pp. 1–13.
18 Harry Eckstein, *Pressure Group Politics*, Stanford 1960, pp. 32–3.
19 Elmer E. Cornwell, Jr, "Bosses, Machines, and Ethnic Groups", *The Annals of the American Academy of Political and Social Science*, Vol. 353, 1964, p. 33.
20 Sklar, op. cit., p. 504.
21 Cf. Bert F. Hoselitz, "Tradition and Economic Growth", in Ralph Braibanti and Joseph J. Spengler, eds., *Tradition, Values and Socio-economic Development*, Durham, NC, 1961, pp. 83–113.
22 'Cooptation is the process of absorbing new elements into a leadership or policy-determining structure of an organization as a means of averting threats to its stability or existence. . . . Cooptation reflects a state of tension between formal authority and social power.' Philip Selznick, "Foundations of the Theory of Organizations", *American Sociological Review*, Vol. 13, 1948, pp. 34–5.
23 David Apter, "Some Reflections on the Role of a Political Opposition in New Nations", *Comparative Studies in Society and History*, Vol. 4, 1962, p. 156.
24 Alexander Leighton, *The Governing of Men*, Princeton 1946.
25 A. L. Epstein, *Politics in an Urban African Community*, Manchester 1958, p. 232.
26 Recent research indicates that not even New York City has been a truly successful melting pot. See Nathan Glazer and Daniel Patrick Moynihan, *Beyond the Melting Pot: The Negroes, Puerto Ricans, Jews, Italians and Irish of New York City*, Cambridge, Mass., 1963.
27 Kurt H. Wolff, trans. and ed., *The Sociology of Georg Simmel*, Glencoe, Ill., 1950, p. 404.
28 Sklar, op. cit., pp. 151–7.
29 Elliot P. Skinner, "Strangers in West African Societies", *Africa*, Vol. 33, 1963, p. 309.
30 Morton A. Kaplan, *System and Process in International Politics*, New York 1957, p. 23.
31 Skinner, op. cit., p. 312.
32 A. Bharati, "Political Pressures and Reactions in the Asian Minority in East Africa", paper presented at the Annual Meeting of the African Studies Association, Chicago 1964, p. 1.
33 Ibid., p. 3.
34 Riggs, op. cit.
35 Bernard R. Berelson, Paul F. Lazarsfeld, and William N. McPhee, *Voting: A Study of Opinion Formation in a Presidential Campaign*, Chicago 1954, p. 131.
36 Dankwart Rustow, *Politics and Westernization in the Near East*, Princeton 1956, p. 10.
37 Lucian Pye, "Administrators, Agitators, and Brokers", *Public Opinion Quarterly*, Vol. 22, 1958, p. 345.
38 Influentials were identified using a combination of the general

reputation technique developed by William H. Form and Delbert C. Miller, and the issue-oriented reputation for participation technique which with variations has been used by Robert Presthus and others. For the purposes reported in this paper, nineteen influentials were identified in Umuahia and fourteen in Mbale.

39 Lloyd Fallers, "The Predicament of the Modern African Chief: An Instance from Uganda", *American Anthropologist*, Vol. 57, 1955, p. 302.

40 See Alvin Magid, "District Councillorship in an African Society: A Study in Role", unpublished PH.D. dissertation, Michigan State University 1965.

41 See chap. 11 of this volume, p. 330.

42 See chap. 6 of this volume, p. 137.

43 Leon Festinger, *A Theory of Cognitive Dissonance*, Evanston 1957, p. 204.

44 See Magid, op. cit.

45 Paul F. Lazarsfeld, Bernard Berelson, and Hazel Gaudet, *The People's Choice: How the Voter Makes up his Mind in a Presidential Campaign*, New York 1944, p. 151.

46 S. N. Eisenstadt, "The Place of Elites and Primary Groups in the Absorption of Immigrants in Israel", *American Journal of Sociology*, Vol. 57, 1952, p. 226.

47 Kenneth Post, *The Nigerian Federal Election of 1959: Politics and Administration in a Developing Political System*, London 1963, p. 48.

48 Cf. Gabriel A. Almond, "Introduction: A Functional Approach to Comparative Politics", in Almond and Coleman, op. cit., p. 51.

49 See William John Hanna and Judith Lynne Hanna, "The Problem of Ethnicity and Factionalism in African Survey Research", *Public Opinion Quarterly*, Vol. 30, 1966, pp. 290–294.

50 Leighton, op. cit., p. 343.

51 Cf. Apter, "Non-Western Government and Politics ...", op. cit., pp. 651–2.

52 See William John Hanna, "Introduction: The Politics of Freedom", in Hanna, ed., *Independent Black Africa: The Politics of Freedom*, Chicago 1964, pp. 25–32.

53 Ronald Lippitt, Norman Polansky, Fritz Redl, and Sidney Rosen, "The Dynamics of Power", in Eleanor E. Maccoby, Theodore M. Newcomb, and Eugene L. Hartley, eds., *Readings in Social Psychology*, New York 1958, pp. 256–7.

54 S. F. Nadel, "The Concept of Social Elites", *International Social Science Bulletin*, Vol. 8, 1956, pp. 413–424.

55 Edward Shils, "Primary Groups in the American Army", in Robert K. Merton and Paul F. Lazarsfeld, eds., *Continuities in Social Research: Studies in the Scope and Method of "The American Soldier"*, Glencoe, Ill., 1950, p. 32.

56 Cornwell, op. cit., p. 31.

57 Charles R. Adrian, "The Community Setting", in Charles R. Adrian, ed., *Social Science and Community Action*, East Lansing, Mich., 1960, p. 4.

58 Donald Kingsley, "Bureaucracy and Political Development, with Particular Reference to Nigeria", in Joseph LaPalombara, ed., *Bureaucracy and Political Development*, Princeton 1963, p. 301; interpolation not implied in the original.

59 See Hanna, op. cit., p. 4 and passim.

60 Cf. Robert K. Merton, "Patterns of Influence: Local and Cosmopolitan Influentials", in Merton, *Social Theory and Social Structure*, Glencoe, Ill., 1957, pp. 387–420.

61 Robert Schulze, "The Role of Economic Dominants in Community Power Structure", *American Sociological Review*, Vol. 23, 1958, pp. 3–9. For a different approach to the same problem, see John K. Hemphill, *Situational Factors in Leadership*, Columbus, Ohio, 1949.

62 Peter Rossi, "Theory, Research and Practice in Community Organization", in Adrian, op. cit., p. 12.

63 Robert Merton, *Social Theory and Social Structure*, rev. edn., Glencoe, Ill., 1957, p. 75.

64 J. L. Moreno, "Foundations of Sociometry", *Sociometry*, Vol. 4, 1941, p. 15.

65 C. I. Barnard, *The Functions of the Executive*, Cambridge, Mass., 1940.

66 Herbert Simon, *Administrative Behavior: A Study of Decision-Making Processes in Administrative Organization*, New York 1947, p. 162.

67 Hoselitz, op. cit , p. 111. Probably not all traditional systems are able to provide such stability. Apter uses the term 'instrumental systems' for those which are able to 'innovate easily by spreading the blanket of tradition upon change itself'. See "The Role of Traditionalism in the Political Modernization of Ghana and Uganda", *World Politics*, Vol. 13, 1960, p. 47. See also Clifford Geertz, "Primordial Sentiments and Civil Politics in the New States", in Geertz, ed., *Old Societies and New States: The Quest for Modernity in Asia and Africa*, New York 1963, pp. 105–57.

8

Bureaucracy and Urban Symbol Systems

LIONEL TIGER

THIS IS AN ESSAY at understanding the relationship of urban symbol systems to bureaucracy and the bureaucratic elite in Ghana. The propositions advanced are not based on 'hard' data, because the collection of information about the urban variable was not a specific goal of the original research and also because of the elusive nature of the material necessary to substantiate the ensuing propositions. The gamble is that in choosing a large territory to explore there exists opportunity for worthwhile discovery, despite the danger of finding nothing and of being lost oneself. At the same time, the argument is lent some reality insofar as it is rooted in a field study of the higher civil service in Ghana between 1960–62.[1]

The thesis of the paper is as follows: the relationship of bureaucracies to cities in contemporary Africa is broadly comparable to the one Fustel de Coulanges[2] proposed in his observation that the ancient European city developed as an essentially religious unit. In both these historical situations, two factors are outstanding: that literacy and high education are fundamental to consideration of the symbol and status systems of each society; and that in each the nuclear social factor in urban coherence is responsible for the management of the peoples' future, i.e., religious destiny or

NOTE: *The notes and references for Chapter 8 will be found on page 211.*

economic development plans. Just as government in the Middle Ages had a religious basis, government in modern Africa has an administrative basis, with the consequence that higher civil servants are the effective leaders of society because only they possess the skill and knowledge to plan and administer the changes people desire. This has not only to do with planning for the future but, retrospectively, with the nature of colonial government.

At the same time as the bureaucracy is the definer of society's mass goals and activity, it is also an elitist group for reasons of income, life style, power and education. Unlike the situation in the Middle Ages, however, the 'peasantry' are able to know of foreign wealth and ways of life because of electronic media of communication which do not require literacy. Thus, they participate in modernity and in the 'revolution of rising expectations'. What bureaucrats do is essential for success in this 'revolution', but, also, what they do is mysterious to non- and semi-literate persons who observe officials living in conditions quite splendid by local standards. The question implied by the wealth of officials and the obscurity of their activity is answered by the creation of a system of magic with some resemblance to the Melanesian cargo cult. Though based on secular activity, this occult image is the crux of an urban symbol system; it also defines the nature of modern life for persons outside the urban area, since in African conditions the distinction is not wholly clear.[3] And at the same time as it is a work-organisation, the bureaucracy is also an elitist system of communication which has consequences for the mass.

The following discussion focuses mainly on Ghanaian material, though, where extension is appropriate, the sub-Saharan region is implied. References to 'civil servants' mean the members of the administrative grade of the service and professional persons of comparable status in ministries such as Justice, Public Works and Health. These will normally be university graduates; a very few will have been promoted through the ranks after no more than a secondary education. 'Elite' means 'national elite' rather than 'local elite', to use the distinction of Lambert and Hoselitz.[4] They define the national elite as the group, based in the capital, which is concerned with integrative and modernisation goals of considerable specificity, while local elites perform in less clear-cut directions. The latter may indeed concern themselves not with modernisation but with the maintenance and extension of traditional behaviours and social groups.

At the risk of over-generalisation it is suggested that, in African urbanisation, the role of bureaucrats and bureaucracy is functionally comparable to the role of church and churchman in medieval cathedral towns, or, less appropriately, to the role of the military in the fortification towns of which Weber wrote.[5] In other words, as the raison d'être of the cathedral town was the cathedral-church, and of the fortress town the castle, so in twentieth-century Africa the bureaucratic apparatus and ministry buildings form perhaps the physical and certainly the symbolic nucleus of the African city.

In Martindale's view: 'The modern city is losing its external and formal structure. Internally it is in a state of decay while the new community represented by the nation everywhere grows at its expense. The age of the city seems to be at an end.'[6] Earlier in the same publication[7] he notes that Weber proposed that the true city could not be a national capital and still be fully urban. Yet Africa is still a relatively unurbanised continent and those urban agglomerations which do exist are primarily centred about administrative capitals.[8] Of course, we are involved here with problems of definition: What is a city? Must the African city differ from the European city, if only because Africa and Europe are different? Or, can it be claimed that the city as a social form is meaningfully the same from place to place? Herskovits[9] argues that European research on African cities has been substantially ethnocentric and proposes that African cities should be studied more in terms of African tradition. While this is a broadly acceptable viewpoint, an important provision (suggested by Herskovits himself) must be made. Because the growth of many African cities was either dependent upon or associated with the colonial system, the real and symbolic role of this colonial input must be identified and examined. Along these lines it can be argued that the bureaucratic administrative system has historically provided a crucial definition of the nature and function of African cities. Unlike India and the new white colonies (such as America, Canada, Australia and New Zealand) in which capital cities have not become dominant metropolitan regions, the relationship has been close between administration and urbanisation in African society. While it may have been more significant when there were no mass communications than it is now, the bond between urbanisation and the style and fact of national administration has been maintained, though at present it assumes a somewhat different form. In effect, it is suggested here that there has been a close historical relationship in Africa between colonial and civil service, the educational system and the patterns of urbanisation.[10] Generally, as Clignet and Foster[11] indicate, the three are linked. Lerner[12] has demonstrated on a world-wide basis how literacy rates, as a symptom of at least minimal education, are tied to urbanisation rates. And in contemporary African societies, within which government service is the major single source of employment for educated persons, the links between bureaucracy and educational system are clear.

The implication of this lies not only in the occupational structure of African societies, but also in the symbol systems of Africans. The process of apprehending what happens in the wider world and achieving any break with tradition is also correlated with living in cities or visiting them, and with working in the civil service or knowing clearly what the civil service does. Less important are the problems involved in political independence; these may matter significantly for only a relative few. Such a contention revises a view which holds that the major sub-system of African societies is political. Instead, it is suggested that, while the political changes of independence are vast and important at one level, what is more important for most Africans now is that they are involved in essentially economic administrative change. We recall Weber's prediction that problems of politics become problems of administration.[13] The important things happening in Africa are not political but administrative; more than political parties and charismatic leaders, administrative cadres define the symbolic conditions of life in so far as they provide the boundaries of possibility and the methods of procedure which politicians must adopt. Because economic development appears central to the meaning of life—in

West Africa at any rate—and because it is bureaucrats who engage in planning and measuring this development, it is they who are the 'leaders' of their society; they are the theologians while the politicians only say Mass. Despite their glamour, affluence and power, politicians have in a real sense become functionaries of the officials they supposedly control. In an environment which is increasingly concerned with information and in which planning is slowly but surely equated with both humaneness and efficiency, experts in the gathering and handling of information combine the central humanitarian concerns of poor societies with the techniques and promises of the wealthy ones. In a complex process of renaissance proportions which is still but vaguely understood, new meanings of life have been rapidly disseminated among African populations; these new meanings are bureaucratic and economic as well as political. Though, for reasons as much connected with Cold War politics as with anything else, considerable scholarly attention has been focused on problems of political integration, the fundamental object of social change in the poor countries is the economic integration of society and individual economic improvement, not political stability and the refinement of nationalism.[14]

The political 'international demonstration effect' has had rapid and profound consequences. In an astonishingly brief period, the example of the first independent African states has been taken and much of the continent has definitively altered its political state; independence is of that nature. But while the change is gross and crucial, the proponents and operators of this change—the politicians—may be of decreasing estimation and importance in African society. Perhaps Nkrumah's 'Dawn Broadcast', in which he sharply chastised his politicians, symptomised an alteration of perspective and redefinition of who was most crucial for the national welfare. This is not to say politicians are unimportant and will cease to be highly rewarded for success in achieving prominence. But just as pre-independence politicians defined their task in terms of the antipathy and power of colonial civil servants, a decade after independence they may once again discover that they operate, not against, but still within the terms of reference of bureaucrats. Not, this time, because officials represent the imperial power, but because they possess skills—perhaps acquired at the imperial universities—to enable politicians to be able to satisfy the wishes of their people for economic and social development. Among the educated, political power and the search for it may be an increasingly unrewarding prospect.*

In a striking suggestion of the diminished prestige of career politicians, Clignet and Foster find that, of a sample of secondary school students in Ivory Coast and Ghana, '. . . very few students envisage a career in politics. In fact, less than 1 per cent of Ivory Coast pupils and only 1·5 per cent of Ghanaians even remotely contemplate political careers.'[15] While they relate this finding in part to the insecurity of West African politics and, paradoxically, to the entrenchment of the current crop of leaders, there is a 'substantial preference for occupations within the public sector: over 69 per cent of Ivory Coast and 85 per cent of Ghanaian students would prefer to work for the government'.[16] When we note that about 60 per cent of employment opportunities in the 'modern' sector of the economy are in public enterprise in Ghana (up from about 40 per cent in 1951)[17] we may appreciate the significance and realism of these students' decisions. Roughly one-half of the students sought medical or scientific-technological careers; this too reveals an emphasis on control and use of information, and a devaluation of control and manipulation of power.

* This was written before the Ghana military coup of 1966 and the other African coups of that period. In general, these events appear to reinforce the view that politicians as a group and force in Ghana and elsewhere are losing some of the predominance which preceded and followed independence. That coups have occurred in countries with considerably different ideologies—such as Nigeria and Ghana—should dispose of the notion quite commonly held that Nkrumah's Marxist-style centralising pattern of administration and his attitude to political dissent were the chief causes of the coup. While these were undoubtedly important and catalytic causes, the suggestion here is that there are others related to larger issues of political development, social change and mass communication which form the essential background to more specific operations of specific political communities. The basically bureaucratic, administrative-based nature of military organisation is also pertinent. I have tried to deal with some of these issues in "Ghanaian Politics and Social Change", *International Journal of Comparative Sociology*, Vol. 7, No. 1, March 1966.

'Both samples are oriented towards government employment in the largest urban centers and attach overwhelming importance to occupational stability.'[18] Though obviously only suggestive, an implication of this kind of material is that students make their own career plans by projecting from current patterns; these encourage them to seek attachment to the bureaucratic infrastructure's involvement in the process of economic development, thus assuring long-term employment of their skills. To use Karl Deutsch's phrase, they appear to aspire to be the 'nerves of government', rather than the government itself. More than that: they aspire to participate in a communication system based on literacy, within which they have been educated, and prefer to leave to others activity in the non-literate sectors of society. That they also look forward to urban life is no accident but an aspect of the triple-factor *Gestalt* of urbanism, education and bureaucracy, referred to earlier and returned to below.

Bureaucracy and Words

Bureaucracy is founded on literacy—on the process of giving and receiving written orders and recording information in a permanent way. As much as the rule book, the filing cabinet and the memo define the nature of bureaucratic interchange. The emphasis on written words in Western culture is profound; perhaps it is this very characteristic which makes it distinctive.

In the religious sphere, 'In the Beginning was the Word', 'The Word of God', 'The Word was made Flesh', the Tablets of Moses and the very notion of the Bible suggest the importance of verbal and written communication. In the Canadian legal system, written libel is more readily and harshly dealt with than unwritten slander. Only comparatively recently have some social scientists approached the study of human behaviour empirically rather than in a literary way. Throughout our culture, written words are endowed with value and certainty beyond that normally granted to spoken words; not a telephone but a teleprinter hot line was installed between Washington and Moscow. In our places of education, the visual contemporary electronic and aural arts have only scarcely achieved some measure of equality with verbal arts, while in many institutions they are still unrecognised. At the University of British Columbia, for example, there are numerous courses on literature, but only part of one course deals with radio and film as media of communication. While there are obviously simple practical reasons for this manner of response to electrically transmitted matter, there may also be profound and extensive ones which symptomise the very way in which educated people apprehend their universe and derive understanding and art from this process.

Self-evidently, structures of thought and the attribution of significance to human relationships must be mediated by this particular form of apprehension. Less evident may be the effect of literacy on the selection of things to know and do, and on what is seen to constitute the real world and the world of the possible. Is it legitimate to suggest that literate communication is inherently more conservative than electronic communication—particularly films, television and radio—and that the mass revolution of rising expectations and frustrations did not get substantially under way until written communication was replaced or accompanied by the more provocative, complex and, at the same time, more meaningful and familiar stimuli of the electronic media? In other words, was the revolution of independence a mandarin movement, stimulated by competence in the craft of literacy and framed by the rules of bureaucratic interchange? And is the successor revolution one in which people demand, not collective political goods, but material ones based on the replacement of ten thousand words by a picture?

Broadly, our concern here is with that skipping-of-steps which David Riesman has called a movement '. . . from pre-literacy or illiteracy to the post-literate stage of the mass-media'.[19] This post-literate condition is dependent upon the technological developments in mass communication. For the first time on an extensive scale, persons unable to read can have information of a relatively complex and direct kind about other societies, new artifacts and different patterns of behaviour. While the nature of the material communicated is important, equally significant may be the nature of the very medium itself and its consequences for personality.

Some intriguing if controversial suggestions of the utility of this approach to the role of technology in human communications have been provided by Marshall McLuhan.[20] While McLuhan's concepts have not been systematically tested by field research, the literary and case-history evidence he adduces is extensive, and several of his observations about the relationship of 'tribal' culture to communications technology appear relevant to this essay.

Sharply sketched, his argument is as follows: the kind of communication which occurs by means of mechanical, linear, typographic modes differs fundamentally from that possible when electricity is the agent for instantaneous contact between people. Electrically transmitted communication is an almost literal extension of man's nervous system. This fact, together with the resources of automation and feedback mechanisms which link action with reaction, reflect an interdependence of man with man which McLuhan decides is tribal and preliterate. Because of their peculiar affinity for the literary and linear rather than the non-literary, scholars have paid far more attention to the transcribed content of the media than to the different social and psychological consequences of various media. But, as McLuhan phrases it, 'the medium is the message'. Though he may overstate this aspect of his case, his view corresponds in part with de Sola Pool's: 'the important thing about a medium is not what it says *per se* but the social function (a) of its existence as an institution and (b) of the statements in it'.[21] McLuhan examines the importance of the existence of a medium in greater detail than is here necessary. What is particularly relevant is his conception of the difference literacy makes. For example:

> Suppose that, instead of displaying the Stars and Stripes, we were to write the words 'American flag' across a piece of cloth and to display that. While the symbols would convey the same meaning, the effect would be quite different. To translate the rich visual mosaic of the Stars and Stripes into written form would be to deprive it of most of its qualities of corporate image and of experience, yet the abstract literal bond would remain much the same. Perhaps this illustration will serve to suggest the

> change tribal man experiences when he becomes literate. Nearly all the emotional and corporate family feeling is eliminated from his relationship with his social group. He is emotionally free to separate from the tribe and to become a civilised individual, a man of visual organisation who has uniform attitudes, habits and rights with all other civilized individuals. . . . To act without reacting, without involvement, is the peculiar advantage of Western literate man.[22]

This medium-centred approach to the affective/affective-neutral dichotomy may reveal a facet of the process of bureaucratisation largely unexamined by students of this process. The relevance of this may be considerable for a society in which literacy is still unusual, and in which literate bureaucrats have enormous responsibility in governments which also require the participation of illiterate persons in what are essentially literate schemes. At this stage in the argument it is principally necessary to suggest that the social implications of the method of communication are at least as important as the message transmitted.

As a consequence of communication facilities, persons making the move to post-literacy are inevitably drawn into urban symbol systems of their own and other societies. As a result, expectations or demands for change are created which can only be satisfactorily met by programmes of development created by highly-trained urban-dwelling bureaucrats. However, the urban world of the bureaucrat is the linear, literary, world-of-the-administratively-possible and differs from the instantaneous, total, everything-is possible-which-I-can-see-and-hear-world of the illiterate. Conceptually, the worlds of the literate higher administrator and the illiterate migrant worker, cook, sweeper or unemployed may both focus on urban life and what it does and can provide. But the routes to this provision are very different for each; they approach the city from different directions and scarcely overlap even upon convergence in the metropolis.

The bureaucrat is concerned with words, not images and sounds; those who cannot read or write are deprived of participation in the communication system within which the bureaucrat works. It is in this sense a closed system—an elitist system in fact —because relatively few can read or write in the first place, and because the nature of bureaucratic communication is secretive. Within the bureaucracy the need to have everything in writing requires that some messages be transmitted publicly but, since privacy must be maintained, there is extensive use of files marked Confidential, Private, Restricted, Top Secret, etc. Information must be written and thus public, but restricted and thus private. Though this may not be so in other bureaucracies, senior Ghanaian bureaucrats appeared reluctant to use the telephone to conduct their business and preferred memoranda transmitted by a messenger system. While this is in part due to the simple fact that the messenger system was efficient and the telephone system somewhat less so, the written form of communication seemed clearly preferable even when the phone system was usable. This is understandable, given the nature of the bureaucratic process; but alongside the traditionally oral mode of conduct of government in Ghanaian society, this choice constitutes a crucial parameter of difference.

The word is not only written but is in English, the second language of most senior bureaucrats; this is presumably of equal significance in distinguishing the bureaucratic view from the reality-perception of the illiterates. In this sense, the medium *is* the most important message. Simply being involved in the bureaucratic operation commits one to a series of relationships, communications and activities which define individuals in a substantial way. While the bureaucracy is not a 'total institution' in Erving Goffman's sense, at least during the working day it functions as a near-total institution in so far as its means of communication are so different from those of the surrounding society. The source of its legitimacy of action is also apart from that of its environment. In these respects the bureaucrats may be functionally equivalent to the Latin-speaking churchmen of medieval Europe who carried on, in an alien and written tongue, procedures devoted to an end with which laymen were in ardent agreement, but which they could not reach without the intermediation of a group defined by education and ordination as qualitatively different from themselves. If Eric Ashby's characterisation is correct, '. . . the universities and their graduates are isolated from the life of the common people in a way which has had no parallel in England since the Middle Ages'.[23] The religious analogy may be appropriate to describe those graduates employed in the bureaucratic government organisations they create and operate.[24]

The 'common people' will not necessarily know exactly or even generally what it is that the higher bureaucracy does; as La Palombara observes,[25] far more important to a citizen's conception of the civil service may be the nature of his treatment by the lower-level officials with whom he comes into contact. At the same time, 'The more local communities have their appetite whetted by the "demonstration effect" for improvements which can be paid for only by the central government, the more unrealistic local politics becomes, and the more extended the central bureaucratic apparatus.'[26] Further, given that not only funds but also the mass media originate in the urban regions, the relationship between rural welfare and the money and power of the city will become more clearly revealed. The central government and its bureaucratic structure will appear to be a uniquely qualified elite, based not on traditional right or colonial conquest, but on its adroitness in exacting taxes and translating them into: (i) public 'shrines' of modernity—schools, roads, hospitals and the infra-structure in general; (ii) constant displays of their effortless competence in unravelling the mysteries of the international scene; and (iii) the private affluence and prestige of the official class. From the viewpoint of the illiterate or barely literate person, these factors combine to encourage the creation of a sense of the importance and symbolic power of high civil servants.

Bureaucratic Status and Self-Conception

Not only the illiterate peasant but the bureaucrat, when he evaluates his own worth in society, will be inclined to conclude that his skills and his income affirm superiority. He has inherited a standard of living defined by 'duty-post housing' and various allowances. In Nigeria, until recently, he also received 'home leave' to the United Kingdom. In the interest of non-discrimination between white and black officials, European standards of payment and perquisite were imposed upon an indigenous revenue and salary structure which could ill-afford such expenditure for even a relatively few higher civil servants.[27]

But perhaps more important than the budgetary implications of this high payment is the standard of living it affords. The cadre of higher civil servants inhabits the bungalows of the former colonial service and indulges in a style of life at least comparable to that enjoyed by their former governors.[28] As factors in the development of symbol systems, wealth and place of residence augment and reinforce the mystique accompanying the hegemony of the civil servant in the symbolic power structure of the community. Given that, as in Ghana, public employment is the dominant form of 'modern' employment, it is understandable that those individuals who supervise this mass of steadily employed and privileged persons will hold considerable power. Various aspects of the Ghanaian prestige structure suggest the important difference in this respect between that structure and the North American one; the Ghanaian is closer to the United Kingdom pattern with its attribution of panache and mandarinesque ability to the administrative grade bureaucrat. In Ghana, advertisements for razor blades and liquor may employ, as the prestigious referrent figure, a civil servant drawn against the background of the ministry buildings. Car advertisements may note that Peugeot is preferred by civil servants or that government officials who travel extensively choose the rugged Vauxhall or swift Renault. While this may represent little more than a maintenance of colonial patterns, there is also evidence that it is a more dynamic reflection of social gradations than simple habit would account for. While it is unimportant in itself (and there are relatively few advertisements in Ghanaian papers anyway) it is apposite to other indications of the place which Ghanaian senior civil servants occupy in the prestige structure of the country.

However significant such projective matter may or may not appear, more directly germane are the incomes and perquisites which higher bureaucrats enjoy. Until 1963–64, fairly liberal car allowances were permitted many officers in the administrative grade of the service, whether or not their job specifically required extensive travel on the job. Another colonial perquisite—low-cost, relatively superior housing—defined and enhanced the conditions of life of higher civil servants. Ghanaian officials inherited the spacious, if not wholly modern, dwellings of departing Englishmen and inherited as well the exclusiveness of residential areas which had once been 'For Whites Only'. The elaborately gardened land around the bungalows and the lack of distracting commercial establishments and lower-status groups in the neighbourhood contributed to an air of privilege which has been largely retained if only because the architecture and landscaping of the most prestigious government residential environs coerce this immodest image. Cooler, quieter and without urban hustle, the living areas reflect the certainty of permanence of their colonial builders. This expectation has now been acquired by the indigenous inheritors of the houses apparently built to recreate Surrey. The fact that higher civil servants are unusually privileged, in so far as they are provided with homes in a situation of widespread shortage, specifies them as an extraordinary group. That efforts were not made to charge the occupants of these houses an 'economic rent' until 1964 suggests how surely the bureaucratic privilege was defended, and how reluctant an otherwise expeditious government was to engage in negotiation with persons presumably their dependents.

A further privilege inherited from their white predecessors was free or relatively inexpensive medical care, usually at 'The Ridge Hospital' in the Ridge residential area where senior officials and their families lived. While it is doubtless financially defensible to assure good health for officials whose time and effectiveness are valuable, a consequence of this perquisite is to emphasise the fact that senior officials are privileged not only because they have high incomes but because they are senior officials.

A constellation of privileges, then, affirms for the community that, while officials are powerful and important persons in the government, they are also special people who are awarded highly desirable goods on a continuous and sanctioned basis. For the officers, their wealth, position and the security of their jobs appear to make them relatively oblivious to these things; the persons interviewed in this study—most of whom would form part of any reckoning of the official elite in Ghana—did not protest about their material working conditions and appeared to consider their high place in the community as their due. There seemed to be a congenial 'fit' between what they received and what they deserved; despite the poverty which surrounded them, they enjoyed their affluence with nonchalance and a sense of rectitude. After all, they were civil servants and thus exploiters of none; more honest than the politicians, they also had the long-run view of things and were managers of the data and the plans which would improve the lot of those less trained than they.

As has been argued about stratification systems, those people who are highly rewarded often reflect a community's values. In the Ghanaian situation, the nature of colonialism determined the reward structure, which the prestige structure apparently followed rather than reflected. While there may be a movement under way in the direction of curtailed reward, particularly for younger officials, the structure of opportunities, rewards and prerogatives of senior civil servants is likely to remain such as (i) to offer these officials a setting in which to create very favourable conceptions of themselves and of their profession; and (ii) to induce members of the surrounding community to continue to regard bureaucrats as important individuals practising an irreplaceable craft, strategic to the nation's development.

Attempts to limit the payment and perquisites of younger officials must be seen in perspective; most of these cadets will have entered the service after three years at the University of Ghana on government scholarships which allow them to live in luxury greater than that enjoyed by most dormitory students in England or Canada. After graduation, scholarship students, which means virtually all, are bonded to serve the government as cadet civil servants or secondary school teachers for periods of three to five years.[29] Because of the still basically elitist nature of the higher education system in Ghana[30] and the cachet which attaches to 'the graduate' in the society, it would be unlikely that such temporary impoverishments of the bureaucratic career as have been proposed would affect significantly its place in the occupational structure of the society. In time, of course, there will be more graduates; simple scarcity will no longer award high status.[31] But given also that the role of the civil service in Ghana will continue to expand and that kudos will attach to those who manipulate the power this will involve, it should continue to be the case that the mass of the population will envy even cadet civil servants, and that the symbol system with which this essay concerns itself will remain substantially unchanged with respect to bureaucratic work.

Politics and the Bureaucratic Profession

The good fortune of civil servants shows no sign of being less secure than it has been. Until 1962, very few Ghanaian senior officials left their posts under overt duress. Apart from a number of careers affected by investigations of probity, it appears that patterns of promotion and reward were generally stable. Amidst all the confusion and despite the fear and rancour engendered by several attempted assassinations of President Nkrumah, one employee of the Ghana Broadcasting System was the only high level official charged with misdemeanour or inefficiency, even though a number of important politicians were accused of treason. The latter even included President Nkrumah's protégé, Tawia Adamafio, and his Foreign Minister and long-time ally, Ako Adjei. In 1961, Kojo Botsio and Krobo Edusei, among others, were asked to resign because of inordinate accumulation of property, and Komla Gbedemah (Finance Minister for seven years) left the country after a variety of insinuations were made about his private enterprise. But throughout all this major movement of politicians at the highest level of government, civil servants were unnamed in any of the formal charges. Also, though this can be less certain, there was none of the rumour and innuendo about bureaucrats which would be predicted had they been discernibly involved. What is important in this is that the bureaucracy was not used as a scapegoat during a difficult period in the nation's life, nor, apparently, were individuals who were unidentified with the Convention Peoples Party subjected to harassment or to the interruption of their careers. Indeed, despite the extremely rapid pace of change in Ghana and the appearance of uncertainty and disorganisation, the civil service has remained stable and yet has been resilient in the face of considerable demands upon it. While some may doubt that it will always be so, there is so far no adequate evidence that party affiliation is essential in ensuring regular advancement and opportunity.[32]

Thus in the one-party polity of Ghana, the role of the bureaucracy has been expanded as the ambitions and needs of the society have expanded. Not only have the activities and responsibilities of the bureaucracy grown, but its influence may well have increased very disproportionately. Elsewhere[33] I discussed what could be seen as a process of 'routinisation of charisma' centring on the Office of the President and based on Nkrumah's tendency, since 1960, to involve civil servants formally in policy-making and decision-making activity to a degree previously unknown in his government. A variety of secretariats, authorities, and Control and Planning Commissions were created which undertake crucial tasks in the government of the nation.[34] In a sense, the Ghanaian system was presidential without high level bureaucratic patronage, and thus without institutionalised turnover of personnel. Over the years the President's confidence in his officials and his concomitantly greater reliance on their decisions and advice, as well as his apparently less enthusiastic use of politicians for the creation of basic plans and operating policy, yielded a situation in which skilled bureaucrats held much effective power, though no clear political involvement was required to achieve high position.[35] Not the political but the administrative apparatus shaped and managed the development schemes. In fact, some concern was expressed that members of parliament had insufficient challenge for their time and competence and some members had been appointed to work within the Seven-Year Development Scheme as 'expeditors'.[36]

Officials, then, sit on boards, committees and authorities as experts rather than as elected representatives. Criticism of a situation which elsewhere could stimulate accusations of 'bureaucracy' or 'socialism' or 'technocracy' are not made in Ghana. Indeed, the impression is offered that this is deemed desirable, that government by expert is thought appropriate to Ghana in its period of development. The persons who have lost most power in this situation are the politicians; it could be suggested that this loss was one of the underlying causes for the assassination attempt involving Adamafio, Adjei and Boi-Doku.[37]

This loss of power may also have been a basis for earlier disruptions in 1961, after economic planners guided by Nicholas Kaldor (now Harold Wilson's adviser) introduced an austerity budget focused on administrative, not political, goals. There have been subsequent efforts to curtail an adverse balance of payments during a period of establishment of industry in the country. These endeavours have been governed by largely administrative considerations and have been politically unpopular. A glance at the *Ghana Times* and the *Evening News* will suggest the emphasis currently placed on the economic development in the country; there is elaborate news of self-help projects, installation of industrial plants, creation of new administrative machinery for co-operative agriculture and promises about the effect of the 'D-plan' on the people of Ghana. Information is prominently available about the movements and actions of foreign advisers hired by the government, or under United Nations or other auspices. The general impression is that what in North America is normally on financial pages is simply news in Ghana. While obviously the earnest journalism about development is in part explicable by the government's propaganda programme and its control over newspapers, it is at the same time a reality of the environment that this reporting exists in almost war-like proportions and intensity. The fact that there is a constant emphasis on communal material acquisitions such as bridges, factories and schools, all of which will ultimately contribute to the general welfare, cannot fail to impress itself on the Ghanaian and the visitor as a symptom of the community's deepest concerns. The constant involvement of government employees with the planning and maintenance of these additions to the society's wealth is inevitably extensive and, while politicians take the credit, on behalf of 'the people', any particular event is placed in the context of a process of planning and administering the nation's programme for attaining prosperity.

I have tried to outline the ideal-typical status and economic position of the senior official, and have suggested some ways in which his work is visible and real to many people. It has been proposed that he is known to be at the centre of a process which involves most people, from which all will gain, though to which only a few can contribute more than a little extra labour or perhaps some small development fund donation.[38] What keeps him in an influential place is his technical knowledge and his experience with the administration of the civil service. At the same time as his expertise is necessary to the public good, and although his services may only be regarded as selfless and constructive, his remuneration and perquisites permit him a style of life far more luxurious than that of virtually all the citizenry of whom he is a servant. While this may not be unusual in itself, the inheritance from the colonial past, the scarcity of his skill and qualifications and the dominance of the government as employer assure the senior official a crucial place in the system of symbols surrounding the national life. Internationally, he is enabled by his competence and training to interact effectively with foreign persons who manage economies at a level to which Ghanaians aspire. The official's ability to do this, because of his familiarity with a literate medium of communication and because of his participation in an organisation predicated on this medium, is a matter of importance to the non-literate citizens of his country, while his expertise defines for semi-literates the extent of their relative inadequacy.

Illiterates and the Bureaucracy as Symbol

Earlier I noted Ashby's observation that the relationship of contemporary West African graduates to non-graduate fellow citizens compared with the relationship of educated persons to their fellows in the Middle Ages. We may use the perspective and scope implied in this remark, bearing in mind Fustel de Coulanges's (albeit controversial) characterisation of the city of medieval times as essentially religious, to examine the relationship of senior bureaucrats in Ghana to their non-literate compatriots, and to their role in the development of national symbol systems.

In medieval times religious reality defined the nature of existential reality for most persons in European society. The Church and its furniture—cathedrals, effigies, paintings, vestments—reflected an other-world which, in many lives, had real implications for this-world. The symbolic system which the Church created, interpreted and manipulated was controlled by the ordained elect, who had both spiritual and literate powers as a result of education. The laity was clearly apart from this special group, and was not only subject to its dicta on mortal and immortal matters but supported it with money in a variety of ways. Because literate communication was largely the province of the clergy, it was the clergy who could determine for most persons the extensions of themselves in time and place, and who could, most significantly, define the possible. If politics is the art of the possible, religion historically has been the creator of the possible; one could go to heaven or hell, have bliss or suffer like Job, be baptised or unsaved, take communion with an historic god or expect to encounter one in the future by taking strategic personal and economic actions. The Church was not only a form of government, it was a programme for the future—a lifetime development plan. Simply being a member of the clergy defined behaviour in a crucial way; the uniform implied that membership in the organisation was more socially significant than what one did in it. To repeat and extend an earlier phrase, the organisation was the medium was the message.

Just as the Church's property, ritual and its promises of heaven and hell functioned in the past, it is argued here that the mass media, as major agencies of the 'international demonstration effect', induce in the population at large the yearnings and frustrations earlier associated with religious cosmologies. As towering churches and mystifying ritual affected people, so also must they be affected by foreign films and picture books, tall office buildings, the chanceries of diplomacy, the complexity of industry—the whole tangible apparatus of modernity. What is also comparable about the two situations is that, in both, the action an individual can take without joining the divine or official elect is very limited. Just as most Catholics in the Middle Ages could not read the Holy Book or lead the Holy Mass, it is impossible for the non-literate Ghanaian to live with or like the citizens of Beverly Hills, or act like the engineers of the Imperial College, or enjoy the catholicity of experience of the jet set and its disciples. His possibility of enjoying these must be vicarious; while he may aspire to share some of their affluence and control-over-environment, he is excluded from the secret of how to do these things. His only direct role in the process—to work harder and more effectively—can provide yields perhaps expanded but relatively trivial nonetheless. The masterful steps—those desirable crucial actions—are undertaken by others who appear to do far less work and manage chiefly by their special competence in the language and practice of learning and administration.

But the onlookers are excluded, like the tragi-comic Cockney in *Beyond the Fringe* who reminisces and complains, 'I would of been a judge but I didn't have Latin, I didn't have the Latin, for the judgin'.' To the Accra 'cockney', the dams, the factories, the laboratories are not available, nor can he participate in them except vicariously. In terms of the scale of these creations and processes, there is relatively little he can do on his own which will be meaningfully satisfying to him. His life permits him only derivative satisfaction from impressive objects and processes representing communal goals achieved through the expertise of foreign or local managers of esoteric information. The prestigious items associated with development and modernisation can be created by members of a knowledge system which excludes him and to which he has no significant means of contribution.

Thus he lacks not only the 'Latin', but literacy and membership in the organisation which, though secular, like a religion defines the possible for him. This 'possible' is sudden and total—a 'non-lineal codification of reality', to use Dorothy Lee's phrase.[39] It does not depend on sequences of cause-and-effect or ordination; it happens all at once. The film provides a way of life with behaviour and environment inexorably linked, in which the new stimuli are regarded as having always been there; the process of their creation is not evident when they are perceived. Buildings, dams, stories on the wireless, television programmes, advertisements: all provide experiences comparable to revelations. They define the possible; they provide instant apprehension of the culmination of a long process. Though it is obscure to them, rural and urban peasants may appreciate that there is a process. It is not however obscure to the ministry officials and their counterparts in other organisations—this the peasantry knows. The essential consequence of this confrontation between the perceptions of reality of non-literates and the skilled actions of senior officials is reinforcement of the sense of exclusion of the non-literate. So different are the wealth, prestige, security, and accomplishments of the officials, in comparison with his own trivial income and creative power, that the non-literate bridges the gap with a mystique, in the cargo-cult style. He sees knowledge as the key to the mystic craft, and demands education for his offspring with remarkable ferocity and direction.

We are already aware of the outcome of this pressure on governments; high school leavers haunt cities seeking the work their apprenticeship to the literate masters promised. Governments despair of providing urban jobs for these partially-trained clerk-aspirants. The government of Western Nigeria[40] promotes a scheme to enable them to return to farming on a rationalised basis. The Ghana government enlists them into the Builders Brigades and moves them about the country; there is insufficient room in Accra for all of them, and many operate collective farms in the kind of environment they educated themselves to leave. Even the secondary school students in Clignet and Foster's sample[41] expressed aspirations unlikely to be met by Ghana's economy.

Just as earlier in Ghana's educational history there was a close association between conversion to Christianity and education, because of the dominance of missionary schooling prior to 1948,[42] there is a current attachment of high ambitions to even low-grade accomplishment in school. Unlike a society such as the United States, which finds the discontinuity between the values of its educational systems and the personalities of some of its students reflected in a significant drop-out rate, Ghanaian youngsters embrace learning, literacy and modernisation as chief values in Ghanaian society. The acceptance of these values is seen as leading to the rewards of conversion of a non-religious kind—a conversion involving more than the acquisition of familiarity with English and the Bible and of an Anglicised name and church membership. Required now is a place at the university, then in the ministries, and finally participation in the appealing round of functions of the senior officer: trips abroad, consultations with United Nations experts, the issue and receipt of splendid documents, telephoning, cabling, receptions, a title in the chief hierarchy of a symbol-minded society, and the basis of all this—life in Accra, the city.

The 'modernizing autocracy'[43] of Ghana is not a rural movement in its symbolism; its central body of operatives does not form a country squirearchy. It is also significant that, over the years since independence, the pattern of civil service staffing of rural and urban District Commissioners' posts has been altered and now these are political posts. Though there are a variety of political and economic reasons for this, one consequence is that civil servants are removed both conceptually and physically from the conditions of rural life. That this situation was likely to manifest itself in urban-oriented development proposals was evident and, for many years of colonial rule in Africa, the agricultural economy was treated with less skill and concern than urban industrial activity.[44] Not until the recent Seven Year Plan did rural regions receive the detailed attention previously devoted to industrial areas. Even now the prestigious projects are urban and industrial[45] while rural regions are increasingly deprived of funds and of people by the urban areas and urban-type development activity. This happens despite the predominantly agricultural economy of the area. Change which has been forthcoming in the planning emphasis may be largely determined by the sophisticated urban need to reduce payment of foreign exchange for agricultural products, so as to permit its use for purchase of industrial capital goods. Less importance would seem to have been attached to the unsophisticated rural view that agriculture is a respectable manner of employment possessing importance and dignity on its own.[46]

Development plans created by persons trained and working in 'modern' city environments on literate schemes, dependent on the bureaucratic process, are apt to be dissociated from the existential reality of farmers. This is not to say agricultural planning is impossible; it does imply that translation is necessary from one sphere to the other, and that this translation requires skills and tolerance apparently unusual in many countries. Since West Africans are relative newcomers to hard agricultural planning, it is too early to know the outcome of their specific efforts. But what is relevant for our purposes here is that this planning takes place in terms of a scheme of wants to which nearly all citizens are exposed. Unlike some societies in Europe which sought to manage their development and planning programmes by stopping, through censorship, the introduction of alien conceptions of desirable living standards, Ghanaians are widely exposed to foreign life-styles, and are in fact encouraged to seek parity with wealthier nations. Inevitably, pre-independence politics defined independence as a time when the living standards of the colonial power would not be supported by the oppressed colonies and when it would be possible therefore to improve life significantly in independent countries. This has not been quite the case and the adverse changes in the relationship between the costs of primary and manufactured goods have exacerbated the difficulties which governments face. The growing differences in wealth between rich and poor countries, coupled with the consequences of the international demonstration effect, force the development process to occur within a situation of tension and invidiousness and with a humbling awareness of the suffering of large populations.

It has been suggested that African countries are fiercely future-oriented[47] and that this defines many of the issues of politics. At the same time as these societies may be looking eagerly to the future, they need not do so with uncertainty. Their future is Spain's or Canada's or Denmark's present. What they can want is clear. How they can achieve it is less clear, but there is sufficient input from international and national aid organisations to clarify procedures and objectives.[48] Furthermore, the involvement of foreign personnel and capital in large projects compels the acceptance of universally-defined bureaucratic methods of accountancy, projection, budgeting and so on. In this connection, it has been suggested[49] that Nkrumah's increased dependence on civil-service-staffed agencies coincided significantly with the start of construction on the Volta River Project. This enterprise was of such complexity, ramification and uncertain profitability that the highest standards of administrative and executive control were required. Politicians were untrained to these standards and could not adequately supervise the work. This principle of administrative centralisation is presumably extensible to other enterprises of cumulative importance.[50]

But whatever the ideological position, the trend is clearly in the direction of centralised government control of economic as well as other activity, and to this end the accumulation of administrative talent in the capital will continue. Whereas in Western nations governments increase in size and influence despite considerable public antipathy to these changes, Ghanaians have entered a period of large-scale government activity without this antipathy. Whereas Western nations live with a suspicion of power,[51] Ghanaians harbour no such suspicion and, contrariwise, appear favourably disposed to extensive government activity.[52] Consequently, centralisation of resources and skilled administrators will continue without ideological impediment. The combination of materialism and socialism may be expected to operate to ensure the growth of centralised administrative units. Linked to a concern with the management of the future is a need for reasonable data and control of the present; under these circumstances, and in the context of world-wide bureaucracies and super-national agencies, it is to be anticipated that trained officials in government capitals, such as Accra, Abidjan, Conakry and Dakar, will take hold of these operations.

That much is obvious. But at the same time as they operate at a pace appropriate to bureaucratic thoroughness, sequence and caution, the persons they serve absorb stimuli from instantaneous electronic contacts with events and things in far wealthier societies. Rural dwellers have contact with urban events in their own society. Not explosion but, as McLuhan puts it, implosion occurs and, in his phrase, people 'live in a global village'. All persons can interact symbolically through the agency of the electronic mass media—mainly radio, television and films—and can be aware of the reality of other societies in a world of expanded possibility. If that possibility is to become locally realised, it will be evident to urban and rural dwellers alike that such developments must come from the city, where persons knowledgeable in the necessary manipulation of the future reside. In the way North American retailers add significance to a product by noting 'Advertised on TV' or 'As Advertised in *Life*', so significance will become attached to facets of materialistic and automated life, i.e., secular matters. Yet for the illiterate and the person not understanding bureaucratic ways, all this may have a style of sacredness to it, because it is based on the non-material mind-work of experts and officials, and because mainly by this method will the possible become real.

Experts and administrators are familiar to Africans in those societies which already possessed administrative elites and functional specialisation.[53] But what may be significant about the newer situation is the manipulative relationship of these elites to exogenous systems of production and consumption which are now displayed by the media to all, including those who may never afford such goods and services but who may feel that they have some right to them.

If 'religion is the opiate of the people', the mass media have a contrary effect. The media stimulate people to sustain some conceptions of the materially possible which will create dissatisfaction rather than promote worldly acquiescence for supernatural gain. But given the structures of contemporary developing societies, the response to this stimulation must depend upon centralised, metropolitan, bureaucratic activity. In the symbol system of non-elite Africans, satisfaction of the wants engendered by the mass media will depend upon the urban-based work of civil servants. At the same time, these officials possess the material welfare which others will have difficulty in achieving. This may have social consequences for which the officials will have no reproach or remedy. We must recall Riggs's synthesis: 'Little enough attention is given to the need for bringing the newly mobilized into community with the elite. Yet this is precisely one of the most acute problems of political development. . . . The internationally encouraged mania for educational development and the spread of mass media is scarcely counterbalanced by pressures for political assimilation.'[54]

Ultimately there may have to be wilful management—possibly

symptomised by the military coups—of the assymetry between popular wants induced by mass media and the popular view of the sacred-type bureaucratic process which is a prelude to satisfaction of these wants. The nature and timing of this management are not the concerns of this essay, but the fact that it will of necessity have an urban focus underlines the tight interdependence of urbanity and world-view.

Notes and References

1 For support of this project, I am grateful to the Foreign Area Training Fellowship Program, the Canada Council, and the Sub-Committee on Comparative Bureaucracy of the Social Science Research Council. These organisations are, of course, not responsible for the contents of the paper.

2 Fustel de Coulanges, *The Ancient City*, Garden City, NY, 1956, pp. 126–7.
3 Daryll Forde, "Methodology in the Study of African Urbanization", in Kenneth Little, ed., *Urbanization in African Social Change*, Edinburgh 1963, p. 3.
4 R. Lambert and B. Hoselitz, eds., *The Role of Savings and Wealth in Southern Asia and the West*, Paris 1962, p. 405.
5 Don Martindale, "Introduction", in Martindale, trans. and ed., *The City*, by Max Weber, London 1960, p. 61.
6 Loc. cit.
7 Ibid., p. 55.
8 M. J. Herskovits, *The Human Factor in Changing Africa*, New York 1962, p. 260.
9 Ibid., p. 297.
10 There are some major Nigerian exceptions, for reasons which do not appear to invalidate the proposition made here. See William Bascom, "Some Aspects of Yoruba Urbanism", *American Anthropologist*, Vol. 64, August 1962, pp. 699–709.
11 Remi Clignet and Philip Foster, "Potential Elites in Ghana and the Ivory Coast: A Preliminary Comparison", *American Journal of Sociology*, Vol. 70, November 1964, pp. 349–62.
12 Daniel Lerner, *The Passing of Traditional Society*, Glencoe, Ill., 1958, pp. 61–5.
13 Reinhard Bendix, *Max Weber: An Intellectual Portrait*, London 1960, p. 433.
14 Ronald P. Dore, "The Search for Modernity in Asia and Africa: A Review Article", *Pacific Affairs*, Vol. 37, Summer 1964, pp. 161–5.
15 Clignet and Foster, op. cit., p. 359.
16 Ibid., p. 361.
17 Philip Foster, "Secondary Schooling and Social Mobility in a West African Nation", *Sociology of Education*, Vol. 37, Winter 1963, p. 152.
18 Clignet and Foster, op. cit., p. 362.

19 David Riesman, "Introduction", in Daniel Lerner, op. cit., p. 4.

20 Marshall McLuhan, *Understanding Media: The Extensions of Man*, New York 1964.

21 Ithiel de Sola Pool, "Mass Media and Politics", in Lucian Pye, ed., *Communications and Political Development*, Princeton 1963, p. 240.

22 McLuhan, op. cit., pp. 82, 86.

23 Eric Ashby, *African Universities and Western Tradition*, Cambridge, Mass., 1964, p. 42.

24 'This uncritical equating of education with special rights and legitimacy has endowed the educated African with an exaggerated sense of superiority and special legitimacy. Politics have been permeated with the presumably uncontestable assumption that the educated have a divine right to rule': James S. Coleman, "The Politics of Sub-Saharan Africa", in G. Almond and J. S. Coleman, eds., *The Politics of the Developing Areas*, Princeton 1960, p. 283.

25 J. LaPalombara, "An Overview", in LaPalombara, ed., *Bureaucracy and Political Development*, Princeton 1963, p. 7.

26 F. W. Riggs, "Bureaucracy and Development: A Paradoxical View", in LaPalombara, op. cit., p. 134.

27 See Thomas Balogh, "What Schools for Africa", *New Statesman*, March 23, 1962; J. Donald Kingsley, "Bureaucracy and Political Development with Particular Reference to Nigeria", in La Palombara, op. cit., p. 315.

28 Hugh H. Smythe and Mabel M. Smythe, *The New Nigerian Elite*, Stanford 1960, chap. 5.

29 This distresses businessmen, who claim that they support the university with their taxes yet receive little benefit in the form of freshly graduated employees.

30 Eric Ashby, op. cit., p. 20. The Ghana government has been trying with some difficulty for several years to 'democratise' the student body and the very meaning of a university education.

31 Colin Legum, "Africa's Intellectuals: The Thin Black Line", *New Society*, December 1964.

32 See *West Africa*, June 22, 1963, and James S. Coleman, op. cit., p. 317.

33 L. Tiger, "Bureaucracy and Charisma in Ghana", *Journal of Asian and African Studies*, Vol. 1, January 1966, pp. 13–26.

34 For example, a recent addition to the list is a central transport organisation to 'promote an effective and modern road transport system in the country'. Membership will consist of: the Chief Transport Officer, the managing director of the National Investment Bank and the Government Statistician, the chief engineer of the Ghana National Construction Corporation, a representative of the State Planning Commission, assisted by two United Nations transport experts and an official of the development scheme institute of the National Investment Bank: *Ghana Times*, April 25, 1964.

35 Colin Legum, op. cit.

36 *Ghana Times*, April 29, 1964.

37 L. Tiger, op. cit.

38 W. Abraham, *The Mind of Africa*, London 1962, p. 166.

39 Dorothy Lee, "Lineal and Nonlineal Codifications of Reality", in E. Carpenter and M. McLuhan, eds., *Explorations in Communications*, Boston 1960, p. 143. In the same volume, see David Riesman, "The Oral and Written Traditions".

40 Western Nigerian Development Plan, 1962–8, Sessional Paper No. 8, 1962, p. 19.

41 Op. cit., p. 360

42 H. O. A. McWilliam, *The Development of Education in Ghana*, London 1957.

43 D. E. Apter, "Political Religion in the New Nations", in Clifford Geertz, ed., *Old Societies and New States*, New York 1963, p. 98.

44 Arnold Rivkin, *The African Presence in World Affairs*, New York 1963, chap. 4.

45 Peter Kilby, "Balancing Town and Country", *West Africa*, August 29, 1964, p. 975.

46 It might be reasonably argued that the almost worldwide failure or indifferent success of economic planners' efforts in the agricultural sphere may depend, as in West Africa, on their acceptance of essentially urban standards of value, buttressed by a literate bureaucratic system of communication into which peasant perceptions and concerns are assimilated only with the exercise of greater sensitivity and flexibility than it is in the nature of bureaucracies to display. See S. C. Dube, *Bureaucracy and Nation-Building in Transitional Societies, Expert Working Group on Social Prerequisites to Economic Growth, Kenia, Cyprus*, Paris 1963, p. 6.

47 J. S. Coleman, op. cit., p. 285.

48 For example, see David Horowitz, "The International Welfare Community", *International Development Review*, Vol. 6, December 1964, and Ralph Braibanti, *Transnational Inducement of Administrative Reform: A Survey of Scope and Critique of Issues*, Bloomington, Ind., 1964.

49 L. Tiger, op. cit.

50 This does not mean that this is necessarily the most effective manner of operation; it is, however, consistent with both the colonial pattern of dirigiste economy, and with those ideological forces which define some form of 'African socialism' as desirable. Berg has argued, for example, that centralisation is dysfunctional to economic growth in sub-Saharan Africa. See Eliot J. Berg, "Socialism and Economic Development in Tropical Africa", *Quarterly Journal of Economics*, Vol. 78, November 1964, pp. 549–73. Berg doubts that contemporary mass media encourage production to satisfy these wants.

51 A. A. Rogow and H. D. Lasswell, *Power, Corruption, and Rectitude*, Englewood Cliffs, NJ, 1963.

52 W. E. Abraham, op. cit., chap. 4.

53 Lloyd Fallers, "Equality, Modernity, and Democracy in the New States", in Geetz, op. cit., p. 179.

54 F. W. Riggs, op. cit., p. 166.

9

Father-Child Relationships and Changing Life-Styles in Ibadan, Nigeria

ROBERT A. LEVINE, NANCY H. KLEIN
and CONSTANCE R. OWEN

EVERY LARGE CITY in Tropical Africa contains an indigenous 'educated elite' that is numerically small but important socially, culturally and politically. The men are high-ranking civil servants and professionals and often community and cultural leaders as well. It is these urban people who, with the university students destined to join their ranks, constitute the educated and internationally aware public of their nations. The style of life of those at the highest levels of Western education and international sophistication seems to depart more radically from indigenous traditions than does that of any other African population. To all appearances, these people represent the farthest point that individual acculturation has reached in Tropical Africa, and the greatest change in behaviour that has taken place there within the span of a single life. They can be viewed as a vanguard of change, exhibiting the results of an acculturative process that will probably continue to be associated with leadership in African nations and that may become widespread in the urban population. The cities in which these people live next to more traditional groups of the same ethnic background are therefore potential laboratories of socio-psychological change in Africa. In the study reported in this essay the

NOTE: *The notes and references for Chapter 9 will be found on page 253.*

city of Ibadan was used as such a laboratory to study the factors involved in socio-psychological change among the Yoruba.[1]

Theoretical Background

The socialisation of the child has most often been seen as a factor in cultural continuity and social stability, i.e., as insuring the transmission and conservation of a socio-cultural tradition from generation to generation. It is equally plausible, however, that when an alteration in social conditions (technological, economic, social-structural or ideological) changes the values, beliefs and life-styles of a given generation of individuals, these changes affect the way in which they socialise their young. If this is true, then the next generation experiences a different pattern of child care and training than its forebears, and socialisation is a process promoting the cumulation of individual change over generations rather than the persistence of tradition. This has been discussed by several social scientists.[2] Inkeles calls attention to 'the role that the parent plays, through both purposive and unconscious adjustments in the child rearing practices, in mediating the influence of social change to his children and consequently in better adapting them for the changed social conditions they meet as adults'.[3] On the assumption that child rearing practices determine modal personality or character, he states: 'There is reason to assume . . . that the influence of large-scale social change occurring at any one time may be reflected in the character of the next generation because of mediation by parents living under and experiencing the change.'[4]

Inkeles has aptly formulated the problems raised for empirical research by this theory:

> To test these assumptions one would ideally want a research design permitting the exploration of two distinct although intimately related questions. The first involves the hypothesis that parents who have experienced extreme social change seek to raise their children differently from the way in which they were brought up, purposefully adapting their child rearing practices

to train children better suited to meet life in the changed world as the parent now sees it. To test this hypothesis we would need detailed information about the child rearing practices utilized by two consecutive generations of parents in the same culture, the first of which lived and raised its children in a period of relative stability, whereas the second lived and brought up its children under conditions of fairly extreme social change. A different requirement is posed by the question of how effective the parents in the second generation are in developing new traits or combinations of traits in their children.[5]

The Nigerian study reported herein was limited to the first question. Unlike Inkeles's study of Russian refugees, the child rearing practices of the first generation were not reconstructed retrospectively but were measured, following Miller and Swanson[6] in their study of 'entrepreneurial' and 'bureaucratic' middle-class parents in Detroit, by taking one contemporary group of parents as representing the pre-change generation that reared the second group. This cross-sectional strategy for the study of social change processes, employed in Redfield's[7] research on the folk-urban continuum in Yucatan and many other studies, presents a number of problems of control and inference that are discussed in detail below.

Our larger study involved two groups of Yoruba parents in Ibadan investigated with respect to: the health and growth of their children;[8] the maternal treatment of, and values concerning, their children;[9] and paternal relationships with, and values concerning, the children. This article deals primarily with the last topic, which is of theoretical significance for the following reasons. Firstly, psychological studies have suggested that the quantity and quality of father-child interaction have an impact on the child's acquisition of behavioural dispositions such as achievement motivation,[10] authoritarianism,[11] sex identity,[12] and the tendency to turn aggression towards the self or towards others.[13] Thus a study of changes in father-child behaviour patterns could help us make predictions concerning possibly ensuing changes in personality. Secondly, in societies generally and contemporary Africa particularly, men, by virtue of their occupational roles and community participation, are more involved in extra-familial institutions and are more directly affected by patterns of institutional change. Thus fathers are likely to be important mediators of change[14] between their extra-familial sources on the one hand and the family and socialisation process on the other. Most previous socialisation studies have concentrated on interviewing mothers, but our data on the child rearing attitudes and practices of both mothers and fathers enables us to compare their conceptions of the socialisation process they are conducting. Differences can be related to their differential exposure to or involvement in processes of socio-cultural change.

The basic theoretical conception involved here can be restated in behaviouristic terms as follows: when there is a change in the stimuli associated with reinforcement—in this case, the complex patterns of social cues, incentives, rewards and punishment comprising the adult social environment and its norms of role performance—adults operating in such an environment perceive the changes and modify their behaviour so as to maximise social reward, minimise social punishment and respond to new incentives under the new conditions. Their new habits and expectancies—i.e., response patterns leading to reward in the new social environment—become generalised behavioural prescriptions perceived as relevant to the future success of their children in adapting to the environment. These changed individuals attempt to reinforce such adaptive behaviour in their children and, in so doing, (i) deviate from the child training practices that constituted their own childhood environment, and (ii) produce in their children behavioural dispositions differing from their own. The children turn out with behavioural dispositions different from those of their parents, even when the parents intend only to reproduce their own adaptive response patterns, because the children acquire them at an earlier age than the parents did, and because the altered child training practices of the parents have many unintended effects on the behaviour of their children. Parents may attempt to reinforce in their children only those behaviour patterns that they have experienced or perceived to be adaptive. Their ability to predict and control the effects of newly-adopted training procedures is limited, however, because, like psychologists, they have trouble identifying many of the reinforcers in the child's social environment. Thus we expect change in the social environment to lead to changes in socialisation as conducted by parents but, in so far as parents are imperfect child psychologists, they will create changes beyond the scope of their conscious goals.

Studies of Trends in Child Rearing

We refrain from applying 'modernisation' or any other term designating a general process to the changes investigated in Ibadan until we can state what those changes are and compare them with changes elsewhere, i.e., until we can assess the extent to which they resemble occurrences independent of the particular cultural setting in which we have observed them. Thus we review briefly what other investigators have found concerning changes in child rearing practices outside Africa.

In the study quoted above, Inkeles, comparing the child rearing values of Russian parents in the tsarist and post-revolutionary periods, found (among other results less generalisable beyond the Russian context) a rise in 'personalistic' values (emphasis on the development of personal qualities in the child) and a decline in traditional values. In comparing the values of tsarist, revolutionary and Soviet generations, he found a marked increase in the value set on self-expression, as opposed to family tradition, in occupational choice.[15]

Bronfenbrenner has summarised the secular trends in American child rearing (1930–55) as follows:

1. Greater permissiveness towards the child's spontaneous desires.
2. Freer expression of affection.
3. Increased reliance on indirect 'psychological' techniques of discipline (such as reasoning or appeals to guilt) *versus* direct methods (like physical punishment, scolding, or threats).
4. In consequence of the above shifts in the direction of what are predominantly middle-class values and techniques, there is a

narrowing of the gap between social classes in their patterns of child rearing.

5. In succeeding generations the relative position of the father vis-à-vis the mother is shifting, with the former becoming increasingly more affectionate and less authoritarian and the latter becoming relatively more important as the agent of discipline, especially for boys.[16]

Prothro conducted a recent interview study of 468 mothers in six Lebanese communities (rural and urban Sunni, Orthodox and Gregorian; each divided again into lower-class and middle-class samples) and found few class differences but a distinct 'modernisation' effect:

> Students of Lebanese society have often mentioned that the Christians of Beirut, and especially those of the middle class, are the most modern of the people to be found there, and that the rural Moslems, particularly those who are peasants, are the most traditional in their outlook and behavior. In the analysis of the answers given by these mothers to our many questions, it was noted that *child rearing practices often reflected the differences between modern and traditional mothers*. On many variables, the mothers expected to be more modern were at one extreme, those considered traditional at the other extreme, and the other mothers at some intermediate point. On a few items, the 'modern' and the 'traditional' mothers were similar to each other and different from the other mothers.
>
> The following characteristics were more likely to be found among 'modern' mothers and less likely to be found among 'traditional' mothers than among Lebanese mothers generally:
>
> 1. Higher education, even when the effect of social class is excluded.
> 2. Warmer treatment of the five-year-old child.
> 3. Shorter duration of breast feeding, with more scheduling of feeding.
> 4. Belief that a child should learn how to fight when necessary.

5. Use of the withholding of favors as a disciplinary technique.
6. Greater emphasis on mothers' decisions in domestic affairs.
7. More reported dependency of the children.
8. Demands and expectations of the sort which in American studies had typified mothers of high achievement need.[17]

The greater warmth, use of non-physical punishment, allowance of dependency and aggression, and egalitarianism in mother-father relations all resemble American child rearing trends of the past twenty-five years as described by Bronfenbrenner. Despite the fragmentary and diverse quality of the evidence from Russia, the United States and Lebanon, there is a remarkably similar thread running through them. The trend has been towards the loosening of formal constraints on behaviour and a greater emphasis on the development of individual choice; the exercise of arbitrary authority in parent-child and husband-wife relations has declined. Kohn's[18] opposition of conformity to external constraints versus self-direction, as value-emphases in child rearing (characteristic of the American working class and middle class, respectively) is relevant here. It raises the question of whether the direction of change everywhere is not determined by an increase in middle-class, bureaucratic and professional occupations for which children are being prepared. This would be consistent with the role of the middle classes as trend-setters in American child rearing.

Other interpretations are possible, however. For example, one might generalise Riesman's[19] view of American trends and say that children are being trained to be discriminatingly self-indulgent consumers in a world economy turning out an increasing variety of goods to satisfy individual tastes. It could also be argued that child rearing practices are reflecting basic trends in world socio-economic and technological development during the twentieth century—most generally, industrialisation and urbanisation; more specifically, the spread of literacy and expansion of schooling, the 'emancipation' of women, as well as the growth of white-collar occupations.[20] These trends have produced in America, Europe and many parts of Asia and Africa an increasing class of people who spend a large proportion of their youth in school, work at jobs requiring a high degree of literate skill, flexibility and technical expertise, and are sophisticated consumers of manufactured goods and the manufactured tastes and styles of the mass media. They value education and social mobility highly and favour modern innovation in many areas of life. They look upon child rearing as the development of the skills, flexibility and tastes that they have found useful themselves; most importantly, they want to give their children the capacities to advance themselves as opportunities occur and to change appropriately under rapidly-changing conditions. Child rearing geared to such aims is expensive in terms of parental attention and stimulation, and often financially expensive as well. Parents find themselves devoting an increasing proportion of their human and material resources to raising a few highly-resourceful children. Although their success in raising such children may be questioned, their goals are fairly clear; the acquisition of the goal of rearing a high-quality, self-directed child we may term 'modernisation' in child rearing practice.

The parents characterised by modern child rearing goals and practices are not distributed randomly within and among nations. Being products and agents of educational and economic development, they are concentrated where these processes have reached their peaks, i.e., more among educated white-collar and professional people than among the manual workers; more in the cities than in the country; more in the industrialised than non-industrialised nations. In many parts of Tropical Africa, a modern class has only begun to form, and the locally recognised 'educated elite' contains a large proportion of persons who have fulfilled minimal educational requirements for clerical positions (or have married such clerks) without showing many other signs of 'psychological modernisation'. In the coastal cities of West Africa, however, one finds groups of people who appear more thoroughly 'modern' in their values and life-styles, and it is the question of how one such group has changed in its child rearing practices that concerns us here. Our fundamental questions are: How have they deviated from tradition? Have their deviations been in the direction of modern child rearing as it is known elsewhere in the world? What factors have been most influential in changing their child rearing?

The Problem and the Setting

The overall aim of the series of investigations carried out in Ibadan was to discover the extent to which a change in style of life (associated with changes in education, occupation and housing) within an ethnic group could affect the physical growth of children and parental values and behaviour. We decided to concentrate on a single ethnic group whose members varied widely in amount of education and other factors associated with modernity, so that more and less modernised individuals could be reasonably assumed to represent different phases in a process rather than differences in culture of origin. The Yoruba were chosen because they are one of the very few African ethnic groups that has a substantial highly-educated segment, with women strongly represented in it. The more common African situation, in which Western-educated men are married to relatively uneducated and more traditional women, would not have permitted us to find out what might happen when enough women are educated to allow whole families to adopt a Western style of life; working with the Yoruba did allow examination of this question.

Of the two Nigerian cities in which the full Yoruba continuum of modernisation is represented, Ibadan was chosen over Lagos because of the research facilities offered by the University of Ibadan and because the Yoruba social organisation and culture of the traditional groups in Ibadan is much more intact. With a population of over a million, Ibadan is the most populous city in West Africa. Founded about 1830 (sixty years before British administration), it has been in turn a large Yoruba settlement, a centre of colonial administration and commerce, and a regional capital and educational centre within the new nation of Nigeria.[21] Each of these 'periods' of its history contributes to the current heterogeneity of the population: the indigenous Yoruba living in their traditional compounds and quarters, diverse peoples from other parts of Nigeria who began coming in during the colonial period, and the growing Westernised elite who manage the modern bureaucratic and intellectual sectors of the city's life. As a pre-colonial Yoruba settlement and a centre of modern economic, political and intellectual activity, Ibadan encompasses within its city limits the traditional-modern gradient that must be studied in many other places by means of a rural-urban comparison.

Although we set out to study groups varying along a dimension of change rather than groups aligned vertically in a system of social stratification, the two axes are not independent in contemporary Ibadan. Those who have deviated most from the traditional culture by virtue of schooling and overseas experience are automatically recruited into elite status positions. Education is the path that leads outwards from traditionalism and upwards towards higher status. The young man with a university degree inevitably (at least up to 1962) obtains a prestigeful job with a relatively high salary and high-status perquisites such as Western-type housing and car allowance. In one fell swoop he is admitted to the highest income and status category in local society, previously occupied only by foreign colonial officials. This system of social mobility presents the investigator with a confounding of modernisation and social status; a low-status modernised group does not exist to be studied. Thus, when one contrasts the most Westernised or modernised segment of the urban Yoruba population with the least, one is also comparing people differing enormously in income and occupational prestige. From one point of view it is a comparison of new and old, but it is also that of high and low, rich and poor.

This confounding of socio-economic status with apparent modernisation presents difficulties in attributing particular contrasts in styles of life to acculturative experience on the one hand or to economic possibilities on the other. The correspondences should not, however, be interpreted in the same light as a similar congruence between acculturation and socio-economic status in older or more stabilised status systems in which the low status groups have suffered severe losses of self-esteem. In Ibadan, the education-based social mobility system is recent and fluid enough, and has promoted to high position a small enough fraction of the population, that the indigenous Yoruba inhabitants still see themselves as bearers of a proud tradition that does not hamper their life chances. Though the outsider might see it differently, they do not yet define their way of life in terms of poverty or servitude, or consider their neighbourhoods slums. Their considerable economic and political autonomy as farmers, small-scale businessmen and participants in a traditional chieftaincy system provides a realistic basis for this self-respect, and their religious beliefs and practices give it symbolic support. Furthermore, the recent expansion of schooling offers hope to all, reinforced by some instances of successful mobility. Ibadan's most modernised families may constitute an exalted group, but its most traditional ones are not an oppressed or depressed class, and differences in life-style between them cannot be a simple function of their respective positions in the status system.

There is another sense in which the status difference between the most and least traditional Yoruba groups in Ibadan is not a serious drawback to the present study. In the United States, according to Bronfenbrenner,[22] the middle class has acted as the trend-setter in child rearing practices, with the working class following. As we noted above, Kohn's formulation[23] of middle-class/working-class differences in parental values resembles the general direction of child rearing trends in several parts of the world, with the middle class appearing more modern. The pattern of socio-economic development in the mid-twentieth century may make it inevitable that higher status groups—in so far as they include those of higher education—will be more modern in their life-styles. As modern technology expands the realm of technical and bureaucratic occupations, so the life-style of the Western middle classes is increasingly identified as modern and is adopted first in underdeveloped nations by those with the education and occupations appropriate to it. If this is so, our Ibadan situation is simply an instance of the inevitable correlation of status with modernisation.

In selecting groups through which to study modernisation in Ibadan, we decided to sample the two extremes of the continuum —i.e., the most traditional descendants of the pre-colonial Yoruba settlers, on the one hand, and the most highly educated Yoruba families on the other. While intermediate groups are necessary for a more conclusive study of the process, the limitation of the initial exploration to the extremes was based on two assumptions: that a small-scale study should at least reveal the baseline from which change began and the farthest point it had reached, and that any similarities found between the two groups would provide more crucial evidence for persistence of traditional orientations than if the groups had been selected closer to one another on the dimension of change. We intended, in fact, to find highly-educated parents who had been reared in extremely traditional circumstances; the differences would then show to what extent education and associated acculturative experiences could affect parental values and behaviour in a single generation. Our degree of success in achieving this aim is discussed below.

Two Contrasting Yoruba Groups in Ibadan

Ibadan seems at first to be a massive, inchoate jumble of overcrowded housing, but it is in fact fairly rigidly segregated into residential areas which have cultural coherence. The original Yoruba settlement is now the crowded eastern portion of the city and contains the vast majority of those descended from the early settlers and least affected by recent change; other sections contain Yoruba from outside Ibadan, and enclaves of Hausa, Ibo, Bini and other Nigerian ethnic groups. Western institutions—missions, schools and colleges, government offices and hospitals—have been built around the periphery on campuses with suburban-style housing developments for their senior staff members. The modern elite, Yoruba and others, live in these areas, in a similarly-styled government housing estate, and in a few neighbourhoods of private housing for higher income families.

The indigenous Yoruba section that was chosen for a community study is the neighbourhood surrounding Ibadan's traditional cloth market; both market and neighbourhood are called Oje. The historical, demographic, and cultural characteristics of this area have been outlined in a paper by Barbara Lloyd[24] and can be recapitulated here only briefly. Oje was first settled about 1840 by the ancestor of the man who is currently the highest-ranking chief in the area. In the past, although tied into the central political system of Ibadan, it had (like other sections of the pre-colonial city) some characteristics of a separate community, e.g., a high frequency of endogamous marriages. Today, it can best be described as an agglomeration of compounds in the vicinity of the cloth market. A traditional Yoruba compound is, physically, a walled residential unit with connected houses arranged around a series of rectangular courtyards. In Oje, relatively few walls exist and many courtyards have been filled in with new houses, but the social reality of the compound persists. Socially, a compound has historical continuity, a patrilineal core group, an hereditary chief —who may or may not have a title in the Ibadan political hierarchy —and a set of self-regulating functions concerning land, succession and internal disputes. It has its own Yoruba tutelary deities and shrines, a traditional role in the annual masquerade associated with spirits of the dead, and its own praise-songs. Most compounds have farm land outside of town and satellite hamlets or villages there that are regarded as rural colonies of the compound, sometimes with the same name. Some Oje compounds have hereditary occupations—notably drumming—that are still passed from father to son.

The compounds in Oje range in size from under forty to more than 340 inhabitants, the smallest being disintegrating units, many of whose members have moved away, the largest that of the senior chief. Each compound is a cluster of nuclear and (patrilocally) extended families, some of them descended from the compound founder and thus part of the patrilineal core, others being 'strangers', who live there but are not compound members. Polygyny is frequent; 58 per cent of the married women are plural wives. Each wife has her cubicle, but shares kitchen facilities with other women. There is much co-operation among women in at least their segment of the compound—in trading, domestic activities and the care of children. A man has a room of his own, perhaps two, and he may spend most of his time in the compound, particularly if he is self-employed (e.g., carpenter, tailor, goldsmith, native doctor) and works at home. Men in traditional occupations like drumming and farming also spend a good deal of time in the compound. To live in a compound is to live in close proximity to a large number of persons doing diverse things and engaging in sociable interaction.

Of the ten Oje men interviewed in the father study, five were small businessmen (small-scale building contractors, produce buyer, shopkeeper), two were craftsmen (carpenter, tailor), one was a truck driver and two were civil servants (hospital messenger, worker at an agricultural experiment station).

Like other traditional Ibadan residents, many Oje men who do not regard themselves primarily as farmers have farms outside the city where they keep a second residence, often with one of their wives or other relatives living permanently there. Some men spend part of the year in a village tending the farm, the rest in the city. Others travel occasionally and briefly to the village to supervise those whom they have left in charge. Each man tries to manage as much land as he can in the rural area and spend as much time as possible in the city. The mobility between town and country has been characteristic of Ibadan for a long time.

Nowadays, most children in Oje get a modicum of schooling, but this was not true of their parents. The vast majority of adult women are illiterate and most men have had no more than a few years of education, although there are some notable exceptions. Three-quarters of the people are nominal Moslems but evidence of a lively interest in traditional Yoruba religion is not hard to find. Yoruba supernatural beliefs, particularly those concerning witchcraft, disease, fertility, infant mortality and reincarnation, are widespread in the population. Offerings are made to deities at their shrines, diviners are consulted, infant twins are the objects of ritual performances. The Christian minority in Oje is less prone to practise Yoruba ritual but remains heavily influenced by traditional belief.

It would be a mistake to assume that Oje and its people have not been profoundly affected by the technological, economic and educational changes in their environment over the past half century. Their contemporary world is one in which modern secondary schools, mass-produced goods and occupations such as truck driver and building contractor are as familiar as the sacred crocodile in the senior chief's courtyard or as street processions and the still-active cloth market. As those who gain higher education move out and as endogamy decreases, Oje is changing from a traditional, village-like sub-community in Ibadan to a dilapidated neighbourhood indistinguishable from others in the city. Yet the burden of our evidence indicates that traditional Yoruba norms, beliefs and practices are preferred to alien ones in a great many spheres of life, and particularly in interpersonal relations. The compound remains the social unit of primary attachment, and it is internally ordered according to traditional ideals. Having acquainted ourselves with the voluminous literature[25] on Yoruba customs of status ranking, marriage and divorce, life cycle rituals and family organisation, we found most of these customs present in Oje. Thus it is not unreasonable to take this Ibadan neighbourhood as representative of the traditional Yoruba way of life for a study of child rearing practices.

Modern elite families do not constitute a local, cohesive community; as noted above, they reside in those dispersed, peripheral enclaves of Ibadan where a middle-class European style of life is possible. In the absence of clear group boundaries, we defined the highly modernised population from which our research samples were to be drawn as those wholly Yoruba families in which the wife had at least some secondary schooling. Our decision to define the population in terms of schooling stemmed from previous acculturation studies[26] that found educational level the best single index of acculturation in Africa, and from our knowledge of the current Nigerian situation in which, as noted above, formal schooling is the main path away from traditional styles of life. The correlates of educational attainment can be clearly seen in our samples for child rearing study, for the Yoruba women selected for their secondary school education are almost invariably married to men with post-secondary education who are in highly prestigeful occupations and reside in the modern, suburban-style sections of Ibadan. Another important correlate of this level of education is overseas experience. In the ten elite families involved in the father study, seven of the men and eight of their wives had lived in England or the United States for at least a year.

All of the ten men in the father study had post-secondary schooling, and three had university degrees (one, a PH.D.). They included a cabinet minister (originally a lawyer), a permanent secretary, two university lecturers and six civil servants in high or middle-range administrative or technical positions. Their wives had all been trained as teachers, nurses, midwives, librarians, or seamstresses, and most were working in addition to being housewives. The level of training, overseas experience and occupational attainment represented by these ten families is typical of the elite population defined by the criterion of the wives having gone to secondary school.

In these elite families, when the husband is a government administrator or works at a school or hospital, government housing is often provided as a perquisite of his position. The lawyers and some civil servants live in housing estates and private residential areas. The residence is generally a one-family house, its size dependent on family income, with a garden and some yard around it, affording a good deal of privacy.

The average cash income of these elite families is more than ten times that of average Oje families. Yet the modern life style in the rather isolated suburban areas has fewer conveniences provided automatically by residence. The educated people are Christian monogamists, living as nuclear families. They must hire servants to care for children and for other domestic tasks that are done co-operatively and with greater trust among kin in Oje compounds. Shops, schools, places of employment, churches, clubs and friends are rarely within easy walking distance and are in diverse parts of the city. Thus daily life involves a great deal of moving about by private car and taxi. The husband's position may determine the family's place of residence, but in general there is a spatial and social disengagement of activities related to kinship, occupation, consumption, education, religion and government. Each type of activity is specialised and carried on in its own place and social context. The multi-functional character of the compound, market and neighbourhood operating within a local environment like Oje has no counterpart in the life style of the elite families. They are primarily oriented to their own status group and its institutions dispersed in various sections of Ibadan.

Does this highly Westernised Yoruba population in Ibadan spring from a background sufficiently similar to that of contemporary Oje that the two groups can validly be considered the same people in different phases of a single process of modernisation? Several considerations favour a negative answer. For one thing, most of the Ibadan elite are not from Ibadan families, but from other Yoruba towns (Lagos, Abeokuta, Ijebu-Ode, Ondo, Ilesha) known to differ sub-culturally from Ibadan. Secondly, some of them are from Lagos or Abeokuta Yoruba families that were Christian and fairly Westernised in their parents' generation. Thirdly, it is possible that the contemporary Oje residents, by virtue of the fact that they have remained traditional while others have changed, are more reluctant to give up traditional customs than were the parents of the moderns. This suspicion is reinforced by the Christian-Moslem difference between the groups, suggesting that those parents who became Christians were self-selected for exposure to modernising influences, while those who chose Islam withheld themselves from such exposure. This is referred to by Doob as the 'spiralled explanation' in acculturation studies.[27]

These qualifications regarding the assumed original similarity of the groups to be compared cannot be set aside, but they can be taken account of in the interpretation of intergroup differences. First of all, although the modern group is not from Ibadan, the characteristics that we are taking as hallmarks of Oje culture—compound life, polygyny, features of Yoruba belief and ritual—are known to be present in all traditional Yoruba groups and not limited to Ibadan. Thus the differences in traditional sub-culture are not serious difficulties.

The question of whether the elite men in the father study are only a generation away from the Oje men in level of acculturation can be answered from an examination of Table 9.1, in which the latter are compared with the parents of the former on education and polygyny. While the Oje men are predominantly unschooled or barely literate (their wives, not appearing on the Table, are all illiterate), the elite men's fathers and even mothers include a few persons with secondary schooling. In fact, since those with educated mothers also had fathers with secondary education, the elite men are divided into two groups, those whose parents resembled the Oje families in education and those whose parents had more education. (It is interesting that the four elite men of the highest educational attainment and occupational position had illiterate parents.) Even the men in the second group, however, probably had grandparents who were illiterate, so the maximum distance in acculturation between Oje and elite men is two generations. This view is supported by the comparison on polygyny in Table 9.1, for the elite men's fathers were very similar to contemporary Oje men in frequency of polygyny. The majority of elite men come from families which, like those of Oje, are polygynous.

TABLE 9.1

Comparison of Men in Oje Sample with Parents of Men in Elite Sample on Education and Polygyny

	Oje Men (N = 10)	Elite Men's Fathers (N = 10)	Elite Men's Mothers (N = 10)
Education			
Illiterate	5	4	7
No schooling but claim literacy	3	2	1
Primary school	2	1	—
Secondary school	—	3	2
Polygyny			
Yes	5	6	
No	5	3	
No information	—	1	

Finally, it may well be that the contemporary Oje residents are less desirous of change than the parents and grandparents of the elite group were, but the impossibility of eliminating self-selection is inherent in the use of a cross-sectional design for the study of culture change. Only a thirty-year longitudinal study could eliminate it and still involve interviews about current child rearing practices. On balance, then, we can conclude that the Oje group can fairly be taken as representative in broad outline of the socio-cultural matrix from which the elite group emerged in one to two generations. There remains, however, the possibility that differences between the two groups may be due in part to the Oje families representing a conservative remnant people rather than a true pre-contact group.

Sample Selection

For the traditional group in Oje, a conventional community study covering history, social organisation, religion and child rearing was conducted over a period of one year. The 1,349 inhabitants of fifteen compounds near Oje market were the subjects of a census and genealogical survey.[28] From this census, mothers with five- or six-year-old children were chosen for interviewing. Although outright refusals were few, temporary migration to the village or natal compound was so frequent that sheer availability determined the nature of the final sample of thirty mothers. The sample of ten fathers, taken from among the husbands of these women, was even more limited by considerations of convenience. Since the interviews had to be conducted within a few weeks, the entire list was gone through, with the availability of the father being the only criterion for inclusion. The sample is biased in favour of those fathers who work at home or spend a good deal of time at home.

Sampling the elite group was more difficult because of its unlocalised nature. As previously indicated, the modernised population was defined in terms of the wives' exposure to secondary schooling. The staff directories of various institutions and government agencies were searched for the names of sufficiently likely candidates to be followed up by a questionnaire. A widespread search was conducted through all of the city's private primary schools that were known at the Institute of Education to draw pupils from the higher status groups. A surprisingly small number of families meeting the criteria was found (so small that the criterion of mother's education had to be lowered for the physical growth study), and an even smaller number had children in the right age bracket. The search was continued until thirty mothers were found.

It should be noted that this definition of the modernised population reflects the emphasis on the cross-sectional study of the modernisation process rather than a sampling of the social strata. If the latter had been our objective, the job would have been relatively easy, for there are perhaps hundreds of socially elite families who meet the educational criteria. This class, however, contains not only many non-Yoruba couples, but a large proportion of Yoruba married to Bini, Sierra Leoneans, British and Americans. Had we compared a sample of this type with the Oje sample, it would have been difficult to tell whether differences were due to variations in ethnic origin rather than modernisation or social status. Consequently, we decided to hold the ethnic group constant and this led to the search for purely Yoruba couples, who turned out to be rare. Their very rarity suggests what is in fact the case, that they are embedded in a network of interaction involving people of less education and varied ethnic origin. The modernised group we finally chose, then, is representative of a category of families, not of a socially interactive group, a choice which is justified on the grounds of attempting to control a source of unwanted variation in our study of cultural process.

The selection of ten fathers in the elite group was subject to the same time pressures operating in the Oje sampling, and more extremely so, because the elite men are busier and more mobile and thus harder to find for an interview. Several of the thirty fathers were out of Nigeria for extended periods; others were continuously involved in a political crisis that was gripping one of the major political parties in the region; most of the lawyers were hardly ever to be found at home, having secondary offices up to a hundred miles away. The only outright refusal was by a senior civil servant who worked long hours and had no intention of wasting an hour talking about the moments he spends with his children. In consequence we took what fathers we could find until we had ten. This resulted in a systematic bias in favour of men who have more leisure time—and spend more time at home—plus university lecturers, who happened to be between terms at the time. The sample includes only civil servants, university lecturers and a regional cabinet minister; the main category of omission is lawyers in private practice, who could not be reached. It should be borne in mind, then, that those elite fathers who are home least, and therefore spend least time with their children, are absent from this sample. Our only consolation on this score is that a similar bias (noted above) operated in the selection of traditional fathers.

Method of Data Collection

In the studies of the mothers and the fathers, the data were collected by interviews on parental behaviour and values. They covered topics that bear on probable antecedents of the behavioural dispositions mentioned above and that have been covered in previous cross-cultural child rearing studies:[29] dependence-independence, aggression and discipline. In addition, questions were added concerning family interaction patterns, family attitudes (polygamy, family planning), child's career choice, certain Yoruba traditional beliefs and practices related to sex and deference. The father's interview was much shorter than the mother's, not only because there is more to ask mothers about child rearing but also because the busy fathers felt they had little time to spare for such an interview.

The mothers were interviewed several months, in some cases as much as a year, before the fathers. The interviews with Oje parents were conducted in Yoruba by an interviewer of the same sex as the respondent;[30] they were recorded on tape and subsequently transcribed and translated into English. The interviews with elite parents were conducted in English by an interviewer of the same sex as the respondent;[31] they were also recorded for subsequent analysis.

Expectations and Findings

On the basis of our ethnographic knowledge of the Oje and elite men, we formulated expectations concerning the specific ways in which their divergent conditions of life and their previous exposure to differing cultural influences might affect their values and behaviour as fathers. The interview responses were systematically examined for these specific differences, sometimes in conjunction with the wife's responses to the mother interview. The expectations and findings are presented below, under four headings: health and family planning, familial and occupational structure, functionality of the domestic group and interpersonal ideology.

(i) *Health.* The contrast here involves what might be called 'effective reproductive capacity'. The Oje families are afflicted with a high frequency of secondary infertility due to gonorrhea and other widespread genital infections. Their malnourished infants, who are shorter and weigh less than their counterparts in modern families, are so beset by endemic malaria, dysentery, measles (a killer of protein-starved children), smallpox, poliomyelitis, kwashiorkor and other infectious and nutritional disorders that only about half of them live to be five years old. In this situation, the Oje father is primarily concerned with having some progeny who live to adulthood, and his anxiety about this is so great that we did not expect him to entertain ideas of family limitation, even if some economic advantage were involved.

In the elite families, health and nutrition conditions are extremely good; fertility is high and infant mortality is low. The latter fact is illustrated in the extreme by a sample family which had managed, by frequent recourse to expert medical care, to keep a child with sickle-cell (hereditary) anemia alive to the age of five; such a child would undoubtedly have died in infancy in Oje. The ease with which the elite couples can have children and raise them to maturity is so great that ultimately they have to consider the expense involved. This is particularly true because their educational standards are so high that each child entails a considerable economic sacrifice. Thus we expected the modern fathers to be favourable to family limitation and planning.

Table 9.2 shows that the Oje fathers have fewer children but want more children than the elite fathers. When asked about their ideal in this regard, most of the Oje men mentioned wanting at least six or, fatalistically, 'Whatever God gives'. Most of the elite men said four or five, which may be higher than Western middle-class ideals but indicates more concern with limiting family size than is shown by their more traditional Yoruba counterparts.

TABLE 9.2

Comparison of Oje and Elite Fathers on Actual and Ideal Number of Children

Group	Number of Living Children		Ideal Number of Children	
			Number of Fathers Responding:	
	Mean	Median	More Than Five or 'Whatever God Gives'	Five or Fewer
Oje	3·4	3·5	9	1
Elite	4·7	5·0	1	9

When asked directly if they believe in family planning, all of the Oje men said no, and all of the elite fathers said yes, although two of the latter qualified their answers so as to indicate that they did not practise it. It was clear that the Oje fathers had not considered family planning as a possibility, and some mentioned infant mortality as precluding it.

It is evident from these data that the elite fathers have deviated from traditional norms in their positive attitude towards family planning and their preference for somewhat smaller families, but they have not embraced an ideal of very small families and drastic limitations on birth. Some of those with six and seven children expressed concern about the financial burden of educating them properly, and admitted regret at not having practised birth control earlier. Our interpretation of their situation is that they yield to traditional pressures to have many offspring without realising that the pressures derive partly from a fear of infant mortality and infertility that is not relevant to their own conditions of life. Serious consideration of economics, education and birth limitation come as an afterthought. Thus the traditionals have difficulty getting as many children as they want, while the moderns have the problem of being able to have more children than they feel they can afford.

The persistence of Yoruba beliefs concerning reproduction is also indicated by half of the elite fathers expressing opposition to sexual intercourse during the lactation period on grounds of its effect on the nursing child. Traditional Yoruba believe that a child can be poisoned this way. We know from the interviews with mothers that the traditional two-year period of nursing and maternal sexual abstinence (still the rule in Oje) is not found among the elite families, and it was surprising to find this associated belief so strong. It was equally surprising that two of the elite fathers, when asked about sexual intercourse during menstruation, spontaneously mentioned—without rejecting—the Yoruba belief that this leads to the birth of an albino child (seven of the ten Oje fathers mentioned it). Our overall impression is that the attitudes and practices concerning reproduction found among the elite fathers, although considerably modified by their changed conditions of life and education, show some traditional influence. They may have embraced quality in the raising of children without giving up the desire for quantity and other traditional reproductive attitudes.

(ii) *Familial and occupational structures*. The traditional family tends to be patrilocal, polygynous and embedded in a residentially localised extended kin group; the elite have isolated, nuclear, monogamous families. In Oje compounds, interaction is often segregated by sex and the nuclear family is not necessarily an interactive cluster. In the elite families, the very isolation of mother, father and children from others brings them into closer contact with each other. Furthermore, while the Oje mothers have numerous women around to help with domestic tasks entailed in infant care, the elite families are dependent on a servant, who is nevertheless occasionally absent. Hence we expected the elite father to participate more in joint activity with his wife and children and to play a greater role in infant care.

The elite father's involvement in a bureaucratic occupational structure takes him out of the home and constantly regulates his life according to office hours and the demands of his job. By way of contrast, many Oje fathers work in the compound or have occupations (e.g., building contractor, produce buyer) that allow them to regulate their own working hours. Our expectation was that the modern fathers would consequently have less time to spend with their children.

Table 9.3 shows several strong contrasts between the two groups concerning family structure. Their preferences for monogamy or polygyny are in fairly close correspondence with their actual marital statuses, for all of the elite men are monogamists and half of the Oje men have more than one wife. The Oje men who endorsed polygyny saw it as entailing a large, happy, family; the desire for numerous progeny is implicit in many of their statements. The elite fathers rejected polygyny on the grounds of its being too expensive and leading to family quarrels; they were not moralistic or absolute about it. Six of them said polygyny was all right in some cases, and in this they diverged from their own wives, who condemned the practice more vigorously. This disagreement between elite husbands and wives in the same families may be related to the reputed incidence among the Ibadan elite of men keeping concubines (locally known as 'outside wives' or 'private wives') of which their legal wives disapprove.

The difference between the role of father in the sex-segregated compound and in the isolated nuclear family is illustrated in the next three comparisons on Table 9.3. Oje fathers do not participate directly in childbirth or infant care, and they eat separately from their wives and children. Their responses left little doubt that they regard their aloofness as proper behaviour and any deviation from it as demeaning to a man. The elite fathers differ in both norms and behaviour. On the normative side, a majority of them endorsed the idea of the father's being present at the delivery of his child, even though most of them had not done so and thought of it as personally distasteful. They had participated in infant care, beginning in some cases when the whole family was overseas and the mother's training course left them no choice. Most of them seemed to regard it as natural that fathers would help their employed wives take care of the children, at least when no one else was available. For the busiest fathers, care of infants was clearly something they had done early in their careers but could not do now. Eating with the family is an important form of social intercourse which the

TABLE 9.3

Comparison of Oje and Elite Fathers on Attitudes and Behaviours Related to Family Structure

	Oje	Elite	χ^2 *	*P*
Prefers Monogamy				
Yes	3	10		
No	7	0	7·09	<·005
Father Present at Childbirth				
Good idea	0	2		
Good, but not for me	0	4		
Not good	10	4	9·3	<·009
Has Fed or Diapered Infant				
Yes	2	9		
No	8	1	8·9	<·002
Eats with Wife and Children				
Sometimes	1	9		
Never	9	1	9·8	<·001
Parental Discussion of Child Rearing				
Democratic or Mutual	1	10		
Father-dominant	9	0	13·7	<·001

* Corrected for continuity.

elite father tries to maintain; only one man habitually eats by himself. The Oje respondents' Islamic religion has acted to perpetuate segregation by sex in ritual; by contrast, half of the elite Christian families at least occasionally find togetherness in prayers at home. Each of these contrasts indicates that interaction in the Yoruba compound is divided along sex lines as much as by family grouping—with infants and small children of both sexes being part of the women's world—and that little of this division has survived the shift to the isolated nuclear family.

The last item in Table 9.3 deals with the authority dimension in family structure in relation to child rearing. Oje fathers, though generally uninvolved in child rearing, regard their participation in terms of giving occasional orders to their wives. The elites speak of discussing it with their wives and making joint decisions. Thus the shift mentioned above is not only towards more participation on the part of the father but more participation as an equal to his wife rather than her superior.

To investigate some outcomes of this change in family interaction, we devised indexes of husband-wife consensus and of their sense of solidarity, with respect to child rearing. Consensus between husbands and wives was measured by rating the interviews with the mother and father of each child for agreement or disagreement on forty-two diverse items of opinion and fact and assigning a total frequency score of parental disagreement. We measured the husbands' and wives' sense of solidarity with their spouses on child rearing issues by counting the number of times they used the plural forms, 'we', 'us' or 'our' (or their Yoruba equivalents) when they might as well have used the first person singular. No more than one plural use was scored for each question; the total scores ranged from 2 to 54 for the mother interviews and from 0 to 34 for the father interviews. The rank order correlation between the sense-of-solidarity scores for the mothers and fathers was 0·78. The scores used in the correlation data reported in Table 9.4 were the mothers' scores.

Table 9.4 shows the correlation of parental disagreement with the use of plural forms and two other aspects of family interaction: number of wives (varying only in the Oje sample, with five as

TABLE 9.4

Correlations* of Parental Disagreement With Other Variables

	Unrequired Use of Plural Forms	Number of Wives	Degree of Father Absence
Total Sample	−0·41	0·60	0·35
Oje	−0·11	0·76	−0·10
Elite	−0·49	—	0·86

* Pearson product-moment correlation.

maximum) and degree of father absence (estimated from the fathers' reports of the proportion of time they spend away from home daily). The fairly high negative correlation between parental disagreement and the use of plural forms for the total sample indicates a positive relation between husband-wife consensus and their sense of solidarity with their spouse on child rearing matters, although the relation is much stronger among the elite than in Oje families. For the latter, parental disagreement varies directly with the number of wives, while for the elites it is strongly related to the amount of time the father spends away from home. These same variations are shown as differences in group means in Table 9.5, where it can be seen that polygynous Oje families have more parental disagreement than the elite (although the difference does not reach statistical significance), whereas monogamous Oje families are much closer to the elite in parental disagreement and

TABLE 9.5

Group Differences in Parental Disagreement and Unrequired Use of Plural Forms

Groups	Parental Disagreement			Unrequired Use of Plural Forms		
	Mean ($\overline{X}$)	t	p	Mean ($\overline{X}$)	t	p
Oje	13·6	1·25	<0·20	13·8	2·66	<0·01
Elite	11·2			31·5		
Polygynous Oje	15·4	1·34	<0·20	4·8	3·94	<0·005
Monogamous Oje	11·8			22·8		
High Father-Absent Elite	14·6	4·69	<0·005	20·4	2·55	<0·015
Low Father-Absent Elite	7·8			42·6		

use of plural forms. Elite parents were much higher than Oje on the use of plural forms, and this index of parental sense of solidarity also significantly differentiates between polygynous and monogamous families in the Oje sample and between families higher and lower in father absence in the elite sample.

These findings support the notion that patterns of father-family interaction for the Oje and elite groups are extremely divergent. In Oje the father's work allows him or forces him to spend a great deal of time in the compound, where he is in close physical proximity to his pre-school children. Oje fathers' estimates of the amount of time they actually spend with their children, however, averaged approximately the same (two to three hours daily) as those of the elite fathers, who are regularly removed from home by their work. Furthermore, as we noted above, the Oje father maintains a good deal of social distance between himself and his family. At the ideational level, this social distance is related to a lack of corporate identity between wife and husband in regard to child rearing, expressed in the infrequent use of plural forms. For interaction the social distance means that physical proximity does not necessarily lead to intimate contact. We find the lack of relation between father absence and parental disagreement in Oje (Table 9.4) because the development of a husband-wife consensus in these families depends not on the physical presence or absence of the father but on the amount of social distance he puts between himself and his family. The more wives he has, the more likely he is to remove himself socially from the several mother-child units, in the interests of impartiality and preventing co-wife dissension. Hence the relation between number of wives and parental disagreement in the Oje group, and the greater parental sense of solidarity in the monogamous families. Thus both sex-segregation and polygyny in the Oje compound seem to favour greater social distance between father and child and less husband-wife consensus on child rearing matters. In the absence of a consensus, the husband resolves disagreements that arise in an authoritarian manner (see Table 9.3).

The elite father has a generally high level of corporate identity with his wife concerning child rearing, as expressed in frequent use of plural forms, which is plausible in terms of his not attempting to maintain social distance between himself and his wife. For him, a consensus with his wife on child rearing matters may be prevented not by factors internal to the family but by the demands of his work, which may keep him away from home—hence the relation between degree of father absence and both parental disagreement and plural usage in the elite families. Since there are no social barriers like sex-segregation and polygyny preventing intimacy between him and his family when he is near them, the sheer amount of time he spends in physical proximity to them becomes a more important dimension of their interaction than it is in Oje families. But the family must compete for his time with the occupational structures in which he also participates. Thus concomitant changes in family structure and the occupational sphere have produced patterns of father-child interaction in the elite families that are sharply discontinuous from their traditional background as represented by Oje.

(iii) *Functionality of the domestic group*. We use the term 'functionality', borrowed from Winch,[32] to designate the extent to which the family or domestic group is charged with carrying out basic societal tasks—economic, educational, religious and political. In Oje, the compound retains many of these functions. In the economic sphere, for example, women collaborate in trade and children are sometimes called upon to help. Hereditary occupation has not died out, the drummers' compound being the most visible example of this. Men gain access to farming land through compound membership and kinship connections. To some extent, then, the compound or a segment of it operates as a corporate unit of ownership and production. Its part in social control, local self-government and access to traditional chieftaincy titles was mentioned above. Its religious importance, though less than in the past, continues through traditional shrines and the *egungun* festival. Also some compounds have their own mosques, which are preferred to the central one, and Christians conduct family prayers in the compound. Greater inroads have been made on the educational function of the compound, due to the spread of schools. Many children drop out early, however, and even when they are not incorporated into the domestic labour force, much of their learning about adult life takes place in the compound.

By contrast, these basic societal functions are discharged in the elite group by specialised institutions—occupational structures, churches, political parties and associations, and schools. The family, 'functionless' in this broader sense, can be seen (as Winch has viewed the American middle-class suburban family) as serving the functions of socialising the young and providing emotional gratification and security, as well as protection, for its members. This is a 'recreational' domestic group, which acts as a unit of consumption and relaxation rather than production and regulation. It is our theory that such a unit necessarily entails a less formal climate of interaction than a highly functional domestic group like the Yoruba compound. Where a family-type group is oriented toward the accomplishment of the relatively impersonal societal goals assigned to formal organisations in more differentiated societies, role relationships must be formalised to assure that the goals are attained. Roles must be explicitly defined and a measure of interpersonal distance must be maintained, for too great intimacy would make the required solidarity, co-operation and deference too contingent on the vagaries of personal attraction to provide a dependable basis for corporate activity. In the Yoruba compound there is strict ranking by age among brothers, co-wives and others, as well as segregation of the sexes. Every person knows what his obligations are in a variety of situations and what the obligations of others are to him. The well-known traditional norms governing interpersonal conduct in the domestic group endow every situation of task performance, ritual and decision-making with a sense of order that is important for goal attainment.

When most important societal functions are allocated to specialised agencies outside the domestic group, the family can afford to be informal, with intimacy more prominent than obligation. The goals involved in emotional gratification are inherently contingent on personal enjoyment and hence subject to improvisation and idiosyncratic variation. Furthermore, in a small group like the educated Yoruba nuclear family, the problem of maintaining order is less, so rigid mechanisms are not required to solve it. By contrast with the traditional compound, there is an easy informality between senior and junior members of the family and a greater degree of intimacy between the sexes.

On the assumption that the traditional family has more economic functions, we hypothesised that Oje fathers would put more emphasis on the assignment of useful tasks to children than would elite fathers. On the assumption that the elite family maintains a less formal climate of interaction, we developed the expectation that modern fathers would express more affection or emotional warmth to their children and take a greater interest in amusing them than would their traditional counterparts. Table 9.6 shows the tests of these hypotheses. More of the Oje fathers assign household tasks to their pre-school children. The elite fathers are very pleased with their children for doing domestic tasks on their own initiative, but for the most part do not order them to do so. One gains the impression that the elite children spontaneously perform such chores more frequently than their American counterparts, but they appear to be under little pressure to do so.

The expression of affection or emotional warmth by the father was measured on the basis of his responses to the following questions:

1. What happens when you come home?
2. What do you find particularly pleasing about your child?
3. What do you think a well-behaved child of . . . . .'s age should be like?
4. Does the child ask to go with you to places? (If so) What do you do?
5. Does the child ask too many questions? (If so) What do you do?
6. What kinds of things do you do with your child?

Each response was copied on to a separate sheet of paper; the sheets from the two samples were then combined, sorted randomly, and rated blindly on a three-point (0–2) scale of emotional warmth by three judges. Inter-judge agreement was extremely high, and the judges' ratings were averaged for each response.

TABLE 9.6

Comparison of Oje and Elite Fathers on Assigning Household Tasks and on Paternal Warmth Ratings

	Assign Household Tasks to Child				Paternal Warmth Rating		
	Yes	No	χ^2 *	p	Mean ($\bar{X}$)	t	p
Oje	8	2	4·8	<0·04	2·83	4·50	<0·01
Elite	3	7			4·75		

* Corrected for continuity.

These final scores on the six items were summed for each respondent and averaged for each group. The means in Table 9.6 show the elite fathers higher on emotional warmth, and the difference is statistically significant, supporting our expectation. It is clear from these data that the elite fathers, on the average, take a more positive interest in their pre-school children, pay more attention to them, seek to amuse them and play with them more often, and respond more favourably to their requests for information and joint activity. The Oje emphasis on child's performance of instrumental tasks has been abandoned in favour of this more affectionate and recreational emphasis in father-child relations.

(iv) *Ideology*. Traditional Yoruba society may be said to have an explicit ideology concerning the allocation of authority in groups. Its basic principles include reverence for age and hereditary position, individual status ranking on the basis of relative seniority and the importance of involving representatives of all subgroups concerned in the formulation of policy. The rather democratic pattern of actual decision-making is at variance with the posture of extreme public deference to those in high position. At the level of compound and family, this posture is adopted by men in relation to the *bale* (chief) of the compound and by women in relation to their husbands, although the actual power of these apparent masters is considerably less than that found in many other African societies. Nonetheless, the symbolic expression of status ranking cannot be discounted and, even if subordinates retain considerable autonomy, there are still distinct prerogatives to higher rank. This is perhaps seen most clearly in the assignment of laborious tasks, which are passed down the hierarchy, in contrast to items of value, which are passed up. A senior person is never expected to perform a menial task when his junior is present to do it; this is true of the *bale* in respect to other compound members, a man in relation to his wives, a senior woman with her junior co-wives (who do the largest share of domestic work), and parents with their children. The most senior person must act with restraint and a sense of noblesse oblige that is less pronounced in other African societies, but the ideology of respect for authority and of meticulous observance of precedence and deference according to rank is very strong—especially by comparison with modern Western values.

The authoritarian elements in traditional Yoruba ideology are bolstered in contemporary Oje by the prevalent Islamic doctrine of obedience to authority and submission to fate as God's will. Without attempting to assess the effect of such values on behaviour, we can state that, when discussing various social and political topics, Oje men emphasise obedience and submission, loyalty to higher authority and respect. The modern Yoruba fathers, by virtue of their Christian schooling and their extended overseas exposure to Western egalitarianism and achievement orientations, have been imbued with an ideology differing drastically from the traditional. It is an ideology stressing personal responsibility rather than fatalism, activism rather than passivity, individual autonomy rather than submission to authority, and social equality rather than hierarchy. Taking into account the higher education of these men, we must also include a resistance to unquestioning obedience as part of their ideological exposure.

On the basis of these ideological differences, we formulated a picture of Oje and elite fathers' conceptions of the child that is similar to Kohn's[33] formulation of American middle and working class values. The Oje fathers should see the child as a passive, obedient servant, who is not expected to have a will or a mind of his own but is expected to conform to social constraints and not to be disruptive. The elite fathers should view a child as a small adult whose individual tendencies require expression, attention and encouragement even if parental authority is occasionally threatened. In terms of this distinction, we predicted that the traditional fathers would put more emphasis on obedience, be stricter disciplinarians, be less responsive to the child's questions, and be more repressive of his aggressive and sexual tendencies than the modern fathers. Several of the findings already presented are consistent with the idea of a transition from an ideology of authoritarian constraint to an egalitarian fostering of self-direction in the child; the elite father is more willing to undertake infant care, less strict in assigning household tasks and more affectionate. We turn now to matters more closely related to authority, discipline, and the child's self-expression.

Table 9.7 shows surprisingly few differences between Oje and elite on authority and discipline, none of them statistically significant. The traditional Yoruba son greets his father every morning by prostration, forehead to the floor; the daughter kneels. These signs of deference are so at variance with Western norms that the father's demand of them was taken as a probable index of lack of Westernisation. Contrary to expectation, the same preponderance of fathers in each group reported that their pre-school children greet them this way. A similar result was produced by our analysis of strictness of paternal discipline, which appears to be almost identical for the Oje and elite. In terms of usual punishment techniques, a few more Oje fathers reported using physical punishment and a few more elite reported isolating the child in a room, but the differences are slight. One elite father boasted of using a whip on his children. Both objective analysis of the interviews and personal impressions point to significant continuities between Oje and elite fathers in terms of deference demands and severity of discipline.

Another aspect of authority, the father's permissiveness of the child's aggression against him, could not be analysed comparatively because the question was asked somewhat differently in the two groups, but the responses exhibited a different pattern than the results in Table 9.7. The elite fathers showed more tolerance of aggression against themselves, while in Oje men the idea aroused

TABLE 9.7

Comparison of Oje and Elite Fathers on Paternal Authority and Discipline*

	Oje	Elite
Child greets father in traditional way		
Yes	7	7
No	3	3
Which parent disciplines more		
Father	8	4
Mother	2	5
Not ascertainable	0	1
Father's usual punishment		
Physical	5	2
Verbal scolding	5	5
Isolation or restraint	0	2
Father's other punishment		
Physical	4	3
Verbal scolding	3	3
Isolation or restraint	0	2

* None of the differences is statistically significant.

extreme emotion. The latter tended to regard such behaviour as almost inconceivable, warranting banishment or supernatural intervention through cursing. Such reactions were rare among the elite fathers, although our impression is that they are less permissive in this regard than their American counterparts. The findings as a whole suggest that the elite fathers are somewhat less jealous of their authority than the Oje men, but are still concerned to instil respect in their children and maintain discipline in the home.

Table 9.8 presents data concerning the fathers' responses to impulses and desires of their children that do not directly involve paternal authority. The Oje fathers are extremely antagonistic to fighting and mutual abuse among children, while the elite are much more likely to tolerate it. Many of the Oje fathers encourage their children to report such attacks, rather than to retaliate. Reactions to sex questions produce a less clear division between the two groups, perhaps because of the concentration on pre-school children, but it is clear that some Oje fathers refuse to answer them, while no elite fathers admit to this. (No statistical test is presented because the categories were created *a posteriori*.) Some of the responses of the elite were evasive, but we gained the impression that they are, on the average, more prepared to be frank about sexual matters with their children. The Oje men seemed to see such questions as a violation of the social distance they are attempting to maintain.

The difference in paternal attitude towards a child's occupational choice is striking (Table 9.8). When asked what they wanted their children to be when they grew up, all of the Oje fathers mentioned a specific occupation, such as doctor (most frequent), nurse or engineer, while most of the elite fathers stated only that the child would have to choose for himself, though perhaps with parental advice. We interpret this to mean, not that the Oje fathers really will choose their children's occupations when the children have

TABLE 9.8

Comparison of Oje and Elite Fathers on Aggression, Sex Questions and Occupational Choice of the Child

	Oje	Elite	χ^2 *	p
Permissiveness for aggression toward other children				
Low	10	1		
Moderate	0	6	16·0	<0·001
High	0	1		
Father answers child's sex questions				
Yes	5	5		
No	5	0		
Hasn't come up yet	0	5		
Names specific future occupation				
Yes	10	2	9·6	<0·001
No	0	8		

* Corrected for continuity.

gained more education than their fathers, but only that the elites are more inclined to see their children as sentient beings who will develop will and judgement of their own.

Thus, the findings on hypothetical effects of ideological differences between the two groups are mixed. The elite fathers have distinctly shifted to greater permissiveness of the child's impulses and desires but they remain closer to their Yoruba background in their insistence on traditional displays of respect and maintenance of fairly strict discipline.

Conclusions

In this exploratory study of two groups of urban Yoruba fathers offered as representing 'traditional' and 'modern' poles of an hypothetical modernisation continuum, we have found evidence of change towards a more intimate and affectionate father-child relationship oriented towards the raising of fewer, more self-directed children. This shift has taken place in the context of a general decline in social distance between the father and his wife and children. Traditionally, this social distance was related to sex segregation in the compound and increased with the number of wives; its sharp diminution under changed conditions has made husband-wife relations more egalitarian, given more paternal attention to the child, and made the amount of this attention dependent not on the internal structure of the family but on the amount of time the father's extrafamilial roles allow him to spend with his family. Given the differences in income and social status, as well as the factors we predicted to make a difference between the groups (fertility, infant mortality, housing, family structure, family functions, education, religion), it is extremely difficult to specify with conclusiveness which aspects of socio-cultural change caused which changes in paternal attitudes and behaviour.

For example, a plausible case could be made for explaining most of the changes in terms of the ideological shift to egalitarianism, without considering social structure and family functions. Rival explanations stressing one of these sets of determinants over the others cannot be tested in the present study. Such specification requires more controlled studies in which some of the socio-cultural factors are held constant.

Without being able to isolate causal influences, we can nevertheless ask whether the changes observed can be validly seen as modernisation in child rearing and father-child relations, as this process has been recorded for other parts of the world. Returning to the studies in Russia, Lebanon and the United States discussed earlier in this article, we find the Nigerian data remarkably concordant on most points: the movement is towards greater permissiveness towards the child's spontaneous desires (his aggresion, his occupational choice, etc.), greater egalitarianism in husband-wife relations and more affection and emotional warmth in father-child relations. The major trend lacking in our Ibadan fathers (or so weak as to be statistically insignificant) is the shift away from physical punishment and towards 'psychological' techniques of discipline. With this exception, we conclude that our Ibadan findings do indeed show a process of modernisation in father-child relationships going on among the Yoruba families there, at least in the most educated stratum of urban society. Movement from the traditional end of the continuum to the modern end can be accomplished in one generation, as illustrated by some of our elite fathers, but may often take two generations of change. Although the effect of this modernisation on the personality of the next generations is beyond the scope of this paper, we might speculate that the loosening of traditional constraints among the Yoruba of Ibadan, accompanied as it is by the persistence of some traditional respect and discipline, will produce fewer disciplinary problems than the modernisation of child rearing in other parts of the world.

Notes and References

1 The study was supported by the National Institute of Mental Health (NIMH), Grant M-4865; by the Ford Foundation Child Development Project, Institute of Education, University of Ibadan; and by the University of Chicago, Committee on African Studies and Committee for the Comparative Study of New Nations (under a grant from the Carnegie Corporation of New York). The principal investigator, Robert A. LeVine, was supported by an NIMH Research Career Development Award and was a Fellow of the Foundations' Fund for

Research in Psychiatry at the time. Dr Barbara B. Lloyd served as field director during much of the research period and carried out much of the background investigation and sample selection that provided the framework for the father study.

2 For example: Margaret Mead, "The Implications of Culture Change for Personality Development", *American Journal of Orthopsychiatry*, Vol. 17, 1947, pp. 633–46; David Riesman, *The Lonely Crowd*, New Haven 1950; D. F. Aberle and K. D. Naegele, "Middle-Class Fathers' Occupational Role and Attitudes Toward Children", *American Journal of Orthopsychiatry*, Vol. 22, 1952, pp. 366–78; Alex Inkeles, "Social Change and Social Character: The Role of Parental Mediation", in N. J. Smelser and W. J. Smelser, eds., *Personality and Social Systems*, New York 1963, pp. 357–66; D. Miller and G. Swanson, *The Changing American Parent*, New York 1958.

3 Inkeles, op. cit., p. 365.

4 Ibid., pp. 358–9.

5 Ibid., p. 359.

6 D. Miller and G. Swanson, op. cit.

7 R. Redfield, *The Folk Culture of Yucatan*, Chicago 1942.

8 The medical and physical growth part of the study was directed by Dr Margaret Janes, Institute of Child Health, University of Ibadan.

9 The study of mothers was directed by Dr Barbara B. Lloyd, who is preparing a monograph on it.

10 cf. B. C. Rosen, "Socialization and Achievement Motivation in Brazil", *American Sociological Review*, Vol. 27, No. 5, 1962, p. 623.

11 Cf. T. W. Adorno, E. Frenkel-Brunswik, D. J. Levinson and R. N Sanford, *The Authoritarian Personality*, New York 1950.

12 Cf. R. V. Burton and J. W. M. Whiting, "The Absent Father and Cross-Sex Identity", *Merrill-Palmer Quarterly*, Vol. 7, 1961, pp. 85–95.

13 Cf. D. Funkenstein, S. H. King and M. E. Drolette, *Mastery of Stress*, Cambridge, Mass., 1957.

14 Cf. Aberle and Naegele, op. cit.

15 Inkeles, op. cit., pp. 361–3.

16 Urie Bronfenbrenner, "The Changing American Child—A Speculative Analysis", in Smelser and Smelser, op. cit., pp. 348–9.

17 E. T. Prothro, *Child Rearing in the Lebanon*, Cambridge, Mass., 1961, pp. 157–8. Italicised as in the original.

18 M. L. Kohn, "Social Class and Parent-Child Relationships: An Interpretation", *American Journal of Sociology*, Vol. 68, 1963, pp. 471–80.

19 Riesman, op. cit.

20 Cf. William S. Goode, *World Revolution and Family Patterns*, New York 1963.

21 Cf. Akin Mabogunje, *Yoruba Towns*, Ibadan 1962.

22 Bronfenbrenner, op. cit.

23 Kohn, op. cit.

24 Barbara Lloyd, "Indigenous Ibadan", in P. C. Lloyd, A. L. Mabogunje and B. Awe, eds., *The City of Ibadan*, Cambridge 1967.
25 Cf. P. C. Lloyd, "The Yoruba of Nigeria", in J. L. Gibbs, ed., *Peoples of Africa*, New York 1965, pp. 547–82, for an ethnographic sketch and comprehensive bibliography.
26 Leonard Doob, *Becoming More Civilized*, New Haven 1961, p. 49.
27 Ibid., pp. 66–70.
28 Cf. Lloyd, op. cit.
29 For example: D. Landy, *Tropical Childhood*, Chapel Hill, NC, 1959; E. T. Prothro, op. cit.; Leigh Minturn and W. W. Lambert, *Mothers of Six Cultures*, New York 1964.
30 Mothers were interviewed by Mrs O. Akinkugbe, fathers by D. O. Oyerinde.
31 Mothers were interviewed by Dr Barbara Lloyd and Mrs Virginia Demos, fathers by Robert A. LeVine.
32 R. F. Winch, *The Modern Family*, New York 1963.
33 Kohn, op. cit.

10

Environmental Change, Types of Descent, and Child Rearing Practices

REMI CLIGNET

URBANISATION is sometimes defined as one manifestation of an increase in scale of society.[1] Such an increase is also associated with growing interdependence of the individuals and segments of society. In the urban context, familial structures cease to be the sole determinants of individual behaviour; the family mediates the influence of other institutions such as schools and corporations which, in turn, modify the family. The present paper examines the first aspect of this inter-relationship, and analyses the degree to which various aspects of environmental change affect the form and intensity of certain familial functions.[2] More specifically, the paper indicates how urbanisation—which I here identify with environmental change—modifies the contrasts between the child rearing practices of two Ivory Coast ethnic groups: the Abure and the Bete.

I. *Aims of the Study*

An analysis of the effects of environmental change upon child rearing practices raises four types of questions: (i) To what aspects of environmental change are individuals and familial groups most likely to react? (ii) Do populations with dissimilar traditional structures respond differently to such influences? (iii)

NOTE: *The notes and references for Chapter 10 will be found on page 292.*

What is the form of the relationship between crucial aspects of environmental change and selected patterns of child rearing practices? (iv) How stable is this relationship?

(i) *The various aspects of environmental change*. First, the changes which affect a modernising society involve a redistribution of its population in space. One might, therefore, equate varying degrees of exposure to environmental change with residence in modern urban centres of differing size. The larger the city, the higher the level of environmental change. However, in the Ivory Coast, there is no real continuum of cities by size and the 'primate' character of the capital city, Abidjan (225,000 inhabitants), is quite evident.[3] Further, the use of the size of an individual's place of residence as an indicator of his exposure to modernising forces requires tight control over other factors, such as the distance between this place of residence and the original locus of his ethnic group. In the present analysis, such control is impossible. Of the three cities to be considered, Grand Bassam (12,000 inhabitants) is located on the fringe of the area where the Abure prevail, Gagnoa (25,000 inhabitants) is situated close to the Bete, while Abidjan is at a distance from both regions. In addition, the distribution of these populations by place of residence does not provide any information about the degree of their residential isolation in the city. For the two smaller cities to be examined here, no accurate data are available on this point. In Abidjan, although Abure and Bete are unevenly distributed among the various sub-areas of the city, neither group seems to be predominant in any one of these;[4] both groups thus seem to be heavily exposed to inter-ethnic contacts.

Second, the urbanisation of a society may refer to the historical depth of the phenomenon. There are at least three possible approaches to this dimension: a comparison of cities of varying age, a comparison of individuals whose stay in an urban environment differs in duration, and an examination of a given urbanised sample through time. None of these approaches was possible here, since all the cities are new and most of the population has lived in such centres for only a relatively short time.[5]

Third, the urbanisation of a society implies an alteration of its occupational structure. More specifically, it involves a decline in the proportion of the population engaged in the primary sector of the economy and a corresponding increase in the proportion of wage earners, especially of those in the tertiary sector. Access to the newer occupations, such as clerical employment, becomes markedly selective. Recruitment into these positions rests upon educational prerequisites which are much higher than those demanded of urban manual workers. The salaries of clerical employees are higher and opportunities for promotion more numerous than for manual workers.[6] In turn, both types of employment enjoy better and steadier incomes than those derived from farming. In short, environmental differences are associated with a selective distribution of the population among productive structures with differing requirements, resources and rewards.

In the present sample survey, I have used both residential and occupational criteria as indicators of differing levels of exposure to environmental change and have distinguished between three subgroups of respondents. The first subgroup includes the wives of cash crop farmers residing in villages and therefore exposed to a minimal level of environmental change. The second comprises wives of manual workers residing in one of the cities involved in the study; they represent a population exposed to a medium level of environmental change. The last subgroup has been exposed to a maximal level of environmental change and involves the wives of clerical workers residing in any of the three cities.

(ii) *Variations in the responses of distinctive societies to modernising forces*. Many authors have contended that traditional systems present organisational features having varying degrees of compatibility with the requirements of modernisation.[7] One possible way of assessing the validity of this proposition is to compare the responses of distinctive ethnic groups to modernising forces of a similar nature and intensity. Thus, the present comparative analysis is based upon data collected in 1960 among Abure and Bete women. Generally, their indigenous geographical environments are alike but, as we shall see, their social organisation differs markedly. An analysis of the reactions of these two peoples to comparable environmental change should enable us to test whether changes in their child rearing practices vary with the structural organisation prevailing in their communities of origin.

What is our rationale for studying such practices? Parents endeavour to raise their children in such a way that they can assume typical adult roles in their own society.[8] Since the social organisation of the Abure and of the Bete are not alike, their child rearing practices should differ accordingly. However, insofar as families from both peoples have experienced various degrees of participation in modern structures, it is crucial to ascertain the degree to which these differential experiences are reflected in the socialising demands imposed upon their offspring. Are these demands increasingly alike or are they still influenced by the specific requirements of these distinctive cultures? To what extent do such demands make modernisation a continuous process built on the acquisitions of successive generations, or is it a discrete experience which must be re-enacted by each cohort of individuals? It is here that the role of women is particularly significant. Since women occupy a low status in many traditional African societies, being the objects rather than subjects of rights, an examination of the impact of environmental change upon their child rearing practices may lead to a better understanding of their domestic position. In more general terms, is it true that individuals with a traditionally low status are most likely to innovate when the environment of their group is changing?[9]

(iii) *Determination of the relationship between environmental change and selected patterns of behaviour.* The simplest model representing the impact of social change is linear in nature. As the participation of an individual in modern structures increases, he tends increasingly to abandon traditional practices or, alternatively, to adopt new patterns of behaviour. The second model assumes a step function and stresses the discontinuities which exist between the effects of traditional and modern environments; individual practices change at a certain threshold point. The third model holds that modernisation fosters new patterns of behaviour, followed by a partial restoration of traditional patterns. This model is curvilinear and indicates that processes of change and stabilisation alternate through time.[10]

(iv) *Variability of the relationship.* These models are not necessarily mutually exclusive. Thus, the effect of environmental change on any pattern of behaviour may vary with the traditional social structure from which the actors come. Similarly, the nature of this impact may differ for various patterns of behaviour. That is, the tensions developed in various components of a given social structure undergoing modernisation are not necessarily uniform. It is possible to imagine that the rates, timing, sequential order and trajectories of change vary in terms of both the area of social life analysed and the innovative qualities prevailing in the group from which urbanised individuals are derived.[11]

I intend in this paper to demonstrate that various aspects of the child rearing practices of the Abure and the Bete—childbirth, weaning and socialisation at home and in school—are differentially affected by variations in the level of exposure to environmental change.

II. Description of the Peoples Compared in this Study

The Abure inhabit a quite small territory around the city of Grand Bassam in the south-east corner of the Ivory Coast.[12] Their society is comprised of 12,000 members, scattered among thirteen villages. It is a very hierarchically differentiated group. Divided into social and political categories based on birth (i.e., slaves, foreigners and members of the founding clans), it is also cross-cut by generation lines. The age classes fulfil definite military, economic and social functions. Potential conflicts among lineages are regulated by a complex network of relationships within social, political and age categories. Ties resulting from seniority or political categories generate more individual obligations than do kin affiliations. The elaborate social and political integration of Abure society probably accounts, at least in part, for the concentration of its population in large multi-lineage villages, such as Bonoua or Mossou.

Although this society usually follows patrilocal rules of residence, the clan structure is matrilineal. The matriclan and its lineages are meaningful units in terms of land tenure, social control and marriage negotiation. The Abure, however, are sometimes considered to follow double-descent rules since, like their Ashanti neighbours, they recognise the implications of the principle, 'Blood is transmitted by women, and bones (or spirit) by men'. As a matter of fact, certain taboos and traditional duties are transmitted along paternal lines. Furthermore, the paternal kin group exerts some control on the education of the offspring. It also chooses the names of children and participates in the negotiations concerning weddings. But the scope of its economic and social influence is by no means comparable to that of the matriclan and its component lineages. The loyalties of the women are directed towards their own maternal descent group. Even after marriage, women maintain strong ties with their brothers, to whom they must report about the upbringing of their children. Usually, married women engage in independent economic activities, so that the only rights acquired by men upon marriage concern exclusive sexual service and the performance of domestic duties. Furthermore, a certain emotional distance between the conjugal partners accentuates the looseness of their ties.

The Bete,[13] who form a subgroup of the Kru family, occupy a large territory in the south-west part of the country, within the districts of Gagnoa, Daloa and Soubre. Numbering approximately 150,000 and scattered among 541 villages, they constitute an unstructured cluster of politically segmented groups. Each patriclan (*digpi*) and each part of a clan occupies a definite territory. Most of the functions of the clan have progressively disappeared, and there is currently no significant social or political unit larger than the village. Thus, although the Bete country may be characterised by its relative linguistic and cultural homogeneity, it does not form a political entity.

The majority of Bete villages are occupied by a segment of a lineage and commonly include several extended families which are able to trace descent from a common agnatic ancestor. The inhabitants of some villages, however, have diverse clan origins. In such cases, the community of their daily experience constitutes an adequate substitute for familial affiliation. Village authority lies in the hands of the eldest man in the lineage segment and each family is supposed to help him maintain the lineage property. Reciprocally, he distributes the land among the heads of the families, settles any conflict between individuals or groups and plays an important role in matrimonial procedures. He receives the bride-wealth claimed for the marriage of the girls of the village and uses it to secure wives for the men. In the past, the gains and the losses resulting from this type of exchange cancelled each other out, but this does not always hold true today. The value of the brideprice claimed by the bride's family has progressed steadily upwards and there is now a temptation for the recipient of these funds to convert them to his own use and thereby violate the traditional rules.

After marriage, a woman usually leaves her community of origin. Since she must marry outside of either parent's clan, the residence of her bridegroom and his family are often remote from that of her family; however, this consequence of exogamy depends upon the composition of the village from which she is derived. Thus the loyalties of the Bete women are split between their natal and marital groups. On the one hand, they enjoy a relatively high status in their village of origin, but, simultaneously, they have to provide their children with a proper position in their husband's patriclan. Moreover, women's economic activities are important to their husbands, whose profits depend to a large extent on the amount of work that their spouses are willing to perform.

In Mitchell's terms, a man's uxorial rights to his wife's services are more numerous and more significant among the Bete than among the Abure. Further, the genetricial rights to offspring are acquired by the husband's clan in the former case, but remain the property of the wife's clan in the latter.[14] Thus, the degree of integration of the wife into her affinal group is greater among the Bete than among the Abure. It can be expected that these variations in genetricial and uxorial rights will be associated with variations in child rearing practices; however, the direction and the intensity of these variations are also likely to be affected by the type of environment in which families live.

The Abure and the Bete have been differentially exposed to European influences. Abure farmers have almost completely abandoned a subsistence economy and are primarily concerned with the growth of coffee, cocoa or pineapples. Although their holdings vary in size, these farmers are often in a position to increase their activities and to use a substantial amount of manpower. By contrast, a large number of Bete men are still engaged in subsistence farming, and only three-quarters of Bete farmers produce any cash crops. The expansion of their holdings remains limited because of inadequate manpower resources.[15] The incidence of formal education within these two groups also differs. Primary school enrolments are much larger in the area of Grand Bassam, where the Abure are concentrated, than in Gagnoa and Daloa, where the Bete are to be found in large numbers.[16]

Geographical factors seem to affect the nature and the form of the migrations of these two peoples towards the capital of the Ivory Coast. Whereas the Abure prevail in an area which is only 20 miles away from Abidjan, there are 200 miles between Abidjan and the Bete area. As a consequence, the patterns of migration of the two groups differ; the Abure are proportionately four times more prevalent in Abidjan than they are in the Ivory Coast as a whole. This contrasts with the Bete, who are only 1.3 times more numerous in the capital than they are in the country as a whole. Thus the volume and distance of migration seem to be related.

Inequalities in the distance of migration of the two peoples were once associated with differences in their respective sex ratios in Abidjan. In 1955, there were 108 Abure men for every 100 Abure women. Among the Bete, the corresponding ratio was 127. By 1963, however, the sex ratio of the Abure had climbed to 113 while that of the Bete had dropped to 118. The age structure of the urbanised segments of the two peoples was not alike either. In 1955 the active elements of the Abure male population of Abidjan—those between 20 and 60 years of age—represented only 45 per cent of the Abure male population in that city. The corresponding figure was 53 per cent in the case of the Bete. The profile of the female population of these two groups was also different. Adult Abure females represented 45 per cent of all Abure females in Abidjan, as against only 36 per cent for the Bete.[17]

The two groups in Abidjan can also be contrasted in terms of their educational level. In 1963, half of the Abure men over fourteen years of age had completed at least their primary studies as compared with one-quarter of their Bete counterparts. With the adult women in these two groups, the contrast is similar. Among the Abure women, 13 per cent had completed their primary studies as against 5 per cent of the Bete. Participation in the modern sector of the economy differed accordingly. In 1955, almost one-quarter of the Abure adult male population worked for the government as opposed to 10 per cent of the Bete. The unevenness of the participation of the two peoples in educational and occupational structures was associated with contrasts in length of stay in the capital. Whereas 58 per cent of the Bete have been in Abidjan for seven years or less, the corresponding proportion is 47 per cent for the Abure. There are also differences in the ecological distribution of the two groups. A substantial minority of the Bete are concentrated in the modern section of the city (Adjame Modern) and in the European-dominated neighbourhoods, while the Abure are more evenly distributed throughout the city.

To summarise the group differences which are indicative of differential exposure to modernising influences, the rural Abure have shifted more completely than the Bete to cash crops; Abure migrants to Abidjan have been in the city somewhat longer, on the average, than have the Bete; and the Abure have had much more exposure to formal education and have entered government employment to a much greater extent. My task is to determine how the contrasts between the two original cultures and the differences in their level of exposure to change affect child rearing practices. The consequences of unequal migration distances from Abidjan are difficult to ascertain. On the one hand, it can be argued that the Abure are in a better position than the Bete to maintain close contacts with their village of origin, and thus will be more inclined, when urbanised, to retain their traditional norms. Alternatively, it can be argued that the proximity of Abidjan to the Abure area facilitates the diffusion of European practices and beliefs to the area.

III. Methodology

The exclusive use of an ethnographic approach would be insufficient in the present case. Based upon participant observation or upon the interview of selected informants, this approach attempts to define a model of the social relationships prevailing in the society under study. The use of such techniques rests upon the implicit assumption that the society is culturally homogeneous and that there are no important spatial or temporal variations in its main social forms. The gathering of ethnographic data constitutes a necessary condition for a complete understanding of inter-personal ties within an underdeveloped area, and provides an indispensable historical background. But this procedure does not accurately depict the situation in developing countries which have been increasingly exposed to foreign norms. The increased degree of social differentiation justifies the use of survey research techniques which will add essential complementary information to the data provided by more traditional approaches.

The present analysis involves 1,207 interviews, or two-thirds of the total number taken. Of those under consideration, 578 were with Abure women and 629 were collected among the Bete. Given such sources of data, the reliability of the interview procedure must be considered. The nationality and sex of the researcher constituted insurmountable handicaps in establishing good rapport with many African women. In the rural areas of the Ivory Coast, the usual reaction of a housewife to the arrival of a European man in the village is to disappear into her compound. Even when a foreigner has been tentatively accepted by the elders of the village, the women are still likely to remain suspicious. Under the circumstances and since I was teaching sociology and psychology in the Ecole Normale Ménagère (Teachers' College of Home Economics) in Abidjan, I asked fifteen female students if they would help me collect the information I needed. They agreed and we started a pilot study of child rearing practices among the mothers of children attending school in the vicinity. After discussing with my students the results of this pre-test, the validity of the questions used and their translation, we jointly constructed the questionnaire for the present study.

The ethnic affiliations and the age of the interviewers could have affected the reliability of the data they gathered. Abure students conducted the majority of the interviews in the Abure area, with the assistance of girls who belonged to somewhat similar tribes (Anyi, Baule and Attie). For the Bete, I asked Malinke girls living in this area to perform the greater part of the work. To be sure, relationships between Bete and Malinke are ambivalent. Yet these girls had mastered the Bete language quite well. They were helped by Kru and Abe girls—members of tribes whose social organisation does not differ drastically from that of the Bete. All of the interviewers were over eighteen years old and approaching womanhood, so they could be looked upon as the age equivalents of the younger sisters of the women interviewed. To clarify the interviewer's role in each village in which the survey was to take place, the goals of the inquiry were explained as thoroughly as possible to the elders, with the help of the local district officer.

Secondly, one may question the validity of responses to questionnaires administered in an African context. Answers to questions constitute verbal behaviour which may be quite remote from the patterns of behaviour they purport to reflect. It should be noted, however, that neither the interviewers nor the interviewees were aware of the nature of the contrasts which were expected. Under these conditions I have no reason to believe that any biases introduced by either interviewers or interviewees have contributed to the response differences observed among the various ethnic, residential and occupational categories.

The third uncertainty raised by the use of survey research techniques concerns the choice of questions, the vast bulk of which provided fixed-answer alternatives in order to simplify the task of the interviewers. The questions were either taken from survey materials already used elsewhere in Africa or else they were based on particularly significant observations made by ethnographers concerning the two tribes. As indicated above, the use of survey research in Africa presupposes the existence of ethnographic data; survey leads only to the measurement of variability within and among patterns reported by ethnographers.

The fourth problem raised by this technique is that of sampling. Interviews were gathered in a large number of villages, in the two smaller cities of Bagnoa and Bassam, and in Abidjan, the capital. The following principles underlay the construction of the sample:

it was assumed that patterns of response would be affected by the type of community being sampled and that responses would be more variable in larger centres than in the smaller villages. It was therefore decided to interview a limited number of women in each of a large number of small villages and, conversely, to increase the size of the sample in larger villages and in the cities. In each village and in Gagnoa and Grand Bassam, women respondents were randomly selected from the census data sheets. In Abidjan, respondents were drawn from a list of owners and tenants which had been made by the Institut Français d'Afrique Noire.

For the purpose of the present analysis, I have eliminated all childless women and all wives of Bete subsistence farmers, in order to increase the comparability of the rural segments of the two peoples. The respondents are in all cases the wives of monogamous men or the senior co-wives of polygynous families. The age structure of the two ethnic samples is different. Among the Abure, the percentage of women below thirty varies from 47 per cent for the wives of farmers, to 75 per cent for the wives of manual workers, to 50 per cent for those of clerical workers. For the Bete, the figures are 54, 82 and 84 per cent respectively.[18] The make-up of the reduced sample is shown in Table 10.1.

IV. The Position of the Women in the Two Groups

I have argued that there is a close relationship between the child rearing practices of a woman and other features of her domestic role. These roles are not alike in the two groups compared here, but the contrast in their main features should be eroded by modernisation for the following reasons. First, modernisation is accompanied by a decline in the functions of the familial group, and correspondingly by a decrease in the social control exerted by this group over its members.[19] This should lead to some deferment of marriage and to an increase in the freedom that women enjoy in the selection of mates. Second, modernisation is associated with participation in an increasing variety of groups, and this cannot but lead to an enlargement of the field of eligible mates; marriages between partners from different geographic and ethnic back-

TABLE 10.1

Source of Interviews

Environment	Abure No. of Sample Units	Abure No. of Interviews	Bete No. of Sample Units	Bete No. of Interviews
Rural Areas	4		45	
Cash crop farmers		430		333
Urbanised areas	2		2	
Manual workers		56		141
Clerical workers		92		155
Total	6	578	47	629

grounds should be more frequent in urban centres than in villages. Third, modern criteria, such as educational status, should play a more important role in the processes of mate selection as one moves from a village to a city. Conversely, traditional forms of marriage, such as plural marriage, should be less common in urban than in rural environments.

Among the Abure, parents' control of their daughter's choice of a mate declines consistently with increases in the level of modernity of the mate's occupation (Table 10.2). Among the Bete also, this form of parental control declines in urban environments, but more markedly among the wives of manual than of clerical workers. In both groups, variations in the degree of parental control in this regard are directly associated with early marriage of the wife. Thus deferment of marriage becomes more frequent as the level of modernisation of the Abure population increases; among the Bete urbanised interviewees married at a later age, but the deferment of marriage is more evident among the wives of manual workers.

As predicted, modernisation increases the frequency of inter-ethnic marriages. The higher degree of modernisation of the entire Abure population probably accounts for the greater incidence of such marriages in this group. However, a maximal level of exposure of this people to environmental changes is associated with a partial restoration of ethnic endogamy among clerical workers. Thus,

TABLE 10.2

Percentage of Subgroups of Abure and Bete Wives Having Specified Characteristics

Characteristic*	Abure Wives of: Farmers %	Abure Wives of: Manual Workers %	Abure Wives of: Clerical Workers %	Bete Wives of: Farmers %	Bete Wives of: Manual Workers %	Bete Wives of: Clerical Workers %
1. Mate selected by parents	85·1	80·4	70·7	70·0	51·8	61·9
2. Married by age of fifteen	83·7	60·7	56·7	55·6	31·9	37·4
3. Ethnically exogamous marriage	2·1	42·9	31·5	0·3	2·8	10·3
4. Locally exogamous marriage	10·7	32·8	23·2	76·1	52·4	68·6
5. Non-French speaking	98·6	91·1	83·7	98·2	82·3	79·4
6. Marriage to a polygynist	41·2	23·2	31·5	52·1	33·6	41·9
7. Gainfully employed	85·6	30·4	38·0	0·6	19·1	23·9

*Chi square values of differences between Abure and Bete for each occupational category and each characteristic.**

	df	Farmers	Manual Workers	Clerical Workers
1.	3	41·1 (P = 0·001)	15·2 (P = 0·01)	2·3 (NS)
2.	3	88·4 (P = 0·001)	15·3 (P = 0·01)	9·3 (P = 0·05)
3.	3	737·6 (P = 0·001)	170·7 (P = 0·001)	185·6 (P = 0·001)
4.	2	324·5 (P = 0·001)	33·7 (P = 0·001)	49·7 (P = 0·001)
5.	2	1·3 (NS)	6·5 (P = 0·05)	3·0 (NS)
6.	1	3·3 (P = 0·01)	2·0 (NS)	2·6 (NS)
7.	1	542·6 (P = 0·001)	2·9 (NS)	5·6 (P = 0·02)

* Each of the numbered characteristics above is one of several response alternatives, the others not being listed here. These sets of response categories also included 'No Answer' for Nos. 1–4. For each set of responses, three values of Chi square were computed for the difference between Abure and Bete, one for each occupational category.

growing social differentiation in the Ivory Coast seems to lead to some social and emotional isolation of people with the highest level of socio-economic development. Among the Bete, who are much less advanced, the frequency of inter-ethnic marriages increases consistently as one moves from the group of cash crop farmers to the sample of clerical workers.[20]

The effect of modernisation upon village exogamy cannot be analysed without reference to the original ecological distribution of the peoples under consideration. Since the population of the Abure village is large and comprises several lineages, the rules of exogamy have no territorial implications. Conversely, in so far as Bete lineages are geographically isolated in separate villages, women of this group are bound to marry outside the territory occupied by their family. For the Abure there is a curvilinear relationship between the prevalence of the village exogamy and the level of exposure to environmental change; the decline of local identity is maximal for manual workers, and this finding is parallel to the previous observation on inter-ethnic marriages in this society. In the case of the Bete, the pattern is also curvilinear and maximal exposure to environmental change leads to a marked tendency to retain the pattern of village exogamy. This might be a consequence of the selective character of urban migrations. It is more likely, however, to result from the maintenance of parental authority in matrimonial negotiations. The continuation of this authority, in turn, reflects a distinctive pattern of adjustment of this group to the pressures of the urban environment. The maintenance of strong familial and ethnic solidarity seems to help the Bete adjust to the more modern urban roles.

As anticipated, Table 10.2 also indicates that the educational level of a woman reflects, somewhat, her husband's occupational status. Thus, among both ethnic groups, the proportion of women who have learned to speak French increases regularly as one moves from the rural to the most urban occupations. The predicted decline in polygyny in the city is also evident in both ethnic groups but, in each, the manual workers show the lowest frequency of multiple marriage. This fact probably reflects the low income of this occupational group and the relative irregularity of their employment rather than distinctive attitudes and aspirations. Clerical employment, even though it presupposes a higher level of education, appears conducive to a somewhat greater incidence of plural marriage.[21]

The lower degree of social attachment of the Abure wife to her affines shows some relationship to her more independent economic role. In rural areas, the Bete women constitute a major source of labour for their husbands and have less economic independence than their Abure counterparts. Although opportunities for female employment remain limited in an urban environment, urbanised Bete wives participate more in the labour market than their rural counterparts, whereas the participation of the corresponding segments of the Abure sample shows a relative decline in the city. Variations in the degree of integration of a woman into her affinal group are also associated with variations in the incidence of divorce, which is almost twice as high for the Abure, among whom over half of the sample has been divorced. These rates of incidence do not vary among occupational subgroups.[22]

In summary, it has been shown that the influence of modernisation on patterns of marriage and on the domestic status of women varies in terms of both the traditional organisation of the two peoples and of the specific pattern of behaviour analysed. Thus in both groups there seems to be a linear relationship between the educational status of women and their husbands' occupations. Among the Bete, there is a similar type of relationship between modernisation and the incidence of inter-ethnic marriage. On the other hand, the relationship between environmental change and the incidence of polygyny seems uniformly curvilinear and the same model describes the distribution of inter-village marriages. Lastly, the fact that the proportion of divorce remains constant among all segments of each ethnic sample indirectly suggests a threshold phenomenon.

V. Fertility and Circumstances Surrounding Childbirth

It must next be ascertained what sort of model best describes the impact of environmental change upon various child rearing practices. For instance, according to the linear model, I posit that, regardless of ethnic affiliations, the fertility of the wives of clerical workers will be lower than that of the wives in any other occupational subgroup. Similarly, I anticipate that parturition in a maternity ward will become more likely as the mother's level of exposure to environmental change becomes more marked.

Before the problem of fertility is analysed, it is well to recall that my samples of women are limited to those who have borne children, thus eliminating some important sources of variability found in more gross comparisons. Also, as noted earlier, the age composition of the various subgroups is not constant. It is approximately the same for the two groups of urban Bete and the wives of Abure manual workers. In these three age-comparable groups, the proportion of women who have had four or more children is 20 per cent for the Abure and 16 per cent, each, for Bete manual and clerical workers' wives. The average numbers of children for the same subgroups are 2·4, 2·4 and 2·3 respectively. This lack of difference appears also in the comparison of the similarly-aged groups of wives of Abure farmers and clerical workers. These somewhat older women have had averages of 3·6 and 3·4 children. The roughly age-comparable rural Bete women, however, have had fewer children (2·9) and the proportions of rural Bete and Abure women with four or more children are 27 and 42 per cent respectively. Two factors contribute to this difference: Abure women are more likely to marry early and to marry a monogamous man. This latter tendency is significant in that monogamy seems to exert a positive influence on fertility.[23]

The social structure of each group is reflected in the circumstances surrounding the birth of children. In both societies, the importance of fertility is evidenced by the anxiety of women who remain sterile or suffer miscarriages. These misfortunes are conducive to divorce or to the husband's acquiring another wife, and they are often interpreted as resulting from malevolent spirits or from sorcery.[24] It is not surprising that pregnancy is a joint concern of all the women of a community. After the death of a pregnant woman, for instance, all other women of an Abure village must mourn, dressed in white gowns and their bodies whitened with

19—TCIMA

kaolin. Under similar circumstances in some Bete villages, men are expelled from their houses for three days, and pregnant women march through the village beating drums, an act usually reserved to males. These differing forms of solidarity are associated with variations in the status of pregnant women in the two groups. Among the Abure, pregnant women are given no special treatment and are not subjected to any restrictions. They do their usual share of domestic chores until the eighth month of pregnancy. Attitudes towards pregnancy are somewhat different among the Bete, where expectant mothers observe dietary restrictions and are not permitted to do heavy work.[25]

The sort of lineal system into which a child is born influences the location of its birthplace (Table 10.3). Among the patrilineal Bete, two-thirds of the rural mothers bear their first child in the compound of their husband. Almost immediately after the delivery, the mother goes into the house from the courtyard where the birth took place. Her infant is carried by the midwife to the front entrance of the house so that her husband's kinsmen may see that there is a new member in the household.[26] By contrast, 60 per cent of rural mothers among the matrilineal Abure delivered their first baby at the residence of their mother. In this case there are usually no female relatives of the baby's father living in the village where delivery takes place.

Parturition at the home of the child's maternal grandmother is a pattern which is more resistant to modernising influences than is delivery in the paternal residence. Despite the lower density of medical facilities in the Bete area, 15 per cent of the rural Bete mothers indicated that they gave birth to their first child in a hospital, as against only 5 per cent of the rural Abure mothers. It is noteworthy that, even among the urban Abure, hospital delivery replaces parturition at the husband's residence much more completely than the matrilocal pattern is replaced.

The latent tensions between spouses are clearly expressed at the time of delivery. In both societies, the difficulties a wife may experience in parturition are frequently considered to be a result of her prior misconduct. Among the matrilineal Abure, if labour is difficult, it implies that the child is that of a lover, whom she is

TABLE 10.3

Birthplace of the First Child of Subgroups of Abure and Bete Women (Percentages of Subgroup)

Location	Abure Wives of:			Bete Wives of:		
	Farmers	Manual Workers	Clerical Workers	Farmers	Manual Workers	Clerical Workers
Hospital	4·7	60·7	68·5	14·7	75·2	82·6
Husband's Residence	30·2	1·8	3·3	69·7	5·7	6·5
Mother's Residence	59·5	25·0	21·7	5·7	11·3	4·5
Others	5·1	10·7	5·4	9·6	7·1	5·2
No Answer	0·5	1·8	1·1	0·3	0·7	1·3
Total	100·0	100·0	100·0	100·0	100·0	100·1
N	430	56	92	333	141	155

Chi square value of differences between Abure and Bete for each occupationa category.

Cash Crop Farmers: 238·8 (P = 0·001)
Manual Workers: 8·5 (NS)
Clerical Workers: 18·2 (P = 0·001)

expected to designate. He is obligat ed to support her, as well as the newborn child. Identical suspicions exist among the Bete, but here, if a woman has a child by a man other than her husband, the latter will keep the child as long as the bridewealth has not been refunded to him.[27] In short, the contrast in the relevant behaviour of the Abure and Bete fathers reflects the dissimilarity of the rules of descent. Urbanised women of the Abure and Bete tend to behave more alike in selecting the locale of parturition. The greater her level of exposure to environmental change, the more apt a mother is to deliver her child in a hospital.

The social organisation of the two ethnic groups also influences whether and for how long a mother visits her own kin group following the birth of a child. Since Abure children belong to their mother's descent group, Abure mothers have more reason than their Bete counterparts to pay a *post partum* visit to their family. In addition, such a visit is much easier for the rural Abure since their husband's residence and that of their own kin group are in the same village. Even taking cognisance of the large 'No Answer' category in Table 10.4, a much larger per cent of rural Bete mothers did not visit their parents after the birth of their first child. The transfer of their genetricial rights to their husband and the distance separating the settlement of their affinal group from their village of origin deters many Bete women from visiting their parents at such a time.

TABLE 10.4

Post Partum Visiting Patterns of Subgroups of Abure and Bete Mothers (Percentages of Subgroup)

	Abure Wives of:			Bete Wives of:		
Length of Visit to Parents	Farmers	Manual Workers	Clerical Workers	Farmers	Manual Workers	Clerical Workers
No Visit	12·3	21·4	13·0	46·5	23·4	21·9
Less than a month	7·0	3·6	1·1	32·1	18·4	11·0
A month or more	54·7	66·1	76·1	19·2	51·8	59·4
No answer	26·0	8·9	9·8	2·1	6·4	7·7
Total	100·0	100·0	100·0	99·9	100·0	100·0
N	430	56	92	333	141	155

Chi square value of differences between Abure and Bete for each occupational category.

Cash Crop Farmers: 275·8 (P = 0·001)
Manual Workers: 8·1 (P = 0·05)
Clerical Workers: 12·9 (P = 0·01)

Furthermore, those women who do return home stay there for a relatively shorter period of time than do the Abure.

Environmental change increases both the frequency and the length of such visits among the Bete. The effect is less marked with the Abure. Thus, far from severing the ties of a woman with her family, modernisation may reinforce them. However, this particular pattern is difficult to interpret. To be sure, the loyalties of the Abure women towards their own kin group are easy to maintain, because of the short distance between Abidjan and their village of origin. On the other hand, urbanised Bete mothers tend to innovate in their increased tendency to visit their home villages. The economic resources of the urban sub-samples seem to have some effect on the visiting pattern in both ethnic groups. The wives of clerical workers are in a better position to take this trip or to stay away longer because their husbands are wealthier and also more likely to have other wives who can assume domestic responsibility while the new mother is absent.[28]

Lastly, I tentatively propose that variations in the level of exposure to environmental change are associated with inconsistencies in the domestic status of women. As a man's participation in modern structures increases, his dependence on and interest in his wife and children declines. This creates domestic strains and often leads a married woman to reaffirm her loyalties to her family or origin. In this way, modernisation increases both the inconsistencies of a woman's status and the number of strategies that she can utilise to cope with them.[29] The effects of modernisation in this regard probably account for the growing similarity in the *post partum* practices of Abure and Bete mothers.

VI. Weaning and Discipline

The family status of a woman influences the length of time she nurses her children. The lower the degree of her social absorption into her affinal group (and thus the more accentuated her economic autonomy) the more likely she is to wean her child as early as possible in order to resume her usual activities.[30] Further, weaning should occur later in the polygynous than in monogamous families since, in the former type of family, domestic chores and sexual obligations are divided among co-wives, which enables the new mother to maintain a close relationship with her infant. This expected difference between the two groups in length of the nursing period is supported by the data. Over one-half of Abure mothers in the rural area say they weaned their last-born child before it was two years old. The corresponding figure is only 38 per cent among the Bete.[31]

Environmental change modifies the time dimension of social action. Urban mothers are prone to nurse their offspring for a shorter period of time. The proportion of mothers weaning their last child before it was two years old increases to 82 per cent among the wives of Abure manual workers and to 58 per cent among the corresponding Bete subsegment. The contrast between the two peoples is not significantly different when the level of their exposure to environmental change increases further; among clerical workers' families, the proportion of mothers weaning their child within this period is 76 per cent for the Abure and 60 per cent for the Bete. The 'Westernisation' of mothers' practices in this regard does not necessarily imply a Westernisation of the related ideology. Thus, whereas European mothers justify earlier weaning in terms of the necessity of raising self-reliant children, urbanised African mothers justify the borrowing of this pattern in terms of their own needs and the requirements of the urban scene.

The next step is to ascertain when the beginning of formal discipline terminates the period of initial maternal indulgence.[32] In rural areas, the behaviour of Abure women seems to be somewhat standardised and three-quarters of them report that they do not begin disciplining their child until he starts to talk. In this society, it seems, weaning usually precedes the initiation of social control over a child's behaviour. In contrast, the norms prevailing among rural Bete mothers are less clear and only 57 per cent of them report that the disciplining of a child is initiated when it begins to talk. However, a quarter of the Bete begin the exercise of discipline as soon as a child can walk, whereas the corresponding proportion does not exceed 15 per cent among Abure mothers.

The practices of the wives of manual workers do not differ from those of women married to cash crop farmers; in each ethnic group, the age at which punishment is initiated remains the same. A maximal level of exposure to environmental change, however, has contrasting effects on Abure and Bete families. The wives of Bete clerical workers show some tendency to start exercising their disciplinary functions later than the wives of other Bete; only a fifth of the former group indicate that they do not punish their children before they begin to walk. Alternatively, over a quarter of Abure mothers in the clerical group start formal discipline by this time. By the time a child can talk, there is no inter-ethnic difference at the clerical level. Thus the contrast along these lines between the two cultures declines with exposure to maximal environmental change. This increased uniformity implies, however, opposite trajectories of change. In short, upward mobility tends to lengthen the period of initial indulgence among the Bete, but has an opposite effect among the Abure. In addition, it should be noted that the lack of difference in behaviour between the wives of cash crop farmers and of manual workers suggests a threshold effect; a certain level of environmental change is required before the discipline pattern changes.

Lastly, the structural differences between the two cultures are reflected in the techniques of punishment used by mothers. The discipline of children in a matrilineal patrilocal society presents special problems. The child is jurally subordinate to his maternal uncle, who usually lives elsewhere in the same village. Yet the child must obey his father, who is responsible for his early socialisation. This asymmetry is conducive to inconsistencies in the demands exerted on the child by his father and by members of his matrilineage. It can be hypothesised that these inconsistencies will lead the mother to be indulgent since her own status is not clear. She must compromise between the expectations of her brothers and her husband. In addition, even in rural areas, social change has increased the ambiguity of the status of married women, who are becoming more dependent upon their offspring in old age.

Inconsistencies in the demands exerted on a child are also indicative of the cross-pressures which characterise such societies.

It is not unlikely that such pressures are internalised and that, in such a context, the manipulation of a child's need for affiliation constitutes an effective disciplinary strategy. The withdrawal of emotional support by the mother is a particularly effective sanction in a society where the loyalties of a child are so easily divided. In short, one might anticipate that Abure mothers would be more indulgent than average and that they would make systematic use of emotional sanctions.[33]

By contrast, although the Bete mother does exercise disciplinary functions over her children, she always acts as a delegate of her husband. The congruence between lines of descent and of authority makes the definition of her rights and obligations very clear. Indeed, a mother is motivated to socialise her children according to her affinal group's expectations, since her own status depends on the position achieved by her children. The interests of both spouses are convergent and their demands are likely to reinforce one another. This situation leads us to expect Bete mothers to be less indulgent than the Abure. Further, Bete society is characterised by highly competitive and aggressive social relations,[34] which should be associated with the prominent use of physical punishment by mothers.

Table 10.5 confirms my predictions: 1 per cent of rural Bete mothers indicate that they never punish their children, compared with 15 per cent of the comparable Abure respondents. Further, in this latter group, 60 per cent of the mothers report that they typically use the kind of emotional punishment described above, as compared with only 42 per cent of the Bete who do so. Conversely, Bete mothers are as likely to punish their children physically as emotionally, but only 22 per cent of Abure mothers use physical punishment.

The effects of environmental change are very clear among the Abure. Mothers abandon traditional practices to adopt more aggressive techniques of punishment. Thus urbanisation not only shortens the period of initial indulgence in this group but also reduces the amount of indulgence displayed by mothers in socialising their children. This may reflect the increasing domestic responsibilities of such wives and mothers. The picture is less clear

TABLE 10.5

Punishment Most Often Used by Subgroups of Abure and Bete Mothers (Percentages of Subgroup)

Type of Punishment	Abure Wives of: Farmers	Abure Wives of: Manual Workers	Abure Wives of: Clerical Workers	Bete Wives of: Farmers	Bete Wives of: Manual Workers	Bete Wives of: Clerical Workers
Emotional	60·2	32·1	19·6	42·0	23·4	34·2
Physical	21·9	33·9	46·7	41·1	52·5	44·5
Deprivational	0·7	5·4	6·5	2·1	5·0	11·0
None	14·7	17·9	8·7	1·2	7·1	5·2
Other* and No answer	2·6	10·8	18·5	13·5	12·0	5·2
Total	100·1	100·1	100·0	99·9	100·0	100·1
N	430	56	92	333	141	155

Chi square value of differences between Abure and Bete for each occupational category.

Cash Crop Farmers: 112·6 (P = 0·001)
Manual Workers: 18·8 (P = 0·001)
Clerical Workers: 20·1 (P = 0·001)

* Includes combinations of the three first items.

among the Bete. Tentatively, I suggest that the greater emphasis upon physical punishment displayed by the Bete wives of manual workers reflects the relative amount of social disorganisation which accompanies an intermediate level of exposure to environmental change.

In summary, this section has enabled the identification of three types of models used to interpret the influence of social change on individual patterns of behaviour: linear, threshold and curvilinear. We have shown also that the applicability of these models varies both with the traditional structure and the pattern of behaviour under study.

VII. Authority Patterns

African families are characterised by a high degree of variability with regard to who can exert authority over children. Even in a single society, there are numerous possible agents of socialisation and discipline. The pattern of authority varies, however, with the structural properties of the group under consideration. In matrilineal societies such as the Abure, it has been observed that the severity and the formality of the ties established between the child and the maternal uncle are in contrast with the friendliness and the lack of restraint which underlie the bond between the child and his father. Correspondingly, in the patrilineal Bete society, the relationships between a child and his maternal relatives are of a pleasant and warm character.[35]

Interestingly enough, the functions of socialisation are not monopolised by descent groups. Thus, almost a third of rural Abure mothers neither rear their first child themselves nor send it to live with maternal relatives, but send it to grow up with paternal relations. In contrast, only 10 per cent of the Abure send the first child to be reared by maternal kin. Thus the socialisation of the child seems to facilitate the development of a complex network of interdependence among lineages and families; the authority which a descent group can exert over one of its members often depends upon the effectiveness of the socialisation practices of non-members of the group. The extent of participation of the extended family in the upbringing of children varies with village residence patterns. In villages which include the lineages of both parents, there is less need to reinforce extended family links through the rearing of children outside the nuclear family. Thus half of the rural Abure nuclear families keep their first child with them, as opposed to a third of the Bete counterparts.

The degree to which children are reared outside their parents' home also varies with the degree of modernisation of the socio-cultural environment. In this respect, environmental changes seem to have a linear effect on the behaviour of Abure parents. The higher the position of the husband in the occupational structure, the more likely he is to keep his offspring with him. The proportion of Abure families where children live most of the time with their parents increases from 52 per cent among rural families to 59 and 64 per cent among the families of manual and clerical workers respectively.

Environmental changes have a minor effect on the corresponding behaviour of Bete nuclear families; there are no marked differences between the families of clerical workers and farmers; one-fifth of clerical workers send their children to their paternal or maternal kin groups and 17 per cent of the farmers follow a similar pattern of behaviour. Yet, here again, manual workers present distinctive features and tend to protect themselves against the pressures of an urban environment by maintaining close contacts with their extended families;[36] at least one-third of them send children back to the community of one or the other parent. Contrasts between urban Abure and Bete suggest, then, that the persistence of traditional affiliations is not only a function of the distance between the present residence of a family and its community of origin, but seems also to vary with the intensity of the pressures exerted on the family by environmental changes.

The structural properties of the two groups compared here also affects the degree to which co-wives, in polygynous families, rear their children co-operatively. Among the Bete, there is a marked hierarchy among co-wives; the first wife is supposed to exert control over the others. She divides domestic tasks among the co-wives, allocates the parcels of land to be cultivated, and determines how frequently and for how long each will sleep with the husband. The hierarchy is often disturbed, however, because the power of each co-wife vis-à-vis the others and vis-à-vis the husband also depends on the domestic status achieved by her offspring. Not only this, but younger wives are often in a position to impose their demands upon the heads of the family.[37] These circumstances are conducive to a climate of competition. Within Abure polygynous families the situation is somewhat different. The hierarchy among co-wives is less formal and competitive feelings are less marked. Whereas Bete women refer to their co-wives as 'rivals', Abure women use the word 'sister'. The status of the Abure co-wife does not depend upon the domestic position achieved by her offspring, for their lineal ties are to her family, not to that of her husband.

As a consequence of these differences, the role of the senior wife in the upbringing of the polygynous husband's children is more prominent among the Bete than among the Abure. In rural areas, over half the senior wives of the former group indicate that they control the rearing of all children in the household, as against only 15 per cent of the Abure senior wives. Further, Abure co-wives are more co-operative and two thirds of them participate jointly in the upbringing of their children.[38]

Environmental change is associated with a decline in the pre-eminence of the role of the senior wife and with a growing individualisation of the relationships among the various actors of polygynous families. Thus, in an urban context, co-operation among co-wives diminished among the Abure; only about 40 per cent of the respondents of this group indicated that they co-operate with co-wives in the rearing of their children. In contrast, co-operation increases among the Bete and this pattern, which characterises only 18 per cent of the rural polygynous families, is evident among one third of the respondents married to either manual or clerical workers. Thus urbanisation tends to reinforce the cohesiveness of the Bete population.[39]

Once more, the effects of environmental change on distinctive types of traditional familial structure are not alike. These types affect the form, intensity, and direction of modernising influences on patterns of individual behaviour.

VIII. Attitudes and Behaviour Towards Formal Education

Although there are variations in the school enrolments of the various ethnic groups in the Ivory Coast, our problem here is to ascertain how lineal structures affect parental reactions to the formal education of their children.[40] Although Abure fathers are traditionally responsible for the socialisation of their offspring, it can be argued that they will be reluctant to take on the expense of a form of education which is not defined by custom, since they cannot expect any return from this type of investment under the matrilineal descent system. Nor is the maternal uncle likely to agree to pay for the schooling of his nephew, for he is not required to assume financial responsibilities for the boy's upbringing. Further, he might be reluctant to have his nephew educated in modern schools since men so trained are said to neglect their traditional obligations.

This situation fosters domestic tensions which can be analysed at various levels. First, I shall discover which member of the family decides whether or not a child should be sent to school. Second, I shall determine who punishes children when they fail to meet academic requirements. Lastly, I shall analyse the relative importance which mothers attach to formal schooling. Table 10.6

TABLE 10.6

Comparison of Subgroups of Abure and Bete with Regard to Who Decides Whether a Child Will Attend School (Percentages of Subgroup)

	Abure Wives of:			Bete Wives of:		
Decision Made by:	Farmers	Manual Workers	Clerical Workers	Farmers	Manual Workers	Clerical Workers
Father	66·4	50·0	64·1	62·8	56·7	54·8
Mother	2·1	5·4	5·4	20·4	10·6	11·6
Parents together	23·5	41·1	28·3	13·5	28·4	31·6
No answer	7·9	3·6	2·2	3·3	4·2	1·9
Total	99·9	100·1	100·0	100·0	99·9	99·9
N	429	56	92	333	141	155

Chi square value of differences between Abure and Bete for each occupational category.

Cash Crop Farmers: 86·4 (P = 0·001)
Manual Workers: 4·4 (NS)
Clerical Workers: 4·2 (NS)

indicates that, in each rural area, about two-thirds of the fathers unilaterally decide whether their offspring will attend school. Yet about 14 per cent of Bete fathers make this decision jointly with their spouse, while the corresponding proportion among the Abure is almost twice as large. This contrast is striking, since one might expect co-operation between husbands and wives to be positively related to the degree of social absorption of the woman into her affinal group. Actually, the greater propensity of Abure parents to co-operate along these lines reflects the necessity of coping with the conflicting pressures in the matrilineal organisation. The Bete father, on the other hand, can delegate the decision to his wife.

Indeed, such pressures increase as the inconsistencies between the requirements of matrilineal descent and of modernisation become more apparent. This may account for the fact that the proportion of Abure families making joint decisions is highest among manual workers, among whom, we have suggested, such inconsistencies are maximal. On the other hand, the inter-ethnic differences seem to disappear in the city, the direction of change depending upon the traditional patterns.

There are other signs of the difficulties met by matrilineal systems in dealing with the formal education of offspring. In rural areas, over half the Abure families do not punish a child who does not meet academic standards, while the corresponding proportion among the Bete does not exceed 15 per cent (Table 10.7). Bete fathers are both more likely to discipline a child for this reason and to delegate this responsibility to their wives. As shown earlier, this delegation is made possible by the relative clarity which characterises the allocation of domestic authority in that society.

Among the Abure, the lack of concern over academic success manifested by absence of punishment declines consistently with the level of exposure to environmental change. Further, the wives of clerical workers perceive a marked accentuation in the disciplinary role of their husband. It may very well be that the inconsistencies built into his domestic role become eroded as the level of his participation in modern structures increases.

The situation is different among the Bete. The father's disciplinary functions are less apparent in urban than in rural areas.

TABLE 10.7

Comparison of Subgroups of Abure and Bete with Regard to Source of Discipline Over Children Who do not Meet Academic Requirements*
(Percentages of Subgroup)

Discipline Exerted Primarily by:	Abure Wives of: Farmers	Abure Wives of: Manual Workers	Abure Wives of: Clerical Workers	Bete Wives of: Farmers	Bete Wives of: Manual Workers	Bete Wives of: Clerical Workers
Father	32·8	39·3	56·5	58·0	37·6	44·5
Mother	4·7	12·5	6·5	14·1	18·4	16·8
No Discipline Exerted	58·6	30·4	18·5	14·4	27·0	18·1
No answer	4·0	17·9	18·5	13·5	17·0	20·6
Total	100·1	100·1	100·0	100·0	100·0	100·0
N	430	56	92	333	141	155

Chi square value of differences between Abure and Bete for each occupational category.

Cash Crop Farmers: 18·7 (P = 0·001)
Manual Workers: 1·1 (NS)
Clerical Workers: 6·5 (NS)

* The future or the conditional tense was used when the interviewees had no child attending school.

The lack of discipline for academic shortcoming is most striking among the manual workers, whose disciplinary pattern is, however, similar to the Abure equivalents. In short, the differences in the responses of Abure and Bete mothers reflect the operation of two distinctive types of forces. First, the attitudes of parents towards formal schooling are influenced by type of descent. In addition, such attitudes also reflect the level of modernisation of the entire ethnic group.

Thus far, some aspects of how the two groups meet the modern requirements of schooling have been analysed. The educational expectations of parents should also be evaluated by comparing this particular demand with others. The majority of Bete mothers in rural areas place higher priority on academic achievement than on other demands (Table 10.8). The proportion of rural Abure mothers who attach primary significance to the academic achievement of their offspring is markedly lower. Regardless of ethnic origin, the shift to an urban environment is uniformly associated with a decline in the importance which mothers attach to their children's participation in domestic chores. Among the Abure, there is a curvilinear relationship between stress on academic achievement and level of exposure to environmental change. We have already observed that the families of Abure manual workers are distinguished by the high participation of both spouses in decisions pertaining to the schooling of their children. This communication between husband and wife seems to reflect the fact that the women in this occupational category tend to emphasise, more than those in any other subsample, the significance of academic achievement.

In this connection, Bete mothers do not seem to be sensitive to changes in the environment. Once more, it is possible to suggest that the relative indifference displayed by the urbanised segments of this group reflects the fact that their access to the most rewarding urban employment is not in proportion to their actual number. Recruitment into these occupations, mainly in the bureaucratic sector of the economy, is characterised by a high degree of ethnic selectivity. In turn, this selectivity affects the individual perceptions of the existing channels for upward mobility.[41] Ethnic groups with a high degree of occupational differentiation are likely to perceive mobility as being dependent upon universalistic criteria such as academic achievement. Ethnic groups characterised by a minimal level of social differentiation will be more likely to perceive the maintenance of familial or tribal solidarity as the principal means of achieving occupational success.

TABLE 10.8

Maternal Ranking of Various Types of Demands Made on Children by Subgroups of Abure and Bete Mothers (Percentages of Subgroup)

	Abure Wives of:			Bete Wives of:		
Most Important that Child:	Farmers	Manual Workers	Clerical Workers	Farmers	Manual Workers	Clerical Workers
Show respect	28·6	19·6	26·1	30·0	34·8	37·4
Participate in domestic chores	19·1	0·0	2·2	9·3	3·5	1·9
Succeed academically	38·4	73·2	63·0	57·7	53·2	52·3
Other*	13·9	7·1	8·7	3·0	8·5	8·4
Total	100·0	99·9	100·0	100·0	100·0	100·0
N	430	56	92	333	141	155

Chi square value of differences between Abure and Bete for each occupational category.

Cash Crop Farmers: 55·3 (P = 0·001)
Manual Workers: 12·7 (P = 0·05)
Clerical Workers: 7·1 (NS)

* Includes 'control of aggression', 'respect for property' and 'no answer'. These categories were separated in the calculations of chi square (df = 5).

IX. Summary and Conclusions

The analysis of the individual responses to environmental change suggests that it is possible to enter them into two categories. On the one hand, urbanisation involves acculturative processes—that is, the incorporation of new sets of norms and practices into the framework of traditional requirements—and this leads to the persistence or even to the accentuation of the original contrasts between ethnic groups. On the other hand, urbanisation implies assimilation and a decline in the distinctiveness of the social networks prevailing in these ethnic groups.

Many studies of urbanisation in Africa have emphasised the second of these processes, but the problem remains of determining the degree to which acculturation and assimilation operate in various segments of the urban population. Since movement into an urban environment is associated with increased social differentiation and with accentuated differences in the access of the various social categories to the resources of the total society, it is unlikely that these categories will respond similarly to the pressures of the new urban environment. I have suggested that the significance of the functions of a group determines how effectively it controls the behaviour of its members. Because of the limited functions of working class families, its members should be particularly innovative and prone to change. This proposition has often been verified in Europe and I hope I have demonstrated that its validity extends beyond the European scene and accounts for differences between manual and clerical workers in the contemporary African context.[42] Indeed, a maximal level of participation in modern structures is not necessarily associated with maximal acceptance of modern values and norms. The more urban and more modernised clerical workers are sometimes more conservative in their familial life than the less urban and less modern manual workers. Thus the incidence of polygyny is higher among clerical than among manual workers.

This should not be interpreted to mean that the curvilinear model is the sole form of relationships observable between level of exposure to environmental change and individual responses. In some cases the urban population is homogeneous and there is no meaningful distinction between the behaviours of the wives of manual and clerical workers. There are many instances, however, where a linear model fits the data more accurately.

All these observations lead to the conclusion that contemporary African cities should not be treated as undifferentiated wholes. I suggest that the contrast between the urban and rural segments of an ethnic group often varies according to the occupational characteristics of the urban segment under study. As the occupational profile of new African cities becomes more differentiated, the norms underlying individual patterns of action become more heterogeneous. In short, if we accept the idea that diverse African societies merge into a common urban culture, we should be willing to entertain the somewhat opposite proposition that differentiation, which is relatively slight in most traditional African systems, becomes more marked as individuals from these systems become exposed to an 'urban way of life'.

I have also demonstrated that ethnicity leads to divergences in the trajectories of change. First, there are variations in the degree to which the requirements of particular traditional cultures conflict with the demands of a modernising society. Thus the matrilineal nature of the Abure society affects the response to schooling of the urbanised segment of that ethnic group. Ethnicity, however, does not imply only variations in the traditional demands imposed upon an individual or in the functions that he performs in his natural setting. It also involves differences in the amount of exposure of the entire group to modernising forces, with consequent disparities in the overall participation of various peoples in modern structures. Thus it is among the Abure that levels of urbanisation vary directly with the likelihood of parents rearing their own children. But, as we have seen, Bete manual workers react to their increased participation in modern structures by showing a greater interest in having their children reared by extended kin. Similarly, the urbanisation of the Abure family is associated with a decline in the co-operation of co-wives, but such co-operation is more manifest among the urban segments of the Bete population. In all these instances, it seems that the Bete take advantage of the rewards of the urban world to intensify their existing network of relationships, rather than to take advantage of the variety of choices which accompanies such rewards.[43] By contrast, the higher general level of modernisation of the Abure people often leads the women to take full advantage of the multiplicity of social choices provided by an urban environment.

Is it possible to extrapolate these observations into the future? Already, we have seen that child rearing practices are sensitive to the effects of environmental change. I have suggested that, to a certain extent, these practices vary with the inconsistencies attached to the domestic status of women in the urban milieu. The problem is now to determine whether or not these inconsistencies will increase as social change becomes more pronounced.

Notes and References

1 On this point see E. Shevki and W. Bell, *Social Area Analysis*, Stanford 1955, pp. 3–15, as well as their precursors, G. and M. Wilson, *Analysis of Social Change*, London 1945.

2 I would like to express my appreciation for the assistance of Professors Roger Bastide and Denise Paulme of the University of Paris, Dr Moreigne (French Navy), Professors Lloyd Fallers, William Hanna, Robert LeVine, Horace Miner and Robert Winch, and all the participants in the Conference on the Methods and Objectives of Urban Research in Africa.

3 This use of the size of a city is indirectly suggested by D. Varley and L. Schnore in their article "Some Concomitants of Metropolitan Size", *American Sociological Review*, Vol. 20, 1955, pp. 408–15. The primate character of a city is defined by B. Berry in "City Size Distribution and Economic Development", *Economic Development and Cultural Change*, Vol. 52, 1961, pp. 573–87.

4 For that matter, Abidjan presents patterns which are at variance with those of many other African cities. See *Recensement d'Abidjan (1963)*, Paris 1965.

5 Ibid.; half of the population has resided in Abidjan for less than seven years.

6 Up to now there has been a sharp contrast along these lines between the two occupational categories in the Ivory Coast. An unpublished survey conducted by the author among the personnel of seven firms of Abidjan shows that at least 81 per cent of manual workers have not completed primary schooling, compared with 9 per cent of their clerical counterparts. Holding the level of skills constant, the wages of the former are significantly lower than those of the latter. Similarly the career pattern of clerical workers shows that they enjoyed more opportunities for promotion than their manual counterparts. Finally, clerical workers have been heavily concentrated in large scale organisations, whereas manual workers have acquired their experience in various types of firms. The distinction between these two types of employment also has implications in terms of length of urban residence and of concentration in the most modern neighbourhoods of Abidjan. On the general significance of this distinction, see R. Simms, *Urbanization in West Africa: a Review of the Current Literature*, Evanston, Ill., 1965, pp. 30–1.

7 Examples of this differentiation are given by M. Levy in "Contrasting Factors in the Modernization of China and Japan", in S. Kuznets, W. Moore and J. Spengler, eds., *Economic Growth: Brazil, India,*

Japan, Durham, NC, 1955, pp. 515–21. Another example would be J. Habbakuk, "Family Structure and Economic Change in Nineteenth Century Europe", *The Journal of Economic History*, Vol. 15, 1956, pp. 1–12.

8 On this point, see for example D. Aberle and K. Naegele, "Middle Class Fathers' Occupational Role and Attitudes Towards Children", *American Journal of Orthopsychiatry*, Vol. 22, April 1952, pp. 366–78.

9 See W. Goode, *World Revolution and Family Patterns*, New York 1963, p. 369. This author states that, whatever are the factors underlying the emergence of a low status (age, sex, social class), the bearers of such a status are most likely to innovate when the environment is changing.

10 For a general analysis of the models of social change, see W. Moore, *Social Change*, Englewood Cliffs, NJ, 1964, chaps. II and V. As an example of the linear model, many authors indicate that the nuclear family tends to be more and more isolated from the extended kin group. It seems important, however, to indicate here that at least two general linear effects of increased exposure to modern forces can be discerned. On the one hand, there may be a decline in traditional patterns of behaviour, and, on the other, there may be a linear emergence of European-like patterns of behaviour. These two consequences of urbanisation have to be kept separate and cannot be equated with a zero-sum effect; the gains of the first are not necessarily the losses of the second. For a review of the authors interested in this type of problem, see R. Simms, op. cit., pp. 24–6.

11 On this point, see A. Feldman and W. Moore, "Industrialization and Industrialism, Convergences and Differentiation", *Transactions of the Fifth World Congress of Sociology*, Washington, DC, 1962, pp. 151–63.

12 See G. Niangoran-Bouah, "Le Village Abouré", *Cahiers d'Etudes Africaines*, Vol. 1, 1960, pp. 113–27, for a more extensive description of this ethnic group.

13 See D. Paulme, *Une Société de Côte d'Ivoire hier et aujourd'hui: les Bété*, Paris 1962, and also A. Kobben, "Le planteur noir", *Etudes Eburnéennes*, Vol. 5, Abidjan 1956.

14 The framework of analysis is that utilised by J. C. Mitchell in "Social Change and the Stability of African Marriage", in A. Southall, ed., *Social Change in Modern Africa*, London 1961, pp. 315–30.

15 The contrast between the two groups along these lines is described in A. Kobben, op. cit., and also in H. Raulin, "Mission d'Etude des Groupements immigrés en Côte d'Ivoire", document, Paris 1957, who analyse the size and the production of Bete farms. The Abure are, like the Anyi, described by Kobben as more 'entrepreneurially oriented' than the Bete.

16 See *Ministère des Affaires Economiques et du Plan Côte d'Ivoire: Supplement trimestriel au Bulletin Mensuel de Statistiques*, Vol. 2, 1961, where the rate of primary enrolments are given by area. It is unfortunate that these figures are not available by ethnic affiliation. There should be a high correlation between the two, however.

17 For a description of Abidjan, see E. Bernus, "Abidjan, Note sur l'agglomération d'Abidjan et sa population", in *Bulletin de I.F.A.N.*, Series B, Vol. 24, 1962, pp. 56–85. See also *Côte d'Ivoire, Ministère des Finances: Recensement d'Abidjan* (*1955*), *Résultats définitifs*, Paris 1960 and *Recensement d'Abidjan* (*1963*), from which all the data in this section are derived.

18 Thus, there is a marked difference in the age of the Abure and Bete wives of clerical workers. Age remains an awkward measure in social surveys conducted in Africa. Many informants do not know their real age; since I did not want the interviewees to indulge in guesswork, there were many 'no answers'.

19 See R. Winch, *The Modern Family*, New York 1964, pp. 4–32.

20 It could be argued that differences in the behaviour of rural and urban Abure, or of urban Abure and Bete mothers, reflect the larger proportion of inter-ethnic marriages among the urban Abure. However, this would suppose that the ethnic status of the father is a powerful determinant of the mother's child rearing practices and this is not certain. Actually, 15 per cent of Abure women marrying 'foreigners' marry Bete.

21 Although many scholars have indicated that 'Westernisation' is associated with a decline of the incidence of polygyny, the available evidence is far from conclusive. See, for instance, P. Mercier, "Etude du mariage et enquête urbaine", *Cahiers d'Etudes Africaines*, Vol. 1, 1960, pp. 21 *ff*. In the Ivory Coast, I have observed that the secondary school population derives as much from polygynous as from monogamous households. Further, there is no significant relationship between the levels of paternal education and occupation and the composition of the household. However, a significantly higher proportion of educated women marry monogamous men than do their illiterate counterparts.

22 Our findings confirm the observations of L. A. Fallers in "Some Determinants of Marriage Stability in Busoga: a Reformulation of Gluckman's Hypothesis", *Africa*, Vol. 27, 1957, pp. 106–21. The Bete have an unusually high rate of divorce for a patrilineal society. In addition, it should be noted that, on the whole, a prior divorce does not influence the relationship of a woman with a subsequent husband and with their children.

23 On this point, see H. V. Muhsam, "Fertility of Polygynous Marriages", *Population Studies*, Vol. 10, 1956, pp. 3–16. In his sample, the ratios of children to married women were about 33 per cent lower for the first and second wives of polygynous husbands than for wives of monogamous husbands. See also V. Dorjahn, "The Factor of Polygyny in African Demography", in M. Herskovitz and W. Bascom, eds., *Continuity and Change in African Cultures*, Chicago 1959, pp. 87–112.

24 D. Paulme, op. cit., pp. 162 *ff*.

25 Ibid., p. 144.

26 Ibid., p. 171.

27 Kobben, op. cit., p. 133.

28 Actually, among the urbanised segments of both groups. the first wife of a polygynous marriage is more apt to take such a trip than is the wife in a monogamous union. Thus, in Abidjan, 66 per cent of the Bete first wives have returned to their village of origin for a period of time exceeding a month, as against 45 per cent of their monogamous counterparts. For the Abure, the figures are 82 and 70 per cent respectively.

29 In Africa, as in British Guiana or in the US, it seems demonstrated that when ascription limits the upward mobility of individuals within a society otherwise based on achievement, the low position of a man in the occupational structure is correlated with the limited amounts of influence he exerts in the field of domestic relations. See R. T. Smith, *The Negro Family in the British Guiana*, London 1956, pp. 253–4.

30 On this point, see L. Minturn and W. Lambert, *Six Cultures: Antecedents of Child Rearing Practices*, New York 1964, pp. 240–80.

31 Here, as elsewhere, the reader should remain aware of the limitations of the data. Verbal behaviour does not necessarily reflect actual behaviour, yet verbal behaviour is certainly indicative of the respondent's norms.

32 The wording of the survey question was, 'How old is your child when you begin to punish him if he does not behave according to your wishes and expectations?'

33 In another matrilineal society, the pattern seems to be similar. See M. T. Knappens, *L'enfant Mukungo: Orientations de Base du Système Educatif et Développement de la Personalité*, Paris 1962, pp. 123 *ff*.

34 The importance of aggressive motivation is stressed throughout D. Paulme, op. cit.

35 On this point see ibid., chap. III, which examines the contrast in relationships with maternal and paternal relatives. The more general question of the diffuseness of socialisation is analysed by G. Murdock and J. Whiting in "Cultural Determination of Parental Attitudes: The Relationship between the Social Structure, Particularly the Family Structure, and Parental Behavior", in M. J. E. Senn, ed., *Problems of Infancy and Childhood*, New York 1951, pp. 13–14.

36 On this point see *Conditions de Vie de l'Enfant Africain en Milieu Urbain et de leur influence sur la Délinquance Juvénile*, Paris 1959, pp. 89 *ff*.

37 On the organisation of polygynous families among the Bete, see E. Dunglas, *Moeurs et Coutumes des Bétés*, Paris 1939, pp. 11 *ff*.; on the more general problem of the relationship among co-wives, see T. Parsons, *The Social System*, New York 1963, p. 419.

38 The wording of the survey question was, 'When there are several co-wives in the house, how are the children of each of these women reared?'

39 This point has been noted by A. Zolberg, *The One Party Government of the Ivory Coast*, Princeton 1964, pp. 39–48.

40 On this problem, see also Barrington Kaye, *Bringing Up Children in Ghana*, London 1962, p. 181.

41 For an examination of the ethnic selectivity underlying access to urban occupations see *Recensement d'Abidjan (1963)*. Indirectly, the same point is covered by R. Clignet and P. Foster, *The Fortunate Few*, Evanston, Ill., 1966, chaps. IV, VI and VIII.

42 See W. Goode, loc. cit.

43 In this sense, the Bete are comparable to the 'Red' Xhosa of East London. See Philip Mayer, *Tribesmen and Townsmen*, Cape Town 1961.

11

Kampala-Mengo

AIDAN SOUTHALL

The Capital of Buganda

The urban agglomeration of Kampala-Mengo is in many respects unusual, if not unique, and therefore immediately raises the question as to how representative or illuminating the data from it can be for the consideration of urban theory in general. My contention would be that, while the combination of factors is somewhat unusual for East Africa, this in itself throws light on the operation of the several components which are individually comparable with their incidence elsewhere. In order to weigh theories and hypotheses against the data from Kampala-Mengo, it will be necessary to give a fairly general description of the community so that the details which become so familiar to the ethnographer may be intelligible to the reader. A concrete historical and topographical framework will give perspective to the facts required to illustrate more abstract social and cultural problems.

Sir Harry Johnston's claim[1] that Kampala was built like Rome on seven hills was perhaps no more than a cultured pleasantry, for clearly it began on fewer while Kampala-Mengo now clothes several dozen. But it is still the hills which provide a good deal of its ecological meaning, as well as its beauty and interest. They are the most convenient pegs for any description of distinctive neighbourhoods and special local functions. Such distinct concentrations, of an ethnic, religious or economic sort, are still significant,

NOTE: *The notes and references for Chapter 11 will be found on page 331.*

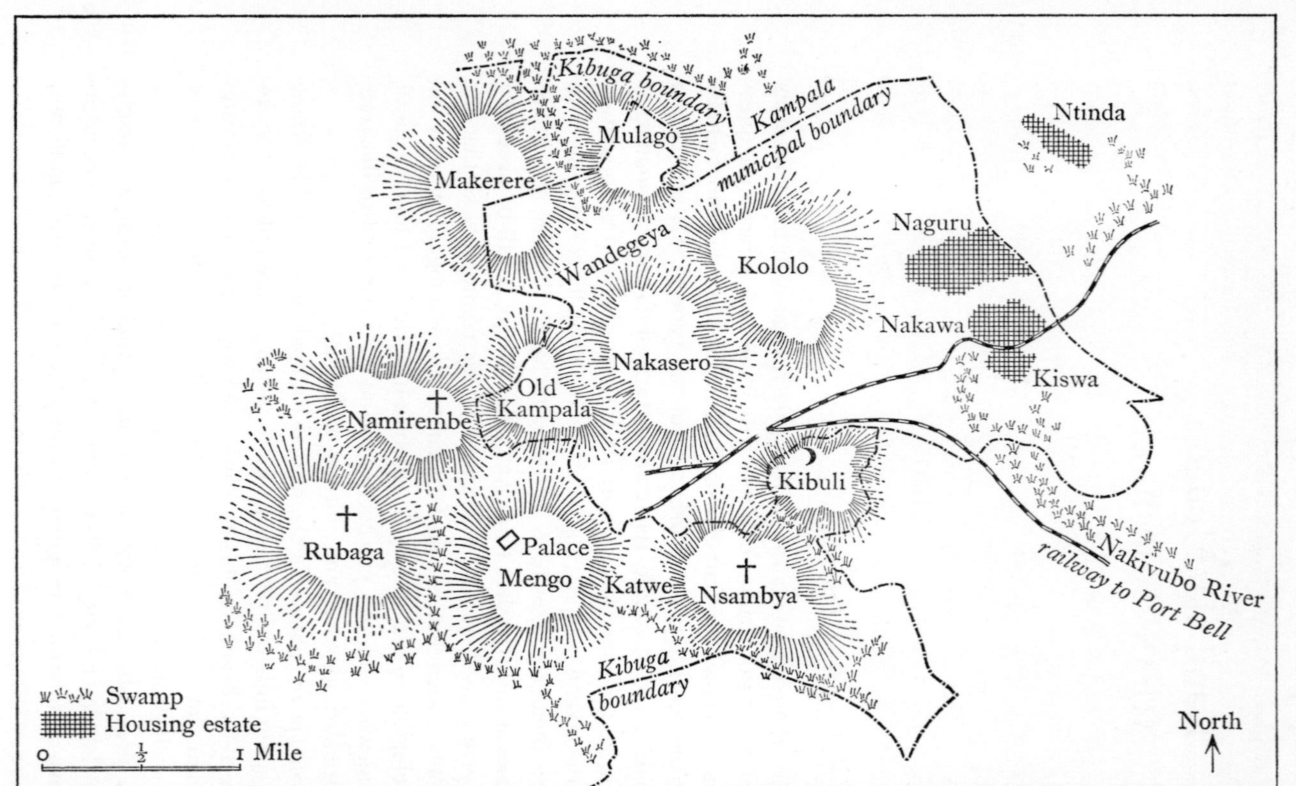

Central Hills of Kampala-Mengo

although to some extent both rich and poor and persons of many tribes or nations can be found on every hill. Since the draining of the swamps some thirty years ago, the valleys between the main hills have also become important parts of the town with characteristics of their own.

This area is the capital district of the ancient kingdom of Buganda. For centuries the capital has been on one or other of these hills. It was moved at least once in each reign, as each site became exhausted or in accordance with other exigencies. From about 1844 onwards, Arab traders began to visit the capital. The explorer Speke was there in 1862, Stanley in 1875, as well as other British, French, American, Russian, German and Italian explorers and adventurers. British Protestants and French Roman Catholics established Christian missions at the court in 1877 and 1879 respectively. It is important to note that, throughout these decades, the kingdom of Buganda not only maintained its political autonomy but steadily increased its power. The corollary is that outside influences, including those with potentially urban implications, were being gradually assimilated by King (the Kabaka), court and people, not forced upon them. The death of the great Kabaka Mutesa I in 1884 marked the end of this golden age. He was succeeded by Kabaka Mwanga. Palace, court and capital moved again, for the last time, from Rubaga hill to Mengo, where they still are.

The population of this traditional Ganda capital can never be accurately established. The problem has been exhaustively explored by Gutkind.[2] It may well be that the King's palace enclosure itself accommodated about 3,000 persons and the so-called 'native town' which surrounded it at least 10,000. In other words, while small by present urban standards, it was an extraordinary phenomenon for East Africa and impressed all who saw it. Yet it was not entirely unique, for the capitals of Bunyoro, Ankole, Karagwe, Rwanda and other interlacustrine kingdoms must have been similar, if smaller.

The capital of Buganda may be considered a proto-city in the sense that it is a very clear illustration of how far an indigenous African people, with a simple technology and without literacy, could proceed in the direction of urban life. It remained essentially temporary, because it was so frequently moved and also because only temporary materials—wood and grass—were used in its construction. Yet it had a very definite cultural and conceptual continuity, for it was quite rigidly structured and was probably reproduced in much of the same form at every transplanting. There were the King's own quarters, his council and audience hall, the guests' reception rooms, the royal harem, the establishments of the Queen Mother, Queen Sister, Prime Minister, ritual officials, treasurer, steward and major chiefs. Each of these had a huge entourage of perhaps as many as a thousand people. The mass population of this proto-city was very fluctuating. Apart from the vast numbers of pages, servants and attendants, there were very large numbers of labourers constantly being brought in to build or repair houses, to maintain roads and fences and to carry out new constructional tasks, such as damming and clearing the lake where the royal crocodiles were kept. There were those involved in bringing tribute and supplies of all kinds, augmented by the hundreds of porters in the trading caravans which were beginning to penetrate from the outside world. There were open markets under the authority of one of the King's officials, at which the crafts and produce of the country were exchanged or sold for cowrie currency.

There are no clear cases of endogenous urban development proceeding further in East, Central or Southern Africa than in the Ganda capital. There, it was essentially the product of political centralisation, transcending a customarily dispersed settlement pattern. It was a closely institutionalised community, quite distinct from the rest of the society of which it was a part, concentrating in itself the highest degree of cultural elaboration and role differentiation. Thus it had a number of the cultural characteristics of a city. It is the only case outside West Africa in which a traditional settlement has continued to exert a profound influence over the development of a large modern city. This was made possible by its own inherent strength, which permitted it to assimilate some external influences without being overwhelmed by them and which in turn led to the siting of a modern city alongside it.

The British Settlement and the Dual System

Lugard reached Buganda in 1890 as agent of the Imperial British East Africa Company at a time when King Mwanga had already sent several requests for British protection. The King might well have changed his mind, but in fact found himself in the grip of opposing pressures from both home and abroad which left him little alternative. The treaty which he signed with Lugard, while far from definitive, marked the end of autonomous sovereignty for Buganda. Lugard had defied the King's authority on arrival by establishing a fort on Kampala hill, which was next to Mengo but not commanded by it, in preference to the more vulnerable site which Mwanga had indicated to him. So the Kampala-Mengo duality was unwittingly inaugurated. In 1893 a Protectorate was declared by Sir Gerald Portal and in 1900 a definitive settlement was worked out by Sir Harry Johnston.

These twin entities have remained inextricably intertwined, essentially opposed yet mutually overlapping. For the first fifteen years Kampala was an insignificant adjunct of the Ganda capital, but, after that, Mengo became increasingly overshadowed by the cuckoo in the nest. In the early years, the name Mengo was taken to include Kampala in popular parlance, and in later years exactly the other way round. Mengo has always feared encroachment by Kampala and officially regarded the latter as an unfortunate temporary concession carved from itself. Kampala has for long regarded Mengo as a backward child, often with the conviction that its separate existence should be terminated as quickly as possible. Similarly, the British were inclined to see themselves as having gone to Buganda on their own accord to trade, to suppress slavery, to establish a sphere of influence, to convert to Christianity and to bring new order and civilisation; the Ganda ideally saw the British as invited tutors, who could be bidden farewell when their job was done. Such a situation of structural cross-purposes could only be legalised by subterfuge, as in the fiction that the British Resident or Governor gave the Kabaka advice which the latter had no right to reject. It is characteristic of the very subtle balance of understanding and of forces between the British and the Ganda that this extraordinary fiction remained unchallenged in the constitution for over half a century, until the crisis over the Kabaka's exile in 1953 brought matters to a head and necessitated an explicit legal interpretation.

Mengo and Kampala have been kept further distinct by radically different systems of land tenure, which still remain. The early missionaries settled, by grace of the Kabakas, on land granted voluntarily to them. The British Settlement founded by Lugard was also regularised by a grant of land from the Kabaka. But, in the agreements of 1900, the mission grants became part of the *mailo* land system of Buganda, while the Settlement became part of the Crown land allocation, redefined as State land when Uganda became independent in 1962. *Mailo* land approximated freehold land, normally tenable only by those legally defined as natives and subjects of the Kabaka. The mission lands were, therefore, something of an exception to this. Crown land was mainly held in lease from the state, except for a few early grants of freehold. The result was that, in general, non-Africans could not legally occupy land in Mengo, but only in Kampala. Conversely, occupation of land in Kampala by Africans was frowned upon, except in their capacity as servants or on temporary sufferance as squatters. As development took place, land in Kampala became exceedingly valuable because of its scarcity, and, even when its occupation by Africans was no longer discouraged, it remained uncommon because any African would-be occupant could acquire land far more cheaply in Mengo. There was thus an effective land segregation, primarily brought about by political exigencies rather than mere race prejudice.

This all-pervading dualism is a very particular instance of a rather general phenomenon. At its most general level it is the localisation of ethnic interests, which has found expression in the ethnic wards of the cities in the ancient and medieval world and even in the ethnic concentration and organisation of immigrants in American cities. But more closely relevant is the joint confrontation of Western with non-Western peoples, embodying at the same time the impact of post-industrial on pre-industrial forms of urbanism.

All over Africa this contrast between the European and the African quarters of towns is manifest in one form or another. In those parts of Africa where traditional experience with urban living was minimal or entirely absent, the European quarters have been dominant. In the process of Africanisation and independence, it is these quarters which the new African leaders feel particularly challenged to incorporate and to imbue with some deeper atmosphere of belonging to Africa. Because of the political power of Buganda, and the near approach of its traditional capital to urban status, the balance was more equal, inviting comparison with common West African situations where, in some cases, the balance could almost be the other way round. In Kano or Zaria the new forms of commercial and industrial urban growth have inevitably been outside the walls of the old city, but the political, cultural and spiritual focus remains within. What was in origin the Western commercial quarter of Ibadan is now highly integrated into Yoruba life.

In Kampala-Mengo, political independence and Africanisation has in no way meant the end of dualism, but only its assumption of many new forms. It is a kind of bi-polar complementary opposition, which generates solidarity at one level while, at another, it often seems on the point of breaking the country apart. The opposed segments and protagonists are no longer the Ganda and the British, but, perhaps even more confusingly, the government of the Kingdom of Buganda against the government of Uganda of which it is a part, or the Ganda against the rest of the Ugandans. In 1966, the struggle between the Prime Minister of Uganda and the Kabaka, who was also President of Uganda, led to a military attack on the Kabaka's palace from which he barely escaped into exile. Lest this appear more an analysis of politics than of urban life, it must be stressed that all these alignments do in high degree correspond to the alignment between Kampala and Mengo. The chief events in the drama must usually be played out in Kampala-Mengo, not only in interpersonal terms, but also in regular institutional activity, such as the proceedings of the Buganda Lukiko (parliament) in Mengo and the Uganda National Assembly in Kampala. In all these respects Kampala-Mengo fulfils the classical urban function of concentrating and at least balancing, if not reconciling, the most crucial elements in the diverse cultural heritage.

The Administrative Structure and Status of Kampala and Mengo

Throughout this account Mengo always refers to the capital of Buganda (the Kibuga) and to the urban community which developed round this core. Kampala always refers to the European and Asian settlement and the urban community which developed round that core. The traditional Kibuga was under the direct administrative charge of the Kabaka's chief minister (Katikkiro). As the urban problems of the Kibuga grew in volume and complexity under the British Protectorate this simple arrangement became unworkable. All the great chiefs of the kingdom had special rights over their traditional establishments in the Kibuga, under the supreme administrative authority of the chief minister, and none of them was willing to give up his rights. It was only in 1922, after years of argument and tiresome negotiation over titles, precedence, jurisdiction and practical duties,[3] that a special chief was appointed to administer the Kibuga at Mengo and was recognised as most senior of the sub-county chiefs of the kingdom. By this time, the traditional complexities of the Buganda administrative hierarchy had been reduced to five distinct ranks of officials: the ministers at the centre, the twenty county chiefs, the sub-county chiefs, parish chiefs and ward headmen. In this framework the ancient patrimonial rights of the fief holders were gradually transformed into a more purely bureaucratic system.

The Kibuga at Mengo, as a sub-county, albeit a unique one, included a number of hills besides the central one of Mengo, each having its parish chief with ward headmen under him. Parish chiefs were also appointed to Kampala and Nakasero hills, pressing the point home that, from the Buganda point of view, these areas were still part of the kingdom and its capital, and were not foreign territory belonging to Europeans and Asians. Since Kampala had its own urban administration, these parish chiefs could hardly operate in a normal manner, but they collected taxes from the African population.

The urban local government structure of the upstart Kampala developed much more rapidly than that of Mengo. It was gazetted as a Township in 1906, administered by officials of the Uganda Protectorate government and financed directly out of government funds. The immediate administrative body was known as a Sanitary Board and consisted mainly of the departmental officials immediately concerned, though it was later expanded and dignified by the title of Township Authority. In 1949 Kampala was raised to the status of a Municipality and in the following year the chairman of its council had the title of mayor conferred upon him. The successive mayors have been an Indian, three Europeans, followed by an African, another European, an Indian, and two Africans.

With municipal status Kampala acquired its own full-time professional Town Clerk, Town Treasurer, Town Engineer, Medical Officer of Health and auxiliary staff. But these executive officers, whose predecessors had constituted the original urban authority itself, were now no longer members of the council. Councillors were still nominated by the central government of Uganda. All three racial groups were represented but, as their numbers in the council were roughly equal, the Asian and still more the European population was correspondingly over-represented while the African population was grossly under-represented. It was only just before the coming of independence that municipal elections were instituted and the council acquired a strong African majority. It was then also that Kampala officially became a City.

Ganda attempts to control the development of Mengo through the establishment of a Sanitary Board in 1931 and of a Planning Board in 1947 were ineffective.[4] Finally, as part of the independence settlement, the Kibuga became the Municipality of Mengo, with most of the constitutional and administrative trappings of a modern urban local government on the British model. But it was not possible to make the municipal council an elected body, nor to separate its executive officers from its membership, so the chief minister of the Kibuga remained chairman of the council and mayor of Mengo.

Hills and Institutions

The basic ecological unit throughout Buganda from ancient times has been the mutala, which is a hill or area of high ground surrounded by valleys usually filled with swamp or forest. Such areas were named; they did not invariably correspond to traditional administrative units but tended to focus community feelings. They were also the usual basis for the political allocation of land. The Kabakas moved their palaces and capitals from hill to hill, while other hills were crowned with their eventual tombs and jawbone shrines. When foreigners began to appear in numbers and for long periods, they were accommodated in the same way by the allocation of a separate hill to each faction, party, religion, race or other special interest group. The practice continued under the British Protectorate, until all the hills within a convenient distance were accounted for. Growing concentration extended settlement down the slopes until, with the added incentive of health control, the swamps were drained and the intervening valley bottoms also brought into use. But by this time the planning authorities had come to appreciate the value of maintaining something of this network of open spaces as a permanent amenity. 'The built up areas will surround the hilly outcrops in the shape of belts, while the valleys between will form the natural green lungs of the town.'[5] Indeed, they provided a hitherto unrealised bonus which permitted a far more advantageous development than would otherwise have been possible in schools, parks, playing fields and main arterial roads.

The settlement of the hills meant, in the first place, that many major institutions were dispersed in this way, rather than concentrated in an urban centre. In the second place, it meant that the personnel of these institutions tended to be concentrated around them, almost in sub-communities, rather than distributed about the town on the basis of diverse factors of choice. There was thus a distinct cellular structure, though it was not rigidly adhered to and has now become almost more of a conventional ideology in Kampala-Mengo than an actuality. The initial functional dispersion also meant that many problems of urban density were slow to develop and present little technical difficulty even today.

Rubaga, Namirembe, Kibuli and Nsambya hills are all regarded as religious or ecclesiastical centres. Rubaga had more than once been the site of the royal capital, but in 1879 was allocated by Kabaka Mutesa I to the French White Fathers for their mission. As the work of the White Fathers extended, they became particularly strong in the south-western district of Buganda, and for a long time they kept their main headquarters there. But Rubaga has always been important because of its position at the capital and now its cathedral has the distinction of being the seat of Africa's first African archbishop. Many leading Ganda Roman Catholic families live and own land on and around Rubaga hill, which is a definite centre of local African Roman Catholic society and culture. The chief justice of Buganda is always a prominent Roman Catholic and his official residence is at the foot of Rubaga hill. The family and descendants of Stanislas Mugwanya, the first chief justice under the agreement between the British and the Ganda, has remained particularly important, and the unofficial lay patron of the Roman Catholics in Buganda.

All the 'ecclesiastical' hills are extraordinarily comparable in a number of structural features. Thus Namirembe hill has similarly been the headquarters of the Church Missionary Society and subsequently the Anglican Church of Uganda. Many prominent Anglican Ganda families have had land and houses on or near the hill for over half a century. The Katikkiro of Buganda is always an Anglican and a number of past Katikkiros are prominent members of the congregation of Namirembe cathedral. It is generally held that the Kabaka himself must also be an Anglican. As frequent ceremonial services are held in the cathedral to commemorate or celebrate the Kabaka's birthday, his Accession Day, his Return from Exile and other notable events in his life, it is very difficult to resist the impression of an Established Church in Buganda, despite the careful distribution of spoils among Muslim and Christian sects which was instituted as a means of preventing further religious strife.

Nsambya hill became the headquarters of the Mill Hill Fathers in 1895, when Roman Catholic work in the area to the east of Kampala was assigned to them, leaving the west to the White Fathers. It was hoped that this move would transcend the identification then made by the Ganda between Anglicans and British on the one hand and Roman Catholics and French on the other. The two denominations were, in fact, openly called 'BaIngereza' and 'BaFransa'. Although now Nsambya also has its cathedral, school and hospitals, it remains socially a secondary focus of the Roman Catholic community in Buganda. It is also diversified by its proximity to the expanding edge of Kampala city and has the main housing estates both of the railways and the Uganda police on its northern slopes.

Kibuli hill has been the headquarters and social focus of African Muslims in Buganda, at least since the 1900 land allocation which made it the estate of Prince Nuhu Mbogo, brother of Mutesa I and leader of the Muslim faction in Buganda. From this estate came the hilltop site for the mosque which is one of the most prominent landmarks round Kampala. Mbogo's son, Prince Badru Kakunguru, inherited his father's position of leadership and continues to reside in a large house on the lower slopes of Kibuli. A very senior post in the Buganda government must always be given to a Muslim.

Prominent as these four hills have been in the history of Uganda and its largest urban centre, all of them lie outside the City of Kampala but within the Municipality of Mengo. The most recent recruit to the religious hills is one on which the All-Africa Headquarters and Temple of the Baha'i faith was established in the late 1950s. It lies several miles outside Kampala to the north and is too new to have attracted any extensive settlement or community around it. Two other important hills with specialised functions, which have continued to determine the nature of their residents, were established in 1921 with the beginnings of the teaching hospital on Mulago, and of the university on Makerere. The latter began as a technical school, but early expanded into the training centre of teachers, surveyors and engineers. It developed continuously and after the Second World War became the university for East Africa, with Mulago hospital as its medical school. Makerere is almost entirely occupied by the students, teachers and auxiliary staff of the university, while Mulago is similarly monopolised by doctors, nurses and large numbers of hospital staff and servants. Even the adjacent area of African houses, shops and market is in countless ways dependent and focused upon the hospital.

The Spread of European and Asian Settlement

Lugard's Kampala Fort at once attracted other settlement around it. There were the few hundred Swahili who had come with him from the coast, plus Emin Pasha's Sudanese soldiers who, with dependents, were rescued by Lugard from their marooned camp on Lake Albert. To these were subsequently added a force of Indian troops. Below the fort grew up the makeshift premises of the Indian traders, on one of whom all the Europeans utterly depended for their material supplies from the outside world. By the beginning of this century a half dozen or so European commercial agencies had been set up—British, American, Italian and Greek. An observer describes the situation at that time:

> Soon after the turn of the century it must have been realised by the government that the space below Kampala Fort was inadequate to meet growing trade and they decided to start a new township on the more expansive hill named Nakasero, half a mile to the east. Already in 1903 a new fort had been built there at the highest part with a high outer wall. It was manned by a company of Punjabis in charge of two British officers. . . . By 1905 practically the whole of government officials and staff and traders' shops had been moved to Nakasero. Thatched roofs gave place to corrugated iron and mud walls to sun-dried or fired bricks.[6]

From this time on, Nakasero became the centre of urban growth and is today the site of the central business district. Kampala hill came to be known as Old Kampala and Lugard's Fort became the site of a museum. At first, the so-called Indian[7] bazaar occupied the lower slopes of Nakasero, near the swamp which separated it from Kampala hill. European and Indian business premises mingled somewhat farther up. Above this were government offices, the High Court and other public buildings, while the upper slopes received the spacious gardens and bungalows of British officials, each with its adjacent quarters for African domestic servants. Near the top of the hill was the European Club, known with unwitting symbolism as the Top Club. The one notable exception to European and Asian commercial dominance was the open market in the midst of the Indian bazaar. There, African cooks and servants of European and Asian families, and even some housewives, purchased their supplies of local produce. At first the market venders were mainly Ganda from the immediately surrounding countryside, but, as time went on, Africans of other tribes began to intrude, especially the Luo from Kenya.

When all the space on Nakasero was taken up, admittedly at very low density by bungalows in spacious gardens, the next area for European and Indian residential expansion was Kololo hill to the east. The first urban impact on Kololo was the settlement there of the Sudanese soldiers' families after the fort on Old Kampala hill was abandoned. When it appeared that Kololo would be required for European and Indian occupation, however, the Sudanese were moved out. Kololo was rapidly covered with various types of new settlements during the 1950s. One large area was built up with official houses for Indians in government service; another area similarly for European officials, but with more spacious houses in larger gardens. The area farthest from Kampala was opened to the highest class of residences, without any racial restriction. This meant that wealthy Europeans and Indians were living in neighbouring plots, but virtually no Africans settled there at first.

The Spread of African Settlement

We have seen Mengo as a focus of Ganda development, with deep historical roots and fundamental continuity, though under the impact of new forces. But the dozens of other African peoples who now make an important contribution to Kampala-Mengo, in addition to the ever increasing numbers of rural Ganda immigrants to the twin cities, have not so far been mentioned.

With Kampala and Mengo divided yet so close together, it was inevitable that the immediate space between them should be subject to particularly intense pressures from both. All along the boundary between the two there sprang up alternating pockets of dense, low-economic residential settlement and of small commerce. These were 'natural' in the sense of unplanned—the net outcome of countless decisions in response to ecological, economic, social and political forces which no coherent authority was controlling in a co-ordinated manner. These interstitial areas were the slopes and valleys rather than the hilltops, and their use was at first severely restricted by the papyrus swamps which, except for a few crossings, separated the major hills. The relative isolation of one hill from another may well have induced a greater solidarity and community spirit in these small hilltop settlements than would otherwise have been the case. But another accompaniment of the swamps was endemic malaria, one of the contributory causes of the very high infant mortality rate among the local population. Whereas those who survived to adulthood had a degree of immunity, European and Indian immigrants ran great risk of succumbing to malaria, especially in its acute form of blackwater fever. Thus Kampala had a bad health reputation in East Africa. This was radically changed by about the time of the Second World War, when the drainage of the swamps was fairly complete.

There was growing pressure in the central interstitial areas, such as Katwe, before the war, though it did not reach high intensity until after it. Katwe not only lay between Mengo, Nakasero and Nsambya, but astride the road from Kampala to the administrative capital at Entebbe—the chief road in the country. Katwe was the earliest and has remained the most important African commercial area in Uganda. It naturally attracted to itself the first African (Ganda) newspaper ventures in the country and the first African political party offices. It also has the largest of the open markets which continue the indigenous market tradition. Here sellers' stalls display every kind of locally available meat, fish, fruit and vegetable, as well as traditional and modern medicines and cheap imported goods. It is one of the main centres of the trade in plantains, which are the staple food of the Ganda and a number of other peoples. As the fruit is both bulky and perishable it poses a fine problem in marketing. Trucks bring daily supplies, in bulk, from as far as two hundred miles away and cut-throat competition prevails among the sellers. The huge volume of transactions in Katwe market presupposes a widely ramifying network of wholesale supply, involving African, Asian and European dealers.

Many similar but smaller areas grew up where there were naturally reinforcing urban influences. The 'hospital hill' of Mulago developed such an adjunct,[8] with retail shops and a small open market, where the Kampala and Mengo boundaries met. The area is as near as possible to the superior urban development of the former, while profiting from the cheaper and freer economic and social conditions of the latter. Also on the Kampala-Mengo boundary, between old Kampala and Namirembe hills and on an important crossroads, the dense quarter of Bakule developed, again with open market and small shops—its name a corrupt Luganda form of 'Buckley', the first manager of the Uganda Company's cotton ginnery, who lived on this spot early in the century.

Round the crossroads and market between Makerere, Mulago and Nakasero is Wandegeya, one of the older unregulated high density areas and, next to Katwe, one of the principal centres of African trading. It became a characteristic bone of contention in 1937 when the Protectorate government and Kampala Township Authority wanted to take over the area because its unregulated condition was held to be a menace to health control in Kampala as well as an affront to planned development. Powerful support came from Kampala traders, who objected to unfair competition from African traders just over the boundary. The latter did not have to buy licences or pay city taxes and, because of lack of stringent or effective building and sanitary rules, had virtually no overhead. Ganda landowners supported the takeover because they knew their property would appreciate in value, but African traders naturally opposed it, and Ganda traditionalists justifiably saw it as the latest threat of encroachment on their capital.

There were also some Asian traders in Wandegeya, an interesting exception to the prevailing segregation. In 1938 the area was taken into Kampala and it was announced that non-Africans would not be permitted to reside or trade there. This provision was never enforced, however, though the restriction was not formally withdrawn until 1950. On the other hand, the Africans were not forced to comply with the Kampala Township rules and, on the grounds that they were making no tax contributions, few public services were provided.[9] Contradictory and irrational as such compromise appears, this muddled arrangement was a sign of things to come: when African shopkeepers would gradually conform to higher standards; when urban authorities would treat them with flexible encouragement rather than with the peremptory imposition of unacceptable rules, or the equally undesirable connivance at total disregard of the legal rules; and when African and Asian shopkeepers would increasingly trade side by side. If this could have happened earlier, Asian traders might be less in jeopardy now.

The major swamp in the centre of Kampala-Mengo was formed by the sluggish Nakivubo river. Rising below Wandegeya and Makerere and reinforced by streams running down from Namirembe, it became a wide expanse of waving papyrus grass between Mengo, Nakasero and Nsambya. As this was drained, it allowed some expansion of inter-hill settlement, and lower down the river there was an ever-widening expanse of railway yards on the drained valley bottom, with the main industrial area of sidings, go-downs, yards, warehouses, workshops, factories and depots growing out in a general easterly direction. From here the railway ran to Port Bell on the shores of Lake Victoria five miles away. From 1902, communication from the coast to Kampala was by railway from Mombasa to Lake Victoria, and thence by boat across the lake to Port Bell. Only in 1931 did the direct railway line from the coast reach Kampala.

The line from Kampala to Port Bell was an inevitable economic focus, but was quite slow to develop. After the Second World War dense slum-like areas grew up near the railway, and a ribbon of African petty shops, bars, tea houses, hovels and renting rooms ran on towards Port Bell. That community is an administratively separate township, linked to Kampala by this narrow band of urban occupation, as Piraeus is to Athens. Uganda's largest prison lies to one side and its main mental hospital to the other. These, with the brewery and port facilities at Port Bell, involve substantial numbers of residents and employees.

Most of the areas of development between Port Bell and Kampala have now been brought into the city. Kenyan immigrants are particularly numerous here. It is the side of Kampala they reach first after crossing the lake from Kenya and so it feels nearest home. Few Kenyans have sufficient commitment to Kampala-Mengo or to Buganda and Uganda to make them willing to involve themselves in the Ganda land system and thereby in the machinations of Ganda society. Temporary occupation of Crown land therefore suited them better than *mailo* land in Mengo. The most numerous and important Kenya group are the Nilotic Luo, whose chief town is Kisumu, a lake port. Although the divergent national interests of Kenya and Uganda tear them apart and job competition may even induce hostility between them, in other respects there is a strong affinity in language, culture and general social intercourse between the Luo and their closest ethnic relatives, the Nilotic Acholi and Alur of northern Uganda.

The African Housing Estates

Much of this African urban growth was as unobtrusive as it was uncontrolled. Immigrants were left to make their own informal adjustments, many thousands living in peri-urban areas where urban and rural conditions blended and accommodation and food were cheap. They rented rooms from other Africans or put up their own simple thatched huts, often living a communal bachelor existence, demanding and getting practically nothing in the way of increased material amenities such as roads, power and light, water, drainage, sanitation, religious and educational services or police protection. While this was true of the vast majority of those involved in the urban community, including the masses of unskilled, uneducated, poorly paid, relatively short-term migrants, it was not true of the middle and upper economic ranks of the Ganda. They evolved their own adjustment to the growing town, whether in the large mansions built by the wealthy landed families in and around Mengo, or the small suburban houses with gardens and banana plantations which every clerical, middle-class Ganda aspires to own. Nor was it true of those supplied with accommodation by major governmental and public bodies such as the police, the railways, Mulago hospital or Makerere University College. Nor, finally, was it true of the increasing numbers accommodated in the government housing estates.

Construction of these estates was under way by 1950 and major extensions have gone on from time to time ever since. This late development shows that public housing has never played the predominant and often hated role which it has in most of the towns of Central and Southern Africa and in Kenya. However, by the time of independence, the population of the housing estates, though still a small minority, was making an important contribution to the social and political life of the urban community. The estates occupy parts of Nakawa, Naguru, Kiswa and Ntinda, on the east side of Kampala. Since they could not have been built on *mailo* land controlled by the Ganda, these were the only areas of suitable Crown land left within reasonable distance of the town. Nakawa was intended for the lower paid, unskilled and most temporary workers; Naguru for the better paid and skilled. Ntinda was also designed for the better off and consisted of various kinds of ownership or tenant-purchase schemes. Houses might be bought on a 20 per cent deposit, the remainder being loaned, or the tenant might purchase the house by monthly instalments over a period of thirty years.

Although there was criticism of the Uganda authorities for being so tardy in developing an African housing policy, and it certainly seems strange that Kampala had no such positive policy until this time, no doubt a great part of the explanation lies in the peculiar relationship between Kampala and Mengo. In that context, the Ganda pursued an independent policy which firmly established a laissez-faire pattern of incorporation for the African population in general, so that it was not until a late stage that the need for planning became urgent. To judge from the slow development of the housing estates in their early years, and despite the very great care and tact expended on them, one can only conclude that any earlier efforts would have been largely a waste of time. Not only were Africans unable to pay for adequate housing by Western standards, and the colonial government unable to subsidise it, but Africans often greatly preferred the homely and congenial, if materially rudimentary, accommodation which they could secure in the laissez-faire situation of Mengo and the peri-urban areas. It would appear that these officially-sponsored housing estates of various types cannot contain more than ten thousand persons today.

After two years of operation, 40 per cent of the houses at Ntinda were occupied by Ganda. On the Kiswa Estate in 1964, 63 per cent of the landlords were Ganda, 20 per cent Luo and 6 per cent Sudanese. At the Naguru Estate, however, only 21 per cent of the houses were occupied by Ganda in 1955 and, although the number of houses almost doubled by 1962, the proportion occupied by Ganda hardly changed. At Nakawa the number of houses nearly doubled during the same period, and the proportion of the houses occupied by Ganda slipped from 13 to 4 per cent. Nakawa also had houses divided into 'bed-spaces' rented to single men. In 1955 Ganda occupied 61 per cent of the bed-spaces and the Luo another 23 per cent.

From these somewhat patchy figures the distinct position of the Ganda nonetheless emerges clearly. They preponderate over other groups in Ntinda and Kiswa, where the residences can be a profitable investment and where a number of householders are in fact absentees. With the exception of the Luo, and of the Sudanese who have lost their tribal home and are dependent upon the town, there are hardly any other peoples who feel sufficiently secure in the town to commit themselves in large numbers to such a long-term proposition. Despite the fact that the Ganda constitute about half the African population of Kampala-Mengo (1959), they make up a minority of the householders in Naguru and Nakawa. But it is interesting that they are the majority in the Nakawa bed-spaces, which house the most temporary and unskilled population. These Ganda must be poor immigrants from rural areas, much like other poor immigrants and very different from the stereotypical Ganda with their reputation for professional, skilled and white collar occupations.

The housing estates were very intensively studied between 1962 and 1964 and the results are now being analysed and written. I am most grateful to be able to refer to D. J. Parkin's manuscript and present some of the illuminating findings. He found that the usual Kampala correlation of topographical and status gradients is repeated in both Nakawa and Naguru. At Nakawa the bed-spaces intended for single migrant labourers are at the bottom of the slope and the inhabitants differentiate the status of Upper and Lower Nakawa. In Naguru also, the newer, larger and more prestigeful houses are fairly consistently on the upper slopes. There is some overlap in socio-economic status between the two estates, and certain ethnic or occupational characteristics tend partly to over-ride status gradients, but in general there is a rise in social status from Lower to Upper Nakawa and on through Lower to Upper Naguru. This is related to objective differences in education, income, occupation and fluency in English, but is also expressed through the behaviour associated with family, marriage and kinship, and associations.

The range of occupation and income (at 1962 levels) runs from the professionals, of whom there are several dozen in Naguru but none in Nakawa, and whose salaries may be above £50 a month, to the skilled, with a good knowledge of English, of whom there are twice as many in Naguru as in Nakawa, and who earn roughly from £15 to £35 a month; then the lower-skilled and semi-skilled who are not able to command higher pay by the use of English, most of whom earn between £10 and £15 a month and who are nearly twice as numerous in Nakawa as in Naguru; the lower-paid semi-skilled, at around £7 to £11, and the unskilled, earning the lowest wages, are very few in Naguru but by far the largest category in Nakawa. Many tribes are represented in both estates. The large Kenya tribes of Luo and Luyia, each with a total population of nearly a million, are almost equally well represented in both Nakawa and Naguru, where they make up a third of the residents. But there are three times as many Acholi and four times as many Kiga-Ankole and Lugbara in the lower status estate than in the higher. The only contrast is the expected one, the Sudanese being twice as numerous, and the Ganda three times as numerous, in the higher status estate of Naguru.

Certain regularities are discernible in the marriage and family life of Nakawa. Stable marriages which are looked upon as permanent are usually established formally through tribal, Christian or Muslim ceremony and are contracted in the country, not the town. Many wives go to and fro between their husband in town and the latter's rural home. The frequency with which wives are brought to town varies somewhat with the ethnic group and its traditional jural rules of marriage, descent and paternity. Also if the husband has become landless, he is more likely to bring his wife, and this situation varies locally both with population density and the demography of particular families.

In contrast, most of the unions contracted in the town are regarded as relatively temporary and based on the urban worker's need for a woman's domestic and sexual services. Very many of these unions are childless. Most inter-tribal unions are also in this category. When a man's country-wife meets his town-wife, quarrelling, violence and the breakup of one or the other union is likely. When a town-wife produces children, unusual though this is, the union is far more likely to acquire stability, even when it is little sanctioned by the respective kin groups and no bridewealth has been paid. Even a wife married in the country with bridewealth and customary ceremony runs into difficulties with her husband in town if she is childless. Mutual suspicion and accusation develop. Such a woman is tempted to try other men in an effort to prove that the inadequacy is not hers. The husband's reaction to this may be to divorce her or to dismiss her to his rural home while he takes another woman in town. It is rare for a man to have more than one wife in town, but there are instances of plural wives housed in different neighbourhoods, or even of men keeping two wives together as long as they are fertile. At higher status levels, as in most of Naguru, polygyny is even less likely, temporary wives are less accepted and bourgeois conventions of respectability seem to be becoming more demanding.

Inhabitants of the housing estates belong to many associations, such as those of tenants, of tribal groups, trade unions, works committees, political party branches, recreational and educational groups and religious bodies. The latter keep themselves rather apart, especially those of evangelistic and fundamentalist movements. Most of the rest are characterised by a general membership of a very nominal kind and small numbers of very active members almost coinciding with the officers and committee membership. The Luo Union, probably the strongest of the tribal associations, was said at one time to have had only about twenty fully paid-up members, though there were more than five thousand Luo who might have belonged and some hundreds who usually turned up for the annual meeting and elections.

The tribal associations express both the exigencies of differing traditional social structures and of the differentiated status levels in town. It is the traditionally segmentary societies which have the strongest and also the most elaborately segmented unions in Kampala. The two most notable cases are the Nilotic Luo and the Bantu Luyia. The fact that both are from across the border in Kenya doubtless adds a greater sense of need for organised solidarity. The Nilotic Acholi and Lango of Uganda also have segmented unions, while the centralised Ganda, Toro, Nyoro and Soga have never had effective unions. The Kiga and Ankole have a combined unitary association, representing the Iru lower caste of Ankole and the segmentary Kiga who have close affinities with them. The Ruanda have a unitary association, which perhaps expresses their special need of solidarity and mutual aid as foreigners from a great distance.

The main Luo Union comprises major branches corresponding to the traditional sub-tribal areas of the Luo, which have been administratively transformed and are known as 'locations'. These in turn comprise minor branches corresponding to the component clans or lineages of the sub-tribes. The Luyia tribal association has a similar three tier structure. These maximal, major and minor levels of associational organisation reflect both different status levels and different functional needs. The clan and lineage associations are formed by people of humble status who particularly feel the need of support from a mutual welfare organisation at times of sickness, misfortune and death. The groups are quite small, rather informal and somewhat ephemeral. A few men of the same lineage and neighbourhood who happen to be friendly in town invoke the confirmatory strength of their agnatic kinship ties. If the group lapses, it will probably rise again on the same basis but with different personnel a few years later. All the time several dozen such bodies are going through this irregular cycle. They are almost completely autonomous for their own purposes, though regarded by the sub-tribal associations as branches.

The leaders and initiators of sub-tribal associations are more ambitious people of higher status, more concerned with organising football matches and basking in the accruing prestige. These associations in turn are hardly at all controlled by the umbrella of the Luo Union, although regarded as its branches. So this largely fictional superordination-subordination suits each segmentary level, since the superordinate group enjoys the sense of importance which the existence of many branches brings, while it is not worth the latters' while to deny their formal subordination as long as it has little or no practical implications in terms of authority and control or finance. Those who lead the Luo Union are important figures, often too busy for more than a token involvement in the concerns of the minor sub-tribal branches, let alone those of the little clan and lineage groups. They are concerned with community, rather than individual, welfare activities: establishing and administering schools and nurseries, organising concerts and dances, making financial collections for either tribal or national causes. Leadership of the Union is obviously the highest level of ethnic leadership and may be used as a springboard to some further role of economic, political or civic leadership. This, once attained, may require tactful withdrawal from direct involvement with the tribal union.

While very limited education makes it exceedingly difficult for anyone to rise far unless he is possessed of quite exceptional countervailing talents, there is this possible ladder of advance for the ambitious through the ranks of ethnic leadership to the point of take-off into more exalted spheres. Parkin has demonstrated how leaders in East Kampala engage in significant multiple role-playing to secure and bind a sufficient following to give them support for the next leap in status. Thus the secretary of a sub-tribal association is also treasurer of a trade union, of the YMCA branch and of the Tenants' Association, as well as an official in the branch of a Kenya political party.

As the structure into which the legion statuses of Kampala-Mengo are built is diverse, multilinear and asymmetrical, so also are the channels and processes by which prestige and status are won. The diversity of structure arises from the weaving together of many factors and every attempt to describe the political, economic, status or other special aspect of social life in Kampala-Mengo tends to become part of a wider account of the same aspect throughout the whole country. It seems easier to make the abstract distinction between the political, economic and status systems of the whole of Uganda than to draw a clear line between political, economic and status structure in Kampala-Mengo and in the rest of Uganda. This is an indication of the general difficulty of distinguishing the intrinsically urban.

Segregation in Kampala-Mengo

The problem of how best to arrange the relationships of many peoples differing in race, language, culture and religion has always dominated the life and development of Kampala-Mengo. It is a particular case of the relation of the Western to the non-Western world. When all the lines of difference are superimposed, the cleavage is particularly deep and integration especially difficult. This is immediately obvious in the juxtaposition of the Negro, Bantu-speaking, plantain-eating, skin-wearing ancestor worshipper with the European Caucasoid, English-speaking, beef-eating, trouser-wearing Christian and with the Indian, Gujerati-speaking, vegetarian, curry-eating, dhoti-wearing Hindu. When such different people are forced by circumstances into some kind of co-operation, their reaction is to restrict their intercourse to a minimum. The most obvious, convenient and effective way of doing this is to live in different areas and, in the early days of Kampala-Mengo, this appears to have been what the majority of Africans, Europeans and Asians assumed was mutually best for all of them. It did not mean that European missionaries did not live in very close association with their African converts, but the majority of the races remained apart. It was long before any voice of criticism was raised against the principle of segregation as such. The earliest complaints, from the Asians, centred only on the classic issue of the provision of 'separate but equal' facilities. Their provision was never equal and in the nature of things could not be.

The dual organisation of the British and the Ganda, which set the early pattern for separate European and African development, was essentially a political and not a racial settlement. Although in a sense the ultimate power lay with the British, they were forced by the circumstances as well as the treaty to deal with the Ganda mainly through Ganda institutions. Inevitably, lower status Ganda became servants in European households and not vice versa. The lower levels of status were not represented among the Europeans. Also the relation between British and Ganda, even at the most respectful level, was to some extent defined as that between teacher and taught. Nonetheless, there was mutual deference and respect between Ganda chiefs and notables and British officials. In certain cases and situations this was accompanied by genuine regard, while in others each inwardly disapproved and heartily despised the other. The King and chiefs expected the Europeans to live in their own settlement in their own way. They became deeply apprehensive at the unexpected growth which that settlement soon began to manifest and they did their utmost to prevent its encroachment on their own capital.

But in Mengo there were not only the true traditionalists, who sincerely wished to preserve their country's heritage, but there were landowners faced with the fact that leasing to non-Africans could be vastly more profitable to them than any other use to which their land could easily be put. On the other hand there was the growing body of African traders and businessmen who saw a relatively secure market if they could use the political situation to prevent any competition from non-Africans. But these three conflicting interests could often be found in the same individual. In the Lukiko he might be moved by patriotism to vote for Ganda national interests and to keep the Asians out of Mengo; as a landowner he would be sorely tempted by highly profitable offers from Asians for leases; as a trader he would be determined to keep them out.

The official procedure for securing a lease in Mengo was so intricate and protracted as to discourage even the keenest. From 1908 till 1948 only nine applications were approved but, officially or unofficially, the Asians gained a footing there. The Kampala Township Authority estimated in 1942 that at least 300 Asians (presumably families) were permanently established in Mengo.[10] Six years later the Lukiko policy was reversed and, in the next decade, the number of approved applications for leases rocketed to 713.[11] As housing became ever scarcer and more expensive in Kampala for those lacking civil servants' privileges, Europeans in professional or commercial occupations were also forced to seek accommodation in Mengo. In view of the mutual advantages, this could be easily and amicably arranged and they were often on excellent terms with their landlord and African neighbours.

From the beginning, the velvet gloved deference of the British Protectorate was regularly given ceremonial expression. The whimsical mixture of intimacy and unconscious prejudice, of humanity and superiority, appears in the following early account:

> On August the 8th, 1903, the infant Kabaka of Uganda [sic], Daudi Cwa, attained his fifth birthday. His birthday was celebrated each year at the Lubiri [palace grounds]. All the few Kampala Europeans were invited to partake of the celebration and the fare was chiefly cakes, biscuits and lemonade. A special guard of honour from the Indian Regiment at Nakasero Fort usually appeared and was duly inspected by the young Kabaka who solemnly walked around holding the European officer's hand. The occasion was always accompanied by the Kabaka's drummers and musicians. Until about 1906 the guardianship of the Kabaka was in the hands of that very fine chief of Kyagwe,

> Hamu Mukasa, and then a European tutor, Mr John Sturrock, a Scotsman, took charge of him. He was an Oxford University man and keen on football. . . . He had a football ground made within the Lubiri on which he taught the Baganda youth, including the Kabaka, the rules of the game. . . . The boys took to football like ducks to the water. Before long we were able to include some of them amongst the European teams at practice matches on the Kampala ground. . . . By 1910 a great number of Church Missionary Society and Roman Catholic Mission Schools had their football teams. The time came when both European teams at Kampala and Entebbe played against Baganda teams and sometimes the latter proved the winners. It was always a concession that Europeans played in tennis shoes against the bare feet of the Africans.[12]

It is intriguing to note the very Protestant definition of the birthday fare, certainly as little in the tradition of many of the British officials as in that of the Ganda chiefs, but the mission influence for a long time pervaded public occasions in Buganda. The Indian soldiers under a European officer doing honour to the infant African ruler symbolises a number of features of local society and race relations. The role of tutor to the king could be occupied successively by the Ganda chief and the Scots schoolmaster. It was equally natural for Ganda and Europeans to play together at first in a mixed team, and later to play against one another in separate teams when growing numbers and organisation permitted.

The Indian bazaar traders who found themselves restricted to the lower slopes of Old Kampala and then of Nakasero hill, nearest to the malarial swamp, complained of the unfairness of the treatment. The Kampala planning scheme of 1919 left the European and Asian trading areas still adjacent on the upper and lower slopes of Nakasero, but aimed at completely separate European and Asian residential areas with green belts not less than a quarter of a mile wide between them. In 1920 the Secretary of State for the Colonies actually approved these 'Scheme C Segregation Proposals', but two years later ruled that there should be no segregation of races. Despite this abolition of segregation in principle, it had little practical effect for some time. By 1926 the Central Town Planning Board recommended 'that there should be no insuperable objection to accommodating in this area [a green belt] an Indian Sports Club and grounds or similar proposals which would not lead to a congestion of buildings'.[13] Thus came into being the Nakasero Recreation Club, most prestigeful of Asian clubs in Kampala. Its rules restricted membership exclusively to persons of British Indian descent but, by the 1950s, some of the younger Indians were inviting European and even African friends to play tennis with them there.

Each major ethnic and religious group built its own clubhouse. The Europeans had two clubs, both with sporting and general social and drinking facilities. Many belonged to both but one had distinctly higher status and prestige than the other and they occupied correspondingly separate positions, the one higher up, the other lower down the slope of Nakasero hill. The Goans had their Institute on the lower slopes, but even farther down was the St. Francis Xavier Tailors' Club of the lower caste Goans. The Patidar Patels, the Lohanas, the Ismailis, the Ithnaashris and the Sikhs all eventually secured separate clubs or sports grounds. Every orthodox and reformist Hindu group and every Muslim sect had its own place of worship, which acted also as a social centre, especially for the womenfolk. Many of these bodies also built hostels for children or families from up-country requiring accommodation while on visits in Kampala or attending school.

Although the town was no longer conceived of as divided into quite separate racial areas, it continued to be laid out in blocks which were clearly envisaged as European, Asian or African. By 1951 Kampala was divided into five types of residential zone according to size of plot, density of building and standard of construction. There was nothing explicitly racial in this definition, but in effect one zone was occupied only by Africans, three zones were almost exclusively Asian, while another included virtually all Europeans and wealthier Asians, with African domestic servants and their families living in quarters behind their employers' houses.[14]

The whole structure of the civil service, in which certain types of job, housing and salary scales had been identified with different races, was rapidly dismantled and transformed in the late 1950s. As more and more Africans were promoted to senior positions in the civil service, they moved into the same houses in the same areas which had previously been identified with Europeans. This process had repercussions on every sphere of social life. Having salaries of a level previously enjoyed only by Europeans, African civil servants began to patronise in much larger numbers the same shops as Europeans previously had; they began to attend the same social functions on terms of greater ease and equality, and to be invited to both public and private parties where previously few of them had been seen. The process was not restricted to civil servants, but in such a highly bureaucratised society the example set by the civil service was of paramount importance. Some business firms had pioneered the same way earlier, but now all followed. Previously despised political leaders were lionised. The intellectual and bohemian fringes of society had long been inter-racial, but now it became the generally accepted convention, even if ridiculed and railed against in private by the diehards. As independence came, an even greater ethnic heterogeneity was brought to the upper reaches of social life by the many foreign diplomats and advisers, all anxious to entertain and get to know the new African leaders.

Conclusions

Kampala-Mengo is interesting because it contains within itself most of the major factors, combined at different strengths, which are found in African cities of quite varied type, such as the older, more traditional West African cities and the newer, European-dominated cities of East and Central Africa. It combines both segregation and the political dominance of a particular African tribe; it includes both European and African controlled land, traditional and modern roles, local African residents of long standing and high status, as well as thousands of temporary migrant labourers of many ethnic backgrounds.

I have presented Kampala-Mengo very much as a temporal and

spatial process and I have been forced to accept antecedent events as major determinants. The neglect of history where it is available is not only absurd but is quite unjustified as a criticism of the recent work of social anthropologists. But I do not regard social anthropology as a kind of history. It is only the history of successive functional networks—the links between a series of synchronic analyses. How far reliance is put upon tracing particular themes through time, how far on linking a series of situations analysed into their components, is a problem of exposition as well as of theory. Although events appear unique, to the social anthropologist they are composed of elements which have regularities, which are his major quest.

The founding of Kampala-Mengo was directly determined by political, not economic factors. The land system, which was fundamental, was similarly the outcome of political bargaining between the Ganda chiefs and Sir Harry Johnston and other British agents, both parties obviously having their own economic interests at heart as they bargained. The hilltop ecology of the site inevitably determined something of the shape of the city, but did not determine which hills were chosen for what, or the combination of uses to which they were all put. Although the swamps must have added to the local isolation of the Europeans and Asians on Nakasero in the early days, Kampala-Mengo was never a collection of villages, as has been said, perhaps dubiously, of such cities as Boston.

The story of segregation here suggests that, where there are deep racial, religious, linguistic and general cultural cleavages, the groups concerned endeavour to live separately from one another in so far as circumstances permit. This provides a fine basis for the imposition of legal segregation by the dominant group but, even if this is not done, the encouragement of ethnic differences through separate residence tends to generalise a model of the whole social system in which an ethnic component enters the interpretation of all differences of wealth, ability and general behaviour. When this is entrenched for several decades, the majority in all groups offer considerable resistance to integration. Nonetheless, I have shown that Kampala-Mengo provides many instances in which personal desires for wealth or power are quite strong enough to overcome racial or ethnic prejudices and separatisms for particular purposes.

It is certainly dangerous to talk about Africa in class terms with Western connotations unless many provisos are made. The immediate problem is that most situations are still in an early phase of transition and the traditional, modern and hybrid components have to be carefully sorted out and their long-term significance assessed. The long-term question is, of course, what elements of Western culture are essential to its technology, productive system and social scale, hence equally inevitable in Africa to the extent that comparable technology, productivity and scale are achieved? Alternatively, what Western elements are not so essential and hence of no necessary relevance to Africa? A more fundamental question is how relevant is the Western model of technology, productivity and scale to Africa anyway, since the current process by which these goals are sought is so different from that which obtained in the Western models? Furthermore, the relevance of the Western model may be based on the unstated assumption that Africa is in some sense catching up with the West. But it seems highly doubtful that this is so. It may be that most of Africa will never catch up to the West economically in the visible future, but in terms of social forms Africa may be working out essentially new answers to new situations, which are in this sense more advanced than those of the West, depending upon one's perspective.

Relativity applies to the cross-cultural as well as to the physical world. Many African economies have expanded and towns grown even faster than Western economies and towns grew in the nineteenth century. But in hardly any sense can this seriously mean that African towns or economies are achieving situations which have the same meaning as in the nineteenth century West. Still less are most African economies catching up to the contemporary West, since the gap between the relative standards of living of the common man in the two situations is in fact widening, not narrowing. It is therefore unlikely that even features which appear formally similar have the same cultural meaning.

Buganda developed a reminiscent squirearchy during the late nineteenth and early twentieth centuries but, while important in some respects, the reminiscence is superficial in many others, so that no comparable development of liberal capitalism, parliamentary democracy or broad churchmanship can be expected. Yet the resemblances are there. What look to Westerners like the slums of African cities may not be the home of the lower-lowers, but rather the very centres of the humbler sort of African commercial enterprise and initiative. In the Kampala housing estates one can see many features developing which are reminiscent of the Western notion of a middle-class, for there is no gainsaying the fact that these people are in the middle range of income, wealth and status. But the context is radically different.

Virtually all the Africans of Kampala-Mengo come from unilineal descent groups. They therefore not only lack, or are free from, the experience of a thousand years of literate, ranked and stratified society, which binds the Anglo-Saxon West, but they approach the industrial age with basically different kinship presuppositions. This does not necessarily mean that they are more or less adaptable to industrial and urban society in any essential ways, but that wherever possible they will manipulate it differently. It is conceivably possible to provide for the spatial and social mobility now required, within an intensive yet flexible kinship framework which both contains widely separated urban and rural areas and includes widely divergent positions of wealth, status and influence.

The ideology of African socialism is sound to the extent that it is prepared to exploit and adapt traditional kinship structures, rather than to appear ashamed and try to deny or conceal them. It can maintain countless lines of solidarity across wide divergencies of wealth and status, as well as across wide spatial distances, and so prevent any clear mobilisation of opposed class interest. But it will be a fragile balance which too many unemployed or landless will quickly upset. The general strike in Nigeria, the unemployed mobs outside ministers' offices in Nairobi and the dissident elements under the Youth Wing aegis in Kampala all demonstrate this clearly. But in so far as a delicate and diffuse interclass solidarity can be maintained through the high valuation of innumerable cross-cutting kinship ties, it has the obvious implication that there will be no place for a multi-party system based on divergent economic interests instead of on ethnic separations, as is the present tendency. It is further to be noted that the possibility of absorbing the great diversity and mobility of modern occupational roles within the wide framework of kinship obligations is greater to the extent that large-scale economic enterprise appears to be inevitably in the hands of either the state or expatriate interests. Although the Ganda have been more successful than any other East African people in incorporating modernisation, rather than capitulating to it, they certainly could not have incorporated large-scale industrial enterprises into fictional extensions of traditional kinship as the Japanese were able to do so remarkably, at least for the first half century of their industrialisation.

Two of the most important aspects of the structure of social relationships which holds together the diverse body of persons and institutions in Kampala-Mengo are the extensive kinship bonds and the playing of multiple roles—the occupancy of cross-cutting statuses.[15] Not only do Africans retain strong kinship bonds from their cultural background, but it is quite possible that these will acquire a new type of valuation, as an African contribution to morality and a distinctive feature of the African cultural personality and mystique. This is despite the fact that many individuals will struggle to limit the burden of such recognition. Multiple role playing and multiple status incumbency confront the most mobile and influential individuals with the necessity of mediating, in their own persons, between the very diverse clients, relatives, cliques, networks, institutions and publics among whom they must move. Nearly all the urban populace is involved in this process, from the humblest migrant worker who must mediate between the demands and expectations of his numerous kin in traditional communities and the exigencies of urban employers, landlords and work situation, with their radically different values, goals and rhythms. It is all the more true of the elite, who still depend fundamentally on the support of the traditionally oriented masses, but are also more deeply involved in a wide variety of modern roles. Thus, fortunately, the strivings of the individual contribute to the maintenance of society, but what this means for personal well-being and mental health in Africa we do not know. The case of Uganda, where the head of a republican state could also be king of one part of it, is only one of the more spectacular anomalies, but the straddling of widely distinct roles is a necessity for most African townsfolk. It has been stated with categorical tautology, to drive home an important truth, that 'an African townsman is a townsman, an African miner is a miner',[16] but having absorbed this truth we can accept the fact that the African townsman brings a lot of cultural and tribal luggage with him to town, on the strength of which he fabricates new relationships to meet new urban needs.

What T. S. Eliot remarked of a nation is true of Kampala-Mengo:

> I may put the idea of the importance of conflict within a nation more positively by insisting on the importance of various and sometimes conflicting loyalties. If we consider these two divisions alone, of class and region, these ought to some extent to operate against each other: a man should have certain interests and sympathies in common with other men of the same local culture as against those of his own class elsewhere; and interests and sympathies in common with others of his class, irrespective of place. Numerous cross-divisions favour peace within a nation, by dispersing and confusing animosities; they favour peace between nations, by giving every man enough antagonism at home to exercise all his aggressiveness.[17]

What is above all important is that the cleavages should indeed cut across at many points and not fall at the same point, as they are in danger of doing when racial prejudice focuses them all. I am convinced that ethnic and cultural differences will remain an important factor at lower status levels for a long time to come, but that these differences will be transcended at the elite level and that this transcendence will proceed further than it has yet had a chance to do, gradually achieving a new cultural integration of the elite.

Notes and References

1 H. H. Johnston, *The Uganda Protectorate*, London 1902.

2 P. C. W. Gutkind, *The African Administration of the Kibuga of Buganda*, The Hague 1963, pp. 13–17.

3 Ibid., pp. 56–67.
4 A. W. Southall and P. C. W. Gutkind, *Townsmen in the Making*, East African Studies No. 9, Kampala, Uganda, 1957, pp. 5–6.
5 E. May, *Report on the Kampala Extension Scheme: Kololo-Naguru*, Entebbe, Uganda, 1947, p. 9.
6 W. E. Hoyle, "Early Days in Uganda" (manuscript).
7 The popular usage of Indian is implied, although it also includes smaller numbers of persons from what is now Pakistan.
8 Fully described in Southall and Gutkind, op. cit.
9 Gutkind, op. cit.
10 Ibid., p. 222.
11 Ibid., p. 229.
12 Hoyle, op. cit.
13 H. Kendall, *Town Planning in Uganda*, London 1955, p. 78.
14 Ibid., p. 57.
15 R. K. Merton, *Social Theory and Social Structure*, Glencoe, Ill., 1957.
16 Max Gluckman, "Anthropological Problems Arising from the African Industrial Revolution", in Aidan W. Southall, ed., *Social Change in Modern Africa*, London 1961, p. 69.
17 T. S. Eliot, *Notes Towards the Definition of Culture*, London 1948, p. 60.

Contributors

William J. Barber, Professor of Economics at Wesleyan University, has conducted research in Kenya and in what are now Zambia and Rhodesia. In addition to *The Economy of British Central Africa: A Case Study of Economic Development in a Dualistic Society*, he has published in *Economic Development and Cultural Change*, the *Canadian Journal of Economics and Political Science* and *Oxford Economic Papers*, among others. Dr Barber also contributed the chapter on "The Movement into the World Economy" in the Herskovits and Harwitz volume on *Economic Transition in Africa*.

Remi Clignet is Assistant Professor of Sociology at Northwestern University and an Associate of the African Studies Program. He has done field-work in the Senegal and Ivory Coast. Among his publications on the latter are contributions to the *International Social Science Review* (1962) and, with P. Foster, to the *American Journal of Sociology* (1964) and the *Revue Française de Sociologie* (1966). They are also co-authors of *The Fortunate Few*.

William John Hanna is Chairman of the Research Advisory Council, Center for Research in Social Systems, the American University. Field-work has lead him and Judith Lynne Hanna, a Research Scientist in the Center, to a number of countries in East and West Africa, with concentrated work in Uganda and Nigeria. In addition to their published articles, the Hannas compiled *Politics in Black Africa: A Selective Bibliography of Relevant Periodical Literature*. William Hanna was author-editor of *Independent Black Africa: The Politics of Freedom*.

Leo Kuper, now Professor of Sociology at the University of California, Los Angeles, was long a resident investigator of the multi-racial scene in South Africa while teaching at the University of Durban. His major publications include *Passive Resistance in South Africa* and *An African Bourgeoisie*, as well as co-authorship of *Durban: A Study in Racial Ecology*, and editorship, with Hilda Kuper, of *African Law: Adaptation and Development*.

Contributors

Daniel Lerner is Ford Professor of Sociology and International Communication at the Massachusetts Institute of Technology, where he is also Senior Research Associate in the Center for International Studies. Dr Lerner's *The Passing of Traditional Society* reports a pioneering series of comparative studies in the Middle East. His other books include *World Revolutionary Elites*, with Harold Lasswell, and *The Human Meaning of the Social Sciences*. His articles have appeared in a spectrum of periodicals ranging from *Sociometry* to *Harper's Magazine*.

Robert A. LeVine is Associate Professor of Anthropology in the Committee on Human Development, University of Chicago. Field-work in East and West Africa resulted in two books: *Nyansongo: A Gusii Community in Kenya*, written with B. B. LeVine, and *Dreams and Deeds: Achievement Motivation in Nigeria*. To Clifford Geertz's *Old Societies and New States*, Dr LeVine contributed a chapter on "Political Socialization and Culture Change". His collaborator, Nancy H. Klein, is Instructor in Sociology at DePaul University and Constance R. Owen is a graduate student at the University of Chicago.

Peter Marris is a member of the Institute of Community Studies, London. His research in Nigeria culminated in his volume on Lagos, *Family and Social Change in an African City*. The results of urban research conducted for the Ford Foundation are reported in *Dilemmas of Reform: Poverty and Community Action in the United States*, of which he is co-author. His publications also include *Widows and their Families* and *The Experience of Higher Education*. Most recently, he has been working from the Institute for Development Studies, University College, Nairobi.

Horace Miner holds professorships in both Anthropology and Sociology at the University of Michigan. Field-work has taken him to Mali, Nigeria and Algeria; he was also a Visiting Professor at Makerere University College, Uganda. Dr Miner's publications include *The Primitive City of Timbuctoo*; co-authorship of *Oasis and Casbah: Algerian Culture and Personality in Change*; the editorship of "Social Science in Action in Sub-Saharan Africa", a special issue of *Human Organization*; and a chapter on "Urban Influences on the Rural Hausa" in H. Kuper's *Urbanization and Migration in West Africa*.

Aidan Southall has been Professor of Anthropology and Associate in the Program of East African Studies at Syracuse University since 1964. Prior to that, he had a score of years' experience as Research Fellow and Professor at Makerere University College, Uganda, where he also served as Chairman of the East African Institute of Social Research and Dean of the Faculty of Social Sciences. Field-work in Uganda led to his publication of *Alur Society*, to numerous articles and to the joint authorship of *Townsmen in the Making*. Following his chairmanship of the first International African Seminar, Dr Southall edited *Social Change in Modern Africa*.

Joseph J. Spengler holds the James B. Duke Professorship of Economics at Duke University, where he is a participant in the African programme. Dr Spengler taught for a brief period in Ethiopia and he has a first hand knowledge of Rhodesia and South Africa. His major publications have tended to be chapters in volumes of collected papers for which, in many instances, he assumed or shared the editorship. Such was the case with his *Natural Resources and Economic Growth* and his collaboration with Braibanti in editing *Tradition, Values, and Socio-Economic Development*. Among his most recent relevant papers are "Population Movements and Economic Development in Nigeria", in Tilman and Cole, *The Nigerian Political Scene*; and "Population Movements and Problems", in E. A. G. Robinson, *Economic Development for Africa South of the Sahara.*

Lionel Tiger, Assistant Professor of Sociology at the University of British Columbia, began his African experience in 1957, followed later by a prolonged period of research and university lecturing in Ghana. His publications include "Bureaucracy and Charisma in Ghana", *Journal of Asian and African Studies* (1966), and "Politics and Social Change in Ghana", *International Journal of Comparative Sociology* (1966).

List of Works Cited

Aberle, D. F., and Naegele, K. D., "Middle-Class Fathers' Occupational Role and Attitudes toward Children", *American Journal of Orthopsychiatry*, Vol. 22, 1952, pp. 366–78.

Abraham, W., *The Mind of Africa*, Weidenfeld and Nicolson, London 1962.

Adams, Robert M., "The Origin of Cities", *Scientific American*, Vol. 203, No. 3, September 1960, pp. 153–68.

Adorno, T. W., Frenkel-Brunswik, E., Levinson, D. J., and Sanford, R. N., *The Authoritarian Personality*, Harper, New York 1950.

Adrian, Charles, "The Community Setting", in Charles Adrian, ed., *Social Science and Community Action*, Michigan State University Press, East Lansing 1960.

Aitchison, J., and Brown, J. A. C., *The Lognormal Distribution*, Cambridge University Press, London 1957.

Allardt, Erik, and Littunen, Y., eds., *Cleavages, Ideologies and Party Systems: Contributions to Comparative Political Sociology*, Transactions of the Westermarck Society, Vol. 10, Helsinki 1964.

Allen, G. R., "The 'Courbe des Populations': A Further Analysis", *Bulletin of the Oxford University Institute of Statistics*, Vol. 16, May 1954, pp. 179–89.

Almond, Gabriel A., "Introduction: A Functional Approach to Comparative Politics", in Almond and Coleman, q.v.; and Coleman, James, eds., *The Politics of Developing Areas*, Princeton University Press, Princeton 1960.

Alonso, William, "The Form of Cities in Developing Countries", paper presented at the Regional Science Association meeting, Chicago, November 1963; "The Historic and the Structural Theories of Urban Form: Their Implications for Urban Renewal", *Land Economics*, Vol. 40, May 1964, pp. 227–31; *Location and Land Use*, Harvard University Press, Cambridge 1964.

Ando, A., Fisher, Franklin M., and Simon, Herbert, *Essays on the Structure of Social Science Models*, Massachusetts Institute of Technology Press, Cambridge 1963.

List of Works Cited

Apter, David E., "The Role of Traditionalism in the Political Modernization of Ghana and Uganda", *World Politics*, Vol. 13, 1960, pp. 45–74; "Some Reflections on the Role of a Political Opposition in New Nations", *Comparative Studies in Society and History*, Vol. 4, 1962, pp. 154–68; "Non-Western Government and Politics: Introduction", in Eckstein and Apter, q.v.; "Political Religion in the New Nations", in Geertz, q.v.

Ashby, Eric, *African Universities and Western Tradition*, Harvard University Press, Cambridge 1964.

Bailey, N. T. J., *The Elements of Stochastic Processes*, John Wiley, New York 1964.

Balogh, Thomas, "What Schools for Africa", *New Statesman*, March 23, 1962.

Banton, Michael, *West African City: A Study of Tribal Life in Freetown*, Oxford University Press, London 1957; "Role Theory and Urbanization", and "Social Alignment and Identity in a West African City", papers presented at Symposium No. 26, under the auspices of the Wenner-Gren Foundation for Anthropological Research, August 27–September 8, 1964; ed., *The Social Anthropology of Complex Societies*, Tavistock Publications, London 1966.

Barber, William J., "Economic Rationality and Behavior Patterns in an Underdeveloped Area: A Case Study of African Economic Behavior in the Rhodesias", *Economic Development and Cultural Change*, Vol. 8, April 1960, pp. 237–51.

Barbour, K. M., and Prothero, R. M., eds., *Essays on African Population*, Routledge and Kegan Paul, London 1961.

Barnard, C. I., *The Function of the Executive*, Harvard University Press, Cambridge 1940.

Barnes, J. A., "The Fort Jameson Ngoni", *Africa*, Vol. 19, 1949, pp. 100–6.

Bartlett, M. S., *Essays on Probability and Statistics*, John Wiley, New York 1962.

Bascom, William, "Urbanization among the Yoruba", *American Journal of Sociology*, Vol. 60, March 1955, pp. 446–54; "Some Aspects of Yoruba Urbanism", *American Anthropologist*, Vol. 64, August 1962, pp. 699–709; and Herskovits, Melville J., eds., *Continuity and Change in African Cultures*, University of Chicago Press, Chicago 1959.

Beckman, Martin J., "City Hierarchies and the Distribution of City Size", *Economic Development and Cultural Change*, Vol. 6, April 1958, pp. 243–8.

Bendix, Reinhard, *Max Weber: An Intellectual Portrait*, Heinemann, London 1960.

Berelson, B., Lazarsfeld, Paul F., and McPhee, William N., *Voting: A Study of Opinion Formation in a Presidential Campaign*, University of Chicago Press, Chicago 1954.

Berg, Elliott J., "Socialism and Economic Development in Tropical Africa", *Quarterly Journal of Economics*, Vol. 78, November 1964, pp. 549–73.

Berghe, P. L. van den, "Toward a Sociology of Africa", *Social Forces*, Vol. 43, 1964, pp. 11–18.

Bernus, Edmond, "Abidjan, Note sur l'agglomération d'Abidjan et sa population", *Bulletin de l'IFAN*, series B, Vol. 24, Janvier–Avril 1962, pp. 56–85.

Berry, Brian J. L., "City Size Distributions and Economic Development", *Economic Development and Cultural Change*, Vol. 9, Pt. I, July 1961, pp. 573–88; et al, "Urban Population Densities: Structure and Change", *Geographical Review*, Vol. 53, July 1963, pp. 389–405; and Garrison, W. L., "Alternate Explanations of Urban Rank Size Relationships", *Annals of the Association of American Geographers*, Vol. 48, March 1958, pp. 83–91.

Bettison, D. G., *Report of the Urban African Affairs Commission, Southern Rhodesia* (Appendix N), 1958.

Bharati, A., "Political Pressures and Reactions in the Asian Minority in East Africa", paper presented at the Annual Meeting of the African Studies Association, Chicago 1964.

Blair, John M., "Technology and Size", *American Economic Review*, Vol. 38, May 1948, pp. 121–52.

Boulding, Kenneth E., "Income or Welfare", *Review of Economic Studies*, Vol. 17, 1949–50, pp. 79–80; "Toward a General Theory of Growth", in Spengler and Duncan, *Population Theory and Policy*, q.v.

Braibanti, Ralph, *Transnational Inducement of Administrative Reform: A Survey of Scope and Critique of Issues*, Occasional Papers, Comparative Administration Group, International Development Research Center, Indiana University, Bloomington 1964, mimeographed; and Spengler, Joseph J., eds., *Tradition, Values and Socio-Economic Development*, Duke University Press, Durham, NC, 1961.

Brazer, Harvey E., *City Expenditures in the United States*, National Bureau of Economic Research, Occasional Paper No. 66, New York 1959.

Breese, Gerald, *Urbanization in Newly Developing Countries*, Prentice-Hall, Englewood Cliffs 1966.

Bronfenbrenner, Urie, "The Changing American Child—A Speculative Analysis", in Smelser and Smelser, q.v.

Brown, Lester R., *Man, Land and Food*, US Department of Agriculture, Washington 1965.

Burke, Fred G., *Local Government and Politics in Uganda*, Syracuse University Press, Syracuse 1964.

Burns, Leland S., and Klassen, Leo H., "The Econometrics of Building a New Town", *Review of Economics and Statistics*, Vol. 45, November 1963, pp. 368–73.

Burton, R. V., and Whiting, J. W. M., "The Absent Father and Cross-Sex Identity", *Merrill-Palmer Quarterly*, Vol. 7, 1961, pp. 85–95.

Carpenter, E., and McLuhan, Marshall, eds., *Explorations in Communications*, Beacon Press, Boston 1960.

Clark, Colin, "The Economic Functions of a City in Relation to Its Size", *Econometrica*, Vol. 13, April 1945; "The Distribution of Labour between Industries and between Locations", *Land*

Economics, Vol. 26, May 1950; "Urban Population Densities", *Journal of the Royal Statistical Society*, Vol. 114, 1951, pp. 490–6; *The Conditions of Economic Progress*, Macmillan, London 1957; and Haswell, M. R., *The Economics of Subsistence Agriculture*, Macmillan, London 1964.

Clawson, Marion, et al, *Land for the Future*, Johns Hopkins Press, Baltimore 1960.

Clignet, Remi, and Foster, Philip, "Potential Elites in Ghana and the Ivory Coast: A Preliminary Comparison", *American Journal of Sociology*, Vol. 69, November 1964, pp. 349–62; *The Fortunate Few*, Northwestern University Press, Evanston 1966.

Coleman, James S., "The Politics of Sub-Saharan Africa", in Almond and Coleman, q.v.

Conditions de Vie de l'Enfant Africain en Milieu Urbain et de leur Influence sur la Délinquance Juvénile, Travaux et Documents XII, Paris 1959.

Cornwell, Elmer E., Jr., "Bosses, Machines, and Ethnic Groups", *The Annals of the American Academy of Political and Social Science*, Vol. 353, 1964.

Côte d'Ivoire, Ministère des Finances, *Recensement d'Abidjan (1955), Résultats définitifs*, Paris 1960; *Recensement d'Abidjan (1963)*, Société d'Etudes et de Mathématiques Appliquées, Paris 1965.

Coulanges, Numa Denis Fustel de, *The Ancient City*, Doubleday, Garden City, NY, 1956.

Curry, Leslie, "The Random Spatial Economy: An Exploration in Settlement Theory", *Annals of the Association of American Geographers*, Vol. 54, March 1964, pp. 138–46.

Davis, Kingsley, and Hertz, Hilda, "Urbanization and the Development of Pre-Industrial Areas", *Economic Development and Cultural Change*, Vol. 3, October 1954, pp. 16–23; "The World Distribution of Urbanization", reprinted in Spengler and Duncan, eds., *Demographic Analysis*, q.v.

Denis, Jacques, SJ, "Le Phénomène Urbain en Afrique Centrale", in Académie royale des Sciences coloniales (classe des sciences morales et politiques), *Mémoires*, Vol. 19, fasc. 1, 1958.

Doob, Leonard, *Becoming More Civilized*, Yale University Press, New Haven 1961.

Dore, Ronald P., "The Search for Modernity in Asia and Africa: A Review Article", *Pacific Affairs*, Vol. 37, Summer 1964, pp. 161–5.

Dorjahn, V., "The Factor of Polygyny in African Demography", in Bascom and Herskovits, q.v.

Dube, S. C., *Bureaucracy and Nation-Building in Transitional Societies, Expert Working Group on Social Prerequisites to Economic Growth, Kenia, Cyprus*, UNESCO, Paris 1963, mimeographed.

Duncan, Beverly, et al, "Patterns of City Growth", *American Journal of Sociology*, Vol. 67, January 1962, pp. 418–29.

Duncan, Otis Dudley, "Optimum Size of Cities", in Spengler and Duncan, eds., *Demographic Analysis*, q.v.; "The Measurement of Population Distribution", *Population Studies*, Vol. 11, July 1957, pp. 39–44; "Population Distribution and Community Structure", *Cold Spring Harbor on Quantitative Biology*, Vol. 22, 1957, pp. 364–7; and Duncan, Beverly, "Residential Distribution and Occupational Stratification", *American Journal of Sociology*, Vol. 60, March 1955, pp. 493–503; and Reiss, Albert J., Jr., *Social Characteristics of Urban and Rural Communities*, John Wiley, New York 1956; and Duncan, Beverly, "The Measurement of Intra-City Locational and Residential Patterns", *Journal of Regional Sciences*, Vol. 2, 1960, pp. 37–54; et al, *Metropolis and Region*, John Hopkins Press, Baltimore 1960.

Dunglas, E., *Moeurs et Coutumes des Bétés*, Larose, Paris 1939.

Dyckman, J. W., "The Changing Uses of the City", *Daedalus*, Vol. 90, Winter 1961, pp. 111–31; "Life in Supercity", *Science*, Vol. 138, December 7, 1962, pp. 1089–91.

Eckstein, Harry, *Pressure Group Politics*, Stanford University Press, Stanford 1960; and Apter, David E., eds., *Comparative Politics: A Reader*, Free Press of Glencoe, New York 1963; "Group Theory and the Comparative Study of Pressure Groups: Introduction", in ibid.

East Africa Royal Commission, *Report*, HMSO, London 1955.

Eisenstadt, S. N., "The Place of Elites and Primary Groups in the Absorption of Immigrants in Israel", *American Journal of Sociology*, Vol. 57, 1952.

Eliot, T. S., *Notes towards the Definition of Culture*, Faber, London 1948.

Epstein, A. L., *Politics in an Urban African Community*, Manchester University Press for the Rhodes-Livingstone Institute, Manchester 1958; "Urbanization and Social Change in Africa", *Current Anthropology*, Vol. 8, 1967, pp. 275–95.

Fallers, L. A., "The Predicament of the Modern African Chief: An Instance from Uganda", *American Anthropologist*, Vol. 57, 1955, pp. 290–304; "Some Determinants of Marriage Stability in Busoga: A Reformulation of Gluckman's Hypothesis", *Africa*, Vol. 27, 1957, pp. 106–21; "Equality, Modernity, and Democracy in the New States", in Clifford Geertz, q.v.; ed., *The King's Men*, Oxford University Press, London and New York 1964.

Farley, Reynolds, "Suburban Persistence", *American Journal of Sociology*, Vol. 69, February 1964, pp. 38–47.

Federation of Rhodesia and Nyasaland, Central Statistical Office, "The African Market in Salisbury, Bulawayo, Umtali and Gwelo", *Monthly Digest of Statistics*, Vol. 5, January 1959; *Second Report on the Urban African Budget Survey in Salisbury, 1957/58*, Salisbury 1959; *Salisbury Demographic Survey, August/September*, 1958, Salisbury 1959; *Monthly Digest of Statistics*, Vol. 6, January 1960; "Occupations and Wage Rates of Africans in the Urban Areas of Southern Rhodesia 1958/59", *Monthly Digest of Statistics*, Vol. 6, July 1960, pp. iii–ix; *Second Report on the Urban African Budget Survey in Bulawayo, 1958/59*, Salisbury 1960; *Second Report on the Urban African Budget Surveys Held in Umtali and Gwelo in July, 1959*, Salisbury 1960; *Second Report on the Urban African Budget Survey Held in Northern Rhodesia, May to August, 1960*, Salisbury 1961; *Preliminary Report on the Federal*

European Family Expenditure Survey, October, 1960, Salisbury 1961; "Preliminary 1961 Census Returns", *Monthly Digest of Statistics*, Vol. 7, November 1961; *Preliminary Report of the April/May 1962 Census of Africans in Southern Rhodesia*, Salisbury 1963; *Economic Report, 1963; Final Report of the April/May 1962 Census of Africans in Southern Rhodesia*, Salisbury 1964.

Feldman, A., and Moore, W., "Industrialization and Industrialism, Convergences and Differentiation", *Transactions of the Fifth World Congress of Sociology*, Washington 1962.

Ferguson, C. E., "A Statistical Study of Urbanization", *Social Forces*, Vol. 37, October 1958, pp. 19–26; "Statics, Dynamics, and the Economic Base", in R. W. Pfouts, ed., *The Techniques of Urban Economic Analysis*, Chandler-Davis, West Trenton, NJ, 1960.

Field, M. J., *Search for Security*, Faber, London 1960.

Forde, Daryll, "Social Aspects of Urbanization and Industrialization in Africa: A General Review", in International African Institute, *Social Implications of Industrialization and Urbanization in Africa South of the Sahara*, UNESCO, Paris 1956; "Methodology in the Study of African Urbanization", in Kenneth Little, ed., *Urbanization in African Social Change*, q.v.

Fortune Magazine, "The Great Urban Tax Tangle", *Fortune*, Vol. 71, March 1965, 106 ff.

Foster, Philip, "Secondary Schooling and Social Mobility in a West African Nation", *Sociology of Education*, Vol. 37, Winter 1963.

Funkenstein, D., King, S. H., and Drolette, M. E., *Mastery of Stress*, Harvard University Press, Cambridge 1957.

Geertz, Clifford, *Old Societies and New States: The Quest for Modernity in Asia and Africa*, Free Press of Glencoe, New York 1963; "Primordial Sentiments and Civil Politics in the New States", in ibid.

Gibbs, J. L., *Peoples of Africa*, Holt, Rinehart and Winston, New York 1965.

Gibrat, R., *Les inégalités économiques*, Librairie du Recuere Sirey, Paris 1931.

Ginsburg, Norton, *Atlas of Economic Development*, University of Chicago Press, Chicago 1961; "Urban Geography and 'Non-Western' Areas", in Hauser and Schnore, q.v.

Glazer, Nathan, and Moynihan, Daniel Patrick, *Beyond the Melting Pot: The Negroes, Puerto Ricans, Jews, Italians and Irish of New York City*, Massachusetts Institute of Technology Press, Cambridge 1963.

Gluckman, Max, "Anthropological Problems Arising from the African Industrial Revolution", in Aidan W. Southall, ed., *Social Change in Modern Africa*, q.v.; *Order and Rebellion in Tribal Africa*, Cohen and West, London 1963; and Mitchell, J. C., and Barnes, J. A., "The Village Headman in British Central Africa", *Africa*, Vol. 19, 1949, pp. 89–106.

Goode, William S., *World Revolution and Family Patterns*, Free Press of Glencoe, New York 1963; Collier-Macmillan, London 1963.

Gordon, Milton M., *Assimilation in American Life: The Role of Race,*

Religion, and National Origins, Oxford University Press, New York and London 1964.

Greenberg, Joseph H., *The Languages of Africa*, Indiana University Research Center in Anthropology, Folklore, and Linguistics, Bloomington 1963.

Greenstein, Fred I., "The Changing Pattern of Urban Party Politics", *The Annals of the American Academy of Political and Social Science*, Vol. 353, 1964.

Gulliver, Philip H., "Anthropology", in Lystad, q.v.

Gutkind, Peter C. W., "African Urban Family Life", *Cahiers d'Etudes Africaines*, Vol. 3, 1962, pp. 149-217; "The African Urban Milieu: A Force in Rapid Change", *Civilisations*, Vol. 12, 1962, pp. 167–91; *The African Administration of the Kibuga of Buganda*, Mouton, The Hague 1963.

Habbakuk, J., "Family Structure and Economic Change in Nineteenth Century Europe", *The Journal of Economic History*, Vol. 15, 1956, pp. 1–12.

Haldane, J. B. S., "On Being the Right Size", in J. R. Newman, ed., *The World of Mathematics*, Vol. II, Simon and Schuster, New York 1956.

Hamdan, G., "The Political Map of the New Africa", *Geographical Review*, Vol. 53, 1963, pp. 418–39; "Capitals of the New Africa", *Economic Geography*, Vol. 10, July 1964, pp. 239–53.

Hance, William A., "The Economic Location and Functions of Tropical African Cities", *Human Organization*, Vol. 19, 1960, pp. 135–6; *The Geography of Modern Africa*, Columbia University Press, New York 1964.

Hanna, William John, ed., *Independent Black Africa: The Politics of Freedom*, Rand McNally, Chicago 1964; "Introduction: The Politics of Freedom", in ibid.

Hatt, Paul K., and Reiss, Albert J., Jr., eds., *Reader in Urban Sociology*, The Free Press, Glencoe, Ill., 1951.

Hauser, Philip M., "Urbanization: An Overview", in Philip M. Hauser and Leo F. Schnore, eds., *The Study of Urbanization*, John Wiley, New York 1965; and Duncan, Otis Dudley, eds., *The Study of Population*, University of Chicago Press, Chicago 1959.

Hawley, Amos H., *Human Ecology*, Ronald Press, New York 1950.

Heer, D. M., *After Nuclear Attack*, Frederick A. Praeger, New York 1965; Pall Mall Press, London 1965.

Hellman, Ellen, *Rooiyard: A Sociological Study of an Urban Native Slum Yard*, Oxford University Press, Cape Town 1948.

Hemphill, John K., *Situational Factors in Leadership*, Bureau of Educational Research, Ohio State University, Columbus 1949.

Herskovits, Melville J., *The Human Factor in Changing Africa*, Alfred K. Knopf, New York 1962.

Hirsch, Werner Z., "Expenditure Implications of Metropolitan Growth and Consolidation", *Review of Economics and Statistics*, Vol. 41, August 1959, pp. 237–41.

Horowitz, David, "The International Welfare Community", *International Development Review*, Vol. 6, December 1964.

Hoselitz, Bert F., "Generative and Parasitic Cities", *Economic Development and Cultural Change*, Vol. 3, April 1955, pp. 278–94; "The City, the Factory, and Economic Growth", *American Economic Review*, Vol. 45, May 1955, pp. 166–84; "Urbanization and Economic Growth in Asia", *Economic Development and Cultural Change*, Vol. 6, October 1957; *Sociological Aspects of Economic Growth*, The Free Press, Glencoe, Ill., 1960; "Tradition and Economic Growth", in Braibanti and Spengler, q.v.; and Moore, Wilbert E., eds., *Industrialization and Society*, UNESCO and Mouton, Paris and The Hague 1963.

Hoyle, W. E., "Early Days in Uganda", manuscript.

Hoyt, Homer, "Is City Growth Controlled by Mathematics or Physical Laws?", *Land Economics*, Vol. 27, August 1951, pp. 259–62.

Inkeles, Alex, "Social Change and Social Character: The Role of Parental Mediation", in Smelser and Smelser, q.v.

Isard, Walter, *Location and Space-Economy*, John Wiley, New York 1956; *Methods of Regional Analysis: An Introduction to Regional Science*, John Wiley, New York 1960.

Jewkes, J., "The Size of the Factory", *Economic Journal*, Vol. 62, June 1952, pp. 237–52.

Johnston, Bruce F., *The Staple Food Economies of Western Tropical Africa*, Stanford University Press, Stanford 1958.

Johnston, Sir Harry Hamilton, *The Uganda Protectorate*, Hutchinson, London 1902.

Kaplan, Morton A., *System and Process in International Politics*, John Wiley, New York 1957.

Kaye, Barrington, *Bringing Up Children in Ghana*, Allen and Unwin, London 1962.

Kazakevich, V. D., "The End of Plant Expansion in American Manufacturing Industries", *Science and Society*, Vol. 2, 1938.

Kendall, H., *Town Planning in Uganda*, Crown Agents, London 1955.

Kendall, M. G., *New Prospects in Economic Analysis* (The Stamp Memorial Lecture, 1960), Athlone Press, London 1960; "Natural Law in the Social Sciences", *Journal of the Royal Statistical Society*, Vol. 124, 1961, pp. 1–16.

Kilby, Peter, "Balancing Town and Country", *West Africa*, August 29, 1964.

Kingsley, J. Donald, "Bureaucracy and Political Development with Particular Reference to Nigeria", in Joseph LaPalombara, q.v.

Knappens, M. T., *L'enfant Mukungo: Orientations de Base du Système Educatif et Développement de la Personalité*, Nauwelaert, Paris 1962.

Kneedler, Grace M., "Functional Types of Cities", in Hatt and Reiss, q.v.

Kobben, A., "Le planteur noir", *Etudes Eburnéennes*, Vol. 5, Institut Français d'Afrique Noire, Abidjan 1956.

Kohn, M. L., "Social Class and Parent-Child Relationships: An Interpretation", *American Journal of Sociology*, Vol. 68, 1963, pp. 471–80.

Kolb, W. L., "The Structure and Function of Cities", *Economic Development and Cultural Change*, Vol. 3, October 1954, pp. 50–2.

Kuper, Leo, "Sociology: Some Aspects of Urban Plural Societies in Africa", in Lystad, q.v.

Kuznets, S., Moore, W., and Spengler, J., eds., *Economic Growth: Brazil, India, Japan*, Duke University Press, Durham, NC, 1955.

Labovitz, Sanford, and Gibbs, Jack P., "Urbanization, Technology, and the Division of Labor: Further Evidence", *Pacific Sociological Review*, Vol. 7, Spring 1964, pp. 3–9.

LaFontaine, J. S., *The Gisu of Uganda*, International African Institute, London 1959.

Lambert, R., and Hoselitz, Bert F., eds., *The Role of Savings and Wealth in Southern Asia and the West*, UNESCO, Paris 1962.

Lampard, Eric E., "Historical Aspects of Urbanization", in Hauser and Schnore, q.v.; "The History of Cities in the Economically Advanced Areas", *Economic Development and Cultural Change*, Vol. 3, January 1955, pp. 123–9.

Landy, D., *Tropical Childhood*, University of North Carolina Press, Chapel Hill 1959.

LaPalombara, Joseph, ed., *Bureaucracy and Political Development*, Princeton University Press, Princeton 1963; "An Overview", in ibid.

Lazarsfeld, P., Berelson, B., and Gaudet, Hazel, *The People's Choice: How the Voter Makes up His Mind in a Presidential Campaign*, Columbia University Press, New York 1944.

Lebergott, Stanley, *Manpower in Economic Growth*, McGraw-Hill, New York 1964.

Lee, Dorothy, "Lineal and Nonlineal Codifications of Reality", in Carpenter and McLuhan, q.v.

Legum, Colin, "Africa's Intellectuals: The Thin Black Line", *New Society*, December 1964.

Leighton, Alexander, *The Governing of Men*, Princeton University Press, Princeton 1946.

Lerner, Daniel, *The Passing of Traditional Society: Modernizing the Middle East*, The Free Press, Glencoe, Ill., 1958.

Leslie, J. A. K., *A Survey of Dar es Salaam*, Oxford University Press, London 1963.

Levy, M., "Contrasting Factors in the Modernization of China and Japan", in Kuznets, Moore, and Spengler, q.v.

Lillibridge, Robert M., "Urban Size: An Abridgment", *Land Economics*, Vol. 28, November 1952, pp. 341–52.

Lippitt, R., Polansky, N., Redl, F., and Rosen, S., "The Dynamics of Power", in Eleanor E. Maccoby, Theodore M. Newcomb, and Eugene L. Hartley, eds., *Readings in Social Psychology*, Henry Holt, New York 1958.

Little, Kenneth, ed., *Urbanization in African Social Change*, University of Edinburgh, Centre of African Studies, 1963, mimeographed; *West African Urbanization, a Study of Voluntary Associations in Social Change*, Cambridge University Press, Cambridge 1965.

Lloyd, Barbara B., "Indigenous Ibadan", in Lloyd, P.C., Mabogunje A. L., and Awe, B., *The City of Ibadan*, Cambridge University Press London 1967.

Lloyd, P. C., "The Yoruba of Nigeria", in Gibbs, q.v.

Lösch, August, *The Economics of Location*, Yale University Press, New Haven 1954.

Lomax, K. S., "The Relationship between Expenditure Per Head and Size of Population of County Boroughs in England and Wales" *Journal of the Royal Statistical Society*, Vol. 106, 1943, pp. 51–9.

Lorimer, F., Brass, W., and Walle, Etienne van de, "Demography", in Lystad, q.v.

Lystad, Robert A., ed., *The African World: A Survey of Social Research* Frederick A. Praeger, New York 1965; Pall Mall Press, London 1965

Mabogunje, Akin L., "Urbanization in Nigeria—A Constraint on Economic Development", *Economic Development and Cultural Change* Vol. 13, July 1965, pp. 413–38; *Yoruba Towns*, Ibadan University Press, Ibadan 1962.

McDonell, Gavan, "The Dynamics of Social Change: The Case of Kano", *Annals of the Association of American Geographers*, Vol. 54 September 1964, pp. 355–71.

McLoughlin, Peter F. M., "The Sudan's Three Towns: A Demographic and Economic Profile of an African Urban Complex", *Economic Development and Cultural Change*, Vol. 12, July 1964, pp. 291–3.

McLuhan, Marshall, *Understanding Media: The Extensions of Man* McGraw-Hill, New York 1964.

McWilliam, H. O. A., *The Development of Education in Ghana*, Longmans, London 1957.

Magid, Alvin, "District Councillorship in an African Society: A Study in Role", unpublished PH.D. dissertation, Michigan State University, 1965

Marris, Peter, *Family and Social Change in an African City*, Routledge and Kegan Paul, London 1961; Northwestern University Press, Evanston 1962.

Martindale, Don, "Introduction", in Weber, UK edn., q.v.; "Prefatory Remarks: The Theory of the City", in Weber, US edn., q.v.

May, E., *Report on the Kampala Extension Scheme: Kololo-Naguru*, Government Printer, Entebbe 1947.

Mayer, Philip, *Townsmen or Tribesmen*, Oxford University Press, Cape Town 1961.

Mead, Margaret, "The Implications of Culture Change for Personality Development", *American Journal of Orthopsychiatry*, Vol. 17, 1947, pp. 633–46.

Medvedkov, Yu V., "Applications of Mathematics to Some Problems in Economic Geography", *Soviet Geography*, Vol. 5, June 1964, pp. 36–53

Melvin, M. Avrami, "Geometry and Dynamics of Populations", *Philosophy of Science*, Vol. 8, January 1941, pp. 113–32.

Mercier, P., "Etude du Mariage et Enquête urbaine", *Cahiers d'Etudes Africaines*, Vol. 1, 1960.

Merton, Robert, "Patterns of Influence: Local and Cosmopolitan

Influentials", in Robert Merton, ed., *Social Theory and Social Structure*, The Free Press, Glencoe, Ill., 1957; and Lazarsfeld, Paul, eds., *Continuities in Social Research: Studies in the Scope and Method of "The American Soldier"*, The Free Press, Glencoe, Ill., 1950.

Miller, D., and Swanson, G., *The Changing American Parent*, John Wiley, New York 1958.

Mills, F. C., "Statistics and Leviathan", *Journal of the American Statistical Association*, Vol. 30, March 1935, pp. 1–11.

Miner, Horace M., "Community-Society Continua", *International Encyclopedia of the Social Sciences*, Crowell Collier and Macmillan, New York.

Ministère des Affaires Economiques et du Plan Côte d'Ivoire, *Supplement trimestriel au Bulletin Mensuel de Statistiques*, Vol. 2, 1961.

Minturn, Leigh, and Lambert, W. W., *Mothers of Six Cultures*, John Wiley, New York 1964.

Mitchell, J. Clyde, "The Yao of Southern Nyasaland," *Africa*, Vol. 19, 1949, pp. 94–100; *The Kalela Dance*, "The Rhodes-Livingstone Papers", No. 27, 1957; "Africans in Industrial Towns in Northern Rhodesia", in *H.R.H. The Duke of Edinburgh's Study Conference*, No. 1, cited in Wallerstein, q.v.; *Tribalism and the Plural Society*, Oxford University Press, London 1960; "Social Change and the Stability of African Marriage", in Southall, ed., *Social Change in Modern Africa*, q.v.; "Theoretical Orientations in African Urban Studies", in Banton, ed., *The Social Anthropology of Complex Societies*, q.v.

Mitchell, N. C., "Yoruba Towns", in Barbour and Prothero, q.v.

Moore, Wilbert E., "Industrialization and Social Change", in Hoselitz and Moore, q.v.; *Man, Time, and Society*, John Wiley, New York 1963; *Social Change*, Prentice-Hall, Englewood Cliffs 1964; *The Impact of Industry*, Prentice-Hall, Englewood Cliffs 1965.

Moos, S., "The Scope of Automation", *Economic Journal*, Vol. 67, March 1957, pp. 26–39.

Moreno, J. L., "The Foundations of Sociometry", *Sociometry*, Vol. 4, 1941.

Morgan, Theodore, "The Theory of Error in Centrally-Directed Economic Systems", *Quarterly Journal of Economics*, Vol. 78, August 1964, pp. 412–13.

Muhsam, H. V., "Fertility of Polygynous Marriages", *Population Studies*, Vol. 10, 1956, pp. 3–16.

Mumford, Lewis, *The Culture of Cities*, Harcourt, Brace, New York 1938; *The City of History*, Harcourt, Brace and World, New York 1961.

Murdock, G. P., and Whiting, J., "Cultural Determination of Parental Attitudes: The Relationship between the Social Structure, Particularly the Family Structure, and Parental Behavior", in M. J. E. Senn, q.v.

Myrdal, Gunnar, *An American Dilemma*, Harper and Row, New York 1962.

Nadel, S. F., *The Foundations of Social Anthropology*, The Free Pres Glencoe, Ill., 1951.

National Resources Planning Board, *The Long-Range Planning of t. Location of New Productive Capacity*, Washington 1940.

Neumark, S. D., *Foreign Trade and Economic Development in Africa: Historical Perspective*, Stanford Food Research Institute, Stanfo 1964.

Neutze, G. M., *Economic Policy and the Size of Cities*, Australian Nation University, Canberra 1965.

Niangoran-Bouah, G., "Le Village Abouré", *Cahiers d'Etudes Africain* 1, 1960, pp. 113–27.

Niedercorn, J. H., and Hearle, Edward F. R., "Recent Land-Use Tren in Forty-Eight Large American Cities", *Land Economics*, Vol. 4 February 1964, pp. 106–10.

Nkrumah, Kwame, *Consciencism*, Heinemann, London 1964.

Northern Rhodesia, *Monthly Digest of Statistics*, May, 1964; Ministry Finance, *Preliminary Report of the May/June 1963 Census of Africans Northern Rhodesia*, Lusaka 1964.

Ogburn, W. F., and Duncan, Otis Dudley, "City Size as a Sociologic Variable", in E. S. Burgess and D. J. Bogue, eds., *Contributions Urban Sociology*, University of Chicago Press, Chicago 1964.

Ornstein, J., "Africa Seeks a Common Language", *Review of Politic* Vol. 26, April 1964, pp. 205–14.

Ottenberg, Simon, "Ibo Receptivity to Change", in Bascom ar Herskovits, q.v.

Parsons, Talcott, "A Revised Analytical Approach to the Theory Social Stratification", in Reinhard Bendix and Seymour Martin Lipse eds., *Class, Status and Power*, The Free Press, Glencoe, Ill., 195 *The Social System*, Free Press of Glencoe, New York 1963; ar Smelser, Neil J., *Economy and Society*, The Free Press, Glencoe, Il 1956.

Paulme, Denise, *Une Société de Côte d'Ivoire hier et aujourd'hui: l Bété*, Mouton, Paris 1962.

Penrose, L. S., "The Elementary Statistics of Majority Voting", *Journ of the Royal Statistical Society*, Vol. 109, 1946, pp. 53–7.

Pfouts, R. W., and Curtis, E. E., "Limitations of the Economic Ba Analysis", *Social Forces*, Vol. 36, May 1958, pp. 303–10.

Pirenne, Henri, *Medieval Cities*, trans. by Frank D. Halsey, Princeto University Press, Princeton 1925.

Polanyi, M., *The Logic of Liberty*, Routledge and Kegan Paul, Londo 1951.

Pool, Ithiel de Sola, "Mass Media and Politics", in Pye, ed., *Communica tions and Political Development*, q.v.

Post, Kenneth, *The Nigerian Federal Election of 1959: Politics an Administration in a Developing Political System*, Oxford Universit Press for the Nigerian Institute of Social and Economic Researc London 1963.

Pred, Allan R., "The Intra-Metropolitan Location of American Manu facturing", *Annals of the Association of American Geographers*, Vol. 54, June 1964, pp. 165–80.

othro, E. T., *Child Rearing in Lebanon*, Harvard University Press, Cambridge 1961.

'e, Lucian W., "The Non-Western Political Process", *The Journal of Politics*, Vol. 20, 1958, pp. 468–86; "Administrators, Agitators, and Brokers", *Public Opinion Quarterly*, Vol. 22, 1958, pp. 342–9; ed., *Communications and Political Development*, Princeton University Press, Princeton 1963.

ashevsky, N., *Mathematical Theory of Human Relations*, Principia Press, Bloomington 1947.

aulin, H., *Mission d'Etude des Groupements Immigrés en Côte d'Ivoire*, Office de la Recherche Scientifique et Technique d'Outre Mer, Paris 1957, document.

eader, D. H., "A Survey of Categories of Economic Activities among the Peoples of Africa", *Africa*, Vol. 34, January 1964, pp. 28–45.

edfield, Robert, *The Folk Culture of Yucatan*, University of Chicago Press, Chicago 1942; and Singer, Milton B., "The Cultural Role of Cities", *Economic Development and Cultural Change*, Vol. 3, October 1954, pp. 53–73.

eiss, Albert J., Jr., "The Community and the Corporate Area", *University of Pennsylvania Law Review*, Vol. 105, February 1957, pp. 443–63; "The Nature of the City", in Paul K. Hatt and Albert J. Reiss, Jr., eds., *Cities and Society*, The Free Press, Glencoe, Ill., 1957.

ex, J., "The Plural Society in Sociological Theory", *The British Journal of Sociology*, Vol. 10, 1959, pp. 114–24.

ichards, Audrey, "Multi-Tribalism in African Urban Areas", in Little, ed., *Urbanization in African Social Change*, q.v.

iesman, David, *The Lonely Crowd*, Yale University Press, New Haven 1950; "Introduction", in Daniel Lerner, q.v.; "The Oral and Written Traditions", in Carpenter and McLuhan, q.v.

iggs, Fred W., "Bureaucracy and Development: A Paradoxical View", in LaPalombara, q.v.; *Administration in Developing Countries: The Theory of Prismatic Society*, Houghton Mifflin, Boston 1964.

ivkin, Arnold, *The African Presence in World Affairs*, The Free Press, Glencoe, Ill., 1963.

ogow, A. A., and Lasswell, H. D., *Power, Corruption, and Rectitude*, Prentice-Hall, Englewood Cliffs, NJ, 1963.

osen, B. C., "Socialization and Achievement Motivation in Brazil", *American Sociological Review*, Vol. 27, No. 5, 1962, pp. 612–24.

ossi, Peter, "Theory, Research and Practice in Community Organization", in Adrian, q.v.

ustow, Dankwart, *Politics and Westernization in the Near East*, Center of International Studies, Princeton University, Princeton 1956.

alisbury, Director of African Administration, *Annual Report, 1963*.

chnore, Leo F., "The Statistical Measurement of Urbanization and Economic Development", *Land Economics*, Vol. 37, August 1961, pp. 229–45.

Schultz, T. W., *Transforming Traditional Agriculture*, Yale Universit Press, New Haven 1964.

Schulze, Robert, "The Role of Economic Dominants in Communit Power Structure", *American Sociological Review*, Vol. 23, 195 pp. 3–9.

Selznick, Philip, "Foundations of the Theory of Organizations", *America Sociological Review*, Vol. 13, 1948, pp. 25–35.

Senn, M. J. E., ed., *Problems of Infancy and Childhood*, J. Macy Foundation, New York 1951.

Shevki, E., and Bell, W., *Social Area Analysis*, Stanford University Press Stanford 1955.

Simmel, Georg, *The Sociology of Georg Simmel*, trans. and ed. by Kur H. Wolff, The Free Press, Glencoe, Ill., 1950.

Simms, Ruth, *Urbanization in West Africa: A Review of the Curren Literature*, Northwestern University Press, Evanston 1965.

Simon, Herbert A., *Administrative Behavior: A Study of Decision-Makin Processes in Administrative Organization*, Macmillan, New York 1947 "The Architecture of Complexity", *Proceedings of the America Philosophical Society*, Vol. 106, December 1962, pp. 467–82; *Model of Man*, John Wiley, New York 1957.

Sjoberg, Gideon, *The Preindustrial City*, The Free Press, Glencoe, Ill. 1960; "Cities in Developing and Industrial Societies: A Cross-Cultura Analysis", in Hauser and Schnore, q.v., "Theory and Research in Urbar Sociology", in Hauser and Schnore, q.v.

Skinner, Elliot P., "Strangers in West African Societies", *Africa*, Vol. 33 October 1963, pp. 307–20.

Sklar, Richard, *Nigerian Political Parties: Power in an Emergent Africar Nation*, Princeton University Press, Princeton 1963.

Slastenko, Ye N., "The Distribution of Productive Forces and the Effacing of Differences between Town and Countryside", *Soviet Geography*, Vol. 5, February 1964, pp. 24–31.

Smailes, A. S., *The Geography of Towns*, Hutchinson House, London 1953.

Smelser, N. J., and Smelser, W. J., eds., *Personality and Social Systems* John Wiley, New York 1963.

Smith, M. G., "Social and Cultural Pluralism", *Annals of the New York Academy of Sciences*, Vol. 83, 1959–1960, pp. 763–77.

Smith, R. T., *The Negro Family in the British Guiana*, Routledge and Kegan Paul, London 1956.

Smith, T. E., and Blacker, J. G. C., *Population Characteristics of the Commonwealth Countries of Tropical Africa*, Commonwealth Papers, No. 9, Athlone Press, London 1963.

Smythe, Hugh H., and Smythe, Mabel M., *The New Nigerian Elite*, Stanford University Press, Stanford 1960.

Sorokin, P. A., and Berger, C. Q., *Time-Budgets of Human Behavior*, Harvard University Press, Cambridge 1939.

Southall, Aidan, ed., *Social Change in Modern Africa*, Oxford University Press, London 1961; and Gutkind, Peter, *Townsmen in the Making*,

East African Studies No. 9, East African Institute of Social Research, Kampala 1957.

Sovani, N. V., "The Analysis of Over-Urbanization", *Economic Development and Cultural Change*, Vol. 12, January 1964, pp. 117–19.

Spengler, Joseph J., "Social Structure, the State, and Economic Growth", in Kuznets, Moore, and Spengler, q.v.; and Duncan, Otis Dudley, eds., *Demographic Analysis*, The Free Press, Glencoe, Ill., 1956; and Duncan, Otis Dudley, eds., *Population Theory and Policy*, The Free Press, 1956.

Steel, R. W., "African Urbanization: A Geographer's Viewpoint", in Kenneth Little, ed., *Urbanization in African Social Change*, q.v.

Stewart, John Q., "Empirical Mathematical Rules Concerning the Distribution and Equilibrium of Population", *Geographical Review*, Vol. 37, July 1947, pp. 461–85; and Warntz, William, "Physics of Population Distribution", *Journal of Regional Science*, Vol. 1, Summer 1958, pp. 99–123.

Stigler, George J., "The Economies of Scale", *Journal of Law and Economics*, Vol. 1, October 1958, pp. 54–71.

Sufrin, S. C., and Paul, S., "Over-Urbanization and Economic Growth", in The National Academy of Economics and Political Science, American University, Washington: Special Publications Series, No. 16, 1960.

Taaffe, Edward J., et al, "Transport Expansion in Underdeveloped Countries: A Comparative Analysis", *Geographical Review*, Vol. 53, 1963, pp. 503–29.

Taeuber, Conrad, and Taeuber, Irene B., *The Changing Population of the United States*, John Wiley, New York 1958.

Taeuber, Karl E., and Taeuber, Alma F., "White Migration and Socio-Economic Differences between Cities and Suburbs", *American Journal of Sociology*, Vol. 69, October 1964, pp. 718–29.

Tawney, R. H., ed., *Studies in Economic History*, Frank Cass, London 1958.

Temporary National Economic Committee, *Relative Efficiency of Large, Medium-Sized, and Small Business*, Monograph 13, Washington 1941.

Thomas, Benjamin E., "Geography", in Lystad, q.v.

Thompson, D'Arcy Wentworth, *On Growth and Form*, ed. by John Tyler Bonner, Cambridge University Press, London 1961.

Thorndike, E. L., *Your City*, Harcourt, Brace, New York 1938; "American Cities and States: Variation and Correlation in Institutions, Activities, and the Personal Qualities of the Residents", *Annals of the New York Academy of Sciences*, Vol. 39, December 1939, pp. 213–98; *144 Smaller Cities*, Harcourt, Brace, New York 1940.

Tiger, Lionel, "Bureaucracy and Charisma in Ghana", *Journal of Asian and African Studies*, Vol. 1, January 1966, pp. 13–26.

Townsend, Peter, *The Family Life of Old People*, Routledge and Kegan Paul, London 1957.

Toynbee, Arnold J., *A Study of History*, Vol. IV, Oxford University Press, London 1939.

Trewartha, Glenn T., and Zelinsky, Wilbur, "The Population Geography of Belgian Africa", *Annals of the Association of American Geographers*, Vol. 44, June 1954, pp. 163–93; "Population Patterns in Tropical Africa", *Annals of the Association of American Geographers*, Vol. 44, June 1954, pp. 135–62.

Ullman, E. L., "The Nature of Cities Reconsidered", *Proceedings*, Regional Science Association, Vol. 9, 1962, pp. 8–11; and Dacey, M. F., "The Minimum Requirements Approach to the Urban Economic Base", *Proceedings*, Regional Science Association, Vol. 6, 1960, pp. 175–94.

United Nations, *Science and Technology for Development*, Vol. 6, 1963.

United Nations, Food and Agriculture Organization, *Survey*, Rome 1962.

United Nations, Department of Economic and Social Affairs, Economic and Social Council, Economic Commission for Africa, *Demographic Yearbook*; "Problems of Size of Plant in Industry in Under-developed Countries", *Industrialization and Productivity*, Bulletin 2, March 1959; "Demographic Factors Related to Social and Economic Development in Africa", E/CN.14, Vol. II, No. 2, *Economic Bulletin for Africa*, Vol. 2, June 1962, pp. 60–4; *Population Distribution, Internal Migration and Urbanization in Africa*, UNESCO, New York, October 16, 1962, E/CN. 14/ASPP/L.3 and E/CN. 9 Conf. 3/13; *Economic Bulletin for Africa*, Vol. 3, January 1963; *Industrial Growth in Africa*, New York 1963; *Provisional Report on World Population Prospects*, New York 1964.

United Nations Educational, Scientific and Cultural Organization, *Social Implications of Industrialization and Urbanization in Africa South of the Sahara*, UNESCO, Paris 1956.

US Bureau of the Census, *Historical Statistics of the United States, 1789–1945*, US Government Printing Office, Washington 1949.

US Department of Agriculture, *Nigeria, Determinants of Projected Level of Demand, Supply, and Imports of Farm Products in 1965 and 1975*, ERS-Foreign 32, Washington, August 1962; *The World Food Budget*, FEA Report No. 19, 1964.

USICA, *Manual of Industrial Development with Especial Application to Latin America*, prepared by Stanford Research Institute, Menlo Park, California, Washington 1958.

Unwin, George, "The Medieval City", in R. H. Tawney, q.v.

Varley, D., and Schnore, L., "Some Concomitants of Metropolitan Size", *American Sociological Review*, Vol. 20, 1955, pp. 408–15.

Vining, Rutledge, "A Description of Certain Spatial Aspects of an Economic System", *Economic Development and Cultural Change*, Vol. 3, January 1955, pp. 147–95.

Warren, Robert, "A Municipal Services Market Model of Metropolitan Organization", *Journal of the American Institute of Planners*, Vol. 30, August 1964, pp. 193–204.

Wallerstein, Immanuel, "Ethnicity and National Integration in West Africa", *Cahiers d'Etudes Africaines*, Vol. I, October 1960, pp. 129–39.

Weber, Max, *The City*, trans. and ed. by Don Martindale, Heinemann,

London 1960; US edition trans. and ed. by Don Martindale and Gertrud Neuwirth, Collier Books, New York 1962.

West Africa, London, June 22, 1963.

Western Nigerian Development Plan 1962–1968, Sessional Paper No. 8, 1962.

Wilson, G., and Wilson, M., *Analysis of Social Change*, Cambridge University Press, London 1945.

Winch, R. F., *The Modern Family*, Holt, Rinehart and Winston, New York 1963.

Winsborough, Hal H., "City Growth and City Structure", to be published.

Woodbury, Coleman, "Economic Implications of Urban Growth", *Science*, Vol. 129, June 12, 1959, pp. 1585–90.

Young, Michael, and Willmott, Peter, *Family and Kinship in East London*, Routledge and Kegan Paul, London 1956.

Yudelman, M., *Africans on the Land*, Harvard University Press, Cambridge 1964.

Zipf, G. K., *Human Behavior and the Principle of Least Effort*, Addison-Wesley, Cambridge, Mass., 1949.

Zolberg, A., *The One Party Government of the Ivory Coast*, Princeton University Press, Princeton 1964.

Index

Index